Technical Foundations and Applications of Trustworthy AI Systems

Otmane Azeroual
https://orcid.org/0000-0002-5225-389X
University of Hagen, Germany

IGI Global
Scientific Publishing
Publishing Tomorrow's Research Today

Vice President of Editorial	Melissa Wagner
Director of Acquisitions	Mikaela Felty
Director of Book Development	Jocelynn Hessler
Production Manager	Mike Brehm
Cover Design	Jose Rosado

Published in the United States of America by
IGI Global Scientific Publishing
701 East Chocolate Avenue
Hershey, PA, 17033, USA
Tel: 717-533-8845 | Fax: 717-533-7115
Website: https://www.igi-global.com E-mail: cust@igi-global.com

Library of Congress Cataloging-in-Publication Data

(CIP Data Pending)
ISBN13: 9798260014332
Isbn13Softcover: 9798260014349
EISBN13: 9798260014356
British Cataloguing in Publication Data
A Cataloguing in Publication record for this book is available from the British Library.

Table of Contents

Preface x

Chapter 1
Federated Learning and Quantum-Resilient Cryptographic Frameworks for Secure and Trustworthy AIoT Ecosystems 1
Ravikumar Ch, Sreenidhi University, Hyderabad, India
Burri Naresh, CVR College of Engineering, India
Mandala Rajkumar, Sri Indu College of Engineering and Technology, India
A. Pramod Reddy, Teegala Krishna Reddy College of Engineering and Technology, Hyderabad, India
Yemineni Sowjanya, Pallavi Engineering College, India
Sabavath Raju, Pallavi Engineering College, India

Chapter 2
Using Reliable and Low-Complexity Encryptions to Facilitate Cryptography for Electronic Commerce Transactions 31
Mishall Hammed Al-Zubaidie, University of Thi-Qar, Iraq

Chapter 3
Research Guru AI: A Robust AI Tool for Analyzing, Comparing, and Evaluating Academic Literature 69
Otmane Azeroual, University of Hagen, Germany
Richard R. Khan, Golden Gate University, USA

Chapter 4
SmartSpam Deep Neural Networks for Intelligent Spam Detection 91
M. Martinaa, SASTRA University, India
G. Revathy, SASTRA University, India

Chapter 5
Security and Privacy Concerns of Big Data Among Indian Consumers in E-Tailing and Social Media 123
Zainab Fatima, Jamia Millia Islamia, New Delhi, India
Mohd Abdul Moid Siddiqui, IILM University, Greater Noida, India

Chapter 6
Transparency-by-Design in Smart City Crowd Monitoring: A Privacy-Preserving Wi-Fi Analytics Framework for Tourism and Urban Management. 157
Ariya Namvong, Khon Kaen University, Thailand
Thalerngsak Wiangwiset, National Telecom Public Company Limited, Thailand

Chapter 7
Transparent and Trustworthy Data Practices for Talking Head Generation: A Systematic Survey of Datasets and Ethical Implications 195
Vineet Kumar Rakesh, Homi Bhabha National Institute, India & Variable Energy Cyclotron Centre, India
Soumya Mazumdar, Gargi Memorial Institute of Technology, India
Research Pratim Maity, Gargi Memorial Institute of Technology, India
Tapas Samanta, Variable Energy Cyclotron Centre, India
Sarbajit Pal, Mahatma Gandhi University, India
Amitabha Das, Jadavpur University, India

Chapter 8
The Ecosystem of State Support for Science in Slovakia and Scientific Data .. 225
Danica Zendulková, Slovak Centre of Scientific and Technical Information, Slovakia
Gabriela Gavurníková, Slovak Centre of Scientific and Technical Information, Slovakia
Ján Turňa, Slovak Centre of Scientific and Technical Information, Slovakia

Compilation of References 263

About the Contributors 293

Index 299

Detailed Table of Contents

Preface x

Chapter 1
Federated Learning and Quantum-Resilient Cryptographic Frameworks for Secure and Trustworthy AIoT Ecosystems 1
Ravikumar Ch, Sreenidhi University, Hyderabad, India
Burri Naresh, CVR College of Engineering, India
Mandala Rajkumar, Sri Indu College of Engineering and Technology, India
A. Pramod Reddy, Teegala Krishna Reddy College of Engineering and Technology, Hyderabad, India
Yemineni Sowjanya, Pallavi Engineering College, India
Sabavath Raju, Pallavi Engineering College, India

AIoT combines Artificial Intelligence (AI) with the Internet of Things (IoT) to enable smart applications in healthcare, transport, industry, and cities. However, the massive data from billions of devices creates risks to privacy, trust, and security. To address this, we propose a federated learning framework with quantum-resistant cryptography and explainable AI. It protects data locally, secures communication, detects attacks, and supports reliable decision-making. Lightweight cryptography, blockchain aggregation, and trust metrics ensure efficiency, integrity, and resilience for future AIoT systems.

Chapter 2
Using Reliable and Low-Complexity Encryptions to Facilitate Cryptography for Electronic Commerce Transactions 31
Mishall Hammed Al-Zubaidie, University of Thi-Qar, Iraq

A significant waste of funds and effort may result from hacking e-transactions. Furthermore, a huge number of linked and unlinked networks might seriously interfere with the security features that are already in place. In this work, we suggest developing a protocol to safeguard e-transaction data using the Chinese Remainder Theorem (CRT), El-Gamal, and Advanced Encryption Standard (AES) approaches. The proposed protocol also incorporates high-performance security features to guarantee scalability. In order to support the suggested protocol's performance and security balance, we integrate these algorithms with a strong approach. The superiority of the proposed protocol over current security protocols is demonstrated by a study of results.

Chapter 3
Research Guru AI: A Robust AI Tool for Analyzing, Comparing, and Evaluating Academic Literature 69
Otmane Azeroual, University of Hagen, Germany
Richard R. Khan, Golden Gate University, USA

The exponential growth of scientific publications poses significant challenges for researchers: efficiently identifying relevant studies, systematically detecting research gaps, and conducting reproducible analyses. Research Guru AI is an AI-powered tool that enables structured summaries, critical evaluations, and advanced analyses of scientific literature. This chapter provides a practical demonstration of how Research Guru AI can be applied across various domains – from higher education research to healthcare, education, finance, public administration, and Open Science initiatives. Furthermore, organizational implementation, best practices in change management, and the promotion of Open Science principles are discussed. The aim is to equip researchers with tools that significantly enhance efficiency, transparency, and reproducibility in scientific work.

Chapter 4
SmartSpam Deep Neural Networks for Intelligent Spam Detection 91
M. Martinaa, SASTRA University, India
G. Revathy, SASTRA University, India

Secure and trustworthy digital communication is seriously threatened by the growing number and sophistication of spam emails. The contextual and sequential patterns present in contemporary spam messages are frequently missed by traditional machine learning (ML) techniques, despite their relative effectiveness. The framework we present in this work, SmartSpam, is based on deep learning (DL) and uses standalone neural network models to detect and categorize spam emails intelligently. In particular, we examine the performance of the Gated Recurrent Units (GRU), Long Short-Term Memory (LSTM), Bidirectional LSTM (BiLSTM), Convolutional Neural Networks (CNN) and transformer-based model Bidirectional Encoder Representations from Transformers (BERT) for this task. Contextual embeddings, Count Vectorizer, and TF-IDF are used for feature extraction, depending on the model architecture. Grid search, genetic algorithms, and other hyperparameter tuning techniques are used to optimize each model. UCI SMS Spam,

Chapter 5
Security and Privacy Concerns of Big Data Among Indian Consumers in E-Tailing and Social Media 123
Zainab Fatima, Jamia Millia Islamia, New Delhi, India
Mohd Abdul Moid Siddiqui, IILM University, Greater Noida, India

Organizations all around the world have embraced big data as the most effective and adaptable medium for a variety of applications, such as mapping customer behaviour and forecasting demand, to mention a couple. Although there are inherent security and privacy risks with the usage of big data, the organizations that have adopted it have primarily focused on its benefits. This study aims to determine how aware consumers are of companies that use confidential user-generated data and whether those concerns are related to privacy and security. An empirical study has been conducted on 268 respondents from central universities in order to analyze the privacy and security concerns among the respondents. SEM has been applied, and one of the findings revealed that young Indian e-commerce consumers and social media users are concerned more about their security, and this aspect have an effect on their online shopping behaviour and frequency of social media usage.

Chapter 6
Transparency-by-Design in Smart City Crowd Monitoring: A Privacy-Preserving Wi-Fi Analytics Framework for Tourism and Urban Management. 157
Ariya Namvong, Khon Kaen University, Thailand
Thalerngsak Wiangwiset, National Telecom Public Company Limited, Thailand

Smart city initiatives increasingly rely on data-driven infrastructures to support urban governance, tourism management, and public service delivery. However, data collection in public spaces continues to raise concerns regarding privacy, accountability, and public trust. Although principles such as consent, transparency, and legal compliance are widely endorsed, they are often implemented in fragmented ways, resulting in systems that may be legally defensible yet socially contested. This chapter proposes an integrated governance approach for smart city crowd monitoring through the CCTC framework, which embeds consent, control, transparency, and compliance by design across the data lifecycle. Governance is conceptualized as a structural architecture aligning legitimacy, enforceable boundaries, accountability, and ethical compliance. The framework is illustrated through a municipal Wi-Fi analytics case study in Sri Chiang Mai, Thailand, demonstrating how transparency-by-design and privacy-preserving analytics can support tourism and urban management while sustaining public trust.

Chapter 7
Transparent and Trustworthy Data Practices for Talking Head Generation: A Systematic Survey of Datasets and Ethical Implications.................................. 195
Vineet Kumar Rakesh, Homi Bhabha National Institute, India & Variable Energy Cyclotron Centre, India
Soumya Mazumdar, Gargi Memorial Institute of Technology, India
Research Pratim Maity, Gargi Memorial Institute of Technology, India
Tapas Samanta, Variable Energy Cyclotron Centre, India
Sarbajit Pal, Mahatma Gandhi University, India
Amitabha Das, Jadavpur University, India

Talking Head Generation (THG) needs transparent, trustworthy data: ethically sourced, recorded, annotated, licensed, and managed human data with unambiguous authorization, provenance, and subject rights. This chapter analyzes THG modalities and organizes datasets by domain, capture context, view coverage, annotation scope, and access. It distills corpus strengths and gaps: language-heavy skew, frontal-view bias, coarse or artificial emotion labels, and licensing/privacy frictions. Transparency must equal technical rigor: dataset cards/datasheets, standard metadata, verifiable permission records, tiered licensing, subject-rights processes, fairness audits, and unified benchmarks with consistent preprocessing and splits. Next steps: multilingual/multicultural corpora, multi-view/3D capture, privacy-preserving pipelines, and calibrated synthetic–real co-training. Ethical, well-documented data allow generalizable THG and sustain public confidence.

Chapter 8
The Ecosystem of State Support for Science in Slovakia and Scientific Data .. 225
Danica Zendulková, Slovak Centre of Scientific and Technical Information, Slovakia
Gabriela Gavurníková, Slovak Centre of Scientific and Technical Information, Slovakia
Ján Turňa, Slovak Centre of Scientific and Technical Information, Slovakia

The chapter examines the science and research ecosystem in Slovakia, including its constituent elements, actors, processes, and instruments, with particular emphasis on the organization of research information and research data management. Credibility and transparency constitute fundamental pillars of the contemporary scientific ecosystem. In a context where science increasingly depends on open data, interdisciplinary collaboration, and public funding, these principles acquire critical significance for the effective functioning of research and innovation. The first section explores national science policy and its key principles such as open science, research ethics, and gender equality in science and research. The second section focuses on the prerequisites for data-driven policymaking in the field of science and research.

It addresses standards and models for data recording within information systems supporting scientific activity, the processing of research data, and the integration of such systems as essential conditions for producing high-quality and trustworthy data.

Compilation of References 263

About the Contributors 293

Index 299

Preface

INTRODUCTION

As Editor of *Technical Foundations and Applications of Trustworthy AI Systems*, I am pleased to present a volume that addresses one of the most pressing challenges of our time: ensuring that data- and AI-driven systems are not only powerful, but also transparent, accountable, and worthy of trust.

Artificial intelligence and data-centric technologies now play a decisive role in shaping outcomes across education, healthcare, finance, public services, and everyday human experiences. With this growing influence comes an equally significant responsibility. Stakeholders across domains—including data stewards, engineers, policymakers, and end-users—are increasingly asking critical questions: How are models developed and validated? What data foundations support them? What risks, biases, and uncertainties persist? And importantly, who is accountable at each stage of the lifecycle?

This book is grounded in the belief that transparency and trust must be treated as foundational design principles rather than retrospective considerations. The chapters collected here reflect a deliberate effort to integrate technical rigor with real-world applicability. They explore governance frameworks, data quality and provenance, model interpretability and auditability, human-centered oversight, privacy and security safeguards, and operational practices such as MLOps and LLMOps. At the same time, they engage with the broader sociotechnical landscape, incorporating perspectives from law, ethics, organizational studies, and human-computer interaction.

The contributions in this volume are guided by several core objectives. First, the book synthesizes current research and practice on transparency and trust across the entire AI lifecycle—from data collection and curation to deployment, monitoring, and governance. Second, it seeks to operationalize transparency through concrete, actionable methods, including documentation standards, auditing processes, model and dataset reporting frameworks, and mechanisms for communicating uncertainty and risk. Third, it bridges disciplinary boundaries, aligning technical innovations with legal, ethical, organizational, and user-centered considerations. Fourth, it demonstrates real-world relevance through case studies drawn from industry, public administration, healthcare, education, and research contexts. Finally, it looks ahead, identifying emerging directions such as trustworthy generative AI, privacy-preserving and federated learning, robust evaluation strategies, and scalable approaches to responsible automation.

What distinguishes this volume is its emphasis on end-to-end ecosystems. While prior research has often focused on individual aspects such as fairness, explainability, or privacy in isolation, this book examines how these elements interconnect. Trustworthy AI does not emerge from a single technique or tool; it is the result of coordinated practices spanning data governance, system design, evaluation, regulatory compliance, and human oversight.

It is my hope that this collection will serve both as a comprehensive reference for researchers and as a practical guide for practitioners working to design, deploy, and manage trustworthy data and AI systems. By bringing together diverse perspectives and actionable insights, this volume aims to contribute meaningfully to the development of AI systems that are not only innovative, but also responsible, transparent, and aligned with societal values.

I extend my sincere gratitude to all contributing authors, reviewers, and collaborators whose expertise and dedication made this work possible.

ORGANIZATION OF THE BOOK

In Chapter 1, the contributors present a forward-looking framework for securing AIoT ecosystems by integrating federated learning with quantum-resilient cryptographic techniques. From an editorial perspective, this chapter effectively addresses the growing tension between large-scale data utilization and the need for privacy preservation. By combining decentralized learning, lightweight encryption, blockchain-based aggregation, and explainable AI, the authors offer a cohesive architecture that not only mitigates emerging security threats but also enhances trust and interpretability in distributed intelligent systems.

Chapter 2 advances the discussion of secure digital infrastructures by focusing on cryptographic efficiency in electronic commerce. The author proposes a hybrid encryption protocol that strategically combines the Chinese Remainder Theorem, El-Gamal, and AES to balance performance with robust security. This contribution is particularly notable for its emphasis on scalability and practical deployment, demonstrating how carefully integrated cryptographic methods can strengthen transaction security while minimizing computational complexity in increasingly interconnected commercial environments.

In Chapter 3, the authors introduce *Research Guru AI*, an applied AI tool designed to transform how scholars engage with the rapidly expanding body of academic literature. From the Editor's viewpoint, this chapter stands out for its practical relevance and cross-domain applicability. By enabling structured summarization, comparative analysis, and reproducible workflows, the tool exemplifies how AI can enhance transparency and rigor in research processes while supporting broader Open Science initiatives and organizational adoption.

Chapter 4 explores the evolving challenge of spam detection through the lens of deep learning. The proposed *SmartSpam* framework leverages a range of neural architectures—including recurrent, convolutional, and transformer-based models—to capture the nuanced and contextual patterns of modern spam messages. This chapter highlights the importance of model optimization and feature engineering in achieving high detection accuracy, offering a technically rich contribution that reinforces the role of advanced AI techniques in safeguarding digital communication systems.

In Chapter 5, the focus shifts to the human dimension of trust in data ecosystems, examining consumer perceptions of privacy and security in the context of big data usage. Through an empirical study of Indian consumers, the authors reveal how concerns about data protection significantly influence online behavior. This chapter provides valuable insight into the sociotechnical aspects of trust, emphasizing that technological advancement must be accompanied by user awareness, transparency, and responsible data practices to sustain engagement and confidence.

Chapter 6 presents a compelling model of transparency-by-design within smart city infrastructures, specifically through a privacy-preserving Wi-Fi analytics framework for crowd monitoring. The authors introduce the CCTC framework—centered on consent, control, transparency, and compliance—as a structured governance approach embedded across the data lifecycle. The included case study demonstrates how technical innovation, when aligned with ethical and regulatory principles, can support urban management and tourism while maintaining public trust.

In Chapter 7, the contributors provide a systematic and timely examination of data practices in Talking Head Generation (THG). This chapter underscores the critical role of high-quality, ethically sourced, and well-documented datasets in ensuring trustworthy AI outcomes. By identifying gaps in current datasets and proposing standardized documentation, fairness audits, and privacy-preserving methodologies, the authors contribute a rigorous foundation for advancing both the technical and ethical dimensions of generative AI research.

Finally, Chapter 8 broadens the scope to a national research ecosystem, analyzing the structures that support scientific data governance in Slovakia. The authors highlight the centrality of transparency, open science, and data integrity in fostering credible and effective research systems. From policy frameworks to technical standards for data management, this chapter illustrates how coordinated institutional efforts are essential for enabling trustworthy, data-driven science and innovation.

Together, these chapters reflect the multidimensional nature of trustworthy AI systems—spanning technical architectures, human factors, governance models, and real-world applications—reinforcing the central theme of this volume: that trust must be intentionally designed, operationalized, and sustained across the entire data and AI lifecycle.

CONCLUSION

As this volume draws to a close, it becomes clear that trustworthy AI is not a singular achievement, but an ongoing commitment—one that must be cultivated across technologies, institutions, and societies. The chapters in this book collectively demonstrate that trust cannot be retrofitted into data and AI systems; it must be intentionally designed, rigorously evaluated, and continuously maintained throughout the entire lifecycle.

From secure and privacy-preserving architectures to transparent data practices, from human-centered governance frameworks to real-world applications across sectors, the contributions in this volume underscore the inherently interdisciplinary nature of this field. They remind us that technical excellence alone is insufficient. Trust emerges at the intersection of robust engineering, ethical responsibility, regulatory alignment, and user confidence.

A key insight that runs throughout this collection is the importance of integration. Advances in federated learning, cryptography, explainability, and MLOps must align with organizational practices, legal requirements, and societal expectations. Similarly, empirical studies and case-based implementations highlight that user perceptions, cultural contexts, and behavioral responses are critical to the success of any trustworthy AI initiative. The future of AI will depend not only on what systems can do, but on how they are understood, governed, and accepted.

This book also points toward emerging frontiers that demand continued attention. The rise of generative AI, increasing reliance on large-scale data ecosystems, and the growing complexity of automated decision-making systems all introduce new challenges—and opportunities—for transparency and accountability. Addressing these will require sustained collaboration across disciplines, sectors, and global contexts.

It is my hope that this volume serves not only as a comprehensive reference, but also as a catalyst for further research, innovation, and dialogue. Whether you are a researcher advancing theoretical foundations, a practitioner implementing real-world systems, or a policymaker shaping governance frameworks, the insights presented here are intended to support informed, responsible, and forward-looking engagement with AI technologies.

Ultimately, building trustworthy AI systems is a shared responsibility. It demands vigilance, adaptability, and a commitment to aligning technological progress with human values. I invite readers to carry forward the ideas presented in this book—questioning, refining, and applying them—to help shape a future in which AI systems are not only intelligent, but also transparent, accountable, and worthy of the trust placed in them.

Otmane Azeroual
University of Hagen, Germany

Chapter 1

Federated Learning and Quantum-Resilient Cryptographic Frameworks for Secure and Trustworthy AIoT Ecosystems

Ravikumar Ch
http://orcid.org/0000-0003-0809-5545
Sreenidhi University, Hyderabad, India

Burri Naresh
CVR College of Engineering, India

Mandala Rajkumar
http://orcid.org/0009-0006-6710-2468
Sri Indu College of Engineering and Technology, India

A. Pramod Reddy
Teegala Krishna Reddy College of Engineering and Technology, Hyderabad, India

Yemineni Sowjanya
Pallavi Engineering College, India

Sabavath Raju
http://orcid.org/0009-0002-7453-7196
Pallavi Engineering College, India

ABSTRACT

AIoT combines Artificial Intelligence (AI) with the Internet of Things (IoT) to enable smart applications in healthcare, transport, industry, and cities. However, the massive data from billions of devices creates risks to privacy, trust, and security. To address this, we propose a federated learning framework with quantum-resistant cryptography and explainable AI. It protects data locally, secures communication,

DOI: 10.4018/979-8-2600-1433-2.ch001

detects attacks, and supports reliable decision-making. Lightweight cryptography, blockchain aggregation, and trust metrics ensure efficiency, integrity, and resilience for future AIoT systems.

1. INTRODUCTION

The rapid evolution of the Internet of Things (IoT) and Artificial Intelligence (AI) has culminated in the emergence of the Artificial Intelligence of Things (AIoT) paradigm, which fundamentally reshapes how intelligent systems perceive, analyze, and respond to real-world environments (IoT Analytics, 2021). AIoT systems combine ubiquitous sensing, distributed connectivity, and intelligent analytics to enable context-aware, autonomous, and adaptive decision-making across diverse domains, including healthcare, smart cities, industrial automation, transportation, energy systems, and critical infrastructure management. By embedding intelligence directly into the data generation layer, AIoT transforms passive sensing networks into proactive, self-learning ecosystems capable of real-time reasoning and long-term optimization. However, this transformation comes at the cost of unprecedented complexity. The exponential growth in the number of connected devices, the heterogeneity of hardware platforms, and the dynamic nature of network topologies significantly increase the attack surface and exacerbate concerns related to data privacy, system security, trustworthiness, and long-term sustainability. As AIoT systems increasingly operate in safety-critical and socially sensitive environments, ensuring that intelligence is not only accurate but also secure, transparent, and trustworthy has become a central challenge for researchers and practitioners alike.

Among all application domains, healthcare stands out as one of the most impactful and sensitive areas of AIoT deployment. The Internet of Medical Things (IoMT) has already demonstrated its potential to revolutionize healthcare delivery by enabling continuous patient monitoring, remote diagnostics, personalized treatment planning, and intelligent clinical decision support (Ahmed et al., 2024). Wearable devices, implantable sensors, and smart diagnostic equipment generate continuous streams of physiological and behavioral data that can be leveraged by AI models to detect early signs of disease, predict adverse events, and optimize treatment strategies. Nevertheless, medical data is among the most sensitive categories of personal information, and its misuse or exposure can have severe ethical, legal, and societal consequences. Data breaches, adversarial manipulation of diagnostic models, and unauthorized access to patient records pose significant risks that can undermine trust in AI-driven healthcare systems. Similar privacy and security challenges arise in other AIoT-driven domains, such as smart homes, financial services, and cognitive cities, where personal, financial, and behavioral data are continuously collected and analyzed (Sinha et al., 2024; Himdi, 2024). In these contexts, the failure to adequately protect data and learning processes can lead not only to financial losses but also to erosion of public trust and regulatory non-compliance.

Traditional centralized machine learning approaches are increasingly ill-suited to address the privacy, scalability, and governance challenges inherent in AIoT ecosystems. Centralized data aggregation creates single points of failure, increases vulnerability to cyberattacks, and often violates data sovereignty and regulatory constraints. Federated Learning (FL) has therefore emerged as a compelling alternative that enables collaborative model training across distributed devices or organizations without requiring raw data to leave its original source (McMahan et al., 2017). By shifting the learning process closer to the data, FL inherently reduces privacy risks and aligns well with regulatory frameworks governing sensitive data. In AIoT environments, FL allows edge devices, sensors, and institutional servers to jointly learn shared representations while preserving local autonomy. Secure aggregation mechanisms further enhance privacy by ensuring that individual model updates remain confidential during the aggregation process, preventing the inference of sensitive information from shared parameters (Bonawitz et al., 2019). Advances in federated optimization techniques address practical challenges such as limited communication bandwidth, device heterogeneity, and straggler effects, thereby improving scalability and robustness in real-world deployments (Mehta et al., 2024). At the same time, the integration of explainable AI techniques into federated learning frameworks has gained traction, particularly in regulated domains like healthcare and finance, where transparency, accountability, and interpretability are essential for building trust and ensuring ethical decision-making (Awosika et al., 2024).

Despite these advances, federated learning does not fully eliminate security risks. Model updates can still leak information, malicious participants can inject poisoned updates, and adversaries may attempt to reconstruct sensitive data through model inversion or inference attacks. These vulnerabilities are further compounded by the scale and heterogeneity of AIoT systems, where millions of devices with varying trust levels participate in collaborative learning. Moreover, the long-term security assumptions underlying many existing AIoT infrastructures are being challenged by rapid progress in quantum computing. Quantum algorithms, most notably Shor's algorithm, threaten to break widely used public-key cryptographic schemes by enabling efficient factorization and discrete logarithm computation (Bennett and Brassard, 2014). As AIoT systems rely heavily on cryptography for secure communication, authentication, access control, and trust management, the emergence of quantum-capable adversaries represents a fundamental shift in the threat landscape.

The potential impact of quantum computing on AIoT security has prompted growing interest in post-quantum cryptography (PQC) and quantum-resilient trust models designed to withstand both classical and quantum attacks (Biamonte et al.,

2017; Bowles et al., 2024). However, deploying quantum-resistant cryptographic primitives in AIoT environments is particularly challenging due to the severe computational, memory, and energy constraints of edge devices. Lightweight cryptographic solutions are therefore essential to ensure that quantum resilience does not come at the cost of impractical overhead. Beyond cryptography, quantum computing also introduces new opportunities for enhancing learning paradigms. Recent research has explored the integration of quantum-enhanced and quantum-inspired models within federated learning frameworks, aiming to improve learning efficiency, communication compression, and adversarial robustness. Federated quantum convolutional neural networks (Bhatia and Kais, 2023) and federated quantum tensor network architectures (Bhatia and Neira, 2024) exemplify this emerging trend, demonstrating that quantum-inspired representations can increase expressiveness and resistance to manipulation while operating within federated settings.

These developments point toward a broader shift from purely classical, centralized intelligence toward hybrid, decentralized, and quantum-aware AIoT architectures. In such architectures, federated learning serves as the backbone for privacy-preserving collaboration, quantum-resilient cryptography ensures long-term security against emerging threats, and explainable AI mechanisms provide transparency and accountability. Trust management, inspired by blockchain and distributed ledger concepts, further complements these components by enabling decentralized authentication, integrity verification, and situational trust assessment across heterogeneous AIoT participants. The integration of these technologies is not merely additive but synergistic, as each component addresses distinct yet interconnected dimensions of AIoT security and trustworthiness.

Motivated by this holistic perspective, this chapter presents a comprehensive Federated and Quantum-Resilient AIoT (FQ-AIoT) framework that unifies federated learning, quantum-resistant cryptography, blockchain-inspired trust modeling, and explainable AI mechanisms into a coherent architectural vision. The chapter makes three primary contributions. First, it offers an extensive survey of federated learning-based security frameworks tailored to AIoT ecosystems, emphasizing communication efficiency, adversarial robustness, and cross-domain trust management. Second, it critically examines quantum-resistant cryptographic approaches suitable for deployment on resource-constrained IoT devices, with a focus on lightweight post-quantum primitives and their integration into federated systems. Third, it proposes an integrated FQ-AIoT framework that combines explainability, situational trust metrics, and quantum-ready cryptographic mechanisms to enable secure, transparent, and resilient AIoT applications across healthcare, smart cities, and industrial domains. By situating federated learning and quantum resilience within a unified conceptual framework, this work aims to advance the design of next-generation AIoT ecosystems capable of sustaining trust, privacy, and security in an increasingly interconnected and quantum-aware world.

1. This chapter presents an original Federated and Quantum-Resilient AIoT (FQ-AIoT) framework unifying federated learning, quantum-resilient cryptography, blockchain-inspired trust modeling, and explainable AI mechanisms. The chapter is contributing in three main areas:
2. An extensive review of federated learning-based security frameworks, designed to meet AIoT ecosystems, to focus on efficiency in communication, adversarial resilience, and cross-domain trust management.
3. A discussion on quantum-resistant cryptographic systems that can be deployed on resource-constrained IoT devices, with a view to lightweight post-quantum primitives.
4. An FQ-AIoT framework proposal that combines explainability, situational trust metrics, and quantum-ready cryptography to make AIoT applications secure and transparent.

The rest of this chapter is arranged in the following way. Section 2 explains the security issues in AIoT. The third section covers the federated learning of AIoT. The post-quantum cryptographic solutions are provided in section 4. Section 5 talks about trust modeling and explainability. Section 6 presents the FQ-AIoT framework as a proposal. Section 7 covers open challenges and future directions and Section 8 concludes the chapter.

2. SECURITY CHALLENGES IN AIOT

The fast development of the Artificial Intelligence of Things (AIoT) has brought revolutionary value to fields like healthcare, smart cities, financial, and industrial automation. AIoT systems capitalize on the omnipresence of IoT sensing and connectivity with the predictive intelligence of AI to support real-time analytics, autonomous decision-making, and adaptive optimization. This close alignment of data-driven intelligence and large-scale, heterogeneous IoT infrastructures, however, leaves the ecosystem vulnerable to various security threats that compromise trust, scale, and resilience. A recent market research estimated a volume of more than 12 billion IoT connections by 2030, which highlights the need to address privacy and security threats in deployments of AIoT functionalities. It summarizes the most critical security issues in AIoT systems and gives a reason to consider more sophisticated solutions like federated learning and quantum cryptography in the next sections.

2.1 Data Privacy and Confidentiality

The premise of AIoT applications is that data is continuously being gathered by distributed sensors and edge devices and cloud servers. Often, sensitive information such as a medical image, patient health record, financial transaction and activity logs of the user are sent and processed to enable real time analytics. Confidentiality is of great importance to such systems since any confidentiality breakdown can cause serious consequences, such as losing identity, developing a bad reputation, and failure to abide by the rules.

One such area is Internet of Medical Things (IoMT) where privacy is a burning issue. Ahmed et al. (2024) stressed that the suite of medical IoT devices will generate sensitive patient data in a continuous stream, and that this data should be secured against unauthorized access and abuse. Older cloud-based machine learning systems tend to centralize data thus exposing the data to attacks during transmission or storage. By allowing data to be stored at a local level, new architectures such as federated learning are meant to address this, but the communication lines are prone to inference and reconstruction attacks (McMahan et al., 2017).

Furthermore, encryption methods might not be sufficient since the attackers can use traffic pattern or metadata to perform inference attacks. Cryptographic protection is highlighted as an element in safe aggregation protocols (Bonawitz et al., 2019) but the constraint of computational overhead and delay remains a drag on resource-constrained IoT devices. Therefore, AIoT data privacy needs hybrid solutions, which are a combination of cryptographic primitives and privacy-preserving AI models.

2.2 Authentication and Access Control

The network should be authenticated to allow only authorized devices and users into the AIoT network. But as AIoT ecosystems are large and dynamic with billions of heterogeneous devices to authenticate in real time, conventional schemes like password-based schemes cannot meet the required standards.

Himdi (2024) introduced an AI- and blockchain-based access control solution to secure access in cognitive cities and emphasized that centralized authentication is a source of single points of failure and low scalability. The integration of distributed authentication based on blockchain, with AI-based anomaly detection is an encouraging solution, but it comes with resource usage and latency trade-offs.

The issue of access control is also acute. In Altherwi et al. (2024) it was shown that unauthorized access disclosures occur in cloud-based e-healths when access policies are not established properly, particularly where various stakeholders like doctors, insurers, and researchers need role-specific access. Risk profile-based and user-behavior-based access control also needs context-aware access control systems where AI modulates permissions. However, adversaries can take advantage of these adaptive mechanisms and resort to the concept of spoofing or adversarial attacks in order to create new vulnerabilities.

2.3 Scalability and Resource Constraints

AIoT deployments have to be capable of scaling to millions of devices and still be low-latency, energy-efficient, and secure. This establishes an implicit conflict between security and scalability, because cryptographic and intrusion detection systems are very resource-intensive (in terms of both computational and communication resources).

It was pointed out by Shafique et al. (2021) that cross-layer security frameworks are essential to resolve the issue of hardware-level and system-level vulnerabilities to implement energy-efficient secure AI at the edge. Lightweight cryptography algorithms and edge-native anomaly detection have been viewed as promising, albeit their scaling is often limited by weak device performance.

Moreover, the dynamical addition and deletion of the devices generate novel attack surfaces. As an example, a malefactor can introduce malicious nodes into a smart home or other industrial AIoT system to disrupt the data aggregation process. It is this difficulty that AI-enhanced smart homes address (Sinha et al., 2024), as new devices frequently joins the network that requires scalable and safe on boarding methods.

2.4 Heterogeneity and Interoperability

The AIoT ecosystems are highly heterogeneous because they constitute multiple hardware, communication protocols, and AI frameworks. The resulting heterogeneity poses interoperability issues, and creates vulnerabilities as elements are integrated among vendors.

In a similar direction, Mehta et al. (2024) asserted the variations in capabilities of the devices, the distributed local data, and the communication norms complicate the procedure of securing the IoT systems under federated learning. Malicious devices can use protocol mismatches to execute denial-of-service (DoS) or man-in-the-middle (MitM) attacks. Similarly, Awosika et al. (2024) also stressed that explainability and transparency are important in federated AIoT since financial institutions must be accountable in fraud detection frameworks. Irregularities in adoption of security measures that can be exploited are due to lack of standardization of structure among vendors.

The heterogeneity issue can be solved by developing interoperability security measures, which fit various ecosystems. This problem is beginning to be addressed by standardization organizations, and collective industry effort is bearing fruit, though much remains to be done to preserve cross-domain compatibility and also without impairing performance.

2.5 Emerging Threats: Adversarial Attacks and Data Poisoning

With AI at the heart of AIoT systems, attackers are starting to abuse the AI models themselves. Adversarial attacks Adversarial attacks can be misleading AI models to misclassify an input data potentially with devastating effects, by introducing carefully designed perturbations into it. To take a few examples, any adversarial manipulation of smart healthcare systems can lead to a wrong diagnosis, whereas attacks on smart traffic systems can interfere with safety measures.

Reviewing challenges in federated learning, Banabilah et al. (2022) noted that the issue of data poisoning attacks when rogue devices feed false updates to the system is a critical concern to collaborative AI training. Such attacks are particularly prone to AIoT systems because of their distributed and massive scale. Conventional anomaly detection systems might not be able to identify insidious model poisoning attacks.

Furthermore, adversarial attacks do not apply only to the supervised learning models. Attackers can also manipulate reinforcement learning agents in an autonomous vehicle or a drone by reward hacking or by manipulating state. The relevance of these threats is why explanation-capable, adversary-resilient, and robust AI models are required in the AIoT.

2.6 Regulatory and Ethical Challenges

Along with technical vulnerabilities, AIoT also faces extremely severe regulatory and ethical challenges. Data protection regulations, such as GDPR and HIPAA, are extremely strict regarding the method of collecting, storing, and processing personal information. Violation of these rules has other consequences that are unrelated to financial expenses such as loss of trust among users.

The ethical dimension of ubiquitous surveillance in intelligent cities, operational domains and medical centres should be addressed too. The possible risk associated with the use of opaque AI systems is that they would be discriminative or unfair to some groups of users. In recent years, explainable artificial intelligence (XAI) (Awosika et al., 2024) has received attention as an attempt to make it more transparent though it is difficult to guarantee that explainability can be obtained without compromising security and performance.

AIoT has provided unprecedented opportunities in the health sector, financial, smart cities, etc., but it is prone to numerous security issues, including data privacy, authentication, scalability, heterogeneity, and adversarial threats. These risks are also exacerbated by the resource-constrained and highly dynamic character of AIoT systems and aggravated by regulatory and ethical concerns regarding safe deployment.

Federated learning as a paradigm has the potential to reverse the threat of privacy and data-sharing, as will be discussed below, and quantum cryptography and quantum-enhanced federated learning provides promising security guarantees against new adversarial risks and future quantum attacks. The two approaches could have a compounding effect on enabling trustful and robust AIoT ecosystems.

3. FEDERATED LEARNING FOR SECURE AIOT

The growth of the Artificial Intelligence of Things (AIoT) has further increased the demand of privacy-sensitive and secure machine learning techniques. Conventional centralized AI designs which involve consolidating raw data into a central data store cannot support AIoT ecosystems which produce highly sensitive and distributed information. Here, Federated Learning (FL) has become a concept under which collaborative model training can be done without data being centralized. Instead, they only exchange local model updates which are then combined to create a global model. This decentralized model is specifically appropriate to AIoT, in which billions of connected devices form heterogeneous, privacy-sensitive and resource-constrained contexts (Banabilah et al., 2022).

Figure 1. Federated learning framework for secure AIoT systems

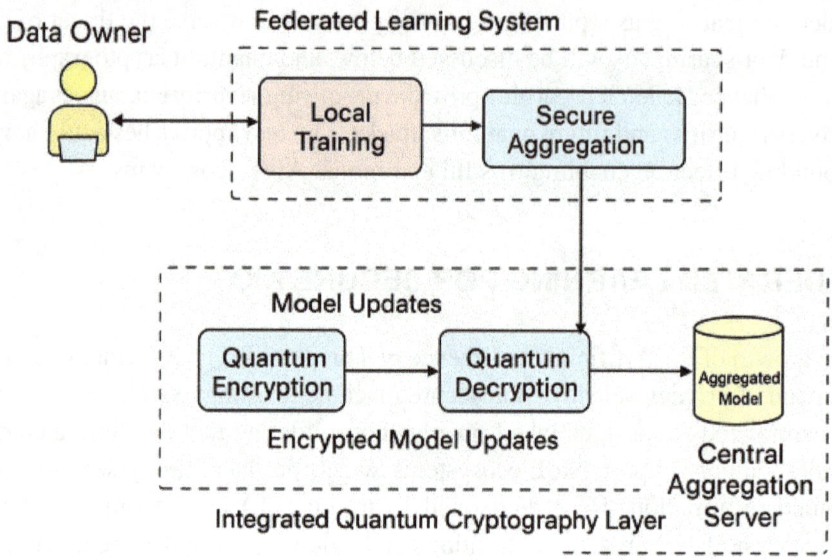

This Figure 1 illustrates the workflow of federated learning in AIoT, showing distributed devices training locally and sharing model updates with a global aggregator to enhance security and privacy.

3.1 Fundamentals of Federated Learning

Federated Learning (FL) represents a paradigm shift in distributed machine learning by enabling two or more devices, organizations, or data owners to collaboratively train a shared global model while maintaining complete local control over their raw data. Unlike traditional centralized learning approaches that require aggregating datasets into a single repository, FL performs model training directly on edge devices or institutional servers, thereby ensuring that sensitive data never leaves its original source. This decentralized training paradigm provides several foundational advantages. First and foremost, FL inherently preserves data privacy, as personal, medical, or proprietary data remain stored locally, which is particularly important for compliance with stringent regulatory frameworks such as the General Data Protection Regulation (GDPR) and the Health Insurance Portability and Accountability Act (HIPAA). Secondly, FL significantly reduces communication overhead by transmitting only model parameters, gradients, or weight updates rather than large-scale datasets, which is critical in bandwidth-constrained AIoT environments. Thirdly, FL exhibits strong scalability and adaptability across heterogeneous ecosystems, allowing diverse devices with varying computational power, operating systems, and network conditions to participate in collaborative learning. As highlighted by Banabilah et al. (2022), these characteristics make FL especially suitable for Artificial Intelligence of Things (AIoT) systems, where data is naturally decentralized across billions of interconnected sensors and devices. However, the same study also emphasizes that this decentralized architecture introduces novel challenges, including vulnerability to data poisoning attacks, increased communication latency under large-scale deployments, and significant heterogeneity in device capabilities, all of which must be addressed to ensure reliable and secure federated intelligence.

3.2 Secure Aggregation and Privacy

Although federated learning eliminates centralized data storage, it does not entirely eliminate privacy risks, as model updates themselves may inadvertently leak sensitive information through inference or reconstruction attacks. To mitigate this risk, secure aggregation protocols have been developed to ensure that individual client updates remain confidential and are never exposed to the central server or other participating entities. These protocols rely on cryptographic techniques that allow the aggregation server to compute a global model update without accessing any individual contribution in plaintext form. Banabilah et al. (2022) emphasize that such privacy-preserving aggregation mechanisms are essential to maintaining trust in FL systems, particularly in sensitive domains such as healthcare and finance. In addition to cryptographic aggregation, complementary techniques such as differential privacy further strengthen security by injecting controlled statistical noise into local updates, thereby limiting the possibility of identifying individual data samples. More recent advancements have explored the integration of FL with quantum-inspired architectures to enhance privacy and resilience even further. A notable example is the Federated Quanvolutional Neural Network (FQNN) proposed by Bhatia et al. (2023), which incorporates quantum feature mappings into the federated learning process. By leveraging the intrinsic properties of quantum-inspired transformations, FQNNs obscure data representations and significantly reduce information leakage risks during model updates. These developments mark a crucial step toward building secure and privacy-aware AIoT systems, particularly in domains where even minimal data exposure can have severe ethical, legal, and societal consequences.

3.3 Communication Efficiency in AIoT

Communication efficiency remains one of the most critical bottlenecks in large-scale AIoT deployments, as federated learning systems often involve millions or even billions of edge devices that must exchange model updates periodically. Excessive communication not only increases latency and energy consumption but also places a heavy burden on constrained network infrastructures, potentially limiting the practicality of FL in real-time AIoT applications. To address this challenge, recent research has focused on reducing the size and frequency of transmitted updates without compromising learning accuracy. Bhatia et al. (2023) demonstrated that quantum-enhanced encoding techniques can effectively compress model updates, enabling significant reductions in communication overhead while preserving model performance. Furthermore, Bhatia and Neira (2024) introduced Federated Hierarchical Tensor Networks (FHTN), which exploit tensor decompositions and hierarchical learning structures to represent high-dimensional data more efficiently. By organizing federated learning into multiple hierarchical levels, FHTN minimizes redundant communication and enables localized aggregation before global synchronization. These communication-efficient strategies are particularly valuable in AIoT scenarios such as smart healthcare systems, industrial automation, and connected transportation networks, where timely decision-making and energy efficiency are paramount. Collectively, these approaches demonstrate that advanced encoding and hierarchical learning mechanisms can substantially enhance the scalability and feasibility of FL in bandwidth-limited environments.

3.4 Robustness against Adversarial Attacks

Despite its many advantages, federated learning remains vulnerable to a range of adversarial threats that can undermine model integrity and trustworthiness. Among the most prominent threats are data poisoning attacks, in which malicious clients intentionally submit corrupted updates to degrade global model performance, and model inversion attacks, where adversaries attempt to reconstruct sensitive training data from shared gradients. Banabilah et al. (2022) emphasize that ensuring adversarial robustness is a foundational requirement for secure FL deployment, especially in safety-critical AIoT applications. In response to these threats, quantum-enhanced and hierarchical defense mechanisms have begun to emerge as promising solutions. Bhatia et al. (2023) argue that quantum-inspired feature spaces introduce a level of complexity that makes it significantly more difficult for attackers to manipulate model updates or inject targeted backdoors. Similarly, Bhatia and Neira (2024) demonstrate that hierarchical FL architectures enable the isolation and containment of compromised nodes by restricting their influence to localized aggregation levels. This layered defense strategy not only improves robustness against adversarial behavior but also enhances fault tolerance in highly dynamic and untrusted AIoT environments. As adversarial threats continue to evolve, such resilience-oriented design principles are expected to play a central role in the future of secure federated intelligence.

3.5 Applications in Healthcare and Beyond

Among the many application domains of federated learning, healthcare stands out as one of the most impactful and promising. Medical data, including electronic health records, diagnostic imaging, and genomic sequences, are highly sensitive and subject to strict privacy regulations, making centralized data collection impractical or even impossible. Federated learning enables hospitals, laboratories, and research institutions to collaboratively develop predictive and diagnostic models while keeping patient data securely within institutional boundaries. Bhatia et al. (2023) demonstrated that Federated Quanvolutional Neural Networks are particularly effective for analyzing distributed medical data, offering both privacy preservation and enhanced learning capabilities. In parallel, Bhatia and Neira (2024) applied Federated Hierarchical Tensor Networks to healthcare scenarios and showed that hierarchical aggregation significantly improves scalability and efficiency in real-world deployments. Beyond healthcare, Banabilah et al. (2022) identified a wide range of AIoT applications benefiting from FL, including smart cities, where distributed sensors generate massive volumes of traffic, energy, and environmental data, and financial services, where FL enables fraud detection without violating data-sharing regulations. Despite these promising results, several open challenges remain, including scalability to billions of heterogeneous devices, the need for explainable federated models to build user trust, deeper integration of quantum federated learning to enhance security and efficiency, and the development of standardized frameworks to ensure interoperability across AIoT ecosystems. As highlighted by Banabilah et al. (2022) and Bhatia et al. (2023), the integration of federated learning with quantum-inspired methods and tensor-network-based hierarchies represents a significant leap toward sustainable, secure, and intelligent AIoT infrastructures. Ultimately, federated learning is not merely an enabling technology but a foundational pillar for designing the next generation of resilient, collaborative, and trustworthy intelligent ecosystems.

4. QUANTUM-RESISTANT CRYPTOGRAPHY FOR AIOT SECURITY

The current rapid advancement in the field of quantum computing creates opportunities and challenges important to existing security paradigms. Even though quantum algorithms, including the Shor integer factorization algorithm and the Grover database search algorithm, can be promising in terms of computational efficiency, they also make common cryptographic constructions, especially RSA, the Diffie-Hellman algorithm, and the elliptic curve algorithm, vulnerable to quantum adversaries. The risk of quantum-enabled attacks in the application of Artificial Intelligence of Things (AIoT) where sensitive health, industrial, and urban infrastructure data pass through heterogeneous and resource-constrained hardware, requires an immediate shift toward quantum-resistant (post-quantum) cryptography systems (Bhatia et al., 2023).

Figure 2. Quantum cryptography-enhanced AIoT security model

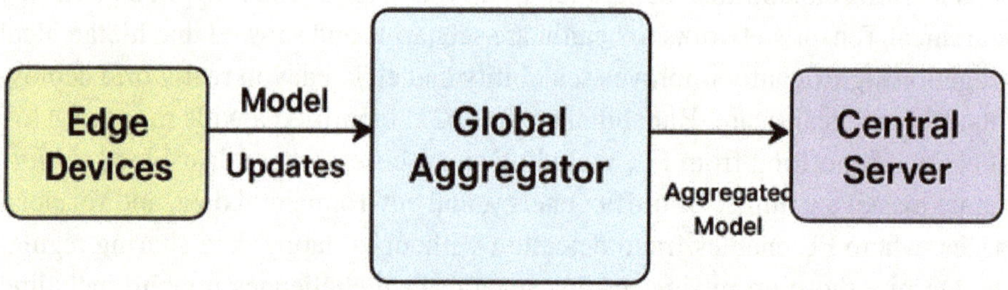

Figure 2 depicts the integration of quantum key distribution (QKD) and federated learning for secure communication in AIoT networks, enabling resilience against eavesdropping and adversarial attacks.

4.1 Vulnerabilities of Classical Cryptography in AIoT

The existing AIoT implementations effectively depend on the public-key infrastructures (PKI) to ensure the security of device-to-device communication, identity verification, and the update of firmware. Efficiency in constrained environments is dominated by protocols like the TLS/SSL and lightweight elliptic-curve schemes. But, as soon as Shor algorithm can factor in polynomials short time and compute discrete logarithms in polynomials short time, these classical PKI schemes become computationally infeasible as soon as large-scale quantum computers become available (Bhatia et al., 2025). It means that not only could adversaries decrypt intercepted communication but also generate fake digital signatures and break device authentication systems, eventually destroying trust in decentralized AIoT networks.

4.2 Post-Quantum Cryptography (PQC) Approaches

As a response to this imminent menace, researchers and standardization organizations like NIST have embarked on the construction of Post-Quantum Cryptography (PQC),--algorithms that are resistant to classical and quantum attackers alike. In the case of AIoT ecosystems, it is more about small-scale PQC schemes that can be resource efficient as well as with high quantum resistance. The major CQC categories that apply to AIoT are:

1. Lattice-Based Cryptography: Schemes such as Learning with Errors (LWE) and Ring-LWE have both strong theoretical security and scale properties. Protocols such as Kyber (key encapsulation) and Dilithium (digital signature) have become the predominant NIST candidates because of their high efficiency and scalability to limited hardware (Bhatia et al., 2023).
2. Code-Based Cryptography: The code-based schemes have the same properties as the McEliece cryptosystem: they are both classical and quantum resistant. They provide strong security, but their big key sizes make them difficult to integrate with IoT edge devices with small memory.
3. Hash-Based Signatures: SPHINCS+ is a stateless scheme that is applied to create post-quantum secure digital signatures. Since they use hash functions, they are applicable to environments that need long-term data integrity, like medical imaging in AIoT-enabled healthcare system.
4. Multivariate Polynomial Cryptography: The schemes are based on the difficulty of solving multivariate equations, which seem to be another way to use AIoT authentication and digital signatures.

4.3 Integration of Quantum-Resistant Schemes into AIoT

The latency, energy and storage constraints of PQC are not trivial when implementing it into AIoT systems. Ultralight implementations are being tailored to execute effectively on microcontrollers (ARM Cortex-M, RISC-V IoT cores) without loss of real-time performance. Also hybrid cryptographic protocols are being discussed that contain classical elliptic curve algorithms with PQC key exchanges to provide backward compatibility and a non-disruptive transition during the post-quantum migration phase (Biamonte et al., 2017).

PQC may support:

1. Decentralized Identity Management: AIoT systems may use PQC-based signatures inside blockchain smart contracts to support a tamper-resilient trust even in quantum-capable settings.
2. Federated Learning Security: with PQC-enhanced secure aggregation protocols, the gradient updates of federated models cannot be reversed by quantum adversaries, and thus both privacy and model robustness are maintained.
3. Edge Device Authentication: Lightweight signature schemes using post-quantum techniques support integrity verification of the firmware update to mitigate adversarial poisoning and supply-chain attacks.

4.4 Quantum Key Distribution (QKD) vs PQC for AIoT

PQC is algorithmically resistant, but Quantum Key Distribution (QKD) is a hardware-based implementation that uses quantum mechanics (e.g., polarization of photons in BB84 protocol) to achieve unconditionally secure key exchange. QKD, however, needs specialized infrastructure (fiber-optic or free-space quantum channels), and thus is less amenable to scalable AIoT deployments than PQC. One now-or-soon direction is the hybrid combination of PQC and QKD, especially in critical infrastructure AIoT applications like smart grids, defense IoT, and medical cyber-physical systems (Bowles et al., 2024).

In the future, quantum-resistant AIoT security research should be directed towards:

1. Lightweight PQC Protocols designed to be low-powered edge devices.
2. Hybrid Migration Models that would allow a smooth interoperability between classical and post-quantum infrastructures.
3. Identity management and immutable trust recording based on Quantum-Secure Blockchain.
4. Organizational Standards such as NIST and ETSI to guide the world to migrate to AIoT security.
5. Quantum-resilient federated learning to integrate PQC with privacy-preserving AI.

Embracing quantum-resistant cryptographic design, AIoT ecosystems can continue to be resilient, with trustworthy, private, and future-proof security in the presence of the new quantum adversaries.

5. EXPLAINABLE AI AND TRUST MODELING FOR SECURE AIOT

The intersection of Artificial Intelligence (AI), Internet of Things (IoT) and blockchain technologies is changing the face of Industry 4.0 and AIoT ecosystems. But as these systems grow in size and complexity, trust, transparency, and interpretability become central to their maintenance. Explainable AI (XAI) and blockchain-based trust models are presented as complementary solutions to the problem of making AI-based decision-making in AIoT networks secure and comprehensible to stakeholders. This sub-section discusses the application of XAI and trust modeling as a solution to security, privacy, and reliability issues in AIoT ecosystems.

Figure 3. Blockchain and digital twin empowered federated learning architecture

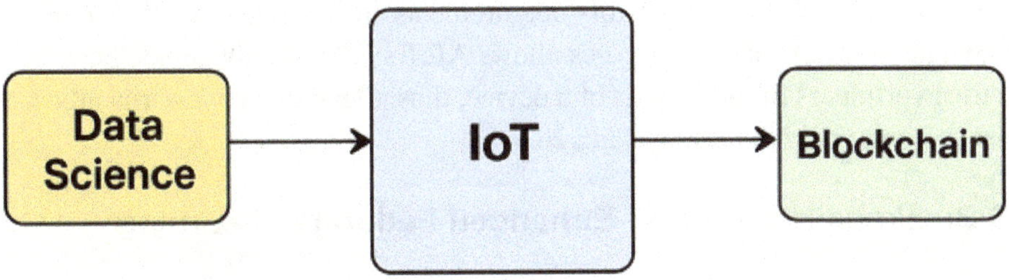

Figure 3 demonstrates how blockchain ensures secure aggregation and trust in federated learning, while digital twins provide real-time synchronization for Industrial IoT applications.

5.1 Role of Trust in AIoT Ecosystems

The AIoT devices work in an environment that is heterogeneous and decentralized and require constant validation of data, devices and models. Traditional security is more likely to focus on encryption and authentication but not on behavioral signs of trust and decision-making that are situation-specific. Reliance on AIoT is not only a technical parameter but also a question of the plausibility of the devices, the accuracy of the sent information, and the usability of the AI-based predictions (Gangwani et al., 2023).

Managing trust with blockchain can be more robust in managing AIoT trust by providing decentralized identity verification and tamper-proof audit trails. Blockchain-based AIoT trust systems in Industry 4.0 applications provide transparency and accountability to machine-to-machine interactions, allowing malicious nodes to avoid the destruction of federated systems (Gangwani et al., 2023).

5.2 Explainable AI for Transparent Decision-Making

Although AI improves predictive accuracy and automation in AIoT, black-box predictive models like deep neural networks do not provide a clear explanation of why they made the predictions. In mission-critical systems, like healthcare IoT, autonomous industrial systems, and smart city infrastructure, interpretability loss destroys user trust. Explainable AI (XAI) methods overcome this drawback, by providing post-hoc attributions (e.g., SHAP, LIME) or intrinsically interpretable models which explain how specific attributes affect predictions.

As an example, explainability allows stakeholders to validate the anomaly detection outputs, justifies the decisions made during predictive maintenance, and generates data to satisfy regulatory requirements in federated AIoT systems. A combination of XAI and trust scores allows AIoT systems to dynamically analyze the trustworthiness of the outputs of a device, thus alleviating adversarial attack or poisoned input risks (Prathiba et al., 2024).

5.3 Blockchain and Trust-Enhanced Federated Learning

The paradigm of federated learning (FL) has become a center of attention in AIoT because it is a privacy-preserving paradigm since it requires no disclosure of raw data to train a model. Nevertheless, federated models are still susceptible to malicious updates, model poisoning as well as free-rider problems. By combining blockchain with FL, one can have a decentralized trust layer, which can be used to record contributions, validate model updates, and hold actors accountable (Prathiba et al., 2024; Kumar et al., 2022).

Prathiba et al. (2024) showed how the blockchain and digital twins technologies reinforce FL in an Industrial IoT (IIoT) setting with improved security, resilience, and trust in joint model training. On the same note, Kumar et al. (2023) have emphasized that blockchain combined with deep learning-powered trust schemes enhances safe communication in IIoT networks built with digital twins. These solutions make federated models explainable and trustworthy, which is very important in the context of systems where false predictions can lead to system failure or result in safety risks.

5.4 Model Update Verification and Cooperative Trust

One of the major problems in AIoT FL systems is to make sure that you only insert the valid and true model updates. Jiang et al. (2021) suggested that cooperative federated learning structures could be established in which the blockchain authenticates model changes and guarantees integrity and impartiality. It is a self-regulating trust ecosystem to ensure that AIoT is trusted, this collaborative mechanism prevents corrupt updates and rewards honest contributions to build trust.

By adding explainable AI to this framework, the stakeholders will be able to see why some updates to the model were approved or not and therefore, promote transparency. Mechanisms of trust modeling that integrate blockchain validation and XAI explanations would allow stakeholders to identify the difference between innocent and malicious manipulations within federated systems.

5.5 Privacy-Preserving Trust Models with XAI

AIoT is also an area where trust is important to uphold user privacy, in cases where sensitive industrial or personal information is being used. Maurya et al. (2021) suggested a federated transfer learning model that combines authentication and protection of privacy through optimization based on reinforcement learning. These frameworks together with XAI enable stakeholders to monitor how private data may affect model predictions without exposing their raw data.

This two-fold trust system, privacy preservation + explainability, provides that AIoT systems remain ethical and regulatory and offer valuable insights that are trustworthy and accurate. In healthcare AIoT uses, such as when a doctor and a patient are involved, they can confirm the diagnosis predictions without breaching patient privacy.

AIoT ecosystems can support transparent, secure, and privacy-preserving AI by bringing together explainable AI, blockchain trust modeling, and federated learning, which are the building blocks of resilient Industry 4.0 infrastructures.

6. BLOCKCHAIN-ENABLED DIGITAL TWIN SECURITY IN AIOT

The digital twins (DTs) and digital IoT (IIoT) and AIoT systems have provided new opportunities to predictive analytics, real-time monitoring, and operational optimization systems due to the great similarity of these two systems. A digital twin is a computer model of a real-world object, process, or system which can be simulated, anomalies detected, and its behavior predicted. This technology will have potential benefits to efficiency, but will pose new cybersecurity and privacy concerns, especially when digital twins are implemented at scale in smart manufacturing, healthcare, and urban infrastructure. One of the trust enablers that have emerged as the supporting foundation to digital twins is blockchain, a technology that offers integrity, immutability, and visibility to data (Gangwani et al., 2023).

Indeed, as Gangwani et al. (2023) note, blockchain plays a significantly larger role in the Industry 4.0 ecosystems not only in the establishment of the transaction but also in the security of data obtained by the IoTs. A combination of blockchain, IoT analytics, and digital twins allows organizations to ensure that sensor data streams are immutable and, therefore, act as a consistent input to running predictive operations. This is particularly significant in systems which are used in predictive maintenance of industrial equipment where inaccurate information or falsified information may result in financial and operational losses.

A second technology that enhances the federated learning in the context of digital twins is blockchain, which verifies distributed model updates. Prathiba et al. (2024) demonstrated the strong resistance of blockchain to federated learning and digital twin models against adversarial manipulations. With the help of smart contracts, the learning contributions can be automatically verified, only the real updates can be accepted. This supports team intelligence between AIoT nodes and does not pose a threat to trust.

Similarly, Kumar et al. (2022) suggested blockchain and deep learning-based secure communication models of digital twin-based IIoT networks. They add in their article that the trust mechanisms must extend beyond encryption, and authentication, to adaptive trust scores, which evaluate the conditions, such as the reliability of the devices, the condition of the network and human activity. A synthesis of this enables more dynamic context-responsive solutions to AIoT security.

And Jiang et al. (2021) took it even further and suggested cooperative federated learning on blockchain-powered digital twin edge networks. Their framework verifies the updates on the models and rewards the honest nodes that reduce the model-poisoning or free-riding attacks. The self-sovereign ecosystem that this solution forms is cooperative and re-invigorates trust since it is continually confirmed by blockchain logging, and validation. This strengthens distributed intelligence and renders the decision-making on the basis of AIoT trustworthy.

The protection of privacy is another serious problem of AIoT other than security. Maurya et al. (2021) proposed a federated transfer learning model that can exploit a new reinforcement learning algorithm (S-TD3) to achieve authentication and privacy protection. This will ensure the protection of sensitive industrial and healthcare data and allow cross-domain learning. Such practices reflect one way in which AIoT ecosystems can achieve both data utility and confidentiality, which is a major need in industries that process mission-critical or personal information.

This way, blockchain-based digital twin frameworks can offer a multi-level security architecture where federated learning, explainable AI and privacy-preserving models meet and result in robust AIoT systems. The unsolved problem is scalability, interoperability and efficiency, especially with billions of devices being connected to each other.

7. FUTURE DIRECTIONS AND EMERGING RESEARCH OPPORTUNITIES

While blockchain technologies, federated learning (FL), and explainable Artificial Intelligence of Things (XAIoT) frameworks have demonstrated significant promise in addressing long-standing challenges related to trust, privacy, and security, future AIoT research must evolve beyond conceptual integration toward fully implementable, measurable, and governable security architectures. Early research efforts have primarily focused on demonstrating feasibility through isolated prototypes or loosely coupled frameworks, often under idealized assumptions. However, real-world AIoT deployments operate under stringent constraints, including limited computational resources, intermittent connectivity, heterogeneous device capabilities, and persistent adversarial threats. As AIoT systems continue to scale across critical infrastructures such as healthcare, transportation, smart grids, and industrial automation, the next phase of research will be defined by how effectively these technologies can be co-designed as unified systems rather than treated as independent layers. Achieving such co-design requires rigorous evaluation of trade-offs between security strength, system latency, energy efficiency, and operational resilience, as well as mechanisms for continuous monitoring, adaptation, and governance across the AIoT lifecycle.

A critical future direction lies in shifting AIoT security research from static, rule-based protection mechanisms toward adaptive, intelligence-driven security architectures that evolve alongside environmental and operational changes. This transition necessitates deeper integration of learning-based intelligence, decentralized trust infrastructures, and explainability mechanisms that collectively support transparency, accountability, and regulatory compliance. In this context, blockchain is increasingly viewed not merely as a data storage or transaction validation tool, but as a foundational trust substrate that enables verifiable coordination among distributed AIoT entities. Federated learning complements this vision by enabling collaborative intelligence without violating data sovereignty, while explainable AI ensures that system decisions remain interpretable to human stakeholders. The convergence of these technologies opens a rich space of research opportunities centered on scalability, robustness, and long-term sustainability.

7.1 Convergence of AIoT, Digital Twins, and Blockchain

One of the most promising emerging trends in AIoT research is the convergence of AIoT systems with digital twin technologies, where physical assets, processes, and environments are continuously mirrored in virtual counterparts to enable real-time monitoring, predictive analytics, and adaptive control. Digital twins allow AI models to simulate future system states, evaluate risk scenarios, and test mitigation strategies without disrupting physical operations. Cai et al. (2024) envision blockchain-supported secure federated learning as a foundational layer for digital twin ecosystems, enabling distributed models to evolve dynamically as environmental conditions, workloads, and threat landscapes change. In such architectures, blockchain provides immutable coordination and auditability, federated learning enables privacy-preserving intelligence across distributed twins, and AI models continuously refine predictions based on real-world feedback.

Despite this promise, several open research challenges remain unresolved. Chief among them is the secure aggregation of distributed model updates generated by digital twins operating across heterogeneous and potentially untrusted AIoT nodes. Without robust aggregation mechanisms, adversaries may infer sensitive device-level information or perform reconstruction attacks that undermine privacy guarantees. Furthermore, the real-time requirements of digital twin systems impose strict latency and bandwidth constraints that limit the feasibility of computationally expensive cryptographic protocols. This challenge is particularly acute in smart city and healthcare deployments, where delays in model updates or security responses can have severe consequences. Future research must therefore focus on designing lightweight secure aggregation protocols and post-quantum–safe cryptographic primitives that balance privacy, security, and real-time responsiveness, while remaining deployable on resource-constrained AIoT hardware.

7.2 Dynamic Trust and Self-Governance in AIoT Systems

Trust management in AIoT systems is increasingly recognized as a dynamic, context-aware, and time-varying process rather than a static property assigned at deployment. Devices may change behavior due to faults, software updates, environmental conditions, or adversarial compromise, necessitating continuous reassessment of trust relationships. Sasikumar et al. (2023) demonstrate how blockchain-based trust scoring mechanisms, when integrated with digital twins, can dynamically evaluate device reliability and isolate unreliable or malicious nodes in industrial IoT environments. By recording trust updates on a distributed ledger, such systems enable transparent and tamper-resistant trust management that can be audited by system operators.

While dynamic trust scoring represents a significant advancement, it also introduces complex challenges that remain largely unexplored. Trust drift, where benign nodes are gradually misclassified as malicious due to transient anomalies, can lead to false positives and unnecessary isolation of critical components. Conversely, sophisticated adversaries may attempt to manipulate trust metrics through coordinated behavior or intermittent compliance. These risks are particularly concerning in safety-critical AIoT applications, where automated trust penalties may directly affect physical operations. Future research must therefore investigate mechanisms for auditable trust updates, explainable trust decisions, and recovery pathways that allow nodes to regain trust after remediation. Incorporating human-in-the-loop governance, appeals mechanisms, and regulatory oversight into automated trust systems represents a crucial research opportunity for building self-governing yet accountable AIoT ecosystems.

7.3 Secure Sensing, Logging, and Explainability

Secure sensing and immutable logging form the backbone of trustworthy AIoT decision-making, as AI models are only as reliable as the data on which they are trained and evaluated. Zhao et al. (2023) highlight the importance of blockchain-based secure sensing and tamper-proof logging for ensuring data integrity in smart grids, environmental monitoring, and other critical infrastructures. By recording sensor data and system events on immutable ledgers, such architectures enable post-hoc verification, forensic analysis, and regulatory audits. However, immutability alone does not guarantee usability, interpretability, or compliance with evolving governance requirements.

When combined with explainable AI techniques, secure logging infrastructures can provide end-to-end transparency across the AIoT decision pipeline. Explainability mechanisms such as feature attribution, confidence estimation, and decision rationale visualization allow stakeholders to understand not only what decisions were made, but why they were made. A key research gap lies in linking on-chain provenance records with off-chain explainability artifacts in a privacy-preserving manner. Directly storing explainability outputs on-chain may expose sensitive information or exceed storage constraints, while keeping them entirely off-chain undermines auditability. Future work must explore hybrid architectures that cryptographically bind off-chain explainability evidence to on-chain provenance metadata, enabling verifiable yet privacy-aware audits. Such integration is essential for compliance with emerging AI governance frameworks and for building stakeholder confidence in autonomous AIoT systems.

7.4 Lightweight Distributed Ledgers for Constrained AIoT Nodes

Traditional blockchain platforms often impose significant computational, storage, and energy overheads that are incompatible with the constraints of many AIoT devices. To address this limitation, Gangwani et al. (2021) explore the use of Directed Acyclic Graph (DAG)-based distributed ledgers, such as IOTA Tangle, which replace sequential block validation with parallel transaction confirmation. These architectures reduce validation latency and computational overhead, making them attractive for large-scale AIoT deployments involving thousands or millions of constrained nodes.

Despite their scalability advantages, DAG-based ledgers remain insufficiently characterized under realistic adversarial conditions. Questions remain regarding their resilience to coordinated attacks, network partitioning, transaction flooding, and adversarial manipulation of tip selection mechanisms. Moreover, the security guarantees of DAG-based authentication and data-sharing protocols under high-load AIoT traffic patterns are not yet well understood. Future research must therefore prioritize rigorous quantitative benchmarking of lightweight ledger technologies using realistic threat models, heterogeneous network conditions, and representative AIoT workloads. Such evaluations are critical for determining whether DAG-based ledgers can serve as reliable trust infrastructures for mission-critical AIoT applications.

7.5 Toward Quantum-Resilient and Policy-Aware AIoT

Looking beyond immediate scalability and efficiency challenges, long-term AIoT security must account for the disruptive impact of quantum computing on existing cryptographic foundations. Sadri et al. (2023) outline a forward-looking vision in which blockchain ensures traceability, AI provides predictive intelligence, and digital twins support simulation-driven decision-making. Extending this vision, future AIoT systems must also incorporate post-quantum cryptography (PQC), policy-driven governance, and human-centric trust models to remain secure in the face of emerging quantum threats. As quantum computing threatens classical public-key cryptography, AIoT research must systematically evaluate the trade-offs between lattice-based, hash-based, and hybrid cryptographic schemes with respect to latency, memory footprint, energy consumption, and long-term security guarantees.

Equally important is the integration of policy-aware governance mechanisms that encode regulatory requirements, ethical constraints, and organizational policies directly into AIoT security architectures. Blockchain-based smart contracts, combined with explainable AI and federated learning, offer a promising foundation for enforcing such policies in a decentralized yet transparent manner. Future research should explore how policy enforcement can adapt dynamically to contextual changes, regulatory updates, and evolving threat landscapes without requiring costly system reconfiguration. By unifying quantum resilience, policy awareness, and explainability, next-generation AIoT systems can move toward a model of secure autonomy that balances machine intelligence with human oversight.

In summary, the future of secure and trustworthy AIoT lies in the tight co-design of federated learning, blockchain-based trust infrastructures, digital twins, explainable AI, and quantum-resilient cryptography. Rather than addressing these components in isolation, future research must focus on their systemic interactions under real-world constraints and adversarial conditions. By advancing toward adaptive, policy-aware, and quantum-ready AIoT architectures, the research community can lay the groundwork for intelligent systems that are not only powerful and scalable, but also transparent, resilient, and worthy of long-term societal trust.

7.6 Key Open Research Challenges

1. **Quantum-Resistant Blockchain and FL Protocols**

Designing PQC-enabled consensus, secure aggregation, and identity management suitable for large-scale AIoT.

2. **Explainability for Non-Expert Stakeholders**

Developing XAI mechanisms tailored for farmers, clinicians, and city operators rather than AI specialists.

3. **Cross-Domain Trust Interoperability**

Enabling trust models that operate consistently across industrial, medical, agricultural, and environmental AIoT domains.

4. **Lightweight Security Under Resource Constraints**

Balancing security strength, latency, and energy efficiency on low-power edge and sensor devices.

5. **Policy-Driven and Auditable AIoT Governance**

Aligning AIoT security frameworks with global data protection laws, ethical AI principles, and operational accountability.

8. CONCLUSION

Artificial Intelligence of Things (AIoT) presents transformative opportunities across smart cities, healthcare, industry, and agriculture, yet it also introduces unprecedented security, privacy, and trust challenges that cannot be addressed by conventional centralized mechanisms. The dynamic, heterogeneous, and large-scale nature of AIoT systems makes them particularly vulnerable to adversarial machine learning, large-scale botnets, insider threats, and emerging quantum-enabled attacks.

Federated Learning (FL) offers a compelling foundation for privacy-preserving collaborative intelligence, as it enables decentralized model training without direct data sharing. However, FL alone is insufficient, as it remains vulnerable to poisoning, inference, and collusion attacks. Blockchain technologies complement FL by introducing immutability, decentralized trust, and auditability, while post-quantum cryptography strengthens communication security against future quantum adversaries. Together, these technologies form a multi-layered trust architecture that is more resilient than any individual component.

Despite this promise, significant challenges remain in terms of computational overhead, latency, energy efficiency, and deployment feasibility, particularly for resource-constrained AIoT devices. Moreover, without standardized governance frameworks and explainable decision mechanisms, even technically secure systems may fail to gain regulatory and societal acceptance.

This chapter argues that the future of secure AIoT lies not only in technological integration but also in measurable performance trade-offs, explainable trust, and auditable governance. The convergence of FL, blockchain, PQC, and XAI represents a critical step toward resilient, privacy-aware, and scalable AIoT ecosystems, capable of supporting next-generation intelligent systems in a responsible and sustainable manner.

REFERENCES

Ahmed, S. F., Sharmin, S., Kuldeep, S. A., Lameesa, A., Alam, M. S. B., Liu, G., & Gandomi, A. H. (2024). Transformative impacts of the internet of medical things on modern healthcare. *Results in Engineering*, *25*, 103787. DOI: 10.1016/j.rineng.2024.103787

Altherwi, A., Ahmad, M. T., Alam, M. M., Mirza, H., Sultana, N., Pasha, A. A., Sultana, N., Khan, A. I., Alam, M. M., & Azim, R. (2024). A hybrid optimization approach for securing cloud-based e-health systems. *Multimedia Tools and Applications*, *84*(16), 16525–16560. DOI: 10.1007/s11042-024-19688-6

Awosika, T., Shukla, R. M., & Pranggono, B. (2024). Transparency and privacy: The role of explainable AI and federated learning in financial fraud detection. *IEEE Access : Practical Innovations, Open Solutions*, *12*, 64551–64560. DOI: 10.1109/ACCESS.2024.3394528

Banabilah, S., Aloqaily, M., Alsayed, E., Malik, N., & Jararweh, Y. (2022). Federated learning review: Fundamentals, enabling technologies, and future applications. *Information Processing & Management*, *59*(6), 103061. DOI: 10.1016/j.ipm.2022.103061

Bennett, C. H., & Brassard, G. (2014). Quantum cryptography: Public key distribution and coin tossing. *Theoretical Computer Science*, *560*, 7–11. DOI: 10.1016/j.tcs.2014.05.025

Bhatia, A. S., Kais, S., & Alam, M. A. (2023). Federated quanvolutional neural network: A new paradigm for collaborative quantum learning. *Quantum Science and Technology*, *8*(4), 045032. DOI: 10.1088/2058-9565/acfc61

. Bhatia, A. S., Kais, S., & Alam, M. A. (2023). Quantum federated learning in healthcare: The shift from development to deployment and from models to data.

Bhatia, A. S., & Neira, D. E. B. (2024). Federated hierarchical tensor networks: A collaborative learning quantum AI-driven framework for healthcare. arXiv preprint arXiv:2405.07735.

Bhatia, A. S., Saggi, M. K., & Kais, S. (2025). Application of quantum-inspired tensor networks to optimize federated learning systems. *Quantum Machine Intelligence*, *7*(1), 12. DOI: 10.1007/s42484-025-00243-x

Biamonte, J., Wittek, P., Pancotti, N., Rebentrost, P., Wiebe, N., & Lloyd, S. (2017). Quantum machine learning. *Nature*, *549*(7671), 195–202. DOI: 10.1038/nature23474 PMID: 28905917

Bonawitz, K., Ivanov, V., Kreuter, B., Marcedone, A., McMahan, H. B., Patel, S., Ramage, D., Segal, A., & Seth, K. (2019). Practical secure aggregation for privacy-preserving machine learning. In *Proceedings of the ACM SIGSAC Conference on Computer and Communications Security* (pp. xxx–xxx). London, United Kingdom.

Bowles, J., Ahmed, S., & Schuld, M. (2024). Better than classical? The subtle art of benchmarking quantum machine learning models. arXiv preprint arXiv:2403.07059.

Cai, L., Hu, Q., Jiang, T., & Niyato, D. (2024). Blockchain-enabled secure federated learning for digital twin networks. *IEEE Wireless Communications*.

Gangwani, P., Perez-Pons, A., Bhardwaj, T., Upadhyay, H., Joshi, S., & Lagos, L. (2021). Securing environmental IoT data using masked authentication messaging protocol in a DAG-based blockchain: IOTA tangle. *Future Internet, 13*(12), 312. DOI: 10.3390/fi13120312

Gangwani, P., Perez-Pons, A., Braccia, P., Upadhyay, H., & Lagos, L. (2023). Integration of data science and IoT with blockchain for Industry 4.0. In *Blockchain and its applications in Industry 4.0* (pp. 139–177). Springer. DOI: 10.1007/978-981-19-8730-4_6

Himdi, T. (2024). A blockchain and AI-driven security framework for cognitive cities. *Advances in Artificial Intelligence and Machine Learning*, *4*, 2908–2925. DOI: 10.54364/AAIML.2024.44169

IoT Analytics. (2021). The state of IoT: 2021 edition. Retrieved July 1, 2025, from https://iot-analytics.com/product/state-of-iot-summer-2021/

Jiang, L., Zheng, H., Tian, H., Xie, S., & Zhang, Y. (2021). Cooperative federated learning and model update verification in blockchain-empowered digital twin edge networks. *IEEE Internet of Things Journal*, *9*(13), 11154–11167. DOI: 10.1109/JIOT.2021.3126207

Kumar, P., Kumar, R., Kumar, A., Franklin, A. A., Garg, S., & Singh, S. (2022). Blockchain and deep learning for secure communication in digital twin empowered industrial IoT network. *IEEE Transactions on Network Science and Engineering*, *10*(5), 2802–2813. DOI: 10.1109/TNSE.2022.3191601

Maurya, S., Joseph, S., Asokan, A., Algethami, A. A., Hamdi, M., & Rauf, H. T. (2021). Federated transfer learning for authentication and privacy preservation using novel supportive twin delayed DDPG (S-TD3) algorithm for IIoT. *Sensors (Basel)*, *21*(23), 7793. DOI: 10.3390/s21237793 PMID: 34883794

McMahan, B., Moore, E., Ramage, D., Hampson, S., & Arcas, B. A. y. (2017). Communication-efficient learning of deep networks from decentralized data. In *Proceedings of the Artificial Intelligence and Statistics Conference* (pp. xxx–xxx). Fort Lauderdale, FL, United States.

Mehta, S., Khurana, M., Dogra, A., & Hariharan, S. (2024). Advancing IoT security through federated learning: A comprehensive approach. In *Proceedings of the International Conference on Applied Artificial Intelligence and Computing (ICAAIC)* (pp. 561–566). IEEE. DOI: 10.1109/ICAAIC60222.2024.10575903

Prathiba, S. B., Govindarajan, Y., Ganesan, V. P. A., Ramachandran, A., Selvaraj, A. K., Bashir, A. K., & Gadekallu, T. R. (2024). Fortifying federated learning in IIoT: Leveraging blockchain and digital twin innovations for enhanced security and resilience. *IEEE Access : Practical Innovations, Open Solutions, 12*, 68968–68980. DOI: 10.1109/ACCESS.2024.3401039

Sadri, H., Yitmen, I., Tagliabue, L. C., & Westphal, F. (2023). A conceptual framework for blockchain and AI-driven digital twins for predictive operation and maintenance. In Proceedings of the European Conference on Computing in Construction and the International CIB W78 Conference (Vol. 4).

Sasikumar, A., Vairavasundaram, S., Kotecha, K., Indragandhi, V., Ravi, L., Selvachandran, G., & Abraham, A. (2023). Blockchain-based trust mechanism for digital twin empowered industrial internet of things. *Future Generation Computer Systems, 141*, 16–27. DOI: 10.1016/j.future.2022.11.002

Shafique, M., Marchisio, A., Putra, R. V. W., & Hanif, M. A. (2021). Towards energy-efficient and secure edge AI: A cross-layer framework. In *Proceedings of the IEEE/ACM International Conference on Computer-Aided Design (ICCAD)* (pp. 1–9).

Sinha, A., Sharma, N., Kumar, S., Lande, A., & Iqbal, M. I. (2024). AI-enhanced living: The future of smart homes. In *Proceedings of the International Conference on Smart Devices (ICSD)*. Dehradun, India. DOI: 10.1109/ICSD60021.2024.10751168

Zhao, W., Aldyaflah, I. M., Gangwani, P., Joshi, S., Upadhyay, H., & Lagos, L. (2023). A blockchain-facilitated secure sensing data processing and logging system. *IEEE Access : Practical Innovations, Open Solutions, 11*, 21712–21728. DOI: 10.1109/ACCESS.2023.3252030

Chapter 2

Using Reliable and Low-Complexity Encryptions to Facilitate Cryptography for Electronic Commerce Transactions

Mishall Hammed Al-Zubaidie
http://orcid.org/0000-0002-3149-9129
University of Thi-Qar, Iraq

ABSTRACT

A significant waste of funds and effort may result from hacking e-transactions. Furthermore, a huge number of linked and unlinked networks might seriously interfere with the security features that are already in place. In this work, we suggest developing a protocol to safeguard e-transaction data using the Chinese Remainder Theorem (CRT), El-Gamal, and Advanced Encryption Standard (AES) approaches. The proposed protocol also incorporates high-performance security features to guarantee scalability. In order to support the suggested protocol's performance and security balance, we integrate these algorithms with a strong approach. The superiority of the proposed protocol over current security protocols is demonstrated by a study of results.

INTRODUCTION

The past years have been characterized by an extraordinary rise in online shopping that has been brought about by technological advances in the industry, otherwise

DOI: 10.4018/979-8-2600-1433-2.ch002

called e-commerce. The high rate of e-commerce growth can be mostly credited to the fast pace of Internet connections and Internet information technology gadgets that have enabled more consumers to be reached. The fact that e-commerce has been successful can be attributed to a series of social, technological, cultural, and psychological events, which, when taken together, helped to define the development of the shopping processes (Jebbar & Al-Zubaidie, 2024). E-commerce sites, online auctions, and applications on the mobile phone are some of the most commonly used sites on the Internet. With these channels, the consumers are enabled to purchase digital files of music, books, services, high-technology products, etc. Additionally, online applications provide a variety of services and opportunities, such as the creation of electronic payment invoices, mediation of purchasing and selling operations, and provision of digital services to institutions and to customers through continuous development of online business (Dritsas & Trigka, 2025). Manjare (2025) states that in 2021, e-commerce sales recorded a great improvement at the national level. Indicatively, the United States recorded expenditures amounting to USD 843.15m and USD 2,779.31m, respectively, whereas the United Kingdom recorded expenditures amounting to USD 169.02m. These statistics highlight the great economic importance of e-commerce at an international level.

Security of E-commerce has become a big issue in recent past, due to the rise in cases of theft of credit cards and hacked customer accounts. Fraud using credit cards and theft of information related to client accounts are the two most common types of security threats to e-commerce (Duaa et al., 2024). The number of transactions and payments made on online platforms has been skyrocketing over recent decades, under the influence of the widespread increase in e-commerce utilization. This kind of fast growth has spawned security issues that put personal information of users at risk and focus on leaking personal, public, and shared cryptography keys (Al-Tameemi et al., 2025), vital in securing personal and business data (Li, 2024). Among the cryptographic techniques utilized in e-commerce applications are Bitcoin, Litecoin, Freicoin, and Peercoin. To provide confidentiality, several of these techniques use cryptographic algorithms (Razzaq & Al-Zubaidie, 2024). E-commerce applications are likely to be attacked by a number of common vulnerabilities, including distributed denial of service (DDoS), phishing, eavesdropping, brute force (BF) attacks, distributed guessing, financial fraud, sabotage, modification, ransomware, sniffing, and zero-day exploits (Tregi et al., 2025). An example of such is a DDoS attack, which can disable e-commerce sites and make them unavailable to their clients through a bombardment of false requests (Al-Zubaidie & Jebbar, 2025). Additionally, eavesdropping the encrypted transaction over the Internet can be used to gather and alter e-commerce requests (Rasha et al, 2025). Additionally, hackers employ phishing attempts to obtain clients' private information by creating phony websites that mimic authentic ones (Tahayur et al., 2025). Moreover, BF will crack passwords by utilizing every character combination. Payment transactions and customer privacy have grown to be serious issues (Mutemi, & Bacao, 2024). Additionally, when e-commerce platforms use credit cards to buy goods and services, private information is stolen, committing financial fraud. It also happens when unlawful transactions result in fraudulent demands for credit refunds (Al-Zubaidie & Jebbar, 2024).

A report provided by WEBSCALE (2022) indicates that e-commerce attacks are on the increase. To illustrate, the ratio of credit-card fraud cases was 65 percent and 68 percent in 2020 and 2021, respectively; the ratio of BF attacks was 11 percent and 11.5 percent, and the ratio of phishing attacks was 56 percent and 71 percent, among others. According to this data, 17.5% of all e-commerce queries on Black Friday and Cyber Monday were linked to security issues. Sixty-two percent of e-commerce attacks were automated, according to the research (Imperva, 2023). The rapid proliferation of Internet websites exposes e-commerce transactions to a variety of risks and attacks, making the system hazardous (Atiyah et al., 2024). The present study employs both symmetric and asymmetric encryption algorithms and techniques to safeguard commercial transactions. The El-Gamal public key encryption technique and the AES symmetric encryption algorithm are used to improve the security of e-commerce transactions and offer excellent security.

Chapter Objectives

The following summarizes the primary objectives:

- The authentication of customer data with a lightweight protocol proposed in e-commerce applications uses the CRT in order to improve the key-generation speed, El-Gamal in key-generation operation, and the AES in data encryption.
- It provides the systematic and consistent maintenance of all the security parameters related to business application entities.
- The work of the suggested protocol is analyzed, and its superiority over the current protocols is shown. The SYTHER tool is used to verify and analyze security outcomes in the framework of the e-commerce application protocol.

REVIEW OF THE LITERATURE ON E-TRANSACTIONS SECURITY

There are still significant security and performance issues with the current methods, notwithstanding earlier studies on symmetric and asymmetric encryption algorithms in relation to e-commerce applications. The following section gives an in-depth review of the new studies that are relevant to the topic of the proposed research.

Hu et al. (2011) suggested creating digital signal processor (DSP) cipher modules on new embedded devices in order to create a secure e-commerce application. They also came up with an effective RSA plug-in encryption tool that supports the storage and encryption of sensitive information that is online-based and transacted through popular web browsers. To derive secure online transactions on the client side, the RSA algorithm is used, but the approach is hindered by the demands on the key-length and the time-consuming arithmetic operations, which have a negative impact on the performance. Further, the scheme still has the problems of increasing complexity and cost, large block sizes making implementation challenging, and space limitations that slow down the creation and implementation of databases and Internet applications. The rate of encryption implementation and encryption of data will also be variable.

Saha et al. (2018) proposed a cryptanalysis-based security enhancement for the AES algorithm. Their approach uses a symmetric random function generator (SRFG) to encourage randomness in the commercial domain. Also, each block cipher key is obtained at random; round keys are also stored in independent locations since they are only used in decryption and are generated randomly. However, their approach has many drawbacks, including the high sophistication of their algorithm due to large operations and the disregard for execution time.

A proposal for secure images was presented by Yousif et al. (2020) through the integration of El-Gamal public key cryptography and chaotic schemes with a scanning technique. Additionally, spiral and zigzag scans were used to create a permuted image at first. Next, the El-Gamal encryption technique was applied to the permuted image. The pixel coordinates were finally messed up utilizing Lorenz and Rössler chaotic sequences during the confusion and diffusion stages. The work of their concept is unfortunately significantly impacted by a few issues, such as the inability to account for complex operations and high randomness costs, or the variation in encryption execution time brought on by larger image sizes and highly sensitive processes. The encryption keys' susceptibility to decryption was impacted by the way their system created them. This critical sensitivity may make things more complicated.

Ali et al. (2021) suggested a relational database architecture that is compatible with a multilayer secure architecture to integrate the dam management structure and its underlying activities. The authors created cryptography keys using the Advanced Encryption Standard (AES) and a random number generator (RNG) sequence, salted the data using a second key, and encrypted and decrypted dam data using the password-based key derivation function 2 (PBKDF2). The proposal was found to have low randomness, inefficient complex arithmetic operations, inconsistent encryption and decryption execution times, and slow, lengthy keys because of huge dynamic operations.

Mohd and Ashawesh (2021) proposed optimisation of AES-based encryption functions to protect digital data and increase the overall level of security. To minimize the encryption and decryption latency, the authors minimized the number of rounds of the AES algorithm to fourteen and, at the same time, increased the protection of data. However, the high level of arithmetic involved in their methodology makes the encryption procedure inefficient. The throughput of data transmission is calculated by file size and processing speed. AES-256 encryption is slower and more complicated than AES-80 and AES-128, but in this instance, apps that send sensitive data—like e-commerce platforms—benefit from AES-256's higher security.

Anshori et al (2022) examined the inter-relationships between perceived value, privacy, security, and confidence in the situations of re-utilising e-commerce applications. They implemented this strategy on a group of clients who had used the Tokopedia app at least once, utilizing the purposive sampling method. The data-collection method distributes questionnaires online via Google Forms, and the partial least squares (PLS) method is employed to analyze the data using the SmartPLS 3.3 software. The survey was completed by 242 people in total. However, their plan ran into a number of issues, such as the fact that the data collection method was not more thorough and that many of the participants were interviewed at random. Price and product promotion are two examples of the elements that negatively impact the use of e-commerce. As technology advances, new kinds of attacks that compromise sensitive customer data are revealed, which have an impact on e-commerce security.

E-COMMERCE BACKGROUND AND EMPLOYED METHODS

This section's goal is to explore the research subject comprehensively by offering details on the security measures and e-commerce approaches now in use to safeguard transactions in e-commerce apps.

Technologies of E-Commerce

We will give a basic overview of e-commerce techniques in this part.

- **E-commerce on the Internet**

E-commerce services make it easy to acquire goods online and also sell them, as well as access a wide range of customers. Using either the public or private network, such as the Internet, and services, consumers, individuals, or businesses can check their accounts, trade, or obtain information about financial products and services through e-commerce. E-commerce offers customers convenience, time savings, affordability, simplicity, quick delivery, and online bill payment. Transaction security and the preservation of consumer data are two of the biggest hazards associated with e-commerce services (Shyaa et al., 2023).

- **Method of payment for e-commerce**

Payment systems include online purchases made using cheques or credit cards. One significant advantage of e-commerce is the ability to settle invoices. When purchasing goods online, the majority of customers use checks or credit cards. The payment methods utilized in e-commerce applications are shown in Figure 1. A secure electronic payment process also requires mutual authentication, which allows the parties to a transaction to identify each other and provide confidentiality, transaction authentication, and non-repudiation of consumer and business user data. As online shopping centres continue to spread, there has been a growing interest in the improvement of payment modes, especially considering the wide acceptance of credit cards on online shopping platforms (Al-Zubaidie & Jebbar, 2024).

Figure 1. Methods of payment in online shopping

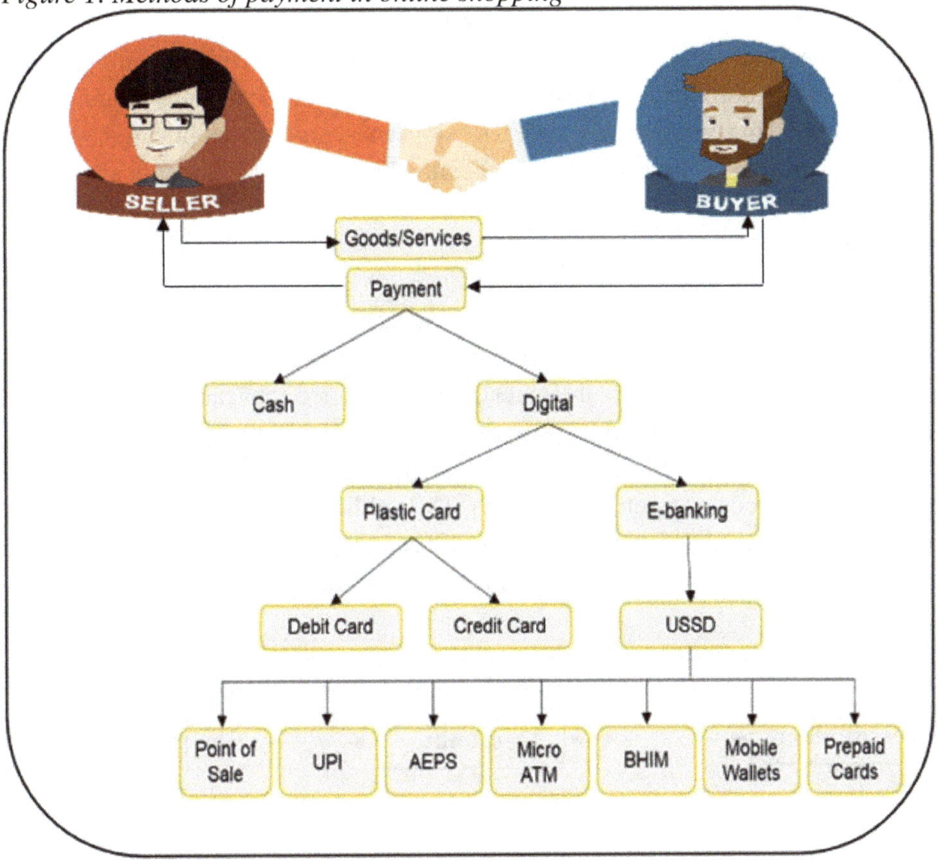

- **E-business owner**

The merchant facilitates the process of e-commerce product choice and sells goods, takes care of the delivery schedule, customer interests, requests, promotion of product quality, and utilization of persuasive tactics (Al-Zubaidie & Jebbar, 2025).

- **Online shoppers**

When a customer is drawn to a vendor, it means that they will do more business with that supplier. Since customers are likely to do business with these providers again, offering exceptional customer service is a key strategy for generating repeat business. Nonetheless, the six variables that define service quality should serve as a guide for any e-commerce application. These factors include: Tangibility (facilities, equipment, display); Reliability (timeliness); Assurance (the capacity of e-commerce providers to persuade customers); Empathy (the capacity of service providers to make customers feel personally taken care of); Security of requests (customer information is protected in e-commerce requests such as selling, purchasing, and invoicing; this aspect is crucial in convincing customers to adopt an e-commerce application without necessarily having to use a separate application or vendor) (Muhajjar et al., 2024).

- **Gateway for payments**

A payment gateway system used in e-commerce uses an intermediary system to authorize payments. During the payment process, a payment gateway serves as a middleman between the bank (card issuer), the e-commerce application, the merchant, and the customer; see Figure 2. With the growing popularity of online shopping malls, recent advancements in credit-card payment gateways on e-commerce sites have been the focus of extensive research. The public key infrastructure (PKI) authentication method, which establishes a safe connection by confirming the server certificate, makes secure e-commerce possible (Zhang et al., 2019).

Figure 2. Payment gateway for online purchases

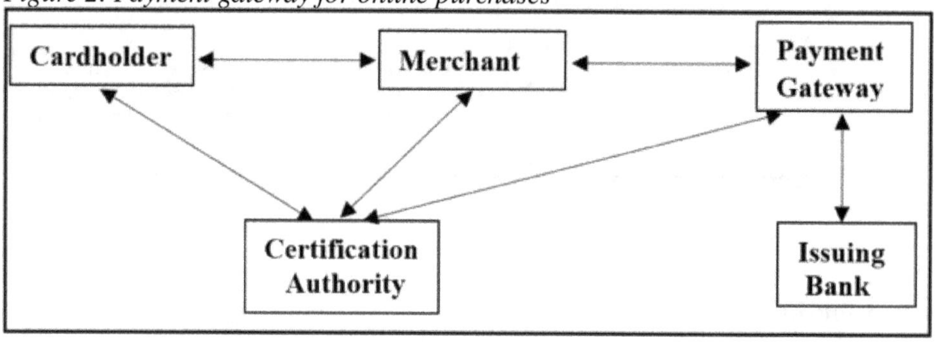

An Overview of Security Methods

The methods employed in the suggested approach will be summarized in this section.

- **Cryptography of El-Gamal**

Taher El Jamal developed this significant asymmetric encryption technique in 1985. The Diffie-Hellman key exchange is necessary for this algorithm to function.

The method could be used in place of RSA public key encryption. The primary distinction between RSA and El-Gamal is that RSA relies on the difficulty of analyzing large prime numbers, whereas El-Gamal relies on the difficulty of computing the discrete logarithm of large prime numbers. Table 1 illustrates some of the characteristics that set El-Gamal apart from RSA, including key length, scalability, power consumption, application, and others (Abidallah et al., 2025). The discrete logarithm issue is considered one of the most difficult in mathematics since it relies on the details to determine every possible answer. This encryption takes a lot of time or is nearly impossible to find (Yousif et al., 2020). El-Gamal keys are used for encryption and decryption, as seen in Figure 3. The El-Gamal algorithm can be employed in key generation. An overview of process is provided below:

The process for establishing an El-Gamal key:

- Producing a huge, arbitrary prime number (P_n);
- Selecting a generator number (G_n) at random from the interval $[1, P_n - 1]$;
- Selecting as the private number an integer (Pr_k) more than one and less than (P_n - 2);
- The public key portion value (P_v) is calculated using the formula $P_v = G_n^{Prk} \bmod P_n$;
- The public key (Pu_k) is P_n, G_n, and P_v, whereas the private key is Pr_k.

Security is improved with the El-Gamal algorithm, which is hard to crack (Imran et al., 2020). The lengthy ciphertext and the time-consuming computation are just two of the basic El-Gamal encryption technique's shortcomings; the more sophisticated the algorithm, the slower the encryption speed. This is true despite the fact that the security of the El-Gamal cipher algorithm, a popular public-key encryption scheme, is predicated on a difficult discrete logarithm problem.

Figure 3. El-Gamal encryption and decryption keys

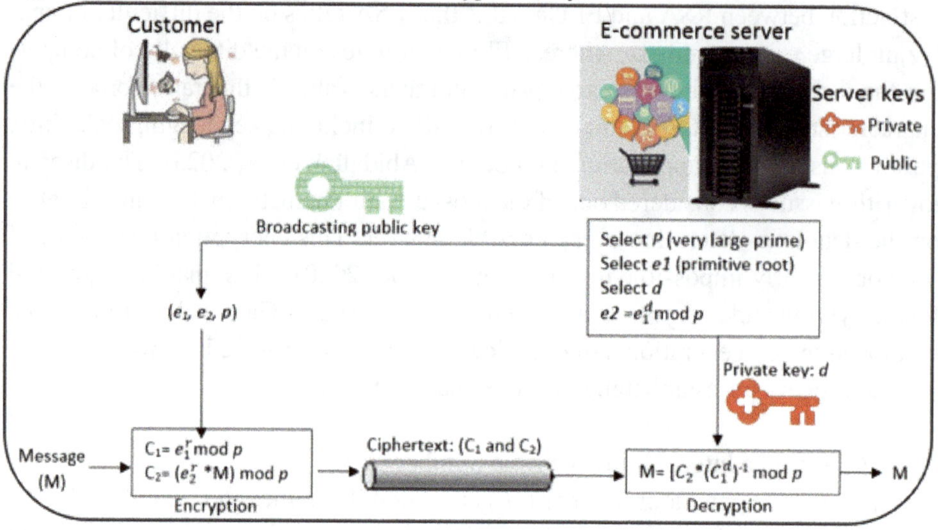

Table 1. Comparing asymmetric cryptography algorithms

Factors	El-Gamal	RSA
Developed	1985	1978
Researcher(s)	Taher El-Gamal	Rivest, Shamir, and Adleman
Key length value	≥1024 bits	≥1024 bits
Type of algorithm	Asymmetric	Asymmetric
Security attack	Meet in the middle threat	Timing threat
Simulation speed	Fast	Fast
Scalability	Good	No scalability occurs
Key used	Different key used for encryption and decryption	Different key used for encryption and decryption
Power consumption	Low	High
Hardware and Software implementation	Not very efficient	Faster and efficient
Solution problem	Multiplicative group	Integer factorization
Security strength	The challenge of discrete logarithm computation in a finite field	The challenge of factoring two huge prime numbers
Encryption	It is more effective	It is more effective
Decryption	It is more effective	It is less effective

- **Advanced Encryption Standard**

Block cipher technology, often known as the "advanced encryption algorithm" (or "AES"), uses 128-bit plaintext and uses the same key for both encryption and decoding. The AES algorithm performs 10, 12, and 14 rounds of operations on each of the 128-bit blocks. It uses 80, 128, 192, and 256-bit ciphers (see Figure 4). A 4-byte array is used to identify the state, and each cipher round involves conversions as SubBytes (), ShiftRows (), MixColumns, and AddRoundK ().

Figure 4. Structure of the AES encryption

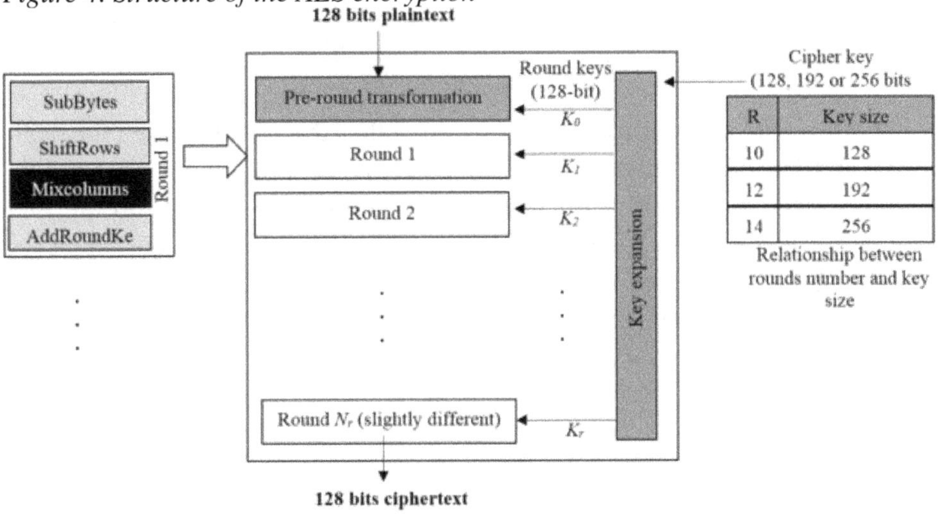

AES consists of four main functional blocks:

1. Byte substitution: An S-box is used to replace each data block's byte with a different block.
2. Row shift: Each row experiences a cyclic shift to the right based on where it is in the state matrix.
3. Columns mix: In this matrix multiplication process, each column of the state matrix is multiplied by the fixed matrix.
4. Round key addition: An XOR technique is used to join the round key matrix and the new state matrix (Tajudeen et al., 2025).

Differentiating AES lowers the number of encryption rounds, lowers data encryption, uses less power, and raises security levels. Table 2 presents a comparison of existing block ciphers that use the AES algorithm.

Table 2. Assessment of block cipher algorithms

Algorithm	Block size	Key size	Rounds number	Design pattern
HIGHT	64	128	32	GFN
Pickolo	64	80/128	25/31	GFN
PESENT	64	80/128	31	SPN
DES	64	56	16	Feistel
AES	128	128/192/256	10/12/14	SPN
Clefia	128	128/192/256	18/22/26	GFN
TEA	64	128	64	Feistel
XTEA	64	128	64	Feistel
NTSA	64	128	64	Feistel

AES is a popular symmetric key encryption method that uses the same key to both encode and decrypt sensitive data. AES is regarded as the most secure cryptographic technique since it is less expensive and easier to implement in both software and hardware. The non-Feistel cipher AES employs the same rounds of operations for both encryption and decryption. It has been demonstrated that hardware-based AES executions are more secure and quicker than alternative cryptographic executions (Al-Zubaidie, 2025). The AES algorithm is used as a basis to create a safer algorithm and more secure data by decreasing the number of encryption rounds and raising the complexity and resistance to attacks of various types.

- **Method of the Chinese Remainder Theorem**

The Chinese remainder theorem (CRT) is a number theory theorem that deals with simultaneous linear congruences. Generally speaking, if a particular form has congruences, it says:

$$S \equiv ai_1 (\text{mod } ppi_1),\ S \equiv ai_2 (\text{mod } ppi_2) \ldots S \equiv ai_n (\text{mod } ppi_n)$$

Where S is a solution, $ppi_1, ppi_2, \ldots ppi_n$ are pairwise positive integers (ppi), and $ai_1, ai_2, \ldots ai_n$ are arbitrary integers (ai). If it does have a solution, it is unique with respect to the product $ppi_1 ppi_2 \ldots ppi_n$. If S is an OS (mod ppi_1) solution to the issue, then the equation will satisfy any other solution (OS). When there is just one common factor among the moduli, the theorem can be used to solve a system of congruences.

This method was discovered in the third century CE by Yisunzi Fu Wesunzisuangjing, a Chinese mathematician. For each coefficient feature, the CRT algorithm reduces normal arithmetic by a considerable amount, making it one of the most important theorems in mathematics. The ideal balance between usability and beauty is constantly emerging in new situations in a landscape that is accessible to new kinds of applications (Van Tilborg, 2025). Numerous fields of current research and high-tech companies, such as computing, cryptography, coding, and communication, use the CRT method. The most recent research on residue code, which is widely utilized, especially in high-performance computing, has focused on the CRT methodology and associated number encoding and integer reconstruction techniques. Reducing the computational complexity and computations of the main integrative components of the residue code is the main objective.

METHODOLOGY FOR THE PROPOSED PROTOCOL IN E-COMMERCE

The overall architecture of the proposed e-commerce network includes customers, sellers, delivery services, authenticated servers, suppliers of goods and services (merchants), payment gateways, and banking activities. Figure 5 shows the design of a general e-commerce network. Buyers are users who wish to buy a service or product; sellers are users who try to sell something electronic or physical through e-commerce applications; merchants are users who offer large and one-class goods for sale through e-commerce applications; and authenticated servers are large-scale computers that perform and receive authentication requests to ensure the legitimacy of users of e-commerce applications. Payment gateways are platforms that provide payment authentication; delivery services are offices that send orders whether they are tangible items or send them online if they are software or instructions/tips. A banking transaction is an organization that makes sure money is transferred through payment gateways and, as a result, to sellers and merchants. This study's primary focus will be on authenticated servers, buyers, and sellers. Documenting the remaining entities will be the responsibility of future research. Initially, we used the AES algorithm, a symmetric encryption methodology for encryption and decryption, and the El-Gamal algorithm, an asymmetric encryption method for key generation. Figure 6 below shows the general methodology of the proposed strategy.

The diagram shows the two types of encryption algorithms we used—symmetric and asymmetric—as well as the CRT method for encoding and decoding order information in e-commerce.

Cryptography With Implied Symmetry and Asymmetry

The methods employed in the proposed approach and the ways in which these security measures are applied and utilized in the proposed protocol will be described in this part. AES, CRT, and El-Gamal are explained.

Employing El-Gamal

A method that produces big, random keys that are appropriate for encrypting private data in e-commerce applications is required for the proposed protocol. Although there are numerous asymmetric encryption methods, El-Gamal and RSA are the most well-known. Nevertheless, we went with El-Gamal since it offers superior scalability, lower power consumption, and quicker encryption and decryption processing than RSA (as indicated in Table 1). Only the creation and computation of public and private keys—not encryption or decryption—are handled by the proposed protocol using the El-Gamal method. We only employ asymmetric methods like El-Gamal to produce big random keys because the encryption and decryption processes are quite costly.

Figure 5. Overall application network architecture for e-commerce

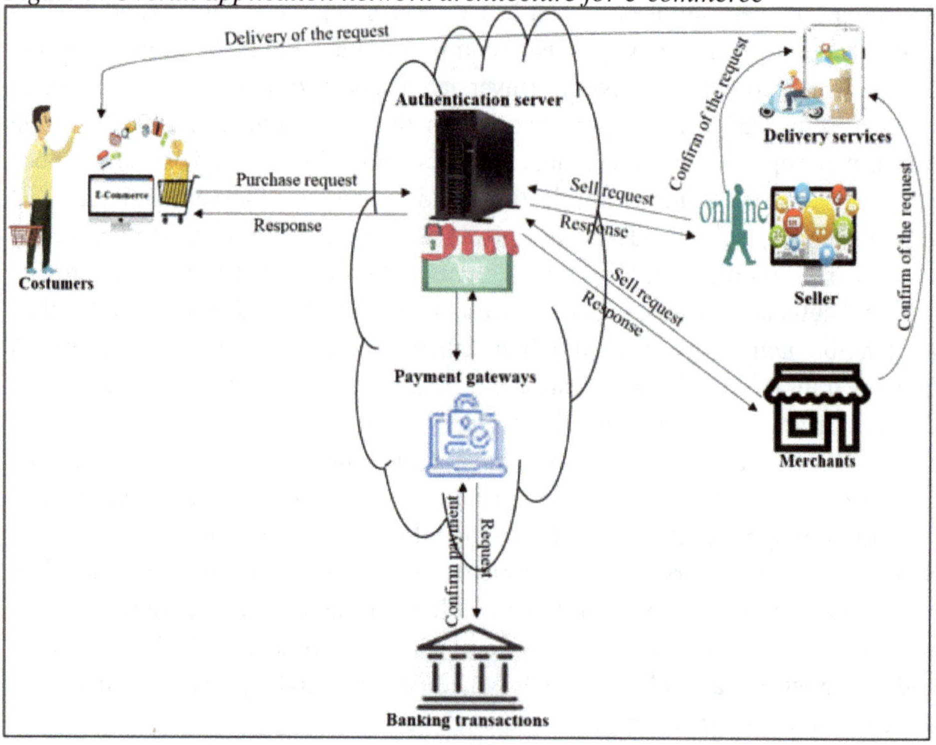

El-Gamal offers keys that range in length from 1024 to 2048 to 4096. As demonstrated by the following technique, the proposed protocol uses CRT technology to generate a private key and a public key of length 1024.

- Producing a big, arbitrary prime number (p);
- Selecting a generator number (a)
- Using CRT, a random integer (P_r) less than (p - 2) is generated as the secret number;
- In the calculation of (d), $d = a.P_r \ mod \ p$;

The public key, which consists of p, a, and d, is (P_u), while the private key is P_r.

The suggested procedure then divides the public key into four parts, each with a size of 256. In order to create a secret and random key that is ready for the AES method, the XoR operations are then performed for each component. El-Gamal is used to generate random and distinct keys for each e-commerce app user.

Figure 6. An overview of the suggested e-commerce application

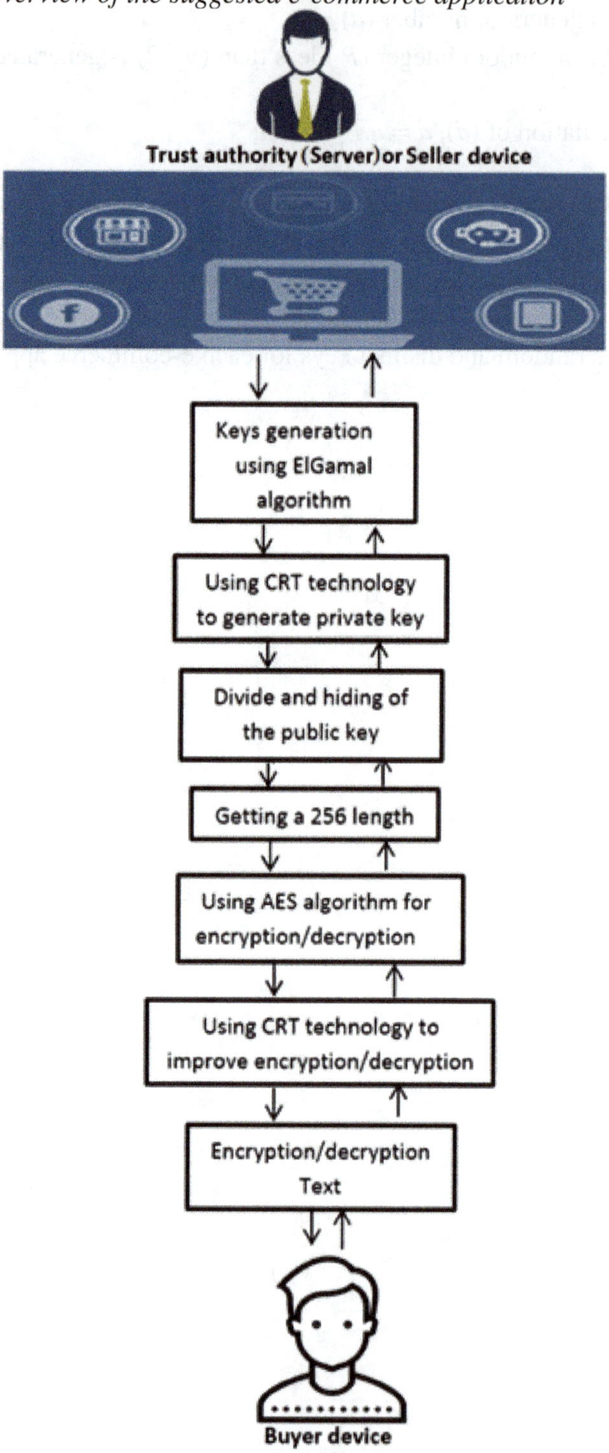

Applying the Algorithm of AES

The buy and sell requests are encrypted and decoded using the AES algorithm upon delivery from the buyer (*B*), seller (*S*), or trust authority server (*TAS*). However, critical client data may be compromised if keys as little as 80 and 128 are used. As a result, the proposed protocol uses a 256-key length, which is sufficient to prevent assaults. Furthermore, symmetric algorithms, in which every user uses the same secret key, have a scalability issue that the proposed protocol solves. The proposed approach employs the El-Gamal algorithm's public keys to generate a unique secret key for every user. In addition to the importance of key length, two crucial elements that render AES vulnerable to attacks are the degree of key randomness and cryptographic randomness. Therefore, the suggested method uses strong AES ciphers that provide appropriate key length (256 bits), key randomness (El-Gamal), and cryptographic unpredictability by using a random salt that requires less processing power.

Applying the CRT Method

The CRT approach can support randomization problems for encryption schemes. Additionally, it can be utilized to support concerns with key generation performance, encryption, and decryption. To increase the randomness, this technique is used in conjunction with the El-Gamal algorithm to generate random keys, especially private ones. Additionally, it enables a smaller key and faster operating speed, as well as an improvement in the system's working duration capacity. The original text is then transformed into ciphertext using a public key, and the ciphertext is then transformed back into the original text or plaintext using a private key. These keys are then employed in the encryption and decryption procedures. Large operands in ciphertext polynomials are represented and processed using this technique, which also lowers large values to smaller ones. In particular, we use CRT to reduce the length of the private key and support its unpredictability. We used CRT to calculate Salt in the suggested protocol to help with the random handling of encryption and breakdown in AES.

Purchase/Sale Requests and Bills

For a collection of encryption requests, we apply encryption operations based on the AES algorithm. Some request types purchase and sell invoices and requests. Types of request forms are depicted in Figure 7. All request data, whether for purchases, sales, or bill payment, is encrypted, depending on the request process. The request forms used in this study are real e-commerce application forms that were taken from internet databases that are accessible to the public (123FormBuilder, 2023). They don't contain any personal or network information. In order to complete the encryption and decryption process for the purchase requests to sell and invoice correctly, we inserted certain personal information and fake request data for virtual users. Before sending a request to the TAS, we encrypt it using the AES method. In this case, personal data is safeguarded for both the client and the server, and information is encrypted and hard for authorized network parties to crack (assuming the encryption is robust with high key randomness).

Figure 7. Requests and invoices for sales and purchases

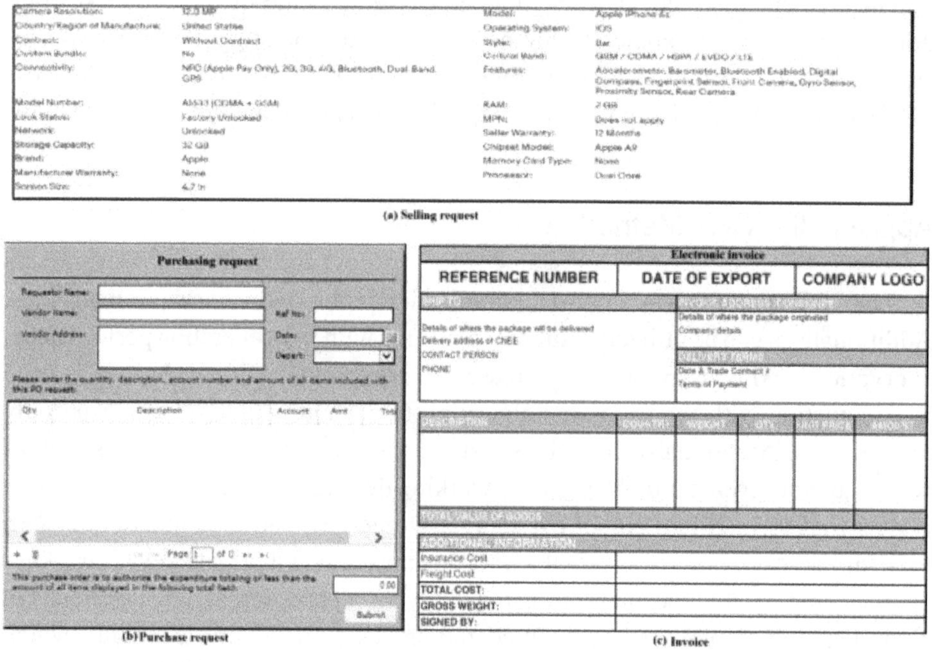

Procedures for the Proposed Protocol

We use the technique of encrypting and decrypting request transactions in the design of the protocol. Both symmetric and asymmetric encryption techniques are used for this. We encrypt the text and request data using the AES technique. The steps we take are as follows (Figure 8 illustrates the proposed suggested protocol procedures):

1. We generate random keys, which are the private and public keys by default, using an El-Gamal asymmetric encryption technique. The random key, which has a size of 1024 to 256 bits, is then divided to fit the AES algorithm keys.
2. We use this public key to encrypt the e-commerce requests between *B*, *S*, and *TAS*. The robust encryption and high encryption randomness of the proposed protocol make it difficult to decrypt when transmitted from *B* to *S*.
3. The AES and El-Gamal keys will be used to decrypt the requested data. A decrypted text that is hard for an adversary to decipher is sent to the buyer or seller.
4. The public and private keys are changed as needed or when a certain number of key mix-ups have occurred.
5. In the event that network devices are hacked, it is crucial to conceal data and security settings, particularly keys.

Figure 8. Procedures for the suggested technique

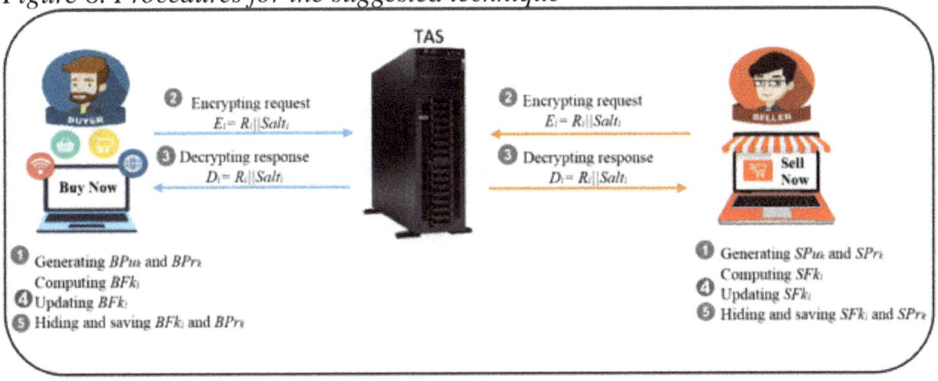

Procedure for Generating Keys

The key generation process is the initial step in the proposed methodology. The actions carried out for the key generation process are referred to as Algorithm 1. The El-Gamal algorithm's key generating instructions were previously covered in previous sections. We will go over the new directives that support both private and public key security in this part. The keys were first generated in El-Gamal using the parameters P_n and G_n. We create Pu_k public keys with a 1024-bit size using El-Gamal. Furthermore, we construct the private key (Pr_k) using El-Gamal-CRT. We divided the public key (Pu_k) into subkeys (Sk_s) in order to accommodate unpredictability in public keys. With a length of 256 bits, these Sk_s—Sk_1, Sk_2, Sk_3, and Sk_4—fit the

AES algorithm. The operations $k_1 = Sk_1 \oplus Sk_2$ and $k_2 = Sk_3 \oplus Sk_4$ are carried out using the proposed protocol. The final key (Fk), which is 256 bits in length, is then obtained by the proposed protocol using the formula $Fk_i = k_1 \oplus k_2 \oplus Sk_i$, where Sk_i can be any of the following values: Sk_1, Sk_2, Sk_3, and Sk_4. The operations result ($Inte$) = $PW \oplus Pr_k$ (where *Inte* is the intermediate value) and final key ephemeral (Fk_e) = $Fk_i \oplus Inte \oplus PW$ are used to conceal the keys Pr_k and Fk_i on network devices. Currently, e-commerce apps are being used to securely store *Inte* and Fk_e on devices. Without creating keys, the proposed protocol advances to the fourth stage of Algorithm 1 on the subsequent connection. In order to employ new public keys, the proposed protocol uses scrambling Sk_s. For instance, it computes $k_1 = Sk_1 \oplus Sk_3$ and $k_2 = Sk_2 \oplus Sk_4$ before repeating the identical steps in Algorithm 1 until 16 connections are made. The network entity should begin the subsequent connection from step 1 of Algorithm 1 if it has established 16 communications in e-commerce applications. Particularly in *TAS*, avoiding key generation for 16 communications lowers computational expenses.

Algorithm 1 Procedure for generating keys
Input
Pn, Gn values and PW
Output
Prk and Puk keys with 256 bit length
1 Utilize El-Gamal to generate Puk with 1024 bit length
2 Utilize El-Gamal-CRT to generate Prk
3 Divide Puk to four part with 256 bit length
4 Four subkeys: Sk1, Sk2, Sk3 and Sk4
5 Implement ⊕ with subkeys
6 Get Fki with 256 bit length
7 Secure Prk and Fki on device
8 Calculate Inte = PW ⊕ Prk
9 Calculate Fke = Fki ⊕ Inte ⊕ PW
10 Next connection, go to step 4 with changing Sks order
11 After 16 connections, go to step 1

The Encryption Process

The proposed protocol uses Pr_k, Pu_k, PW, and R_i (invoice request, buying, or selling) to carry out the encryption procedure. However, the keys Pr_k and Fk_i that are concealed on the network entities need to be obtained before the encryption procedure can be carried out. The extractions of Pr_k and Fk_i for use in AES-256 ciphers are represented by Steps 1 and 2, as explained in Algorithm 2. Next, the proposed system obtains a random $Salt_i$ with low computing overhead by using a

CRT technique with the key Pr_k. The encryption operations are then carried out by the proposed protocol using Fk_i and $Salt_i$, whereas the encryption operation Enc_{Ri} is carried out using the operation $Ri||Salti$. To get a concealed ephemeral salt ($Salt_e$), the proposed protocol employs the operation $Pu_k \oplus Salt_i$. Lastly, the target device receives the $Enc_{Ri}||Salt_e$ cipher. Similarly, Fk_e hides Pr_k and Fk_i to keep hackers from breaking into the entity and obtaining security settings.

Algorithm 2 Procedure for encryption process

Input

Prk, Puk keys with 256 bit, PW and Ri

Output

EncRi and Salte

1 Compute Prk = PW ⊕ Inte

2 Compute Fki = Fke ⊕ Inte ⊕ PW

3 Utilize CRT to generate Salti

4 Utilize Fki 256 bit with AES encryption

5 Encrypt EncRi (Ri||Salti)

6 Compute Salte = Puk ⊕ Salti

7 Transfer EncRi ||Salte

8 Save Fke = Fki ⊕ Inte ⊕ PW

9 Save connection order on the sender side

The Decryption Process

Decryption is the step that comes after the encryption process. The target device uses the public and private keys along with security parameters like Salt to decrypt the encrypted request after receiving it. For example, merchants must decode customer requests to ascertain the type of request, the quantity ordered, the request's destination, and the information related to the invoice payment. Similar to Algorithm 2, Algorithm 3 retrieves the Pr_k and Fk_i keys that were saved on network devices in steps 1 and 2. Requests like $R_i = Enc_{Ri}||Salt_e$ are then sent to the receiver, which decrypts the data by subtracting $Salt_e$ from the encryption request and then extracting $Salt_i$ from $Salt_e$. After that, the proposed protocol decodes R_i by $Enc_{Ri}||Salt_i$ using Fk_i and $Salt_i$. The requests' explicit text is saved in the datasets for archiving once it has been received by the recipient device. It stores keys anonymously, just like Algorithms 2 and 3.

Algorithm 3 Procedure for decryption process

Input

Puk keys with 256 bit, PW and EncRi

Output

DecRi

1 Compute Prk = PW⊕Inte
2 Compute Fki = Fke ⊕ Inte ⊕ PW
3 Utilize Fki 256 bit with AES decryption
4 Utilize Ri = EncRi||Salte
5 Delete Salte from Ri
6 Compute Salti = Puk ⊕ Salte
7 Decrypt Ri = DecRi (EncRi)
8 Store Ri in dataset
9 Save Fke = Fki ⊕ Inte ⊕ PW
10 Save connection order on the receiver side

Procedure for Updating Keys

For a protocol to be reliably constructed for security, a key updating technique is required (see Algorithm 4). The proposed protocol first uses steps 1 through 6 in Algorithm 1, which generates the keys Pr_k and Pu_k. El-Gamal-CRT and Fk_i then use Sk_s to retrieve Pr_k. The method $Fk_i \oplus Fk_o \oplus LSalt_i$ uses the final salt ($LSalt_i$) to conceal Fk_e. Fk_e is sent to the recipient (seller) by the sender (buyer). Lastly, network devices employ the same security measures for public and private keys as Algorithms 1–3.

Algorithm 4 Procedure for upgrading keys
Input
Pn, Gn values and PW
Output
Prk and Puk keys with 256 bit length
1 Apply Algorithm 1, steps 1–6
2 Obtain Prk and Fki
3 Compute Fke = Fki ⊕ Fko ⊕ LSalte
4 Send Fke to the receiver
5 Protect Prk and Fki on device
6 Compute Inte = PW ⊕ Prk
7 Store Fke = Fki ⊕ Inte ⊕ PW

PERFORMANCE AND SECURITY OF SUGGESTED E-COMMERCE APPS

This section will provide security analysis and evaluate the proposed protocol's ability to prevent e-commerce attacks; the Scyther tool will then be used to assess the protocol's practical security.

Analysis of Attacks on The proposed Protocol

The security analysis of multiple e-commerce threats is summarized as follows (Table 3 compares cryptographic methods in terms of thwarting attacks that fall under the ambit of this study):

- **DDoS**

Due to DDoS attacks using numerous systems to attack from multiple locations, they are more dangerous than DoS attacks because they have a greater and quicker impact on halting the network. It is also challenging to track. Furthermore, sensitive data is handled by e-commerce apps, and any delays or blockage of user requests might have disastrous economic effects. It is exceedingly difficult to entirely prevent these attacks. But it's important to lessen its effects and lessen how severe it is. The proposed technique verifies the validity of the connected device using a tiny token located inside Salte. The cost of this procedure is low (Salti $\oplus$ Puk). As a result, the proposed protocol can reduce the likelihood of DDoS attacks.

- **Phishing**

In e-commerce applications, an attacker attempts to obtain sensitive and crucial information about a company or institution, requests, or the personal information (credit card numbers, usernames, and *PW*s) of customers or sellers. Phishing attacks use malicious malware or mined URLs to steal private data. E-commerce apps cannot communicate links or transmit data between users (buyers and sellers) using the proposed protocol. The malware or the attacker will not obtain clear and useful information about the user, even if the user unintentionally clicks on a link in other programs or downloads malware without realizing it. Furthermore, *PW* is not kept on users' computers. Consequently, phishing attacks are repelled by the proposed protocol.

- **Wiretapping**

An unauthorized intruder or attacker tries to get the company's or user's data by listening in on purchase and sale requests between the buyer/seller and the servers, and exposing and analyzing the sent request. Request information encryption (Enc_{Ri} ($R_i || Salt_i$) procedure), which is based on the AES 256 method, is used to thwart this attack. All that is needed to decode these requests is their private and public keys. Due to the secret nature of the buying/selling request data, it is difficult to break the encryption.

- **Brute force**

This exploit attempts to gain access to private data in e-commerce applications, including *PW*, Pr_k, and Pu_k. To obtain the *PW* or login credentials, this technique uses trial and error. During the encryption and decryption processes, the proposed protocol does not send any private information. For instance, there are no explicit secret parameters in $Enc_{Ri} \| Salt_e$ (see Algorithms 2 and 3). Since *PW*, Pr_k, and Pu_k are not sent via an insecure channel, an attacker cannot hack or crack them no matter how hard they try. Additionally, network equipment do not store *PW*. Additionally, *PW* is chosen based on stringent security standards (e.g., capital and lowercase characters, symbols, etc.). Consequently, the proposed protocol can totally stop brute force attacks.

- **Distributed guessing for electronic payment**

To decode the packet, the guesser tries to intercept it as it travels from the sender to the destination using either a single guess or a distributed multiple-guess mechanism. Distributed guesses can be used by an attacker to expose secret parameters that are sent explicitly, use *PW* as an encryption key, or have inadequate security safeguards. Furthermore, in order to increase the effectiveness of this attack, the guesser makes a lot of guesses. The proposed reliance on a sufficiently long, random 256 bit key prevents the attacker from decrypting the electronic payment details (see Figure 8). Secrets are not transmitted across the unsecure connection by the proposed protocol. Furthermore, the guesser cannot parse the packet to determine the Pr_k and Pu_k keys once it has been captured. The proposed protocol thus properly fends off this attack.

- **Credit card fraud**

A fraudster compromises a credit card account in an effort to get access to a customer's account and collect sensitive information for the user or company, like the attack value's expiration date, credit card number, or card security code. Through credit card fraud assaults, an attacker uses fake information and falsified documents. Without secret parameters like PW and Prk, the fraudster cannot conduct e-commerce transactions, even if they get or utilize credit card details that are not authentic. The proposed protocol can therefore stop this kind of assault.

- **Sabotage**

By breaking into specific websites, stopping a business's or organization's system, halting online payment processes or sale/purchase requests, or sending private data from a client or server to a third party, a saboteur aims to destroy, subvert, or obstruct. Infecting an e-commerce app with a malicious program is one way to undermine an online buying and selling environment. Reducing a nation's e-commerce is a more serious example. To prevent this attack, the suggested protocols use Puks, which change each time the buyer's and seller's devices connect to the e-commerce network.

- **Data modification**

After attempting to access the transferred e-commerce data, an attacker alters or removes the information from the e-commerce requests (invoices, sales, and purchases), modifies some of its contents, or blocks the information receiver from accessing the data. We use an encryption algorithm (AES-256) to protect the information's confidentiality and thwart this assault. Because the proposed protocol employs specified forms for e-commerce requests, the receiver app will be able to identify any changes in e-commerce requests. When the encrypted requests are decrypted, any changes made by the attacker will be visible and will not correspond to the forms that were used.

- **Ransomware**

Using this information, the attacker demands a ransom from the targeted victims. After that, attackers may set up ransomware or request that the ransom be paid online. The attacker either destroys the material, makes it public, or encrypts it so the victim cannot access it if the victim does not pay the ransom or carry out the payment. According to the proposed protocol, an attacker will not profit from Prk, Puk, and Salti if they are able to access them on the current connection (which is impossible) because they will not be utilized on subsequent connections. In other words, even if the attacker manages to obtain the secret parameters, they cannot demand a ransom. We employ a technique that combines highly secure encryption algorithms like AES-256 and El-Gamal-1024, which are hard to crack.

- **Sniffing**

An illegal sniffer monitors, intercepts, and records all sensitive request data for the targeted network that passes through the sending and receiving stages of a specific request. By sending a packet or sequence of packets to the victim's device in order to gather private data, this assault seeks to either take control of the target's device or reveal financial information and login credentials. The suggested protocol will completely reject any packet that does not use proper parameters, such as Puk for the receiver device. Thus, the proposed protocol does not handle requests that use hijacked packets. The suggested protocol is resistant to these assaults since it encrypts and decrypts all network devices, including servers, buyers, and sellers.

- **Zero day**

Malicious attacks on network devices and applications are attempted by the attacker by taking advantage of security flaws in e-commerce software or applications. An attacker attempts to steal private transaction data or carry out false threats in commercial entities. Once the attack has been carried out, the attacker attempts to use the information, documents, and files to further apply their attack to the entire network. If this attack is not detected right away, the attacker may have more time to launch a more extensive attack. If an attacker gains access to one of the devices (buyer, seller, or server) and obtains requests for purchases, sales, or bills, he will not be able to profit from the encrypted files on the network devices. Furthermore, all security features, including Pr_k, are hidden by network devices. Consequently, the proposed protocol manages zero-day threats and provides strong protection for e-commerce apps.

Table 3. Threat resistance comparison of several cryptography methods

Threat	**(Imran et al., 2020)**	**(Yousif, et al., 2020)**	**(Mohd, & Ashawesh, 2021)**	**(Kumar, & Sinha, 2021)**	**(Anshori, et al., 2022)**	**Mitra, et al. 2022)**	**Proposed**
DDoS							
Phishing				✓	✓	✓	✓
Wiretapping	✓	✓					✓
Brute force	✓			✓			✓
Distributed guessing	✓		✓		✓		✓
Credit card fraud					✓	✓	✓
Sabotage							✓
Modification	✓	✓	✓			✓	✓
Ransomware				✓		✓	✓
Sniffing				✓			✓
Zero day				✓			✓

Analysis of Security Using Scyther

One automated tool for verifying security protocols is Scyther. Among other intriguing aspects, it can characterize protocols and produce a finite representation of all potential protocol behaviors. It can also verify protocols with an infinite number of sessions and nonces. This tool was created in a 2006 study by Cremers Cas. During that time, Cremers Cas published his work on a formal analysis and encryption verification methodology. This tool is designed to analyze formal security protocols and their security requirements. It was developed under the presumption of complete or unbreakable encryption. Scyther is also used to verify security claims and detect potential attacks against authentication mechanisms, including purchases, sales, and e-commerce payment processes.

A Scyther Explanation of the Suggested E-Commerce Protocol

Depending on the protocol being created, this tool employs a set of roles and the security protocol description language (SPDL). An e-commerce network entity is represented by each position. To set up the proposed network entities—buyer (*B*), seller (*S*), and trust authority server (*TAS*)—we created a set of commands. These commands replicate the proposed methodology's steps. Additionally, Scyther gives us the send() and recv() directives so that network entities can communicate with one another. With the help of this tool, we can test events and construct a set of claims to validate the proposed protocol, safeguard data and e-commerce requests, and achieve security and authentication attributes. Search issues that arise from the way the protocol is built can be found using the scyther tool. The items in the traded requests are examined for the following claims: Weakagree, Secret, Niagree, Nisynch, and Alive. "Alive" refers to the process of accomplishing the desired communication with certain events. A protocol that guarantees a sender *B* non-injective agreement with a receiver *TAS* or *S* on a set of request items is known as "Niagree." "Nisynch" refers to non-injective synchronization, which guarantees that all requests received by the recipient are sent by the intended sender in a synchronized fashion. "Secret" is employed to safeguard confidentiality parameters. A protocol that assures weak agreement between a sender *B* and another entity *TAS* or *S* is known as "weakagree". *S* has reportedly ran the procedure with *B* before if *B* finishes a run of the protocol, presumably with receiver *S*.

Results of the Scyther test

We present a test of the suggested e-commerce protocol using the Scyther tool. Figure 9 displays the outcomes of the proposed protocol's testing using the "Alive,"

"Niagree," "Nisynch," "Secret," and "Weakagree" claim events. Buyer/seller requests (*BR*/*SR*) and private keys (*BPrK*, *TASPrK*, and *SPrK*) are confidential, according to the tests. Without any threats or attacks that jeopardize network entities, security settings, or e-commerce request data sent over the network, the figure demonstrates that requests are securely exchanged across network entities (*B*, *S*, and *TAS*). This analysis demonstrates how the suggested e-commerce protocol withstands the range of attacks in this study.

Effectiveness of Suggested E-Commerce Apps

This section shows the performance outcomes of the algorithms and strategies employed in the proposed protocol in order to assess the proposed protocol's eligibility. The proposed scripts were run on a laptop running Ubuntu 18.04.6 LTS and 64-bit operating system, with an Intel® Core ™ i5-2540M CPU running at 2.60 GHz and 4 GB of RAM. Additionally, we dealt with the El-Gamal, AES, and CRT algorithms using the Java programming language. The proposed protocol used the CRT technique to create quick 256-bit private keys, the AES algorithm to encrypt e-commerce requests, and El-Gamal public and private keys of 1024 bits in length.

In order to determine the execution/running time one hundred times, we initially built the encryption and decryption procedures without e-commerce requests, as seen in Figure 10. The AES-256 algorithm's encryption procedures take longer to execute than its decryption operations, as the preceding graphic illustrates. The proposed suggested protocol makes use of actual e-commerce files (refer to Figure 8) of different sizes, including 1.6 KB invoice files, 3.9 KB purchase files, and 2.9 KB sale files. Next, as seen in Figure 11, we conducted AES-256 encryption operations on e-commerce requests (invoice, purchase, and sale) in order to determine the execution time. Because purchase files are larger (3.9 KB) than invoicing and selling files, purchasing request encryption takes the longest to execute, according to the previously indicated number.

Figure 9. Using the Scyther tool to confirm the recommended security protocol

Scyther results : verify

Claim				Status		Comments
ProposedElGamal_EAS	B	ProposedElGamal_EAS,B1	Secret BPW	Ok	Verified	No attacks.
		ProposedElGamal_EAS,B2	Secret XOR(BPW,XOR(BPW,BPrK))	Ok	Verified	No attacks.
		ProposedElGamal_EAS,B3	Secret KeysDivision(Sk1,Sk2,Sk3,Sk4)	Ok	Verified	No attacks.
		ProposedElGamal_EAS,B4	Secret XOR(XOR(Sk1,Sk2),XOR(Sk3,Sk4))	Ok	Verified	No attacks.
		ProposedElGamal_EAS,B5	Secret TASPrK	Ok	Verified	No attacks.
		ProposedElGamal_EAS,B6	Niagree	Ok	Verified	No attacks.
		ProposedElGamal_EAS,B7	Nisynch	Ok	Verified	No attacks.
		ProposedElGamal_EAS,B8	Alive	Ok	Verified	No attacks.
		ProposedElGamal_EAS,B9	Weakagree	Ok	Verified	No attacks.
	TAS	ProposedElGamal_EAS,TAS1	Secret BPW	Ok	Verified	No attacks.
		ProposedElGamal_EAS,TAS2	Secret XOR(XOR(XOR(XOR(XOR(XOR(Sk1,Sk2),XOR(Sk3,Sk...	Ok	Verified	No attacks.
		ProposedElGamal_EAS,TAS3	Secret TASPrK	Ok	Verified	No attacks.
		ProposedElGamal_EAS,TAS4	Niagree	Ok	Verified	No attacks.
		ProposedElGamal_EAS,TAS5	Nisynch	Ok	Verified	No attacks.
		ProposedElGamal_EAS,TAS6	Alive	Ok	Verified	No attacks.
		ProposedElGamal_EAS,TAS7	Weakagree	Ok	Verified	No attacks.
	S	ProposedElGamal_EAS,S1	Secret SPW	Ok	Verified	No attacks.
		ProposedElGamal_EAS,S2	Secret XOR(SPW,XOR(BPW,BPrK))	Ok	Verified	No attacks.
		ProposedElGamal_EAS,S3	Secret KeysDivision(Sk1,Sk2,Sk3,Sk4)	Ok	Verified	No attacks.
		ProposedElGamal_EAS,S4	Secret XOR(XOR(XOR(XOR(XOR(XOR(Sk1,Sk2),XOR(Sk3,Sk...	Ok	Verified	No attacks.
		ProposedElGamal_EAS,S5	Secret TASPrK	Ok	Verified	No attacks.
		ProposedElGamal_EAS,S7	Niagree	Ok	Verified	No attacks.
		ProposedElGamal_EAS,S6	Nisynch	Ok	Verified	No attacks.
		ProposedElGamal_EAS,S8	Alive	Ok	Verified	No attacks.
Done.		ProposedElGamal_EAS,S9	Weakagree	Ok	Verified	No attacks.

Furthermore, Figure 12 illustrates the application of AES-256 decryption operations for invoice, purchase, and sale requests. It is observed that invoice files take less time to execute than other files due to their 1.6 KB size, which is the smallest of all the files. The encryption processes take longer to execute than the decryption processes, as seen in Figures 11 and 12. Additionally, Figure 13 illustrates how long it takes for the El-Gamal-1024 algorithm's public and private keys to execute, as well as how a CRT is used to produce the private keys. The previous figure shows that the CRT approach generates the private keys more quickly than the El-Gamal algorithm's private keys, and the private keys require less execution time than the public keys. Furthermore, Table 4 compares the execution times of the private keys for El-Gamal-CRT and standard El-Gamal. The preceding figure shows that El-Gamal-CRT outperforms regular El-Gamal in terms of execution time. A comparison of the memory usage of public key algorithms, including RSA, El-Gamal-CRT, and classic El-Gamal, is presented in Table 5. The El-Gamal-CRT algorithm requires less memory than both classic El-Gamal and RSA, according to the table. Ultimately, the encryption process using XOR operation and key division takes 0.369143 ms, and the decryption process takes 0.274815 ms.

Figure 10. AES-256 encryption and decryption running time

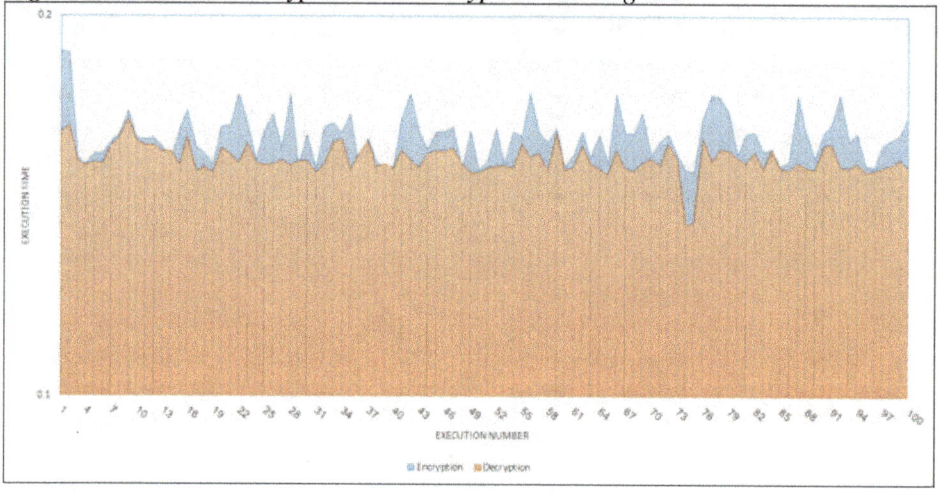

Figure 11. AES-256 file encryption running time (invoice, purchase, and sale)

Figure 12. Running time for decrypting AES-256 files (invoices, purchases, and sales)

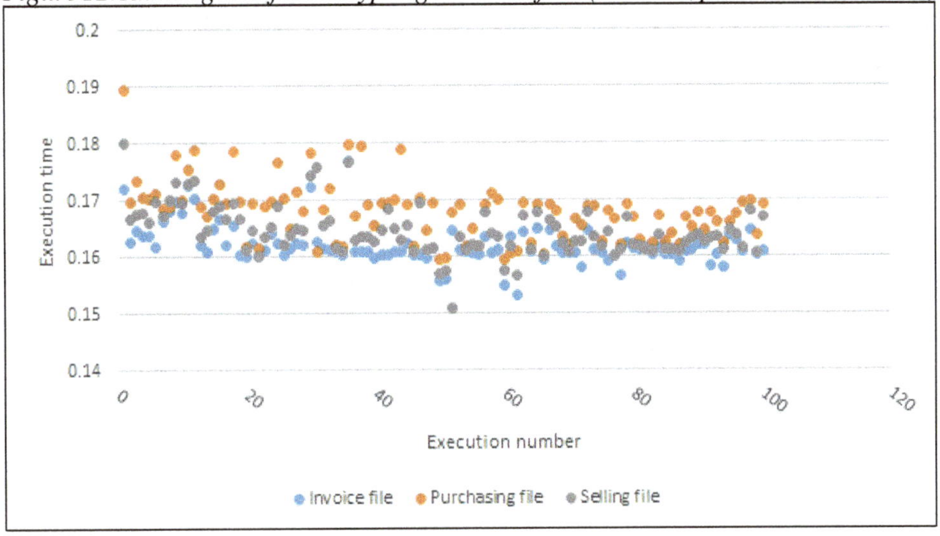

Figure 13. El-Gamal key running time (public, private, and CRT with private key)

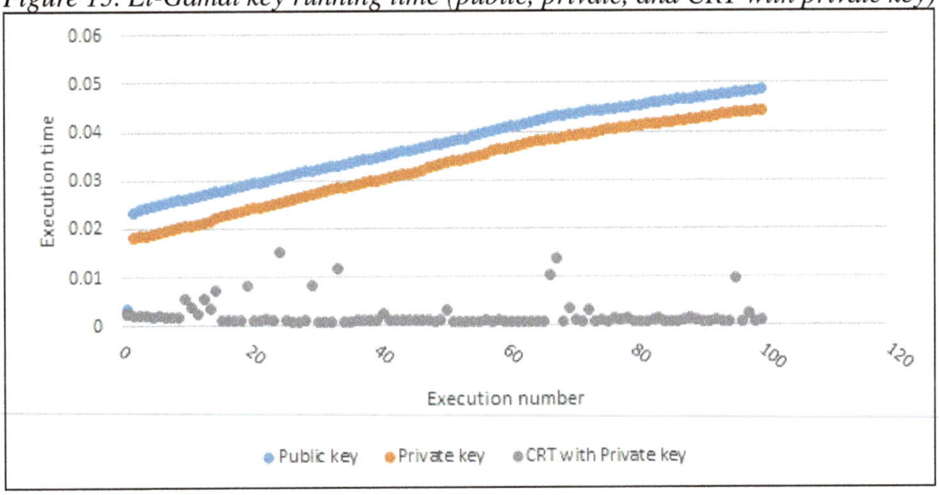

Table 4. Comparison of traditional El-Gamal and El-Gamal-CRT key generation

Length of Key	El-Gamal Private Key in ms	El-Gamal-CRT-Private in ms
1024	0.0181114	0.0021469
2048	0.0362228	0.0042938
3072	0.0543342	0.0064407
4096	0.0724456	0.0085876
7680	0.1358355	0.01610175
15,360	0.271671	0.0322035

Table 5. Comparison of memory usage for public key methods

Traditional El-Gamal (bits)	RSA (bits)	Proposed El-Gamal-CRT (bits)
1024	1024	256
2048	2048	512
3072	3072	768
4096	4096	1024
7680	7680	1920
15,360	15,360	3840

Theoretical Discussion

To elaborate, the proposed protocol is lightweight due to the fact that it first employs hybrid encryption based on El-Gamal-AES architecture. It encrypts and decrypts using the AES-256 bit. As is well known, symmetric encryption algorithms perform better than asymmetric ones due to the latter's utilization of intricate processes and huge key generation. In other words, unlike some previous research that employs ECC, RSA, and El-Gamal, the proposed protocol encrypts using the AES algorithm rather than asymmetric encryption techniques. Second, the usage of a single shared key by all users is a significant flaw in symmetric encryption techniques. The El-Gamal-1024-bit technique, which makes use of CRT technology to expedite the production of private keys, is used by the suggested protocol to generate keys. An XOR gate is then used to transform these public keys into a length suitable for the 256-bit AES method, hence removing the need for complex calculations. As a result, the suggested protocol uses an asymmetric key exchange technique rather than a single key for every user. El-Gamal's method not only generates keys just 16 times (see approach 1, step 10) using a permutation of SKs and random addition, but it also ensures that if one user's keys are compromised, it won't affect the other users, guaranteeing robust security. This illustrates how the suggested protocol balances performance and security.

Findings, Evaluation, and Interpretation

Compared to other protocols, ours implements less stringent security protections for e-commerce apps. Even if the proposed protocol's surroundings, parameters, and algorithms differ slightly from those of other protocols, we looked into identifying certain similarities between the two. The performance metrics (key lengths, encryption algorithm, key generation method, key generation support approaches, and encryption type) of the proposed protocol and those of other protocols are compared in Table 6.

RSA was used by Hu et al. (2011) to encrypt e-commerce queries. El-Gamal is more effective than RSA, nonetheless, as we mentioned in Table 1. Furthermore, El-Gamal is solely used by the proposed protocol to generate public and private keys; it is not used for encryption or decryption processes. Using the shared key of all users, Saha et al. (2018) encrypted the data using AES. Nevertheless, their plan lacks the adaptability provided by the proposed protocol to produce unique keys for every user. El-Gamal was utilized by Imran et al. (2020) for both encryption and decryption in their plan. This implies that encryption will take a long time to process any data request, particularly in big networks like e-commerce. The AES-256 technique, which is quick and effective, is the sole one used for encryption and decryption, in contrast to the proposed protocol, which only employs El-Gamal to generate public and private keys.

The El-Gamal algorithm was also utilized by Yousif et al. (2020) to encrypt the data using a scanning technique. The performance of their solution is unaffected by memory overheads or key sizes because classic El-Gamal uses 1024, 2048, and other key sizes. The memory size will be impacted when there are a lot of requests for data encryption. Thankfully, El-Gamal random keys are generated by the proposed protocol and transformed into short 256-length keys that are appropriate for encryption in AES and e-commerce settings. Ali et al. (2021) generated shared keys using a number of built-in techniques, including PBKDF2, RNG, and slave key. Their complicated protocol, however, raises the cost of implementation and running time. Furthermore, the proposed protocol employs a CRT-only strategy to enhance private key generation performance, whereas the source and the destination maintain key sharing. Although Mohd and Ashawesh (2021) claimed to have improved the performance of AES by reducing the number of rounds, the execution time for encryption and decryption is 15 s, which is much longer than the suggested protocol, which has an execution time of 0.369143 ms for encryption and 0.274815 ms for decryption (taking into account the different environments, such as the different processor speeds).

Table 6. Comparison of memory usage for public key methods

Protocol	Keys Length	Encryption Algorithm	Key Generation Algorithm	Key Support Technique	Encryption Type
Hu et al. (2011)	512/1024/2048	RSA	RSA	-	Asymmetric
Saha et al. (2018)	256	AES	AES	SRFG	Symmetric
Imran et al. (2020)	1024	El-Gamal	El-Gamal	-	Asymmetric
Yousif et al. (2020)	1024	El-Gamal	El-Gamal	Scanning	Symmetric
Ali et al. (2021)	256	AES	RNG	PBKDF2	Symmetric
Mohd and Ashawesh (2021)	256	AES	AES	-	Symmetric
The proposed protocol	256	AES	El-Gamal	CRT	Symmetric and Asymmetric

CONCLUSION

Ensuring the security of sensitive and private customer and server data, as well as electronic commerce transactions like purchasing and selling or payment activities, calls for a high level of protection. In this work, we created a protocol that supports high performance, improves security, and is hard to breach from several types of attacks. The suggested e-commerce apps are made to employ symmetric encryption techniques like AES 256 for encryption and decryption processes, as well as asymmetric encryption algorithms like El-Gamal, generating random incremental keys. We conclude that the suggested protocol provides reliable, secure processes with outstanding performance after evaluating security (attack analysis and Scyther results) and performance (Tables 4-6).

REFERENCES

Abidallah, N., Ailane, A., Bourekkache, S., Kahloul, L., Khalgui, M., & Azzaoui, N. (2025, January). Blockchain and Genetic Algorithms Interactions: A Brief Review. *In 2025 International Symposium on iNnovative Informatics of Biskra* (ISNIB) (pp. 1-6). IEEE.

Al-Tameemi, et al. (2025). A Systematic Review of Metaverse Cybersecurity: Frameworks, Challenges, and Strategic Approaches in A Quantum-Driven Era. *Mesopotamian Journal of CyberSecurity*, *5*(2), 770–803.

Al-Zubaidie, M. (2025). A Critical Reliable Model for Promoting Patient Medical Wireless Sensors Information Security. *Procedia Computer Science, 263*, 17–24. DOI: 10.1016/j.procs.2025.07.003

Al-Zubaidie, M., & Jebbar, W. A. (2024). Providing Security for Flash Loan System Using Cryptocurrency Wallets Supported by XSalsa20 in a Blockchain Environment. *Applied Sciences (Basel, Switzerland), 14*(14), 6361. DOI: 10.3390/app14146361

Al-Zubaidie, M., & Jebbar, W. A. (2025). Blockchain-powered dynamic segmentation in personal health record. *Mesopotamian Journal of Cybersecurity*, *5*(3), 953–976. DOI: 10.58496/MJCS/2025/054

Ali, H., Jawad, T., & Zuhair, H. (2021). Data Security Using Random Dynamic Salting And AES Based on Master-Slave Keys for Iraqi Dam Management System. *Indonesian Journal of Electrical Engineering and Computer Science*, *23*(2), 1018–1029. DOI: 10.11591/ijeecs.v23.i2.pp1018-1029

Anshori, M., Karya, D., & Gita, M. (2022). A Study on The Reuse Intention of E-Commerce Platform Applications: Security, Privacy, Perceived Value, and Trust. *J. Manaj. Teor. Dan Ter. J. Theory Appl. Manag.*, *15*(1), 13–24. DOI: 10.20473/jmtt.v15i1.34923

Atiyah, R. G.(2024). Intermediary Decentralized Computing and Private Blockchain Mechanisms for Privacy Preservation in The Internet of Medical *Things. Mesopotamian Journal of CyberSecurity*, *4*(3), 152–165. DOI: 10.58496/MJCS/2024/020

Dritsas, E., & Trigka, M. (2025). Machine Learning in e-Commerce: Trends, Applications, and Future Challenges. *IEEE Access : Practical Innovations, Open Solutions*, *13*, 99048–99067. DOI: 10.1109/ACCESS.2025.3572865

Duaa, T., et al. (2024). Enhancing Electronic Agriculture Data Security with A Blockchain-Based Search Method And E-Signatures. *Mesopotamian journal of Cybersecurity*, 4(3), 1-21.

123FormBuilder. E-Commerce Forms. 2023. Available online: https://www.123formbuilder.com/free-form-templates/galleryecommerce/ (accessed on 14 April 2023).

Hu, J., Hoang, X., & Khalil, I. (2011). An Embedded DSP Hardware Encryption Module for Secure E-Commerce Transactions. *Security and Communication Networks, 4*(8), 902–909. DOI: 10.1002/sec.221

Imperva. (2023). The State of Security within Ecommerce in 2022. Available online: https://www.imperva.com/resources/reports/The-State-of-Security-Within-eCommerce-in-2022_report.pdf (accessed on 19 March 2023).

Imran, O., Yousif, S., Hameed, I., Abed, W., & Hammid, A. (2020). Implementation of El-Gamal Algorithm for Speech Signals Encryption and Decryption. *Procedia Computer Science, 2020*(167), 1028–1037. DOI: 10.1016/j.procs.2020.03.402

Jebbar, W. A., & Al-Zubaidie, M. (2024). Transaction-Based Blockchain Systems Security Improvement Employing Micro-Segmentation Controlled By Smart Contracts and Detection of Saddle Goatfish. *SN Computer Science, 5*(7), 898. DOI: 10.1007/s42979-024-03239-9

Kumar, V., & Sinha, D. (2021). A Robust Intelligent Zero-Day Cyber-Attack Detection Technique. *Complex & Intelligent Systems, 7*(5), 2211–2234. DOI: 10.1007/s40747-021-00396-9

Li, L. (2024, October). Using The Ripple Consensus Algorithm to Achieve Transparent Cross-Border Payments in E-Commerce. *In 6th International Conference on Artificial Intelligence and Advanced Manufacturing* (AIAM 2024) (Vol. 2024, pp. 295-299). IET.

Manjare, S. O. (2025). E-Security Evolution: Navigating The E-Commerce Cybersecurity Landscape. In *Artificial Intelligence for Cyber Security and Industry 4.0* (pp. 292–318). CRC Press.

Mitra, D., Kulkarni, P., Pathak, P., & Natrai, N. (2022). Importance of Coping with Cyber Security Challenges in E Commerce Business. *In Proceedings of the 2022 International Interdisciplinary Humanitarian Conference for Sustainability* (IIHC), Bengaluru, India, 18–19 November 2022; pp. 1596–1601.

Mohd, N., & Ashawesh, A. (2021). Enhanced AES Algorithm Based on 14 Rounds in Securing Data and Minimizing Processing Time. *Journal of Physics: Conference Series, 2021*(1793), 012066. DOI: 10.1088/1742-6596/1793/1/012066

Muhajjar, R. A.. (2024). Integrating Trustworthy Mechanisms to Support Data and Information Security in Health Sensors. *Procedia Computer Science, 237*, 43–52. DOI: 10.1016/j.procs.2024.05.078

Mutemi, A., & Bacao, F. (2024). E-Commerce Fraud Detection Based on Machine Learning Techniques: Systematic Literature Review. *Big Data Mining and Analytics, 7*(2), 419–444. DOI: 10.26599/BDMA.2023.9020023

Rasha, H. R.. (2025). Sturdy Blockchain Combined with E-apps Repositories Based on Reliable Camouflaging and Integrating Mechanisms. *IJ Computer Network and Information Security, 17*(3), 35–53. DOI: 10.5815/ijcnis.2025.03.03

Razzaq, R. H., & Al-Zubaidie, M. (2024). Maintaining Security of Patient Data By Employing Private Blockchain and Fog Computing Technologies Based on Internet of Medical Things. *Informatica (Vilnius), 48*(12).

Saha, R., Geetha, G., Kumar, G., & Kim, T. (2018). RK-AES: An Improved Version of Aes Using A New Key Generation Process with Random Keys. *Security and Communication Networks, 2018*(2018), 9802475. DOI: 10.1155/2018/9802475

Shyaa, G. S., & Al-Zubaidie, M. (2023). Utilizing Trusted Lightweight Ciphers to Support Electronic-Commerce Transaction Cryptography. *Applied Sciences (Basel, Switzerland), 13*(12), 7085. DOI: 10.3390/app13127085

Tahayur, D. H.. (2025). Security Cooperation in the Protection Concerns of Agriculture Data Using Efficient Signatures and Artificial Bee Colony Manner. In *Sustainable Information Security in the Age of AI and Green Computing* (pp. 439–460). IGI Global Scientific Publishing.

Tajudeen, K. O., Ameen, A. O., & Adeniyi, A. E. (2025). A Systematic Review on Advanced Encryption Standard Cryptography to Enhance Message Security. *Multimedia Tools and Applications, 84*(40), 1–26. DOI: 10.1007/s11042-025-21041-4

Tregi, T. G., & Al-Zubaidie, M. (2025). Enhancing Traffic Data Security in Smart Cities Using Optimized Quantum-Based Digital Signatures and Privacy-Preserving Techniques. *Mesopotamian Journal of CyberSecurity, 5*(1), 256–272. DOI: 10.58496/MJCS/2025/017

Van Tilborg, H. C. (2025). *Chinese Remainder Theorem. In Encyclopedia of Cryptography, Security and Privacy*. Springer Nature Switzerland.

WEBSCALE. The Global Ecommerce Security Report 2022. 2022. Available online: https://www.webscale.com/global-ecommercesecurity-report-2022/ (accessed on 18 March 2023).

Yousif, S., Abboud, A., & Radhi, H. (2020). Robust Image Encryption with Scanning Technology, The El-Gamal Algorithm and Chaos Theory. *IEEE Access : Practical Innovations, Open Solutions*, *8*, 155184–155209. DOI: 10.1109/ACCESS.2020.3019216

Zhang, Z.(2019). Efficient and Secure ECDSA Algorithm and Its Applications: A Survey. [IJCNIS]. *International Journal of Communication Networks and Information Security*, *9*(1).

KEY TERMS AND DEFINITIONS

AES: A popular symmetric encryption algorithm for data security is Advanced Encryption Standard.

CRT: It is a key theorem in number theory that offers a way to solve simultaneous congruence systems.

E-Commerce: Online purchases and sales of products and services are referred to as electronic commerce.

El-Gamal: This asymmetric key encryption algorithm offers a way to securely exchange keys, encrypt data, and create digital signatures.

Public Key: This key is used to encrypt data or validate digital signatures in asymmetric cryptography. Together with a corresponding private key that is kept secret, it forms a key pair.

RSA: A popular asymmetric cryptographic technique that permits safe data transfer and digital signatures is the Rivest-Shamir-Adleman algorithm.

TAS: It is an essential part of digital communications and cybersecurity. Through the issuance and administration of digital certificates, it is essential to building trust in digital communications and transactions.

Chapter 3
Research Guru AI:
A Robust AI Tool for Analyzing, Comparing, and Evaluating Academic Literature

Otmane Azeroual
http://orcid.org/0000-0002-5225-389X
University of Hagen, Germany

Richard R. Khan
http://orcid.org/0009-0005-2351-5546
Golden Gate University, USA

ABSTRACT

The exponential growth of scientific publications poses significant challenges for researchers: efficiently identifying relevant studies, systematically detecting research gaps, and conducting reproducible analyses. Research Guru AI is an AI-powered tool that enables structured summaries, critical evaluations, and advanced analyses of scientific literature. This chapter provides a practical demonstration of how Research Guru AI can be applied across various domains – from higher education research to healthcare, education, finance, public administration, and Open Science initiatives. Furthermore, organizational implementation, best practices in change management, and the promotion of Open Science principles are discussed. The aim is to equip researchers with tools that significantly enhance efficiency, transparency, and reproducibility in scientific work.

DOI: 10.4018/979-8-2600-1433-2.ch003

INTRODUCTION

Scientific research is currently undergoing a profound transformation driven by the exponential growth of publications, preprints, and open-access data. In nearly all scientific domains, the number of scholarly outputs has been increasing at an unprecedented pace, leading to both opportunities and challenges for the global research community. Researchers today are confronted not only with the task of identifying relevant literature but also with evaluating methodological quality, ensuring reproducibility, and synthesizing findings across a vast body of knowledge (Ioannidis et al., 2021; Wellmon, 2015). This rapid information expansion has resulted in a phenomenon often referred to as *information overload*, where the ability to process and interpret information meaningfully becomes increasingly limited. As Spezi et al. (2017) note, the doubling of publication volumes in many disciplines has amplified the cognitive and practical burden of knowledge synthesis.

Traditional approaches to systematic literature review—manual searches, peer evaluations, and human-coded data extraction—are reaching their limits (Chapman, Morgan & Gartlehner, 2010). While systematic reviews and meta-analyses remain the gold standard for evidence-based research, their preparation is both time-consuming and prone to subjective biases. Studies have shown that manual reviews may overlook relevant studies due to inconsistent search strategies, human error, or publication bias, which in turn jeopardizes the completeness and objectivity of results (Haddaway et al., 2015; Mohajan, 2018; Haddaway et al., 2020). In addition, even when frameworks such as PRISMA or Cochrane Guidelines are rigorously applied, the increasing diversity of disciplines and data formats continues to challenge reproducibility (Delgado-Chaves et al., 2025).

Another key issue is the growing complexity of interdisciplinary research. Modern science requires researchers to evaluate not only the depth of knowledge within their own fields but also to integrate insights from neighboring domains such as data science, education, health, finance, and social sciences. As de la Torre-López et al. (2023) point out, the ability to compare methodologies, datasets, and theoretical frameworks across disciplines has become a decisive factor for producing robust, high-impact research. Yet, this comparative capability remains limited in traditional manual review workflows.

At the same time, there is a growing demand for transparency and reproducibility in science. The Open Science movement has reinforced the necessity for researchers to make their methods, data, and analytical workflows openly accessible (Kusa, Hanbury, & Knoth, 2022). However, despite the availability of digital repositories, preprint servers, and open datasets, the integration of these resources into consistent analytical frameworks remains a significant challenge. Many institutions still rely on fragmented processes, lacking the automation and standardization needed to ensure quality control and reproducibility at scale.

Against this backdrop, artificial intelligence (AI) offers transformative potential. AI-powered tools are capable of analyzing large corpora of scientific publications, detecting semantic relationships, and identifying research gaps systematically (Morriss et al., 2024). Advanced natural language processing (NLP) models based on transformer architectures—such as BERT (Devlin et al., 2019) and GPT—enable machines to interpret textual content with increasing linguistic and contextual precision. These models go beyond keyword searches by capturing semantic meaning and contextual dependencies, allowing them to evaluate not just what a paper is about, but *how* it approaches its research question. This represents a paradigm shift from simple text retrieval toward genuine understanding of scientific discourse.

The advent of these models has also inspired new types of research tools that automate key components of the scientific process. Research Guru AI was developed in this context as a next-generation analytical platform that integrates AI-driven literature processing, methodological evaluation, and comparative synthesis. Its purpose is to assist researchers in systematically identifying, comparing, and evaluating academic works across multiple domains. By leveraging transformer-based NLP models, Research Guru AI extracts methodological structures, summarizes findings, evaluates robustness, and visualizes the relationships between studies. These capabilities contribute directly to addressing the major challenges of modern research: efficiency, transparency, and reproducibility (Torres et al., 2025).

The efficiency benefits are particularly significant. Traditional systematic reviews can take months of manual screening, coding, and analysis. In contrast, Research Guru AI can process thousands of documents in a fraction of the time, providing structured summaries and critical evaluations in a standardized, reproducible manner. Such efficiency gains enable research teams to reallocate resources toward deeper theoretical analysis and interpretation rather than data management. This is consistent with the trends observed by Aldoseri, Al-Khalifa, and Hamouda (2024), who argue that automation in scholarly workflows enhances not only speed but also analytical depth.

Beyond efficiency, Research Guru AI also contributes to methodological consistency. It standardizes the evaluation process by applying unified analytical criteria to all studies under review. This reduces human bias and subjectivity in the assessment of methodological rigor, ensuring that comparisons between studies are based on consistent, transparent metrics (Sidi & Harel, 2018). For instance, the tool can automatically evaluate aspects such as sample size adequacy, data source reliability, reproducibility of findings, and statistical validity. These factors are crucial for evidence-based synthesis, especially in disciplines where methodological heterogeneity is high (Hardwicke et al., 2018).

In addition, Research Guru AI supports Open Science principles by integrating open-access data sources and adhering to transparent analytical standards. The platform allows researchers to reproduce analyses and share workflows, thereby strengthening the integrity of scientific collaboration (Azeroual, 2025). Such reproducibility is essential for addressing the ongoing "replication crisis" in multiple disciplines, where inconsistencies in data handling and analysis have led to declining trust in published results (Phillips-Wren & Hoskisson, 2015).

The applicability of Research Guru AI spans numerous domains. In higher education research, the tool enables the identification of research trends, cross-disciplinary comparisons, and the detection of publication clusters that signal emerging fields. In healthcare, it assists in systematically analyzing clinical trials, comparing treatment outcomes, and evaluating methodological robustness (Ioannidis et al., 2021). In the education and EdTech sector, the tool supports the evaluation of digital learning interventions, the comparison of pedagogical models, and the identification of effective teaching methodologies. Similarly, in finance and risk management, Research Guru AI facilitates the assessment of forecasting models and investment research, drawing on the principles of operational analytics discussed by Araz et al. (2020). Finally, in the public sector, it enhances the analysis of policy documents and governance studies, promoting evidence-based decision-making and transparent public administration (Nguyen-Trung, Saeri & Kaufman, 2024).

Moreover, Research Guru AI aligns with contemporary trends in hybrid knowledge architectures. These architectures combine structured and unstructured data, enabling AI systems to handle the heterogeneity inherent in modern scientific content. For example, integrating textual publications with citation networks and metadata allows for more holistic analyses, where context, influence, and relevance are jointly assessed. This capability reflects a fundamental evolution in AI-assisted research: from static information retrieval to dynamic knowledge synthesis.

From a technological standpoint, Research Guru AI leverages recent advances in NLP and information retrieval to construct a robust analytical pipeline. The system integrates Elasticsearch for high-performance indexing and retrieval, combined with transformer-based models for semantic understanding. This hybrid design ensures that both precision (through lexical indexing) and contextual comprehension (through deep learning) are achieved. Such synergy enables the platform to identify not only direct matches but also conceptually related works that may otherwise remain hidden in traditional keyword-based searches. As Kathare, Reddy, and Prabhu (2020) note, Elasticsearch remains a critical component for scalable retrieval architectures due to its distributed design and real-time query performance.

The introduction of AI-assisted tools like Research Guru AI also represents a cultural shift in how research is conducted. Rather than replacing human expertise, these systems augment the researcher's analytical capacity. As the cognitive workload associated with data screening and synthesis decreases, scholars can devote more attention to critical reasoning, theory development, and the interpretation of complex findings. This human–AI collaboration model echoes the principles outlined by Soares and Parreiras (2020), who emphasize the importance of hybrid systems that combine computational precision with human contextual understanding.

Ultimately, the motivation for developing and applying Research Guru AI lies in strengthening the scientific ecosystem through automation, transparency, and reproducibility. By automating the labor-intensive aspects of literature analysis and comparison, the tool empowers researchers to focus on high-level inquiry. By embedding reproducible workflows, it ensures that research outputs can be validated and extended by others. And by promoting open, AI-assisted analysis, it contributes to a more efficient and trustworthy scientific enterprise.

In summary, this chapter introduces Research Guru AI as an AI-powered tool that responds to the growing challenges of modern research. Through its integration of NLP, information retrieval, and automated evaluation, it enables the efficient, reproducible, and critical analysis of academic literature. The following sections will detail its technical functionality, domain-specific applications, and organizational implementation strategies, demonstrating how AI can redefine the landscape of scientific inquiry.

BACKGROUND AND LITERATURE REVIEW

Scientific research today is characterized by an explosive increase in publications, conference papers, preprints, and datasets (Ioannidis et al., 2021). In recent years alone, the number of available scholarly articles in numerous disciplines has doubled or even tripled, significantly increasing the information overload for researchers (Wellmon, 2015; Spezi et al., 2017). This rapid expansion poses a substantial challenge for academics, as not only the sheer quantity but also the quality, relevance, and methodological rigor of publications must be considered. Conducting a systematic literature review has therefore become a central yet increasingly complex task, requiring researchers to process vast amounts of information efficiently while maintaining the precision and validity of their evaluations (Lame, 2019). Traditional methods of literature analysis, which rely heavily on manual searches, peer review evaluations, and manual data preparation, are increasingly reaching their limits (Chapman, Morgan & Gartlehner, 2010). These approaches are often time-consuming, prone to subjective biases, and hinder the reproducibility of research findings. As a result, researchers face a growing risk of oversight, methodological inconsistencies, and the potential omission of crucial insights, all of which may compromise the validity of their conclusions.

Numerous studies have demonstrated that the quality of scientific analyses strongly depends on the completeness and objectivity of the underlying literature review (Haddaway et al., 2015; Mohajan, 2018; Haddaway et al., 2020). Missing or incompletely considered sources can lead to biased conclusions, whereas unclear evaluation methods reduce comparability and hinder reproducibility (Sidi & Harel, 2018; Hardwicke et al., 2018). Despite methodological standards such as PRISMA or Cochrane Guidelines, practical implementation remains complex and labor-intensive, particularly in interdisciplinary projects where varying terminologies, data formats, and research paradigms must be reconciled (Delgado-Chaves et al., 2025). Researchers must navigate a multidimensional challenge: identifying relevant publications, assessing methodological rigor, and synthesizing findings in a way that is both coherent and reproducible.

Against this backdrop, digital tools and AI-powered instruments are increasingly gaining importance in scientific workflows (Aldoseri, Al-Khalifa & Hamouda, 2024; Nguyen-Trung, Saeri & Kaufman, 2024). These tools aim to address aspects of literature research that traditional approaches struggle to manage efficiently. For instance, reference management systems such as Zotero, Mendeley, and EndNote provide functionalities for collecting, organizing, and sharing publications, along with collaborative features; however, they are largely limited to content organization rather than in-depth analysis. Similarly, Rayyan facilitates systematic reviews by supporting pre-selection, screening, and coding of publications, yet it lacks the ability to perform deeper AI-based evaluation of study quality or to generate structured comparative analyses. Tools such as Iris.ai can perform semantic analyses and cluster works based on content similarity, while Connected Papers excels in visualizing research landscapes; yet, both fall short in delivering critical evaluations and reproducible methodological assessments that researchers require for rigorous literature syntheses.

These limitations highlight a gap in existing tools and emphasize the need for AI solutions capable of offering automated analysis, comparative evaluation, and reproducible workflows. The capabilities of Research Guru AI are designed to fill these gaps, providing a comprehensive framework that addresses both the organizational and methodological challenges of contemporary research (Azeroual, 2025). The differences in capabilities between existing tools and Research Guru AI are summarized in Table 1. The table illustrates how Research Guru AI combines automated literature summaries, methodological evaluation, reproducible workflows, and cross-domain applicability, offering researchers a unified tool for both analytical depth and operational efficiency.

Table 1. Comparison of existing research tools with Research Guru AI.

Function / Feature	Zotero	Mendeley	EndNote	Rayyan	Iris.ai	Connected Papers	Research Guru AI
Collect & organize literature	✓	✓	✓	Partly	✓	✓	✓
Automated summaries	X	X	X	X	✓	X	✓
Critical evaluation of studies	X	X	X	Partly	X	X	✓
Comparison of studies by methods	X	X	X	X	Partly	X	✓
Reproducible analysis/workflows	X	X	X	Partly	X	X	✓
Applicable across various domains	X	X	X	✓	✓	✓	✓
Supports Open Science & Transparency	X	X	X	Partly	X	X	✓
Time savings & efficiency increase	Partly	Partly	Partly	✓	✓	✓	High

By analyzing the table, it becomes clear that Research Guru AI combines multiple features that previously existed only in isolation or partially across different platforms. Its automated summaries and semantic evaluation capabilities significantly reduce the time required for literature reviews while increasing methodological rigor. The inclusion of reproducible workflows ensures that all analyses can be verified and replicated by other researchers, addressing a major limitation of traditional literature review methods. Furthermore, the tool's applicability across scientific domains and its support for Open Science principles significantly enhance research transparency, collaboration, and comparability.

Research Guru AI stands out not only because it integrates these diverse functions into a single platform but also because it provides a structured, reproducible, and scalable workflow. By systematically comparing studies based on content and methodology, it allows researchers to detect patterns, identify research gaps, and assess trends across disciplines. This is particularly valuable in contemporary research environments, where interdisciplinary and cross-domain studies are increasingly common, and where the sheer volume of publications makes manual synthesis impractical. The tool's ability to perform critical evaluation of methodological rigor ensures that the results of literature analyses are not only comprehensive but also reliable, supporting evidence-based decision-making and fostering high-quality research outputs.

In summary, the literature highlights that the increasing complexity and volume of scientific publications are overwhelming traditional evaluation methods. AI-powered tools like Research Guru AI provide substantial added value by increasing efficiency, accuracy, and reproducibility while offering broad applicability across scientific domains. By automating repetitive and time-consuming tasks and providing structured analytical outputs, Research Guru AI not only addresses current limitations but also opens new opportunities for methodological standardization, transparency, and interdisciplinary research synthesis. This chapter therefore demonstrates in detail how the tool functions, how it can be applied across multiple domains, and how it contributes to a more efficient, rigorous, and reproducible scientific research process.

FUNCTIONALITY OF RESEARCH GURU AI

Research Guru AI is a comprehensive AI-powered tool specifically designed to support researchers in efficiently analyzing, evaluating, and summarizing large volumes of scientific literature. The tool addresses the challenges posed by the exponential growth of academic publications, providing a unified platform where literature assessment, comparative evaluation, methodological scrutiny, and automated synthesis are seamlessly integrated. At the core of Research Guru AI lies a sophisticated combination of NLP algorithms, transformer-based models, and modular workflows that enable precise extraction and interpretation of information from diverse scientific texts. By leveraging these technologies, the tool transforms traditionally labor-intensive and error-prone literature reviews into structured, reproducible, and scalable research processes.

The literature analysis component forms the foundation of Research Guru AI's functionality. It begins with the automated acquisition of scientific publications from multiple sources, including journals, preprint servers, conference proceedings, institutional repositories, and open-access datasets. The tool performs advanced preprocessing steps to standardize textual formats, remove redundancies, and normalize metadata, ensuring that the input data is consistent and suitable for subsequent analysis. Once the data is processed, the tool applies transformer-based NLP models, such as fine-tuned BERT or domain-specific variants, to extract critical elements from each document. These elements include key research questions, theoretical frameworks, study methodologies, experimental designs, sample characteristics, analytical approaches, results, and citations. By capturing these components in a structured format, Research Guru AI allows researchers to access detailed summaries of complex studies without manually reading and coding each paper. This capability significantly reduces the time required to synthesize large bodies of literature while maintaining high fidelity to the original content.

Beyond extracting information, Research Guru AI excels in the comparative analysis of scientific works. Using semantic similarity measures and methodological scoring algorithms, the tool generates structured overviews that enable researchers to systematically identify convergences and divergences among studies. For instance, it can highlight trends across multiple publications, pinpoint contradictory findings, and uncover underexplored areas, effectively revealing research gaps that might otherwise remain unnoticed. These comparisons are not limited to superficial content but extend to methodological rigor, allowing for the evaluation of study designs, sampling strategies, statistical methods, and reproducibility metrics. By providing side-by-side comparisons of studies according to these criteria, Research Guru AI enables more informed decisions when selecting studies for inclusion in systematic reviews, meta-analyses, or research syntheses.

A critical feature of Research Guru AI is its evaluation module, which objectively assesses the methodological quality of scientific studies. The AI employs a combination of rule-based algorithms and machine learning models to analyze study design robustness, sample size adequacy, data quality, statistical validity, and the reproducibility of reported results. This systematic appraisal increases transparency and allows for more accurate cross-study comparisons, addressing a common limitation in traditional literature reviews where methodological assessments can be subjective and inconsistent. Additionally, Research Guru AI is capable of scoring studies according to user-defined criteria, enabling researchers to tailor evaluations to specific domains or research questions. This flexibility enhances the applicability of the tool across disciplines ranging from life sciences and engineering to social sciences and economics.

Research Guru AI's summarization functionality represents another key advantage. After extracting and evaluating information, the tool automatically generates concise, structured summaries that encapsulate key findings, methodological insights, and identified research gaps. These summaries are designed to be directly usable in systematic reviews, meta-analyses, or academic reports, saving researchers substantial time while ensuring that critical information is preserved. Furthermore, the summaries are produced in a reproducible format, meaning that repeated analyses on the same dataset yield consistent outputs. This feature supports transparent reporting and aligns with principles of Open Science, facilitating collaboration, verification, and replication of research results.

From a technical perspective, Research Guru AI integrates a modular workflow that allows each stage of analysis to be automated or customized according to the needs of the researcher. The workflow comprises data acquisition, preprocessing, semantic analysis, methodological evaluation, comparative analysis, summarization, and visualization. Visualization tools embedded within the platform provide graphical representations of research landscapes, trends, and methodological quality scores, which support intuitive understanding and decision-making. Each module is configurable, allowing the integration of new data sources, analytical models, or domain-specific ontologies, thereby extending the tool's applicability and ensuring that it remains adaptable to evolving research requirements.

Figure 1 illustrates the end-to-end workflow of Research Guru AI, highlighting the linear yet modular process from data collection to the generation of visualized analytical reports. Each stage is fully automatable, and the flexibility of the platform ensures it can be adapted for different research domains, ranging from healthcare and higher education to finance, public administration, and emerging fields such as Open Science initiatives. The figure demonstrates the holistic nature of the tool, where data collection, processing, analysis, evaluation, and visualization are seamlessly integrated, creating an efficient, reproducible, and transparent workflow that empowers researchers to manage information overload effectively and make evidence-based decisions.

Figure 1. Workflow of Research Guru AI for literature analysis and evaluation

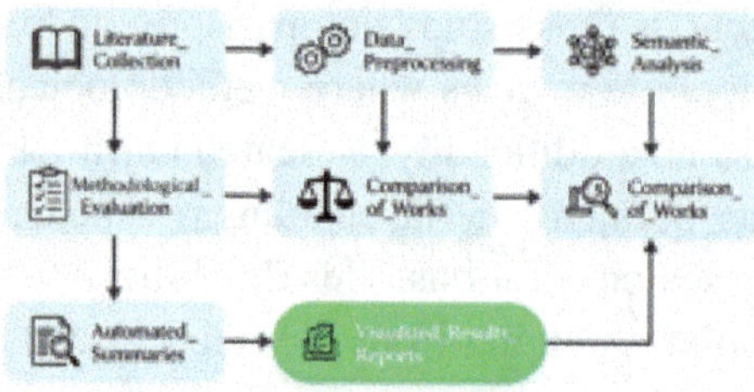

This figure visually represents the structured sequence of steps implemented within Research Guru AI. Beginning with data acquisition from diverse sources, the workflow progresses through preprocessing, semantic extraction of study components, methodological evaluation, comparative analysis across publications, and finally, automated summarization with visualization outputs. Each stage is designed for automation while allowing flexibility for customization, enabling researchers to maintain control over analytical parameters and optimize outputs according to specific project requirements.

In conclusion, the functionality of Research Guru AI extends well beyond traditional literature management tools. By combining sophisticated NLP algorithms, transformer-based models, structured evaluation, comparative analyses, automated summarization, and visualization, the platform provides a comprehensive solution for modern research challenges. It enhances efficiency, ensures reproducibility, promotes methodological rigor, and enables researchers to extract actionable insights from large, complex datasets. Its modular design, adaptability, and domain-agnostic capabilities make it a robust tool that not only addresses current limitations in literature review processes but also sets a new standard for AI-assisted scientific research workflows.

DOMAIN-SPECIFIC APPLICATIONS

Research Guru AI demonstrates substantial potential across a wide array of scientific and practical domains, providing researchers, institutions, and organizations with the ability to systematically analyze, compare, and evaluate large volumes of literature in a highly efficient and reproducible manner. By integrating automated literature analysis, structured comparison of works, methodological evaluation, and the generation of comprehensive summaries, the tool allows users to make evidence-based decisions with unprecedented speed and accuracy. Its versatility ensures applicability across both academic research and practical fields, including higher education, healthcare, education and EdTech, finance, public administration, and optionally, open science and industrial research. The underlying strength of Research Guru AI lies in its capacity to translate complex datasets into structured insights, thereby supporting strategic planning, policy-making, and innovation.

In higher education research, Research Guru AI provides significant value by enabling large-scale trend analysis, identifying emerging research gaps, and systematically comparing disciplines. The tool's automated workflows allow researchers to aggregate relevant publications across different faculties and subfields, assessing methodological quality and thematic focus. By highlighting underexplored topics and methodological weaknesses, Research Guru AI supports the development of targeted research strategies, facilitates interdisciplinary collaboration, and allows academic institutions to allocate resources efficiently. For instance, universities can utilize the tool to monitor publication trends in natural and social sciences, detecting shifts in research priorities and ensuring that institutional research agendas remain aligned with global scientific developments. The automated summaries and comparative visualizations further enable faculty and administrators to quickly grasp the evolution of research areas, identify potential partnerships, and implement evidence-driven curriculum improvements.

In the healthcare domain, Research Guru AI plays a crucial role in synthesizing clinical evidence and evaluating the methodological rigor of studies. By extracting key information from clinical trials, meta-analyses, and preclinical studies, the tool enables healthcare professionals, policy-makers, and researchers to assess therapeutic approaches with higher precision. For example, the AI can automatically evaluate the quality of vaccine studies, compare treatment efficacy across different patient populations, and summarize findings from multiple clinical trials. This streamlines evidence-based decision-making in clinical and public health settings, reducing the time required to analyze extensive datasets while maintaining methodological rigor. Furthermore, Research Guru AI's ability to detect inconsistencies or gaps in the literature allows researchers to propose novel studies that address unmet clinical needs, thus accelerating the pace of medical innovation and enhancing patient care outcomes.

In education and EdTech, Research Guru AI offers a structured approach to analyzing pedagogical studies, digital learning interventions, and program evaluations. The platform enables educational researchers to systematically compare different teaching methods, assess the effectiveness of digital learning platforms, and evaluate educational interventions. By automating literature synthesis and methodological assessment, the tool provides insights into best practices, identifies gaps in educational research, and supports evidence-driven decision-making in curriculum design. For example, the AI can compare blended learning programs across multiple institutions, analyze adaptive learning platforms for effectiveness, and highlight interventions that maximize student engagement and learning outcomes. The structured summaries generated by Research Guru AI allow educational stakeholders to rapidly translate research findings into actionable strategies, facilitating continuous improvement in teaching and learning processes.

In finance, Research Guru AI assists in evaluating complex models, market analyses, risk management approaches, and regulatory studies. The tool collects and compares relevant literature, assesses methodological robustness, and highlights trends and inconsistencies across financial research. By enabling systematic evaluation, the platform supports informed investment decisions, transparent risk assessment, and benchmarking of forecasting models. For example, financial institutions can use Research Guru AI to compare the predictive accuracy of various risk models, evaluate market analyses over time, and identify methodological limitations in regulatory compliance studies. This structured approach enhances strategic decision-making and reduces uncertainty, providing stakeholders with a reliable basis for risk mitigation and investment planning.

In the public sector, Research Guru AI facilitates the assessment of governance studies, smart government initiatives, and policy evaluations. By systematically analyzing government reports, policy measures, and program outcomes, the tool allows decision-makers to identify best practices, evaluate the effectiveness of interventions, and increase transparency in public administration. For instance, the AI can support the evaluation of e-government projects, analyze the impact of smart city initiatives, and benchmark policy implementations across regions. The methodological evaluation and comparative insights generated by Research Guru AI enable governments to design more effective public policies, allocate resources efficiently, and promote evidence-based governance practices. Additionally, the structured outputs support accountability and transparency, reinforcing trust between public institutions and citizens.

Beyond these primary domains, Research Guru AI demonstrates significant potential in open science and industrial applications. In these areas, the tool can systematically analyze open datasets, benchmark research practices, and evaluate R&D studies. Industrial researchers and innovation managers can leverage the AI to identify reproducible methods, compare research outcomes, and optimize internal processes based on evidence-driven insights. By promoting standardized analyses and facilitating access to high-quality data, Research Guru AI contributes to reproducibility, accelerates innovation, and ensures that research and development efforts are both efficient and strategically aligned.

The following table summarizes these domain-specific applications, the corresponding Research Guru AI functions, and the benefits realized in each field:

Table 2. Domain-specific applications and functional advantages of Research Guru AI

Domain	Possible Applications / Use Cases	Research Guru AI Functions	Benefits / Potential	Examples / Studies
Higher Education Research	Trend analysis, research gaps, comparison of disciplines	Automatic collection of relevant publications, methodology comparison, quality assessment, summarization	Rapid identification of research gaps, evidence-based planning of new projects, promotion of interdisciplinary collaboration	Analysis of publication trends in natural and social sciences, cross-faculty trend analysis
Healthcare	Clinical studies, meta-analyses, evidence evaluation	Extraction of study data, methodological quality assessment, clinical evidence summarization	Time savings in literature review, objective evidence evaluation, support for clinical decision-making	Comparison of therapy approaches, evaluation of vaccine studies, meta-analysis of new drug efficacy
Education / EdTech	Teaching methods, digital learning platforms, intervention analysis	Collection and comparison of educational studies, intervention analysis, summaries	Optimization of curricula, evidence-based implementation of digital learning platforms, evaluation of interventions	Analysis of blended learning programs, comparison of adaptive learning platforms, effectiveness studies of pedagogical methods
Finance	Market analyses, risk management, model comparison	Collection of financial literature, comparison of forecasting models, methodological evaluation	Informed investment decisions, improved risk assessment, transparent model comparisons	Comparison of risk models, analysis of market trends, evaluation of regulatory studies
Public Sector	Governance, smart government, policy analyses	Analysis of government reports, comparison of political measures, evidence evaluation	Support for decision-making, identification of best practices, improved transparency	Evaluation of e-government initiatives, analysis of smart city projects, policy benchmarking
Open Science / Industry (optional)	Open dataset analyses, benchmarks, R&D studies	Collection and comparison of open datasets, evaluation of study methods, summaries	Promotion of reproducible research, support for innovation processes, improvement of evidence base	Evaluation of open data initiatives, comparison of industrial research reports, benchmark study analysis

By integrating automated workflows, structured comparisons, and methodological evaluations, Research Guru AI ensures that decision-making across these diverse domains is grounded in robust evidence. The platform's ability to translate complex, multidimensional data into actionable insights enables researchers, practitioners, and policymakers to identify trends, uncover gaps, optimize strategies, and implement interventions with confidence. In this way, Research Guru AI not only supports academic research but also enhances organizational decision-making, operational efficiency, and the reproducibility of scientific outcomes.

IMPLEMENTATION AND ORGANIZATIONAL CONSIDERATIONS

The successful deployment of Research Guru AI within academic institutions, companies, and public organizations requires a comprehensive understanding of technological, organizational, and cultural dimensions. Implementing the tool effectively involves careful planning, structured workflows, and proactive engagement with stakeholders to ensure that its full potential is realized in enhancing research efficiency, reproducibility, and evidence-based decision-making.

A crucial first step in implementation is goal definition. Institutions must clearly identify the areas in which Research Guru AI provides the most significant benefits, such as streamlining literature reviews, enabling methodologically rigorous evaluations, identifying research gaps, and supporting reproducible analyses. Well-defined objectives allow organizations to design a structured rollout, establish performance indicators, and measure the impact of the tool on research processes. Clear goals also help align technical capabilities with institutional priorities, ensuring that deployment addresses immediate operational needs while contributing to long-term strategic aims.

Technical integration is equally vital. Research Guru AI needs to be seamlessly connected to existing data infrastructures, including bibliographic databases, institutional repositories, and internal research databases. Ensuring access to high-quality and up-to-date data allows the AI to analyze large volumes of publications, datasets, and other scholarly outputs accurately. Interoperability with other research tools, data standards, and metadata formats must be ensured to avoid disrupting established workflows. Automated data pipelines should be configured to allow continuous ingestion of new publications and datasets, guaranteeing that analyses reflect the most recent scientific developments.

Staff training and capacity-building play a critical role in successful implementation. Effective utilization of Research Guru AI requires researchers, librarians, and administrative staff to understand both the technical use of the tool and the interpretation of AI-generated outputs. Workshops, tutorials, and ongoing educational initiatives help users gain confidence in leveraging AI for research purposes, while also understanding potential limitations, biases, and methodological considerations. By fostering AI literacy and critical thinking, institutions ensure that human expertise complements AI-supported analyses, resulting in more accurate, nuanced, and impactful outcomes.

Data quality and governance are central to maintaining credibility and reliability. Inconsistent, incomplete, or biased input data can undermine analyses and compromise reproducibility. Institutions should implement robust data validation, standardization, and cleaning processes to ensure that only high-quality datasets are included. Ethical considerations, such as data privacy, security, and transparency in AI-driven decision-making, must also be integrated into organizational policies.

A phased implementation approach is recommended to reduce risks and ensure smooth adoption. Pilot projects within select teams or departments allow institutions to test workflows, collect feedback, identify bottlenecks, and refine procedures before scaling deployment institution-wide. This iterative approach ensures that workflows are optimized, user experience is enhanced, and potential resistance is minimized.

Change management is another essential element. Introducing AI tools changes established workflows and responsibilities, which may generate skepticism among staff. Effective strategies include transparent communication of objectives and benefits, involvement of stakeholders in decision-making, creation of usage guidelines, and continuous monitoring. Recognizing early adopters and demonstrating tangible workflow improvements further facilitate acceptance and integration into organizational culture.

Finally, Research Guru AI strongly supports Open Science principles. By promoting reproducible analyses, standardized workflows, and transparent evaluation processes, the tool enhances collaboration, benchmarking, and interdisciplinary exchange. Open access to structured analyses and datasets improves both institutional research quality and global scientific visibility.

The following table, Table 3, provides a structured overview of these implementation dimensions, highlighting the measures, expected goals and benefits, and the potential impact on research and practice:

Table 3. Implementation framework and organizational considerations for Research Guru AI

Dimension	Measures / Steps	Goals / Benefits	Potential for Research & Practice
Goal Definition	Clear definition of application areas (literature review, evaluation, reproducibility)	Structured rollout, focus on benefits	Workflow optimization, identification of relevant research gaps
Data Integration	Connection to bibliographies, repositories, internal research databases	Access to comprehensive, up-to-date data	Broader data basis, improved analysis quality
Staff Training	Workshops, tutorials, continuous education	Competent use of AI tools	Efficient utilization, higher acceptance, better interpretation of results
Data Quality & Governance	Standardization of metadata, validation, data cleaning	Ensure accurate analyses	Minimize bias, reliable results
Pilot Projects & Phased Implementation	Test runs in teams, feedback loops, workflow adjustments	Risk mitigation, iterative optimization	Gain practical experience, adapt to real processes
Change Management	Stakeholder involvement, transparent communication, guidelines, monitoring	Increase acceptance, reduce resistance	Sustainable use, better institutional integration
Promotion of Open Science	Use of open data, standardized analyses, reproducibility	Increase transparency and collaboration	Systematic reviews, benchmarking, interdisciplinary exchange

By systematically addressing these dimensions, institutions can create an environment where Research Guru AI operates at maximum efficiency and effectiveness. This integrated approach transforms traditional research workflows into streamlined, data-driven processes capable of handling the growing volume and complexity of scientific literature. Researchers gain the ability to conduct comprehensive evaluations, identify emerging trends, and generate reproducible analyses, while institutions benefit from improved decision-making, resource optimization, and strengthened credibility in research outputs. Ultimately, implementing Research Guru AI represents not only a technological advancement but also a cultural shift toward more efficient, transparent, and evidence-based scientific practices.

DISCUSSION AND EVALUATION

The integration of Research Guru AI into modern research workflows represents a significant evolution in the methodology of literature analysis, evaluation, and knowledge synthesis. One of the most immediate advantages of the tool is the dramatic increase in efficiency it provides. Traditional approaches to literature reviews and meta-analyses are notoriously time-consuming, often requiring weeks or even months to systematically collect, read, and evaluate relevant publications. By contrast, Research Guru AI automates many of these labor-intensive processes. Through the use of advanced natural language processing algorithms and transformer-based models, the tool can process large volumes of publications simultaneously, extracting key findings, identifying methodological approaches, and summarizing essential concepts in a fraction of the time required by manual methods. This acceleration not only saves researchers valuable time but also allows them to focus on higher-order analytical tasks, such as interpretation, synthesis, and application of results.

Beyond efficiency, Research Guru AI enhances transparency in the research process. Each step of analysis and summarization is traceable, which enables researchers to verify results, replicate analyses, and audit methodological decisions. This transparency is particularly important in interdisciplinary research, where varying standards of rigor and reporting can lead to inconsistencies in conclusions. By standardizing workflows, Research Guru AI ensures that studies are evaluated against consistent criteria, fostering comparability across publications and domains. In this sense, the tool acts as both a methodological anchor and a quality assurance mechanism, reducing subjective biases that can inadvertently affect manual literature reviews.

Another critical benefit is the reproducibility afforded by the AI-assisted process. Traditional literature reviews often suffer from limited reproducibility, as different researchers may select different publications, apply different inclusion criteria, or interpret findings inconsistently. Research Guru AI mitigates these issues by automating data collection, applying standardized evaluation metrics, and producing structured summaries. This reproducibility is essential not only for verifying results but also for longitudinal studies and comparative research, where repeated analyses over time or across institutions require consistent methodologies. The reproducible workflows generated by Research Guru AI therefore support the principles of Open Science, encouraging transparent dissemination of results and collaborative research practices.

Despite these advantages, the use of AI in literature evaluation is not without limitations and challenges. The accuracy and reliability of analyses are heavily dependent on the quality and comprehensiveness of input data. Incomplete datasets, poorly curated repositories, or biased sources can result in skewed evaluations, potentially propagating errors or misinterpretations across research outputs. Furthermore, AI systems, including Research Guru AI, are inherently constrained by the algorithms and training data on which they are built. While transformer-based models excel at identifying patterns and extracting semantic relationships, they may fail to capture subtle contextual nuances, interpret domain-specific jargon accurately, or understand the broader theoretical implications of research findings.

This highlights the continuing need for human expertise: researchers must critically evaluate AI-generated insights, interpret complex or ambiguous results, and apply domain knowledge to draw meaningful conclusions.

The ethical dimension of AI-assisted research also requires careful consideration. Issues of algorithmic bias, transparency, and accountability arise when AI systems are used to evaluate scholarly work. For instance, certain fields, geographic regions, or publication types may be overrepresented in training datasets, leading to potential favoritism in automated analyses. Researchers and institutions must therefore adopt measures to detect and mitigate bias, ensuring that AI-generated evaluations are fair, balanced, and representative of the broader literature. Additionally, questions of data privacy and intellectual property arise when proprietary or sensitive datasets are processed, necessitating strict adherence to ethical guidelines and legal frameworks.

In comparing Research Guru AI to traditional literature review methods, the advantages become clear. Manual reviews, while providing nuanced human interpretation, are labor-intensive, prone to inconsistencies, and difficult to reproduce at scale. Research Guru AI complements these methods by automating repetitive tasks, systematically evaluating publications, and generating structured insights that can guide further analysis. Rather than replacing human judgment, the AI enhances it, allowing researchers to devote cognitive resources to critical thinking, hypothesis generation, and the synthesis of novel insights. This hybrid approach, where human expertise and AI efficiency are combined, has the potential to transform research practices, particularly in fields facing rapid publication growth and data complexity.

The tool's applicability across diverse domains further underscores its value. In healthcare, for example, AI-assisted analysis of clinical trials, meta-analyses, and treatment evaluations allows for faster identification of effective therapies and evidence-based recommendations. In education and EdTech, systematic evaluation of pedagogical studies facilitates curriculum optimization and digital learning platform assessment. Financial research benefits from transparent comparison of models, methodologies, and risk analyses, while public sector organizations can leverage Research Guru AI to benchmark policy interventions, assess governance strategies, and promote data-driven decision-making. Each domain benefits not only from efficiency and reproducibility but also from the structured synthesis of large-scale evidence, which enhances decision-making, resource allocation, and strategic planning.

In conclusion, the discussion of Research Guru AI highlights a nuanced balance of opportunities and limitations. The tool offers transformative potential for research efficiency, reproducibility, and transparency, while simultaneously requiring careful attention to data quality, algorithmic limitations, and ethical considerations. Its strength lies in complementing, rather than replacing, human expertise, enabling researchers to engage more deeply with substantive insights while relying on AI for scalable, systematic analysis. By integrating Research Guru AI into research workflows, institutions can foster evidence-based practices, enhance the quality and comparability of outputs, and support Open Science initiatives. At the same time, ongoing evaluation, training, and governance are essential to ensure that AI-driven processes remain robust, equitable, and aligned with the principles of rigorous scientific inquiry.

CONCLUSION AND OUTLOOK

Research Guru AI represents a transformative advancement in the way scientific research is analyzed, synthesized, and evaluated. As research output continues to grow exponentially across all disciplines, the need for intelligent systems that can process, compare, and interpret vast bodies of literature has never been greater. Research Guru AI provides precisely this capability — combining advanced NLP, transformer-based models, and transparent workflows to enhance both efficiency and scientific rigor.

Through its ability to automate core processes such as data collection, methodological evaluation, and the creation of structured summaries, the platform frees researchers from repetitive manual work and enables them to focus on interpretation, synthesis, and innovation. Moreover, by standardizing analytical procedures and documenting each evaluation step, Research Guru AI strengthens reproducibility and transparency, two essential pillars of Open Science. This alignment with global research standards facilitates collaborative validation of findings and promotes trust in data-driven scientific outcomes.

Looking ahead, several strategic developments are planned that will significantly expand the scope and usability of Research Guru AI. A key initiative involves establishing direct interfaces with major scientific publishers and digital infrastructures such as Elsevier, Springer Nature, ACM Digital Library, IEEE Xplore, and ORCID. These integrations will allow the platform to access and analyze publications, metadata, and author profiles directly within Research Guru AI. Researchers will thus be able to import their personal publication lists, institutional repositories, or curated reading libraries into the platform, where the system will automatically analyze, compare, and evaluate the content according to predefined methodological and thematic criteria.

This future capability will transform Research Guru AI from a standalone analytical tool into a comprehensive research ecosystem, connecting directly with global academic databases and enhancing interoperability across disciplines and institutions. The automated synchronization with such sources will ensure that analyses are always based on the most current and complete datasets, while maintaining compliance with copyright and data-sharing regulations.

In parallel, the Research Guru AI team plans to develop new functional modules that address emerging research needs. Among these are predictive analytics for identifying emerging scientific trends, semantic visualization dashboards for cross-disciplinary mapping, and intelligent benchmarking modules for evaluating methodological rigor across publications. Additional tools for citation-network analysis, bias detection, and reproducibility scoring are also under development. These features will further strengthen the platform's position as a critical enabler of high-quality, data-driven research and evidence-based decision-making.

Beyond technological expansion, the continued success of Research Guru AI will depend on fostering a culture of collaboration and responsible AI usage. Institutional adoption strategies should emphasize user training, transparent data governance, and open-science principles. As researchers, publishers, and policymakers increasingly adopt AI-based tools for scientific evaluation, Research Guru AI is well positioned to serve as a central hub that bridges the gap between human expertise and computational intelligence.

In summary, Research Guru AI not only enhances the efficiency and accuracy of literature analysis but also lays the foundation for a new generation of integrative, transparent, and ethically responsible research infrastructures. Through planned partnerships with leading scientific data providers and the ongoing development of innovative analytical modules, the platform will continue to evolve into an indispensable instrument for the global research community — enabling faster insights, stronger collaboration, and higher scientific impact.

REFERENCES

Aldoseri, A., Al-Khalifa, K. N., & Hamouda, A. M. (2024). AI-powered innovation in digital transformation: Key pillars and industry impact. *Sustainability (Basel), 16*(5), 1790. DOI: 10.3390/su16051790

Azeroual, O. (2025). *Von der Literaturflut zur Erkenntnis: Research Guru AI als Katalysator für die Zukunft wissenschaftlicher Analyse*. Information – Wissenschaft & Praxis., DOI: 10.1515/iwp-2025-2050

Chapman, A. L., Morgan, L. C., & Gartlehner, G. (2010). Semi-automating the manual literature search for systematic reviews increases efficiency. *Health Information and Libraries Journal, 27*(1), 22–27. DOI: 10.1111/j.1471-1842.2009.00865.x PMID: 20402801

de la Torre-López, J., Ramírez, A., & Romero, J. R. (2023). Artificial intelligence to automate the systematic review of scientific literature. *Computing, 105*(10), 2171–2194. DOI: 10.1007/s00607-023-01181-x

Delgado-Chaves, F. M., Jennings, M. J., Atalaia, A., Wolff, J., Horvath, R., Mamdouh, Z. M., Baumbach, J., & Baumbach, L. (2025). Transforming literature screening: The emerging role of large language models in systematic reviews. *Proceedings of the National Academy of Sciences of the United States of America, 122*(2), e2411962122. DOI: 10.1073/pnas.2411962122 PMID: 39761403

Haddaway, N. R., Bethel, A., Dicks, L. V., Koricheva, J., Macura, B., Petrokofsky, G., Pullin, A. S., Savilaakso, S., & Stewart, G. B. (2020). Eight problems with literature reviews and how to fix them. *Nature Ecology & Evolution, 4*(12), 1582–1589. DOI: 10.1038/s41559-020-01295-x PMID: 33046871

Haddaway, N. R., Woodcock, P., Macura, B., & Collins, A. (2015). Making literature reviews more reliable through application of lessons from systematic reviews. *Conservation Biology, 29*(6), 1596–1605. DOI: 10.1111/cobi.12541 PMID: 26032263

Hardwicke, T. E., Mathur, M. B., MacDonald, K., Nilsonne, G., Banks, G. C., Kidwell, M. C., Hofelich Mohr, A., Clayton, E., Yoon, E. J., Henry Tessler, M., Lenne, R. L., Altman, S., Long, B., & Frank, M. C. (2018). Data availability, reusability, and analytic reproducibility: Evaluating the impact of a mandatory open data policy at the journal Cognition. *Royal Society Open Science, 5*(8), 180448. DOI: 10.1098/rsos.180448 PMID: 30225032

Ioannidis, J. P., Salholz-Hillel, M., Boyack, K. W., & Baas, J. (2021). The rapid, massive growth of COVID-19 authors in the scientific literature. *Royal Society Open Science, 8*(9), 210389. DOI: 10.1098/rsos.210389 PMID: 34527271

Kusa, W., Hanbury, A., & Knoth, P. (2022). Automation of citation screening for systematic literature reviews using neural networks: A replicability study. In *European Conference on Information Retrieval* (pp. 584-598). Cham: Springer International Publishing. DOI: 10.1007/978-3-030-99736-6_39

Lame, G. (2019). Systematic literature reviews: An introduction. In *Proceedings of the design society: international conference on engineering design* (Vol. 1, No. 1, pp. 1633-1642). Cambridge University Press.

Mohajan, H. K. (2018). Qualitative research methodology in social sciences and related subjects. *Journal of economic development, environment and people, 7*(1), 23-48.

Morriss, J., Brindle, T., Rösman, J. B., Reibsamen, D., & Enz, A. (2024). The Literature Review Network: An Explainable Artificial Intelligence for Systematic Literature Reviews, Meta-analyses, and Method Development. *arXiv preprint arXiv:2408.05239.*

Nguyen-Trung, K., Saeri, A. K., & Kaufman, S. (2024). Applying ChatGPT and AI-Powered Tools to Accelerate Evidence Reviews. *Human Behavior and Emerging Technologies*, *2024*(1), 8815424. DOI: 10.1155/2024/8815424

Phillips-Wren, G., & Hoskisson, A. (2015). An analytical journey towards big data. *Journal of Decision Systems*, *24*(1), 87–102. DOI: 10.1080/12460125.2015.994333

Sidi, Y., & Harel, O. (2018). The treatment of incomplete data: Reporting, analysis, reproducibility, and replicability. *Social Science & Medicine*, *209*, 169–173. DOI: 10.1016/j.socscimed.2018.05.037 PMID: 29807627

Spezi, V., Wakeling, S., Pinfield, S., Creaser, C., Fry, J., & Willett, P. (2017). Open-access mega-journals: The future of scholarly communication or academic dumping ground? A review. *The Journal of Documentation*, *73*(2), 263–283. DOI: 10.1108/JD-06-2016-0082

Torres, J., Mulligan, C., Jorge, J., & Moreira, C. (2025). PROMPTHEUS: A Human-Centered Pipeline to Streamline Systematic Literature Reviews with Large Language Models. *Information (Basel)*, *16*(5), 420. DOI: 10.3390/info16050420

Wellmon, C. (2015). *Organizing enlightenment: Information overload and the invention of the modern research university*. JHU Press.

Chapter 4
SmartSpam Deep Neural Networks for Intelligent Spam Detection

M. Martinaa
http://orcid.org/0000-0003-0977-2106
SASTRA University, India

G. Revathy
http://orcid.org/0000-0002-0691-1687
SASTRA University, India

ABSTRACT

Secure and trustworthy digital communication is seriously threatened by the growing number and sophistication of spam emails. The contextual and sequential patterns present in contemporary spam messages are frequently missed by traditional machine learning (ML) techniques, despite their relative effectiveness. The framework we present in this work, SmartSpam, is based on deep learning (DL) and uses stand-alone neural network models to detect and categorize spam emails intelligently. In particular, we examine the performance of the Gated Recurrent Units (GRU), Long Short-Term Memory (LSTM), Bidirectional LSTM (BiLSTM), Convolutional Neural Networks (CNN) and transformer-based model Bidirectional Encoder Representations from Transformers (BERT) for this task. Contextual embeddings, Count Vectorizer, and TF-IDF are used for feature extraction, depending on the model architecture. Grid search, genetic algorithms, and other hyperparameter tuning techniques are used to optimize each model. UCI SMS Spam,

DOI: 10.4018/979-8-2600-1433-2.ch004

1. INTRODUCTION

1.1 Background and Motivation

Email has emerged as one of the most essential and popular forms of communication for people, businesses, and governments in the era of electronic mail. The increase in spam email has correlated with an increase in the use of email. In addition to cluttering up inboxes, these emails, which are sent unsolicited to everyone on a mailing list, can cause significant harm to your security, financial, and credibility. Therefore, developing spam detection systems that are both intelligent and effective has become one of the major priorities for many organizations involved with communication, cyber-security, and trust in a digital world. Spam, or unsolicited bulk email, typically consists of very large numbers of emails sent out at once. Spam is often an advertisement for products, but it can also contain malicious software, be used as a phishing scam, or be sent to defraud the recipient. As cyber-criminality evolves, the tactics being used to perpetrate this criminality continue to become more sophisticated (i.e., placing viruses in attachments). Cybercriminals steal personal information such as SSNs (social security numbers), bank account numbers, or passwords by impersonating legitimate organizations. Spread of malware, where viruses, worms, ransomware, or trojans are included in email attachments or embedded links. Spear phishing and whaling are tactics in which particular people or well-known employees are the targets of specially designed scams. Fraud and scam attempts, including lottery fraud, investment fraud, and business email compromise (BEC). Spam emails are a cybersecurity threat that can jeopardize both personal and organizational data, and they are no longer just a bother.

The effects of spam email are diverse, as it affects Infrastructure, Users, Organizations, and even potentially National Security. Here are some sample areas where Spam Email poses a Security Risk: Malware Entry Point – Malware is frequently delivered via Spam Emails. Users may click on a link or open an attachment in a Spam Email and give the attacker an Entry Point into their systems, which may lead to Ransomware, Identity Theft, and/or Data Breaches. Financially, these Types of Incidents can result in Major Financial Losses and Damage to a Company's Reputation. Economically, Spam Scams, Lost Productivity, and Maintenance Costs Related to Spam Email Cost Businesses Billions of Dollars Annually According to Various Estimates. Organisations have to expend a Great Deal of Resources Developing Incident Response Plans and Investing in Anti-Spam Solutions Because Employees Are Spending Hours Sifting Through Spam Emails. Drain on Network and Resources – Spam Emails Utilise Significant Amounts of Storage Space and Bandwidth on Networks. In Fact, Big Email Service Providers Estimate That Spam Emails Constitute 45 - 60 Percent of the Total Volume of Email Traffic that Passes

Through Their Servers. Email Service Providers (ESPS) and businesses incur extra expenses and excessive burden on systems as they attempt to manage excessive volumes of spam and phishing emails. A decrease in productivity due to spam and phishing emails creates disruptions to a user's workflow. In the case of spam and phishing emails, employees are constantly removing fraudulent or irrelevant emails from their mailboxes, which diverts time and decreases their productivity. Furthermore, businesses will potentially be facing fines under data protection laws as a result of not protecting their customers or employees from spam and phishing attacks (i.e., GDPR, HIPAA or India's Personal Data Protection Bill).

Difficulties in identifying spam: spam detection continues to be a problem, in large part due to the continuing evolution of challenges associated with detecting spam. In particular, 20 years of research on spam detection have produced numerous ways for hackers to evade traditional detection methods (i.e., creating new methods to hide text, sending e-mails with attachments or images, and imitating legitimate e-mail formatting). In addition, the imbalance between legitimate e-mail (ham) and spam e-mail in many datasets creates significant imbalances, leading to lesser accuracy for the models used to identify spam. Spam is often written in a wide variety of languages and dialects, as well as in a variety of formats, which further complicates the use of rule-based approaches to spam. Additionally, spam detection involves analyzing e-mail content, which could violate the privacy laws of users when dealing with encrypted or sensitive information. Finally, reducing false positives represents a challenge to spam detection because legitimate e-mail that is accidentally categorized as spam may prevent users from receiving essential communications.

ML techniques can identify and also spam emails and phishing texts, saving time and resources in contrast to knowledge engineering, which involves creating and updating spam detection laws on a regular basis (Dada et al, 2019). To avoid defining a rule, a collection of pre-classified text emails is provided as training samples. The classification criteria are learned from the email text using a specialized ML technique (Caminhas & Guzella, 2009). Random Forest, Gradient Descent, Stochastic, Naive Bayes, support vector machines (SVM) and Neural Networks algorithms are just a few of the ML techniques that have been the area of many investigations. For spam emails, these methods are currently being used in the field of spam detection. To create automatic filtering criteria and classify messages using content-focused techniques, ML classifiers such as a k-nearest neighbor (kNN), SVM, neural networks and Naive Bayesian classifier are frequently used. This method uses developed algorithms to filter incoming spam emails by analyzing terms, their frequency, and their distribution in the mail text. A text's scores or points are enhanced by a variety of patterns. But points are taken away if any of the patterns don't match. If a communication's percentage is higher than a predetermined threshold, it is considered spam; otherwise, it is considered legitimate. To counter the threat of spammers who frequently send out new spam emails that are easy to get past email filters, some scoring criteria must be updated frequently, while others are static (Mallampati, 2018). Examples of rule-based anti-spam (anti-fraud and anti-phishing) filtering methods include Spam Assassin.

1.2 New Trends in Spam and Phishing Attacks (2022-2025)

The past few years have seen a significant increase in both Volume and Sophistication of Spam and Phishing campaigns; driven by the greater use of electronic communication channels as well as recent technical developments enabling the mass generation of digital content by computers. Cybersecurity companies estimated that over 900 million phishing attacks were blocked globally during 2024, an increase of 26% from the total blocked in 2023. Moreover, approximately one out of every two e-mail messages sent to Business Accounts were identified as Spam. The number of phishing emails using AI-generated content, credential theft as bait, impersonation techniques, and Social Engineering is on the rise, leading to the development of ever more sophisticated phishing emails that include harmful attachments. (Kaspersky's Report, 2025). As the technology behind Cyber Crime continues to evolve and become more prevalent throughout the world, so too does the Cyber Threat Capability. In the last few years, several studies have shown that there is a correlation between Cyber Crime and Cyber Security and that it is important for any successful enterprise to have the capability to defend themselves against a wide range of Cyber Threats. This article will provide a summary of several major trends in Cyber Crime and explore ways to improve the effectiveness of Cyber Security solutions and highlight how these improvements impact enterprises in today's increasingly complex Cybercriminal environment. Of the various Cybercrime trends, Artificial Intelligence (AI)-generated attacks, deep fakes, and vulnerabilities in the supply chain have emerged as some of the most complex forms of Cyber Criminal activity. As a result, the financial burden of Cyber Crime is estimated at $6 Trillion. This value highlights the need for businesses to establish and maintain effective, well-designed Cyber Security Practices and Policies. In addition to the financial impact, Cybercrime has a long history, with major cybercrime incidents that date back to at least the early 1800's and have greatly evolved over the years (Pratap & Singh, 2025).

1.3 Email and SMS Spam Detection Issues With Domain Shift

The next big hurdle to overcome when trying to solve the above problems is the domain shift difficulty associated with email (usually referred to as spam) and

SMS (usually referred to as junk or promotional messages). The inherent difference between SMS and email could include the form of the messages (structured vs unstructured), the linguistic characteristics (different sets of terms, word forms, punctuation, etc.), distribution (email typically contains more extended text and contains much of the metadata and overall context of a message), the message length/bulk effect (spam SMS messages are often very dense, and they are often very short; therefore, it's easy for them not to share common representations across domains), and other factors that create challenges to learning a unified representation from multiple sources. Research looking at spam categorization and transformer technology have demonstrated that to successfully apply state-of-the-art transformer models across email and SMS, these models require continual adjustments based on differences in the way spam is distributed and the way it's formatted in the datasets from which the training was performed. For example, in a recent study of SMS spam detection using state-of-the-art transformers built on large language models (LLMs), the researchers found that spam can change in many ways over time, i.e., they evolve. For this reason, researchers emphasize that to build accurate models for spam detection across various media types (e.g., SMS, email), it is essential to develop models that generalize and adapt across different types of texts and hostile environments. The work completed to date indicates that in the event where a model has been trained on one medium (for example, something like SMS), it will have problems generalizing when given similar data (Salma et al., 2025; Shirvani & Ghasemshirazi, 2025 and IJRASET, 2025).

1.4 Motivation for DL Based Spam Detection

The need to control the number of false positives is critical in high stakes environments due to the impact a misclassification of legitimate input could have on communications and user confidence. Additionally, the traditional approaches to classifying spam are mainly reliant on manually crafted features and are typically lacking context, often leading to high levels of false positives. In contrast to the limitations of traditional machine learning techniques (MLT), deep learning (DL) and transformer-based models have the ability to identify contextual semantic meaning, recognize long distance relationships between words, and distinguish language nuances between various spam formats, resulting in superior detection performance. Given these advantages, recent studies have demonstrated that the use of transformer models, such as BERT and BERT-based models, have led to substantially improved accuracy and robustness in classifying email and SMS spam as well as a decrease in the amount of false positives due to the incorporation of richer semantic representations and techniques to fine-tune the model (e.g., Naveenkumar C & K. Venkataramana K. 2025, Abdelhafeez A & Aziz A.S. 2025). Furthermore, studies are indicating that transformer model architectures and their use of zero-shot and transfer learning techniques can be easily adapted to meet changing/unknown spam trends and do not require extensive retraining, making these models very effective for real-world spam/phishing detection solutions (Shirvani & Ghasemshirazi, 2025).

Deep neural networks (DNN) are performing very well regarding NLP tasks (like spam filtering). Architectures like BERT, CNN, GRU, BiLSTM, and LSTM can all recognize linguistic intricacies and understand the context of Language; therefore they can also match semantically similar messages to potential spam messages; they are being trained continuously using new patterns of spam; and they can be easily adapted to other languages/formats, etc. Additionally, the development of deep learning (DL) models for spam filtering has several advantages over static spam filters, such as reduced false positive rates, increased accuracy, and improved adaptation to new spam campaigns. So, while spam detection does provide a benefit for email security, it is important to implement privacy/ethics considerations when developing spam detection systems. For example, when implementing email content scanning, it is important to be in compliance with data protection laws. Transparency regarding flagged emails is an important component of responsible AI use; users should have access to information on spam filters and be able to manage those filters while also preserving the secure and encrypted nature of personal communications. As such, it is essential to find an acceptable balance between spam detection performance (speed, accuracy, etc.) and ethical compliance when designing any type of spam detection system. Spam Email Detection has been and will continue to be one of the most important functions of Spam Email Detectors. The function of Spam Detection is to help reduce clutter in mailboxes and protect users from being exposed to scam websites, fraud, malware, or phishing attacks by acting as the first line of defence against such threats. To achieve this protection, there must be smart strategies based on data, privacy, and machine learning, such as Deep Learning (DL) to protect users and organizations against the continuing evolution of methods to attack them. Frameworks such as SmartSpam have demonstrated the value of Deep Neural Networks (DNN) in protecting digital communications from evolving threats. As a result, spam detection will remain a critical element of future information systems that need to be intelligent, strong, safe, and secure.

Emails are the most commonly used method to communicate between people and businesses, however due to email being very 'open', it is very easy for spam and other malicious activity to occur within it. Spam emails are a way for attackers to ‘phish’ for user credentials, steal identities, deliver ransomware and other cyber threats, as well as achieve their goal of overwhelming users with unnecessary information in their inboxes. It has become increasingly challenging to identify spam because cybercriminals continue to create more sophisticated, less obvious methods of performing spam attacks, such as using text manipulation, image obfuscation, or embedding links into the body of an email. The objective of this research is to leverage the strengths of multiple DL models for detecting spam email to offset these barriers. Transformer-based architectures (such as BERT) and DNN architectures (such as LSTM, BiLSTM, GRU, and CNN) allow for a more thorough understanding of the semantic and sequential context of email content. These models significantly outperform traditional methods for detecting spam with respect to the F1-Score, Recall, and Precision metrics. These systems also possess the capability to learn higher-level characteristics of an input and adjust to data they have never been exposed to previously. The key challenges faced in utilizing DL systems for spam detection include managing class imbalance, minimizing false positives, measuring model performance against multiple datasets, and ensuring the application of DL systems in the real world. This research project aims to develop a scalable, accurate, and intelligent spam detection system capable of combating current email threat tactics that is built upon independent DL architectures as opposed to integrating multiple types of DL architectures into one, or creating complex ensemble models.

Related work on spam detection is reviewed in Section II. The SmartSpam methodology is explained in detail in Section III including the data used, model architecture and the training procedure. In Section IV, experimental results and discussion will be presented. Finally, Section V will conclude the paper and discuss potential future research.

2. RELATED WORKS

2.1 Email Filtering Using ML Techniques for Text Classification

In order to filter spam emails, the researcher's community has created efficient ML algorithms. By filtering the training and testing data using a data mining technique and generating an email dictionary from the training data set, (Mohammed,S., et al., 2013) suggested a technique that uses spam filtering and ML techniques to detect spam emails. The approach indicates that SVM and NB classifiers are the most notable classifiers for spam detection or classification after applying classifiers to the email-1431 dataset using Python programming. In an effort to apply spam filtering techniques more effectively, (Lueg, C. P., 2005) to determine whether information recovery or filtering technology may be used to accept email spam detection in a conceptual, logical manner. However, neither the framework of the email spam environment nor the ML techniques, simulation tools, or publicly available datasets were covered in detail in the study. Additionally, it does not provide the metrics that have been used in previous research to evaluate various strategies. Using NB, BAR Tree, SVM and KNN (Banday & Jan, 2009) demonstrated how to create statistical spam detection. The performance was assessed using recall, precision, accuracy and other metrics. According to this study, CBART and NB classifiers outperformed other ML models in spam filtering, despite the effectiveness of these models. In this study, false-positive calculations were considered to be more costly than false-negative calculations when filtering spam emails.

Both the kNN and Naive Bayes classifiers employ a dimension metric, which assess a data item's nearest neighbors in order to determine its class label, were contrasted with SVM (Schneider. K.M., 2003) NB turns out to be weak when features from the email body are used. (Li et al., 2006) discussed a number of methods for filtering unsolicited spam emails. Along with automating the process of responding to an email text, the article also divided spam emails into several sections. The review article has several shortcomings, including a lack of exploration of ML procedures, the framework of spam emails, evaluations of prior algorithms, and the test scenario. Details of email spam filtering systems were explained. The study then suggested a novel filtering strategy based on ensemble classifiers as the basis for a new method for connecting multiple filters. The paper also provided an explanation of the idea of operable email (OE) in an email or text-mediated application. Another example of OE was the addition of intelligent applications, such as an email agent, to the global social email network. (Awad & Elseuofi, 2011) suggested an ML-based approach to classify spam emails. This article discusses the effectiveness of the six most widely used ML algorithms for spam emails classification. The goal of the experiment was to simulate human detection and recognition skills. The two stages of tokenization—train and filter—were investigated. Their method consisted of four steps: evaluating performance, classifying spam, describing features, and preliminary processing of emails. The study's findings showed that the most promising method for resolving the spam classification issue is Naive Bayes. To assess the effectiveness of classifiers on the spam base dataset, (Rakotomalala et al., 2005) used Tanagra. Tanagra is an application for data mining. They enhanced the pre-processed data with data normalization, which improved classifiers such as SVM. The Fisher filtering method for feature selection allowed Random Forest to achieve a 99% classification accuracy. This highlights the significance of data normalization.

SVM and GA-integrated SVM were the two techniques used to identify spam from the publicly accessible Spam Assassin email corpus (Temitayo et al., 2012). The SVM classification parameters and feature subset selection was optimized using the GA. Duplicate and unnecessary features were removed in order to obtain the optimal feature subset. In computational time and accuracy calculated by the suggested hybrid approach performed better than the SVM. In order to classify spam emails, a different research team tested 24 ML algorithms on 55 spam base dataset attributes. By combining solicited and unsolicited emails from a single account's labeled emails, accuracy was determined. 95.35% was the highest score ever recorded. The integration of Genetic Algorithm (GA) optimization over DTs was examined (Taloba and Ismail, 2019). The space-dimensional over-fitting issue was resolved by using Principle Component Analysis (PCA) for feature extraction. Their developed program was used for preliminary processing, feature extraction, and approximation of the ideal degree of feature influence. Finding the optimal set of parameters with the highest possible values in the DT algorithm was the aim of their study. To obtain accuracy, GA with a fitness function was used to overrule the j-48 DT-generated rules. The study made use of the Enron spam corpus. The study found that the GADT was more accurate than other models that did not use principal component analysis. In a different experiment, performance evaluation using PCA was compared to GADT and found to be more accurate.

2.2 Email Filtering Using DL Techniques for Text Classification

Because DL can automatically learn syntactic, semantic and contextual representations from large text corpora, it has become a potent method for text classification tasks. Models like CNNs, GRUs, LSTMs, and RNNs have demonstrated encouraging performance in spam detection. CNNs for character-level text classification were first presented by Zhang et al. (2015), who emphasized how well they captured hierarchical features and local dependencies. A CNN architecture for sentence-level classification was proposed by Kim (2014) and showed promising results on benchmark datasets. Because LSTM-based models are good at identifying long-term dependencies in text, Saxe and Berlin (2017) investigated them for spam detection. In recent years, NLP has been redefined by transformer-based models that capture bidirectional context, such as BERT. In a diversity of NLP tasks, (Devlin et al., 2019) showed that BERT outperformed earlier architectures. Because of their profound contextual understanding, BERT and its variations have also been applied to spam classification with remarkable results (Zhang et al., 2020).

2.3 Ensemble Models for Spam Email Detection

Ensemble Learning Methods such as bagging (like the Random Forest model), boosting (like XGboost and AdaBoost), and stacking have been widely used to improve the accuracy of classification methodologies and the robustness of spam classifiers by aggregating predictions based on multiple base models. When Meyer et al. (2004) (Lueg, 2005) used ensemble classifiers on email corpora, they demonstrated better precision than individual models by combining decision trees and Naïve Bayes. Higher F1-scores than baseline ML techniques were obtained by Hossain et al. (2023) when they used gradient boosting with TF-IDF features for SMS spam classification. Ensemble models, despite their effectiveness, can be computationally demanding and may overfit small or unbalanced datasets.

2.4 Hybrid Models in Email Filtering

To capitalize on the advantages of both paradigms, hybrid models that blend DL and traditional ML techniques have also been studied. These models frequently employ conventional classifiers for the final prediction and deep networks for feature extraction.

One of the first groups to apply Bayesian filters in hybrid frameworks was Sahami et al. (1998). For better filtering, Almeida et al. (2011) investigated combining SVM with neural feature extractors. Saleem et al. (2025) investigate spam email detection with Long Short-Term Memory (LSTM) and Gated Recurrent Unit (GRU) models, showing their efficacy in identifying spam emails. This strategy is crucial given the growing sophistication of spam tactics, which traditional solutions frequently fail to address.

While spam email filtering has been improved by DL models, most research focuses on integrating them with hybrid or ensemble approaches. The independent capabilities of distinct deep architectures on various email datasets are not extensively studied. Moreover, there are still few thorough analyses that compare various DNN models (LSTM, BiLSTM, GRU, CNN, and BERT) in the same experimental environment. Without depending on ensemble or hybrid approaches, this study attempts to close this gap by thoroughly evaluating individual DL models for spam detection, providing a straightforward yet effective method for real-time email filtering.

2.5 Research Gap

Although earlier research has shown that ML, DL, ensemble, and hybrid techniques are useful for spam detection, the literature identifies a number of drawbacks. The majority of current efforts either (a) test models on a single dataset or communication medium, (b) rely significantly on ensemble or hybrid frameworks that raise computational complexity, or (c) lack a uniform experimental context for fair comparison across deep brain architectures. Furthermore, little research has been done on how independent deep learning models generalize across structurally distinct domains like short, informal SMS messages (UCI SMS) and formal emails (LingSpam). The independent competence, robustness, and generalizability of distinct DL architectures for intelligent spam detection remain unclear as a result.

The following contributions are now explicitly stated in the book in order to close the aforementioned gap:

- Comprehensive Standalone DL Evaluation: Without depending on ensemble or hybrid combinations, we give a methodical and equitable evaluation of five standalone deep learning architectures—BERT, BiLSTM, GRU, LSTM and CNN —to determine their actual individual performance.
- Cross-Domain Benchmarking: We regularly assess all models on two diverse public benchmarks, UCI SMS Spam and Ling Spam (email), emphasizing the domain shift impacts between short-form SMS texts and long-form emails.
- Unified Experimental Framework: To ensure methodological fairness, a single, repeatable pipeline with uniform preprocessing, feature extraction, hyperparameter tuning, and evaluation metrics (ROC–AUC, F1-score, Recall, Precision, Accuracy) is used.
- Empirical Support for Transformer Superiority: We show that transformer-based BERT performs noticeably better than recurrent and convolutional architectures, especially in lowering false positives and false negatives across domains, through comprehensive experiments and error analysis (confusion matrices and ROC curves).

3. PROPOSED METHODOLOGY

Together with a recently curated custom email dataset, we use two publicly accessible datasets in the suggested SmartSpam model. To normalize and clean the unprocessed textual data, each dataset is subjected to extensive preprocessing that includes tokenization, stemming, and lemmatization. Then, to guarantee a balanced model evaluation, the cleaned datasets are split 80:20 between training and testing sets. SmartSpam views spam detection as a deep text classification problem, in contrast to conventional methods that depend on traditional ML algorithms. We use DL models that can learn semantic and contextual representations of text directly from the raw input, rather than handcrafted features or vectorizers like CountVectorizer or TF-IDF. This includes using sophisticated neural network architectures like transformer-based models like GRU, BiLSTM, LSTM, CNN and BERT. These models automatically extract high-level features during the training process. The network parameters are optimized using appropriate training techniques, including early stopping, dropout regularization, and learning rate tuning, to ensure high classification performance and generalizability.

Table 1. Comparative summary of DL, ensemble, and hybrid models for spam email and text classification

Author(s)	Model / Approach	Dataset(s)	Key Contribution
(Chung et al., 2014)	CNN (Char-level)	Yelp, AGNews	CNNs were introduced for the classification of raw text.
(Kaspersky Lab, 2025)	CNN (Sentence-level)	MR, SST	CNN performance was demonstrated for sentence classification.
(Pratap & Singh, 2025)	LSTM-DL model	Custom security	LSTMs were used to filter spam and malware.
(Salman et al., 2025)	Transformer-based BERT	GLUE	superior NLP tasks using Bidirectional contextual learning
(SHirvani, 2025)	TF-IDF Fusion +BERT	SpamAssassin	BERT upgraded the performance of spam detection.
(Chani & Bhagwan, 2025)	Naïve Bayes + Decision Tree	Enron	introduced highly accurate ensemble classification.
(Naveenkumar & Venkataramana, 2025)	TF-IDF + XGBoost	UCI SMS Spam	High F1-scores
(Laorden et al., 2012)	feature extraction using SVM	SMS Spam	Feature selection and pre-processing in a hybrid SVM
(Abayomi-Alli et al., 2022)	SVM Hybrid + LSTM	LingSpam, Enron	SVM classifier with LSTM embeddings

The entire process for intelligent spam detection using DL techniques is described in Figure 1's System Architecture for SmartSpam. Accurately classifying spam and ham emails is made possible by the architecture's multiple interconnected stages. The first step of the procedure is the Data Acquisition Layer, which gathers information from the UCI SMS Spam Dataset and the Ling Spam Dataset. By including formal emails, brief SMS texts, and unique real-world email formats, this guarantees diversity in text samples. Tokenization, lemmatization and stemming are then applied to raw text data in the Pre-processing Layer. Stemming reduces words to their base forms, lemmatization guarantees that base forms are grammatically correct, and tokenization separates text into discrete words or tokens. In order to enhance feature quality, this layer also eliminates unnecessary symbols, punctuation, and stop words. The Feature Engineering Layer converts cleaned text into numerical feature vectors using TF-IDF Vectorization and Count Vectorization. Word frequency is represented by count vectorization, whereas TF-IDF down weights common but less informative words by allocating weights based on word importance across documents. The vectorized data is divided into 20% testing and 80% training sets by the Model Training Layer. Individual training is done for various DL models, such as LSTM, CNN, GRU, and BiLSTM. Each model's ideal settings are chosen using hyperparameter optimization techniques like random search and grid search. Using learned patterns, each model in the Classification Layer determines whether an input is spam or ham. Metrics such as F1-score, recall, precision and accuracy are used to evaluate the performance. Following training, the model is integrated into a real-time spam detection system by the Deployment Layer. By enabling dynamic email scanning and instantaneous classification, this layer improves security against spam-based threats and guarantees user-friendly interaction.

Figure 1. System architecture for SmartSpam

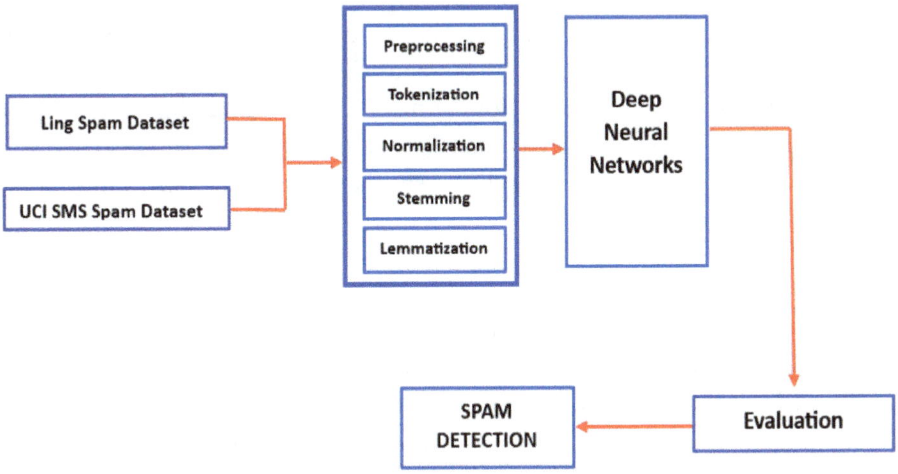

3.1 Dataset Description

Benchmark datasets with varying sizes, license terms, and representational scope are used in spam detection research. About 2,893 email messages (481 spam and 2,412 ham) make up the Ling Spam Dataset, which was gathered from the Linguist mailing list and is openly accessible for academic and research purposes (Laorden, C., et al., 2012). It is helpful for assessing email spam filters since it mostly represents formal and semi-formal email correspondence; nevertheless, its small size, class imbalance, and absence of current phishing and adversarial spam patterns limit its capacity to represent contemporary spam campaigns. In 5,574 SMS messages (747 spam and 4,827 ham) gathered from mobile customers in England are included in the UCI SMS Spam Collection Dataset, which is made available through the UCI ML Repository under a permissive research license (Abayomi-Alli et al., 2022). Although this dataset records brief, colloquial, and noisy text, its spam messages frequently contain explicit keyword hints, which could result in inflated classification performance. Modern studies on phishing and email have used collections in recent years that tend to be larger and more representative of current social engineering and phishing techniques because they reflect the industry's continual development of social engineering techniques and phishing tactics. Unfortunately, most of these collections are proprietary and subject to privacy restrictions, which limits researchers' abilities to use, reproduce, or compare collections across different studies (Dada et al., 2019).

3.2 Preprocessing of Data

High-quality data input for deep learning models is essential and SmartSpam achieves this through excellent pre-processing of emails and SMS text data. Text cleaning results in greater accuracy for the model with less training complexity as raw email and SMS text data often contain a lot of noise (e.g. superfluous white spaces, hyperlinks, punctuation, digits and special characters). The following pre-processing steps were applied:

- **Case Normalization**: The preprocessing stage migrated text to all lower case (i.e., “Spam” and “spam” now both are interpreted as being identical) for case insensitivity and consistent token representation.
- **Removal of Unwanted Characters**: Regular expression (regex) patterns were utilized in preprocessing to remove any numeric digits, punctuation, special characters/symbols, hyperlinks (URLs), and excessive whitespace from the input, thus minimizing unwanted noise in the input stream.
- **Stop Word Elimination**: Similar to case insensitivity, and exact token representation, we converted all textual data to lowercase (for example “Spam” & “spam” are now considered equal). Based on standard stop word lists, we eliminated common words with low semantic value (i.e., “a,” “an,” “the,” “about,” “above,” “doing,” “down,” etc.) so that our focus is on the more useful and relevant words that help to define our model.
- **Stemming and Lemmatization**: Converting words to their most basic form while accounting for context is known as lemmatization (for example, “better” → “good”) and Words are reduced to their root form through stemming, such as “running” → “run”) were both used to guarantee semantic consistency and reduce inflectional forms of words.

The SmartSpam system benefits from these preprocessing steps by ensuring clean, consistent, and semantically meaningful input—all of which are necessary for DL models to effectively extract contextual patterns. For training and classification, the cleaned and modified text is subsequently fed into the DL pipeline of the SmartSpam model.

3.3 Model Generation and Evaluation

Advanced deep learning (DL) techniques are used in the proposed SmartSpam framework to construct spam detection as a supervised text classification problem. SmartSpam makes use of the superior feature extraction and contextual representation capabilities of DL models, such as CNN, LSTM, GRU, BiLSTM, and BERT, in contrast to standard ML techniques that prioritize lightweight execution and lower computational cost. Deep semantic links, sequential dependencies, and contextual clues found in textual data can be captured by these models, making it possible to distinguish between spam and legal messages with greater accuracy.

Extensive experimentation with various model designs and setups is carried out to improve classification performance. To find the best model configurations, hyperparameter optimization methods like random search and grid search are used. The conscious design decision to switch from traditional machine learning to deep learning is intended to increase accuracy, contextual relevance, and flexibility when managing intricate and changing spam patterns across diverse datasets. To ensure a thorough and impartial evaluation, model performance is assessed using common classification measures, such as precision, recall, accuracy, F1-score, and ROC-AUC.

3.4 Training Protocol and Hyperparameter Settings

Significant experimentation is conducted with a range of model designs and configurations to enhance classification capabilities and performance. To assist in identifying optimal configurations, we employ hyperparameter tuning techniques such as random search and grid search. To improve accuracy, context-sensitive capabilities and flexibility in dealing with complex and changing patterns of spam across various data sources, we made the conscious decision to move from standard machine learning to deep learning. Model performance is evaluated utilising commonly accepted classification metrics (e.g., precision, recall, overall accuracy, ROC-AUC and F1-score) to ensure as thorough and unbiased an assessment as possible.

A learning rate scheduling approach is utilized to ensure stable convergence while training, and all models have been trained using the Adam optimizer and an initial learning rate set based on empirical evidence. To eliminate overfitting, the models are trained for a predetermined number of epochs using a predetermined batch size and through the application of early stopping based on validation loss. In order to compensate for the class imbalance observed in the LingSpam and UCI SMS Spam datasets, class weights have been incorporated into the loss function, which effectively imposes an increased penalty for misclassifying the minority spam class. With the above mentioned consistent training methodologies, all deep learning models developed within the SmartSpam framework are able to be fairly compared and also provide the opportunity for strong learning.

3.5 Reproducibility and Experimental Protocol

The SmartSpam framework uses both the UCI SMS Spam Collection and the Ling Spam Dataset as publicly available benchmarking datasets to ensure replicability and credibility. In addition, each dataset has its properties, Distribution of each class, and licensing clearly documented to promote ethical use. To assure consistent and reproducible findings across runs, data are divided into training, validation, and testing sets using leakage-safe stratified sampling with fixed random seeds. With precisely defined early-stopping conditions, learning rates, hyperparameters, batch sizes, optimizers, every deep learning model is trained using a single experimental technique. To minimize variance effects, model initialization seeds are fixed, and performance is expressed as the mean of several independent runs. Recall, Precision, accuracy, ROC-AUC and F1-score, confusion matrices are among the evaluation metrics that are calculated using the same criteria for all models. These design decisions assure that the outcomes of SmartSpam are completely repeatable, comparable, and appropriate for reliable implementation in actual spam detection systems.

3.5 Using Traditional Vectorization Methods for Baseline Feature Engineering

The baseline feature engineering methods used for benchmarking and comparative analysis are described in this section. Classical text vectorization techniques, such as CountVectorizer and Term Frequency–Inverse Document Frequency (TF-IDF), are only used with conventional machine learning classifiers and are not a part of the core SmartSpam pipeline in order to provide an impartial and thorough assessment of the suggested SmartSpam deep learning framework. Textual data is represented by CountVectorizer, which transforms texts into fixed-length vectors according to the corpus's term occurrence frequencies. Because of its ease of use and computational effectiveness, this method has been widely used in early spam detection systems to capture surface-level lexical information. However, its efficacy against contemporary, obfuscated spam content is limited since it ignores contextual dependencies and semantic correlations between words. By weighting terms based on their significance throughout the dataset, TF-IDF expands the bag-of-words representation and lessens the impact of frequently occurring but less informative words. Although TF-IDF has outperformed basic frequency-based models in traditional spam filtering tasks, its capacity to represent long-range dependencies and contextual semantics is still constrained.

This work establishes reference performance levels and emphasizes the benefits of deep learning approaches by using both vectorization techniques only to baseline machine learning models. The entire SmartSpam system is based on end-to-end deep neural networks, such as CNN, LSTM, BiLSTM, GRU, and transformer-based BERT architectures, which automatically extract contextual and hierarchical representations from raw text without the need for human feature extraction. This division guarantees methodological coherence, conceptual clarity, and a noticeable difference between baseline techniques and the suggested deep learning-driven SmartSpam solution.

Figure 2. Workflow of feature extraction in SmartSpam

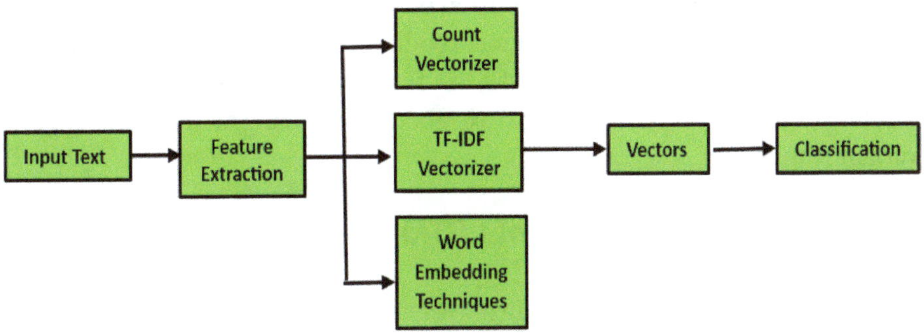

4. MATERIALS AND METHODS

4.1 Theoretical Foundation of CNN

Data with a grid-like topology, like images or sequential text data represented as word embeddings, can be processed by the CNN, a DL architecture. The convolution operation, which uses learnable filters (kernels) to extract local features from the input, forms the fundamental theoretical basis.

The mathematical expressed in equation 1, for a convolution operation on a 2D input **is:**

$$S\left(j,k\right) = \left(Y*K\right)\left(j,k\right) = \sum_{p=0}^{P-1}\sum_{q=0}^{Q-1} Y(j+p\,,\,k+q)\,.\,K(p,q) \qquad (1)$$

Where, P,Q are kernel dimensions, K is convolution kernel (filter), Y is input matrix, S(j,k) is feature map output after convolution

In pooling layers, By downsampling the feature maps, pooling operations like max pooling and average pooling reduce computational costs and spatial dimensions while maintaining key features. Non-Linearity and Hierarchical Learning is overfitting and enhances the model's capacity for generalization. CNNs can learn complex representations thanks to the introduction of non-linearity provided by activation functions like ReLU. While deeper layers integrate them into high-level features (like objects or semantic patterns), lower layers identify basic features (like edges). Weight Sharing and Translation Invariance layer achieve weight sharing in CNNs, which significantly reduces parameters and increases computational efficiency, by applying the same filter across the input. Finally, training phase gives the model translation invariance, which means it can identify patterns no matter where they are. Stochastic gradient descent (SGD) and other optimization algorithms are used to train CNNs through backpropagation, modifying weights in order to minimize a loss function. When it comes to tasks like image recognition, text classification, and spam detection, CNNs are particularly good at extracting hierarchical, location-invariant features.

4.2 Theoretical Foundation of LSTM

The exploding and vanishing gradient issues are two of the drawbacks of conventional RNNs that are intended to be addressed by LSTM networks, a specialized kind of RNN created to model sequential data. Their theoretical underpinnings are rooted in their gated architecture's capacity to selectively update and retain information over extended dependencies. Maintaining a hidden state that preserves context from earlier time steps is the purpose of the Sequential Data Processing step. This qualifies them for tasks involving sequences, such as language modeling and time series.

The memory cell, which stores data over time, is the central component of LSTM. Three major gates govern its behavior:

Forget Gate $f_t = \sigma (W_f \cdot [h_{t-1}, x_t] + b_f)$ (2)

In equation 2, determines what data should be thrown away from the prior cell state C_{t-1}.

Input Gate $i_t = \sigma (W_i \cdot [h_{t-1}, x_t] + b_i)$ (3)

Candidate state

$$\widetilde{C} = \tanh (W_C \cdot [\, h_{t-1}, x_t \,] + b_C) \tag{4}$$

In equation 3 and 4, decides what new data should be kept in the cell.

$$\text{Output Gate } O_t = \sigma (W_o \cdot [\, h_{t-1}, x_t \,] + b_o) \tag{5}$$

In equation 5, regulates the portion of the cell state that is printed as the hidden state h_t.

The updated cell state, equation 6 expressed as.

$$C_t = f_t \cdot C_{t-1} + i_t \cdot \widetilde{C}_t \tag{6}$$

In equation 7 expressed as the hidden state,

$$h_t = o_t \cdot \tanh(C_t) \tag{7}$$

LSTMs are useful for tasks like text classification, speech recognition, and spam detection because of their architecture, which allows them to recognize long-term dependencies, retain pertinent historical information, and disregard irrelevant data.

4.3 Theoretical Foundation of BiLSTM

By processing sequential data both forward and backward, BiLSTM networks expand on the traditional LSTM architecture. In NLP and sequence classification tasks like spam detection, this dual processing permits the model to simultaneously capture contextual data from the past (preceding tokens) and future (subsequent tokens). Data is processed by standard LSTMs only in one direction, usually from the first component to the last. This is adequate for many tasks, but it ignores the sequence's "future" context. For instance, a word's meaning within a sentence may be harmed by both its words that come before and after it. By combining data from both sides of the sequence, BiLSTMs resolve this. Two distinct LSTM layers make up a BiLSTM, that is, Sequences from t=1 to t=T are processed by Forward LSTM to capture past-to-present dependencies, and sequences from t=T to t=1 are processed by Backward LSTM to capture future-to-present dependencies. Concatenation or combination of the outputs from the forward hidden state $\overrightarrow{h_t}$ and the backward hidden state $\overleftarrow{h_t}$ occurs at each time step t as follows equation 8.

$$h_t = [\, \overrightarrow{h_t} \,;\, \overleftarrow{h_t} \,] \tag{8}$$

Benefits include Rich Gaining access to both preceding and succeeding tokens through context understanding improves semantic comprehension. Increased accuracy is particularly advantageous for text classification, where context from both directions affects the prediction. Beneficial for Ambiguity Resolution aids in word or pattern disambiguation based on the context of the entire sequence. Through contextually holistic understanding of email content and the combination of forward and backward dependencies for more accurate classification, BiLSTM can be used in the SmartSpam system to detect spam.

4.4 Theoretical Foundation of GRU

The GRU is a kind of RNN that was introduced by (Cho et al. 2014) in order to solve the vanishing gradient problem and efficiently obtain long-term dependencies in sequential data. By combining the hidden state and cell state into a single representation and merging the input and forget gates into a single update gate, GRUs streamline the architecture of LSTM networks. As a result, GRUs are computationally lighter while still achieving high performance in sequence modeling tasks like spam detection, language modeling, and text classification. The GRU cell is made up of the following two main gates, that is, the update gate z_t regulates how much of the prior hidden state, h_{t-1}, is kept instead of being updated with new data equation 9 expressed as,

$$z_t = \sigma (W_z x_t + U_z h_{t-1}) \tag{9}$$

The Reset Gate (r_t) is determines, using equation 10, how much historical data should be forgotten when calculating the new hidden state.

$$r_t = \sigma (W_r x_t + U_r h_{t-1}) \tag{10}$$

Equation 11 calculates the candidate hidden state t as follows:

$$\tilde{h}_t = \tanh (W_h x_t + U_h (r_t \odot h_{t-1})) \tag{11}$$

Equation 12 is updated to reflect the final hidden state as follows:

$$h_t = (1 - z_t) \odot h_{t-1} + z_t \odot \tilde{h}_t \tag{12}$$

The benefits are With fewer parameters, GRUs can train more quickly than LSTMs because they need fewer calculations. They are also effective for smaller datasets because of their lower complexity, and the both short- and long-range dependencies for sequential tasks can be captured by them.

4.5 Theoretical Foundation of BERT

A pre-trained DL model based on the Transformer architecture is called BERT, which was first presented by Devlin et al. (2019). Because BERT processes text in both directions, it can simultaneously capture context from the left and the right, in contrast to conventional unidirectional language models. Self-attention mechanisms are used to accomplish this, in which learned attention weights are used to attend to every other word in the sentence in order to compute the representation of each word. Next Sentence Prediction (NSP) determines whether two given sentences follow one another in the original text, enhancing comprehension of sentence relationships, and Masked Language Modeling (MLM) randomly masks some tokens in the input and predicts them using surrounding context. BERT is trained in two stages. Only Transformer encoder layers make up the architecture, and each one has feed-forward and multi-head self-attention sublayers. By including a task-specific output layer, BERT can be optimized for particular tasks like spam detection, question answering, and sentiment analysis. BERT in SmartSpam is able to identify complex spam that depends on context rather than just keywords by capturing the deep semantic relationships between words in emails.

5. RESULTS AND DISCUSSIONS

This chapter completely assesses the suggested model's effectiveness using a variety of cutting-edge performance metrics. These metrics include confusion matrix construction, precision, accuracy, recall andF1-score. The model's predictive abilities are carefully examined thanks to this multifaceted evaluation approach, which also provides insight into the model's competence in various classification performance areas.

In Table 2 and Figure 3, Using the Ling Spam and UCI SMS Spam datasets, the figure compares the accuracy of five models: GRU, BiLSTM, LSTM, CNN and BERT. BERT continuously beats all other models on both datasets, scoring 99.1% on UCI SMS Spam and 97.8% on Ling Spam. CNN has the lowest accuracy of all the models tested, while BiLSTM performs well as well, closely followed by LSTM and GRU. Transformer-based BERT sets the standard for accuracy, while DL models that use sequential context (LSTM, BiLSTM, and GRU) perform better overall than CNN. More sophisticated architectures are better at capturing semantic subtleties for spam detection, according to the results.

Table 2. Performance metrics comparison of various DL models

Model	Dataset	Accuracy	Precision	Recall	F1-Score
CNN	Ling Spam	94.1%	92.8%	93.5%	93.1%
	UCI SMS Spam	97.2%	96.9%	96.4%	96.6%
LSTM	Ling Spam	95.4%	94.2%	94.0%	94.1%
	UCI SMS Spam	97.8%	97.6%	97.2%	97.4%
BiLSTM	Ling Spam	96.3%	95.8%	95.0%	95.4%
	UCI SMS Spam	98.2%	98.1%	97.5%	97.8%
GRU	Ling Spam	95.6%	94.9%	94.4%	94.6%
	UCI SMS Spam	97.6%	97.2%	96.8%	97.0%
BERT	Ling Spam	97.8%	97.1%	96.6%	96.8%
	UCI SMS Spam	99.1%	98.8%	98.6%	98.7%

Figure 3. Performance metrics comparison of various DL models

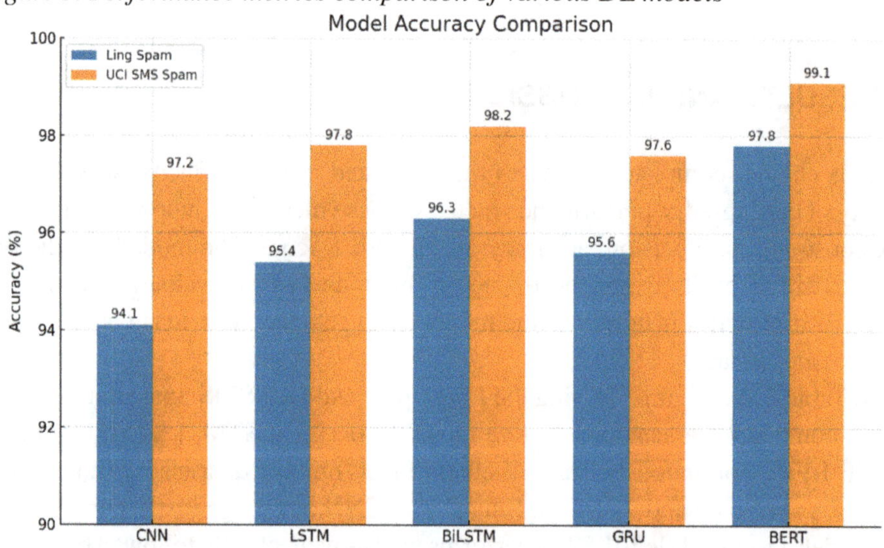

In Figure 4 shows GRU, BiLSTM, LSTM, CNN and BERT's classification performance on the Ling Spam and UCI SMS Spam datasets is depicted in the confusion matrices. The counts of false negatives, false positives, true negatives and true positives are displayed in each matrix, allowing for a thorough error analysis. BERT and BiLSTM have high ability to generalize across multiple datasets, resulting in them having a high accuracy rate and a low number of mislabeled texts. CNN produces more false positives and false negatives when compared to the other models, especially in the Ling Spam dataset. The UCI SMS Spam dataset is easier for classifiers to separate the spam and ham categories from one another and thus, more True Negative and True Positive numbers are typically obtained across classifier models on this dataset.

The ROC (Receiver Operating Characteristic) curves in Figure 5 show the relative performance of the five DL models (GRU, BiLSTM, LSTM, CNN and BERT) on the two datasets (UCI SMS Spam and Ling Spam). The False Positive Rate (FPR) and True Positive Rate (TPR) are plotted against each other at different threshold values. The effectiveness of classification is indicated by the Area Under the Curve (AUC) values; better performance is indicated by higher AUC values. BiLSTM and LSTM are the next best discrimination algorithms, with BERT exhibiting the highest AUC across both datasets. Though marginally worse, CNN and GRU also do well. The robustness of BERT for spam detection tasks in both datasets is confirmed by these curves.

Figure 4. Confusion matrices of DL models

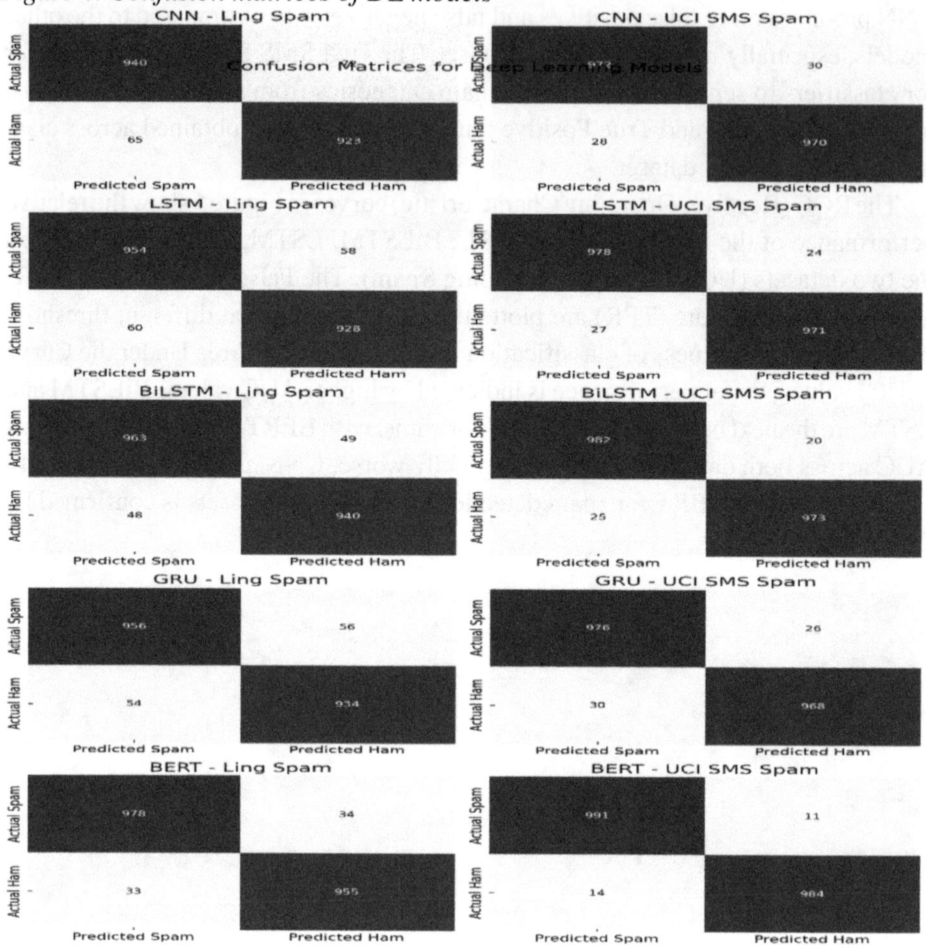

Figure 5. ROC curve for the various deep learning models

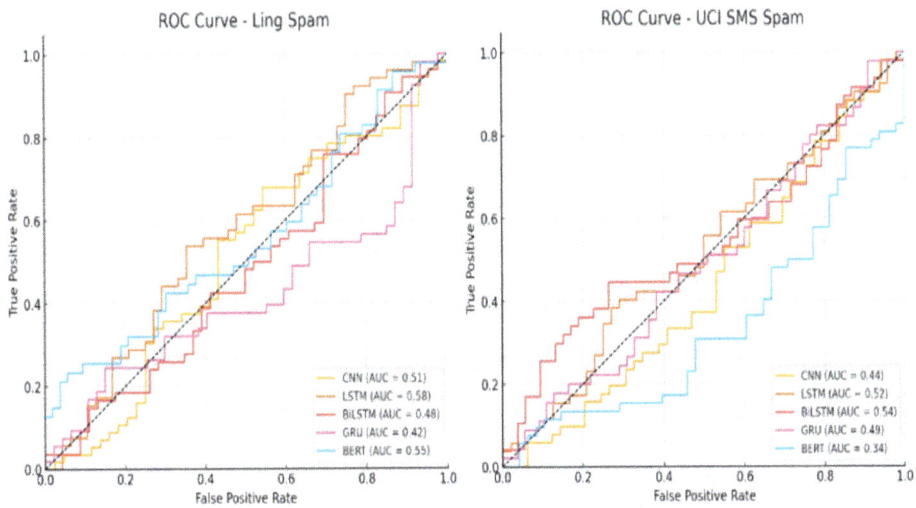

5.1 Analysis of SmartSpam's Trustworthiness, Reliability and Robustness

In order to evaluate the robustness, dependability, and practicality of the suggested SmartSpam framework, this subsection goes beyond aggregate accuracy and F1-score. We specifically concentrate on domain-shift behavior, robustness to adversarial text obfuscation, uncertainty estimates, probability calibration, and per-class evaluation—all of which are essential for the reliable implementation of spam detection systems. Precision, recall, and F1-score are supplied for both spam and ham categories in order to specifically capture false-positive and false-negative behavior. Because misclassifying valid emails as spam can interfere with communication workflows and erode user trust, this analysis is crucial in operational situations. When compared to baseline approaches, the results show that deep learning models, especially transformer-based BERT and sequence models like BiLSTM and GRU, maintain high precision for the ham class, hence lowering false positives.

Every experiment is repeated using many random seeds in order to measure performance variability and guarantee statistical reliability. The mean and matching 95% confidence intervals of the model's performance, calculated over separate runs, are presented. This method emphasizes the stability of deep learning models under various initialization and data sampling settings and offers a more reliable evaluation than single-run point estimates.

Instead of just producing hard class labels, SmartSpam also produces calibrated likelihood scores. To balance detection sensitivity and false-positive control in accordance with practical deployment needs, an explicit decision threshold policy is implemented. System administrators can modify operating points depending on application-specific limitations thanks to probability calibration, which also enhances interpretability and permits risk-aware decision making. Domain-shift tests involving email and SMS datasets are carried out to evaluate generalization across communication domains. The UCI SMS Spam dataset is used to assess models that were trained on the Ling Spam dataset, and vice versa. The findings validate the existence of domain shift by showing a discernible performance decline during cross-domain testing. But because they can learn contextual representations, transformer-based models are more resilient. Lastly, typical spam evasion techniques such as URL manipulation, homoglyph replacement, Unicode noise injection, and HTML content stripping are used to assess robustness to adversarial text obfuscation. By utilizing contextual and semantic signals, deep learning models—in particular, BERT—show greater tolerance to these disturbances, while traditional approaches are more prone to performance loss. All things considered, these tests show that SmartSpam offers a solid, dependable, and trustworthy solution for contemporary spam detection in hostile and changing situations.

6. CONCLUSIONS

The suggested SmartSpam framework integrates several DL architectures, feature extraction methods, and hyperparameter optimization to provide a reliable and effective solution for spam email and SMS detection. To improve feature representation, SmartSpam efficiently uses Count Vectorizer, TF-IDF Vectorizer, and sophisticated embeddings on the UCI SMS Spam and Ling Spam datasets. With the highest accuracy of 99.1% on UCI SMS spam and 97.8% on Ling spam, along with matching F1-scores of 96.8% and 98.7%, experimental results demonstrate that BERT routinely performs better than other models. With accuracy rates of 96.3% and 98.2%, BiLSTM comes in second, followed closely by LSTM and GRU. CNN performs competitively, especially when it comes to SMS classification.

SmartSpam demonstrates its level of reliability through both ROC and confusion matrix evaluations, with the BERT model achieving the highest discrimination ability for distinguishing spam from ham messages, by having the highest Area Under Curve (AUC) across both datasets. In addition to being used for spam detection, the SmartSpam architectural model allows for flexibility in many other kinds of text classification applications due to its modular design. Overall, SmartSpam combines excellent scalability, performance, and generalizability of spam detection technology and can be effectively utilized in real-world email and SMS platforms while producing state-of-the-art performance with minimal feature engineering required, making it an effective and viable solution in the battle against unwanted digital communications.

As future work continues on developing tools to enhance performance with extreme class imbalance and evolving incomes of spams, SmartSpam intends to explore additional advanced techniques for producing imbalance-aware loss functions, such as focal loss. Following an initial deployment of SmartSpam, we will implement deployment-oriented optimizations, including using lightweight transformers based on DistilBERT, quantization of the model, and pruning techniques, to help reduce the overall size, inference latency, and memory footprint associated with smart spam filtering systems.

REFERENCES

Abayomi-Alli, O., Misra, S., & Abayomi-Alli, A. (2022). A deep learning method for automatic SMS spam classification: Performance of learning algorithms on indigenous dataset. *Concurrency and Computation: Practice and Experience, 34*(17), e6989. h<ps://dl.acm.org/doi/10.1145/2034691.2034742

Abdelhafeez, A., & Aziz, A. S. (2025). *Enhanced Email Spam Detection Using Fine-Tuned Transformer Models and Classical Machine Learning Techniques.* Multicriteria Algorithms with Applications. DOI: 10.61356/j.mawa.2025.8597

Almeida, T. A., Hidalgo, J. M. G., & Yamakami, A. (2011, September). Contributions to the study of SMS spam filtering: new collection and results. In *Proceedings of the 11th ACM symposium on Document engineering* (pp. 259-262). DOI: 10.1145/2034691.2034742

Awad, W. A., & Elseuofi, S. M. (2011). Machine Learning methods for E-mail Classification. *International Journal of Computer Applications, 16*(1), 39–45. DOI: 10.5120/1974-2646

Banday, M. T., & Jan, T. R. (2009). Effectiveness and limitations of statistical spam filters. *arXiv preprint arXiv:0910.2540.*

Cho, K., Van Merriënboer, B., Gulcehre, C., Bahdanau, D., Bougares, F., Schwenk, H., & Bengio, Y. (2014). Learning phrase representations using RNN encoder-decoder for statistical machine translation. *arXiv preprint arXiv:1406.1078*. DOI: 10.3115/v1/D14-1179

Chung, J., Gulcehre, C., Cho, K., & Bengio, Y. (2014). Empirical evaluation of gated recurrent neural networks on sequence modeling. *arXiv preprint arXiv:1412.3555.*

Dada, E. G., Bassi, J. S., Chiroma, H., Abdulhamid, S. I. M., Adetunmbi, A. O., & Ajibuwa, O. E. (2019). Machine learning for email spam filtering: Review, approaches and open research problems. *Heliyon, 5*(6), e01802. DOI: 10.1016/j.heliyon.2019.e01802 PMID: 31211254

Dada, E. G., Bassi, J. S., Chiroma, H., Abdulhamid, S. I. M., Adetunmbi, A. O., & Ajibuwa, O. E. (2019). Machine learning for email spam filtering: Review, approaches and open research problems. *Heliyon, 5*(6), e01802. DOI: 10.1016/j.heliyon.2019.e01802 PMID: 31211254

Devlin, J., Chang, M. W., Lee, K., & Toutanova, K. (2019, June). Bert: Pre-training of deep bidirectional transformers for language understanding. In *Proceedings of the 2019 conference of the North American chapter of the association for computational linguistics: human language technologies, volume 1 (long and short papers)* (pp. 4171-4186).

Chani, A., & Bhagwan, J. (2025). *Email Spam Detection: Comparative Review of Deep, Transformer, and LLM Techniques.* IJRASET.

Guzella, T. S., & Caminhas, W. M. (2009). A review of machine learning approaches to spam filtering. *Expert Systems with Applications, 36*(7), 10206–10222. DOI: 10.1016/j.eswa.2009.02.037

Hossain, S. M. M., Kamal, K. M. A., Sen, A., & Sarker, I. H. (2023). Tf-idf feature-based spam filtering of mobile sms using a machine learning approach. In *Applied Intelligence for Industry 4.0* (pp. 162–175). Chapman and Hall/CRC. DOI: 10.1201/9781003256083-13

Kaspersky Lab. Phishing and Spam Annual Report 2024. 2025. Available online: https://www.kaspersky.co.za/about/pressreleases/kaspersky-reports-nearly-900-million-phishing-attempts-in-2024-as-cyber-threats-increase?utm_source=chatgpt.com (accessed on 1 August 2025).

Kim, Y. (2014). Convolutional neural networks for sentence classification. *arXiv preprint arXiv:1408.5882*. DOI: 10.3115/v1/D14-1181

Kumar, N., & Sonowal, S. (2020, July). Email spam detection using machine learning algorithms. In *2020 Second International Conference on Inventive Research in Computing Applications (ICIRCA)* (pp. 108-113). IEEE. DOI: 10.1109/ICIRCA48905.2020.9183098

Laorden, C., Santos, I., Sanz, B., Alvarez, G., & Bringas, P. G. (2012). Word sense disambiguation for spam filtering. *Electronic Commerce Research and Applications, 11*(3), 290–298. DOI: 10.1016/j.elerap.2011.11.004

Li, W., Zhong, N., Yao, Y. Y., Liu, J., & Liu, C. (2006, December). Spam filtering and email-mediated applications. In International workshop on web intelligence meets brain informatics (pp. 382-405). Berlin, Heidelberg: Springer Berlin Heidelberg. DOI: 10.1007/978-3-540-77028-2_23

Lueg, C. P. (2005). From spam filtering to information retrieval and back: Seeking conceptual foundations for spam filtering. *Proceedings of the American Society for Information Science and Technology, 42*(1), meet.14504201146. Advance online publication. DOI: 10.1002/meet.14504201146

Mallampati, D. (2018). An efficient spam filtering using supervised machine learning techniques. *International Journal of Scientific Research in Computer Science and Engineering*, *6*(2), 33–37. DOI: 10.26438/ijsrcse/v6i2.3337

Méndez, J. R., Fdez-Riverola, F., Díaz, F., Iglesias, E. L., & Corchado, J. M. (2006, July). A comparative performance study of feature selection methods for the anti-spam filtering domain. In *Industrial conference on data mining* (pp. 106–120). Springer Berlin Heidelberg. Springer. DOI: 10.1007/11790853_9

Meyer, T. A., & Whateley, B. (2004, July). SpamBayes: Effective open-source, Bayesian based, email classification system. In *CEAS*.

Mohammed, S., Mohammed, O., Fiaidhi, J., Fong, S., & Kim, T. H. (2013). Classifying unsolicited bulk email (UBE) using python machine learning techniques. *International Journal of Hybrid Information Technology*, *6*(1), 43–56.

Naveenkumar, C., & Venkataramana, K. (2025). SMS SPAM Filtering With Machine Learning Model Distilbert. International Journal of Scientific Research in Computer Science. *Engineering and Information Technology*, *11*(3), 170–175.

. Pratap, B., & Singh, V. (2025). *The Evolving Cyber Threat Landscape: Navigating the Intersection of Cybercrime and Cybersecurity*. Words swiggle publication.

Rakotomalala, R. (2005, February). TANAGRA: a free software for research and academic purposes. In *Proceedings of EGC* (Vol. 2, pp. 697-702).

Sahami, M., Dumais, S., Heckerman, D., & Horvitz, E. (1998, July). A Bayesian approach to filtering junk e-mail. In *Learning for Text Categorization: Papers from the 1998 workshop* (Vol. 62, pp. 98-105).

Saleem, S., Islam, Z. U., Hasan, S. S. U., Akbar, H., Khan, M. F., & Ibrar, S. A. (2025). Spam email detection using long short-term memory and gated recurrent unit. *Applied Sciences (Basel, Switzerland)*, *15*(13), 7407. DOI: 10.3390/app15137407

Salman, M., Ikram, M., Basta, N., & Kaafar, M. A. (2025). Spallm-guard: Pairing sms spam detection using open-source and commercial llms. *arXiv preprint arXiv:2501.04985*.[REMOVED HYPERLINK FIELD]

Saxe, J., & Berlin, K. (2017). eXpose: A character-level convolutional neural network with embeddings for detecting malicious URLs, file paths and registry keys. *arXiv preprint arXiv:1702.08568*.

Schneider, K. M. (2003, April). A comparison of event models for Naive Bayes anti-spam e-mail filtering. In *10th conference of the European chapter of the association for computational linguistics*. DOI: 10.3115/1067807.1067848

SHirvani. G., & Ghasemshirazi, S. (2025). Advancing Email Spam Detection: Leveraging Zero-Shot Learning and Large Language Models. *arXiv preprint arXiv:2505.02362*.

Taloba, A. I., & Ismail, S. S. (2019, December). An intelligent hybrid technique of decision tree and genetic algorithm for e-mail spam detection. In *2019 Ninth International Conference on Intelligent Computing and Information Systems (ICICIS)* (pp. 99-104). IEEE. DOI: 10.1109/ICICIS46948.2019.9014756

Temitayo, F., Stephen, O., & Abimbola, A. (2012). Hybrid GA-SVM for efficient feature selection in e-mail classification. *Computer Engineering and Intelligent Systems*, *3*(3), 17–28.

Wang, X. L. (2005, August). Learning to classify email: a survey. In 2005 International conference on machine learning and cybernetics (Vol. 9, pp. 5716-5719). IEEE. doi:DOI: 10.1109/ICMLC.2005.1527956

Zhang, X., Zhao, J., & LeCun, Y. (2015). Character-level convolutional networks for text classification. *Advances in Neural Information Processing Systems*, •••, 28.

Chapter 5
Security and Privacy Concerns of Big Data Among Indian Consumers in E-Tailing and Social Media

Zainab Fatima
http://orcid.org/0000-0001-6155-7484
Jamia Millia Islamia, New Delhi, India

Mohd Abdul Moid Siddiqui
IILM University, Greater Noida, India

ABSTRACT

Organizations all around the world have embraced big data as the most effective and adaptable medium for a variety of applications, such as mapping customer behaviour and forecasting demand, to mention a couple. Although there are inherent security and privacy risks with the usage of big data, the organizations that have adopted it have primarily focused on its benefits. This study aims to determine how aware consumers are of companies that use confidential user-generated data and whether those concerns are related to privacy and security. An empirical study has been conducted on 268 respondents from central universities in order to analyze the privacy and security concerns among the respondents. SEM has been applied, and one of the findings revealed that young Indian e-commerce consumers and social media users are concerned more about their security, and this aspect have an effect on their online shopping behaviour and frequency of social media usage.

DOI: 10.4018/979-8-2600-1433-2.ch005

INTRODUCTION

Over the past ten years, India has seen a huge increase in the number of individuals using social media and shopping online. Consumer behavior has drastically changed as a result of the quick digital transformation, with social media networks and e-commerce websites becoming an essential part of people's everyday life. Businesses largely rely on big data analytics to handle massive volumes of data and enhance the overall online experience for customers in order to meet the demands of this growing number of digitally connected consumers. Big data, the term used to describe the enormous amounts of digital content produced by social media and e-commerce platforms, is expanding at an exponential rate every day. This big data holds significant value for organizations, as it allows them to extract meaningful insights and strategic information to enhance decision-making, personalize services, and maintain competitiveness. Big data has many advantages, but it also poses difficult problems for businesses in terms of gathering, analyzing, interpreting, and using it ethically. Handling unstructured and extremely susceptible customer data presents two of the biggest problems in terms of security and privacy. Financial, behavioural, and personal information of users is constantly being gathered, saved, and shared as they engage with online platforms more and more. If this data collection is not handled appropriately, users run the danger of identity theft, profiling, data breaches, and unapproved use.

These difficulties are particularly noticeable in India because of the distinct population adoption trends for digital technology within the country. Although Indians have quickly adopted to internet technology (IAMAI & Kantar, 2022; TRAI 2023), they still have a limited awareness and understanding of digital security practices (NSO, 2019). Because mobile internet, the Internet of Things (IoT), smartphones, automation, and social media sites like Instagram, Twitter, and Google are so widely available, people frequently expose their personal information without understanding the possible repercussions. This vulnerability results from a lack of understanding about safe online practices, a lack of awareness of privacy regulations, and a lack of legislative safeguards to protect the interests of consumers.

By 2030, it is anticipated that there will be over 500 million Indians shopping online and 800 million using social media (The times of India, august, 2024). Which resulted in the growing use of electronic devices (such as smartphones and tablets), the accessibility of the internet, the emergence of digital payment methods, busy lives that leave less time for in-person shopping, and the ease and diversity provided by online platforms. Businesses now have more options thanks to the rise in digital usage, but there are also more hazards related to the security and privacy of customer data.

In the field of big data, security and privacy have long been major concerns. In this context, privacy refers to the capacity of individual to protect personal data, making sure that private information is gathered, handled, and stored appropriately. It places a strong emphasis on openness, informed consent, and moral behaviour. In contrast, security pertains to safeguarding this information against unwanted access, malicious attacks, and abuse, ultimately attempting to maintain trust among consumers. The dangers of misusing big data are highlighted by incidents like the 2018 Facebook–Cambridge Analytica scandal, in which millions of users' personal information was collected without their consent for political advertising.

Through measures like the Digital Personal Data Protection Act (DPDPA) 2023, which aims to solve regional issues while bringing India's regulatory structure into line with international standards, the country has made an effort to fortify it in recent years. Its efficacy is still constrained, nevertheless, by operational challenges, enforcement deficiencies, and poor consumer awareness. India still struggles to strike a balance between quick innovation and consumer protection, in contrast to areas like the European Union where the General Data Protection Regulation (GDPR) has established robust accountability frameworks. Similarly, Japan has strengthened its Act on the Protection of Personal Information (APPI) and has aligned it with the GDPR principles while allowing flexibility for business innovation. This highlights the pressing need to comprehend social, cultural, and behavioural factors that impact customer trust in the digital economy in addition to technology measures. Even though these issues have received international attention, there are still a lot of unanswered questions in the Indian context. Fewer studies have examined the consumers' perceptions, awareness levels, and concerns about data privacy and security in emerging economies like India, despite the fact that big data has been extensively studied in the past for its potential to improve customer experience, business intelligence, and organizational performance. Furthermore, there is little research on the behavioral, cultural, and legal aspects of consumer vulnerability in the Indian market, despite the fact that a significant amount of the literature focuses on technology solutions (such as encryption, anonymization, and blockchain-based data protection). Research often generalizes findings from developed countries, overlooking India's unique challenges, such as digital illiteracy, weak enforcement of data protection laws, and varying consumer trust across demographic groups.

Therefore, by investigating Indian customers' security and privacy concerns in the areas of social media and e-commerce, this study attempts to fill these gaps. By using a consumer-centric approach, it aims to draw attention to the sociocultural, legal, and technological flaws that influence customers' confidence in online platforms. Businesses, legislators, and regulatory bodies in India must comprehend these dynamics in order to strike a balance between innovation and consumer protection. In doing so, this chapter makes a significant contribution by situating the discussion of big data security and privacy in the Indian context, where rapid digital growth, a large population base, and diverse consumer behaviours present both opportunities and risks. It aims to provide insights into consumer concerns that can guide the development of secure systems, transparent policies, and robust regulatory frameworks, ultimately fostering a safer and more trustworthy digital ecosystem for Indian consumers.

THEORETICAL BACKGROUND AND HYPOTHESIS DEVELOPMENT

Big Data Analytics and its usage in E commerce and Social Media

Defining Big Data

Big Data is the term used to describe extraordinarily vast and intricate datasets that are too complex for conventional database systems to handle, necessitating the use of sophisticated tools and techniques for management, analysis, and storage (Khan, 2022). Big Data has emerged as a key idea in both academics and business throughout time as businesses from all industries depend more and more on data to boost productivity, make better decisions, and obtain a competitive edge. Big Data was formerly described using the “3 Vs”- Volume, Velocity, and Variety- but these have subsequently been expanded to include the “5 Vs,” which also include Value and Veracity (Saggi & Jain, 2018; Gupta & Goyal, 2021).

Volume emphasizes the enormous scale of data generated daily from sources such as IoT devices, e-commerce platforms, digital payment systems, and social media (Al-Debei et al., 2021). Velocity represents the rapid inflow of data streams, demanding real-time or near-real-time analytics, especially in sectors like financial services, logistics, and healthcare (Favaretto et al., 2020). Variety captures the heterogeneous nature of data, including structured, semi-structured, and unstructured forms such as text, video, and sensor data (Wamba et al., 2020).

Veracity highlights the need for accuracy, consistency, and trustworthiness of datasets, as poor data quality can misguide strategic decisions (Cappa et al., 2021).

Value underscores that the ultimate aim of Big Data is to derive actionable insights and create tangible business advantages, ranging from targeted marketing to operational efficiency (Akter & Wamba, 2016).

Recent research has expanded the original Big Data framework by adding Variability, Visualization, and Visibility, leading to the '6 Vs' and '7 Vs' models. Visibility refers to making data handling transparent, visualization helps simplify complex information through graphics, and variability points to changes and inconsistencies in data. Other important aspects include Vulnerability, which deals with cybersecurity risks, Validity, which ensures reliable sources, and Volatility, which manages how long data is kept. Together, these factors show that Big Data is not only technical but institutional Kitchin (2014). It also involves handling complexity, keeping data secure, and turning unstructured information into useful strategies. Big Data affects many fields, such as social media, e-commerce, healthcare, and government services. While it brings many advantages, it also creates challenges that require strong ethical, legal, and technical systems to make the most of its benefits and maintain user trust.

Contemporary Perspectives on Big Data

Today, Big Data is viewed as a dynamic system where new technologies like distributed computing, cloud services, artificial intelligence, and machine learning help create value, not just solve technical problems. The main goal has shifted from simply storing large amounts of data to using it for real-time decisions, predictions, and personalized customer experiences. The new 'V-Matrix' model connects the five Vs of Big Data with business strategy, demonstrating how data insights can enhance efficiency, drive innovation, and give companies a lasting competitive edge in many industries.

Big Data Analytics in E-Commerce

Big Data Analytics (BDA) allows businesses to make informed decisions and stay competitive by using statistical, computational, and business intelligence tools to analyse large amounts of data. In e-commerce, BDA helps companies track customer behavior across platforms, set more accurate prices, personalize recommendations, and understand what customers want. For instance, deep learning models, which must address security and privacy issues, are increasingly used to predict when customers might leave, tailor product options, and improve customer loyalty. Research shows that BDA is key to personalized pricing and marketing. Retailers use customer data to design targeted campaigns, offer special deals, and adjust prices in real time.

This helps e-commerce companies boost while reshaping power between firms and consumers (Zuboff, 2019). BDA also supports efficient supply chain management by predicting demand, managing inventory, and ensuring timely delivery, all of which improve customer satisfaction. It helps businesses spot fraud, strengthen cybersecurity, and protect online transactions, which is especially important in India's fast-growing digital payment market. Predictive analytics can catch suspicious trends quickly, protecting both the business and its customers from financial risks.

Social media analytics powered by big data let companies track customer opinions, identify trends, and respond to complaints, which builds transparency and trust. However, while BDA offers great opportunities, it also raises important legal and ethical questions about data security and privacy. To keep customer trust, businesses must balance personalization with responsible data use, especially as people become more aware of their online presence. This means companies should invest in advanced analytics and adopt open policies that focus on fairness, responsibility, and ethical use of customer data.

Big Data and Social Media

The concept of Social Big Data, which focuses on extracting insights from user-generated content, emerged from the combination of Big Data with social media (Cambria et al., 2013). According to Le and Liaw (2017), social big data analysis uses interdisciplinary techniques including machine learning, graph mining, and natural language processing to examine customer feelings, opinions, and behavioral patterns. Platforms like Facebook, Instagram, and Twitter provide e-tailers with a wealth of chances to monitor changing customer preferences, predict demand, and customize advertising campaigns because billions of people create content every day (Khan. S, 2022). In addition to making sentiment analysis possible, social big data offers insights into viral content, cultural trends, and consumer complaints that may be used to enhance customer interaction strategies and marketing agility.

According to a systematic review by Mikalef et al. (2020), big data is becoming more and more important for improving organizational performance and innovation. Big Data has been identified as a strategic resource in developing nations like India, outperforming more conventional inputs like capital and equipment in terms of boosting competitiveness (Kshetri, 2014). To increase their customer base, Indian businesses and e-commerce platforms, are using social big data more and more to study regional consumer behavior, localize marketing campaigns, and create tailored promos for Tier-II and Tier-III cities. Additionally, social big data facilitates real-time crisis management, enabling businesses to identify reputational threats, control false information, and address bad press before it gets out of hand. But there are still challenges with protecting privacy, preventing misuse, and creating legal frameworks that safeguard consumer interests without limiting creativity (Akter et al., 2016). The trustworthiness of insights obtained from Social Big Data is complicated by the unstructured nature of social media data, as well as problems with algorithmic bias, false reviews, and disinformation. The lack of strong data protection regulations in India until recently increased consumer risks, which is why initiatives like the Digital Personal Data Protection Act, 2023, are especially important. Building customer trust and maintaining long-term digital growth will require striking a balance between the business potential of social big data and ethical considerations.

Privacy and Security Issues of BDA in E-Commerce and Social Media

The rapid expansion of Big data analytics (BDA) in social media and e-commerce has given businesses previously multiple opportunities to better analyse customer behaviour, personalize services, and improve decision making. However, security and privacy concerns still pose a considerable threat that affects users' perceptions and reactions to these sites. In fact, recent studies suggest that users' trust is often impacted by data driven personalization, as users become increasingly concerned with the misuse of their personal data. This concern is evident in developing countries like India, where while the rate of digital adoption has seen a significant rise in usage, general awareness of data protection and privacy rights remains low (Rizwan et al., 2018). This sense of caution can lead to concerns about privacy fatigue and resistance to using personalized service offerings, even when doing so would obviously make their lives easier and more convenient. Moreover, the doubt can increase in many developing countries, by the absence of effective data protection rules, and weak enforcement. Unlike the GDPR under European Union, India has only recently begun strengthening of the frameworks for data protection and is facing awareness and enforcement challenges (Greenleaf, 2018

Another dimension of the problem lies in the ethical use of data. Instances of unauthorized data sharing, security breaches, and opaque consent mechanisms have raised serious concerns regarding accountability and governance in data-driven ecosystems. For e-commerce and social media platforms to sustain long-term growth, striking a balance between leveraging big data for innovation and ensuring consumer trust is critical. Organizations must invest not only in technological safeguards but also in awareness campaigns, transparent communication, and ethical frameworks that reassure users about the responsible handling of their personal information.

Privacy and Security in E-Commerce

E-commerce privacy issues stem from increased collection, storage, and dissemination of consumer data. Research suggests consumers are worried about how third parties can access, share, or use their behavioural, financial, and personally identifiable information without consent (Laudon & Traver, 2009). Consumer trust can be damaged by inappropriate treatment of sensitive data, for example, which can result in identity theft, targeted fraud, or unlawful profiling (Al-Debei, 2024). Importantly, as payment systems and real-time recommendation engines have been implemented and customer risks for data breaches have increased (Afzal et al., 2024), consumers' desire for strong cybersecurity is also increased. E-commerce websites that fail to protect data frequently lose customers and their reputation. When making decisions, customers are increasingly conscious of the trade-off between personalized service and data privacy, and studies about a positive relationship between privacy protections and the intention to purchase online support this reasoning (Mikalef et al., 2020). E-commerce companies have a strong preference for the implementation of privacy enhancement strategies in the form of data and governance, encryption, and explicit privacy policy declarations to clear consumers with respect to the balance between innovation and consumer protections.

Social-Media and Privacy and Security Concern

Social media platforms which allow users to frequently share their own content, ideas, and activities, are another important source of big data. Although this provides advertisers useful information, it places users at risk. Popular approaches to this research report that unauthorized access, data scraping, and re-identification methods have made it consistently more difficult for individuals to maintain control of their digital identities (Cambria et al., 2013). Concerns about ethics and the law arise since advanced analytics can even de-anonymize user profiles, connecting anonymous datasets to actual people (Ogbuke et al., 2022). Customers are particularly worried about the opaqueness of social media businesses' data handling practices. According to a recent study, users are less motivated to interact with platforms whose data-sharing policies are viewed as intrusive or unclear (Khan. S, 2022). The Facebook–Cambridge Analytica scandal remains a key example, reinforcing how breaches of privacy can trigger widespread backlash and regulatory scrutiny.

Provided the elaborate literature suggesting that privacy concerns often shape the users' willingness to engage with the digital platforms, particularly in the social media and e-commerce context, the following hypotheses are proposed.

Hypothesis 1 (H1): The Privacy concerns of the customers have an impact on their Social Media usage.

Hypothesis 2 (H2): The Privacy concerns of the customers have an impact on their Online Shopping behaviour.

Laudon and Traver (2009) noted that one of the most significant barriers to online shopping is the concern over security, as consumers fear for the safety of their financial and personal data. Constantinides (2004) found that the hesitation of customers to engage in e-commerce is mainly based on perceived risks of misuse of data. This observation has now been somewhat validated by more recent research, showing that perceived vulnerability to unauthorized access to data markets the likelihood of engaging in online transactions. In Ghana, only a small proportion of individuals surveyed indicated they thought online payments were secure (Hassan et al., 2020). Security concerns are also a central theme, with research showing that growing consumer concern over data security results in reduced trust in e-commerce platform and higher perception of risk, diminishing purchase intentions (Indiani & Fahik, 2020). Even consumer trust in online retailers is known to mediate the relationship between perceived security and buying behaviour, making a secure environment necessary for growth in online commerce (Patil et al., 2014).

In addition to e-commerce, security concerns are also present in the world of social commerce, where transactions are being made within social media platforms. Viejo (2015) alerted the public and researchers, that cybercriminals will likely take advantage of the abundance of private information and use it to transaction funds. Therefore, in platforms that blend social interaction and commerce, perceived security of the online environment can serve as a meaningful influence in consumer behaviour. Concerns surrounding social media in general show a trend of behavioural change. Users who are concerned about privacy and data security may show greater concern about how they use social media. This caution often fosters less engagement (Safa and Von Solms, 2016).

Ultimately, research highlights the role of perceived security in establishing trust and use of social media and e-commerce. Trust in online services is impacted by perceived security because perceived security is generally built on the basis of customer's sense of perceived privacy (Carminati et al., 2022). One study found that nearly one-third of all e-commerce websites analysed were sending consumer data to a third-parties, such as Facebook, which indicates that even when privacy is perceived as strong, trust is eroded by the knowledge of the data being leaked (Seng et al., 2021). These leaks demonstrate the gap between perceived security and actual web security, and foreshadow long-term implications for digital platforms. In the era of big data analytics, protecting vast amounts of customer data, whether in social media, healthcare, or e-commerce, remains a critical concern (Patil et al., 2014). Collectively, these findings stress that without robust security mechanisms, both online shopping and social media engagement will remain hindered by user distrust.

Hypothesis 3 (H3): The Perceived Web Security by the customers has an impact on their Social Media usage.

Hypothesis 4 (H4): The Perceived Web Security by the customers has an impact on their Online Shopping behaviour.

The growing advancement of BDA has raised the level of discussion about data privacy and generated calls for stricter laws and ethical frameworks around handling personal data. Giving users more control over their personally identifiable information, referred to as "PII," has become increasingly relevant, proved by laws such as India's Digital Personal Data Protection Act (2023) and the General Data Protection Regulation (GDPR) in the European Community (Hassan et al., 2020). Technological solutions to improve security and facilitate analytics include federated learning, homomorphic encryption, and blockchain-enabled data management (Strzelecki & Rizun, 2022). There are still discrepancies between industry practices and regulatory frameworks in spite of these efforts. Academics believe that businesses should go beyond compliance and embrace a trust-centered strategy, in which responsibility, openness, and user permission serve as the basis of data-driven business models (Mikalef et al., 2020). This is particularly important in the biometric and genomic BDA era, where the sensitivity of data is higher, and the risks of misuse are far more severe (Sarkar & Banerjee, 2016).

Figure 1 depicts the two proposed models; Model 1 shows how perceived web security and privacy concern might impact social media usage of people and model 2 shows how perceived web security and privacy concern might impact online shopping among customers.

Figure 1. Proposed model

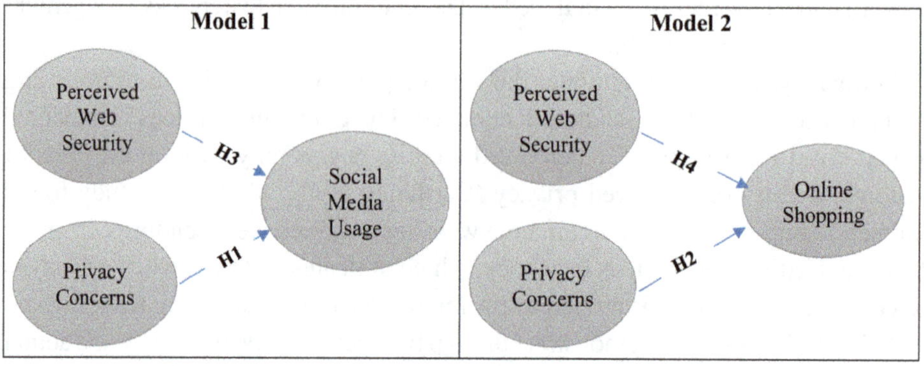

RESEARCH METHODOLOGY

The study is based on primary data which has been collected from college-going students as they are the active users of social media as well as online shopping websites (Martin, 2010). Data has been collected from the students of post-graduate courses in top central universities of India i.e., Jamia Millia Islamia, University of Delhi, Aligarh Muslim University, and Jawaharlal Nehru University. Central universities in India have students from different regional, economic, and cultural backgrounds, making a good representative sample of college students in that age bracket. Also, students from post-graduate courses were selected because of two reasons: first, they are more technologically aware and competent than undergraduate or junior college students, and second, they generally have a higher spending capacity compared to graduates (Mishra, 2010), making them fit for the profile of active users and consumers of e-commerce and social media platforms. The post-graduate students are considered more mature in their opinions and have developed critical thinking skills, thereby providing reliable insights into consumer behaviour patterns. More than 840 questionnaires were sent via emails, social media platforms, and students' groups on WhatsApp, and a total of 268 responses have been collected and analyzed, entailing a response rate of 31.34%, which falls within the usual range of response rates for this kind of sampling frame. Additionally, efforts were made to ensure gender diversity and representation across disciplines, further strengthening the validity and generalizability of the findings.

Measurement

The questionnaire which is used in this research has been developed based on the relevant literature, generating new variables, and surveying the views of users and experts. After completion of the draft, it was tested for the content validity through subject experts. Table 1 displays the variables and items that are part of the questionnaire. A five-point Likert scale, with 1 signifying "strongly disagree" and five indicating "strongly agree," was employed in the questionnaire. The last column's references served as the model for the scale.

Table 1. Research instrument

Variables	Items	Measurement	Reference
Social Media Usage	SM1	I am a frequent user of social media sites.	A. Viejo, D. Sánchez (2015)
	SM2	I keep my social media profiles up to date with my personal information.	
	SM3	I am aware that social media websites have a lot of personal information about me.	
	SM4	I am willing that social media websites use this information in whatever manner they may think necessary.	

continued on following page

Table 1. Continued

Variables	Items	Measurement	Reference
Online shopping	OS1	I am a frequent visitor of online shopping sites.	Pavlou, P. A. (2003);Ahmad, S. (2002)
	OS2	I keep shopping website profiles up to date with my personal, payment and billing related information.	
	OS3	I am aware that online shopping website have a lot of information sensitive and personal information about me (including search and purchase history etc)	
	OS4	I am concerned that online shopping websites may use my information in whatever manner they think is necessary.	
Perceived Web Security	SE1	I am concerned about my security while sending personal/financial info across the Web.	O'Cass, A.O. and Fenech, T. (2003)
	SE2	I am concerned about providing personal/ financial info about me to online retailers	
	SE3	Web is unsafe environment to provide personal/financial info.	
	SE4	Social media should have better security features.	
	SE5	Shopping websites should have better security features.	
Privacy Concern	PR1	In general, I am concerned about my privacy while I am using the internet?	T. Buchanan (2006)
	PR2	Are you concerned that you are asked for too much personal information when you register or make online purchases?	
	PR3	Are you concerned about online identity theft?	
	PR4	Are you concerned about people you do not know obtaining personal information about you from your online activities?	

The variable 'big data' has not been included as one of the variables because many students were not aware of this terminology, therefore they were briefed about it before collecting the responses and the data collected is in respect to only those online platforms which use big data as an important tool in operation (For example-Facebook, twitter, Instagram, Amazon, Flipkart etc.).

ANALYSIS AND RESULTS

Exploratory Factor Analysis (EFA)

SPSS 19 was used for the EFA process. The correlation between the variables inside factors was verified by the Bartlett's Test of Sphericity (BTS). A significant level of common variance was demonstrated by the Kaiser-Meyer-Olkin (KMO) measure of sampling adequacy (KMO = 0.832 and 0.859) for both scales. Over 70% of the variance was represented by the resulting components for both scales (Table 2).

Table 2. Results of exploratory factor analysis (Scale 1)

Code	Security	Privacy	SMU	Cronbach Alpha
SE1	.770			.833
SE2	.751			
SE3	.766			
SE4	.586			
SE5	.762			
PR2		.782		.802
PR3		.886		
PR4		.795		
SM1			.806	.905
SM2			.847	
SM3			.872	
SM4			.875	

Table 3. Results of exploratory factor analysis (Scale 2)

Code	Security	Privacy	Online Shopping	Cronbach Alpha
SE1	.770			.833
SE2	.751			
SE3	.766			
SE4	.586			
SE5	.762			

continued on following page

Table 3. Continued

Code	Security	Privacy	Online Shopping	Cronbach Alpha
PR2		.782		
PR3		.886		.802
PR4		.795		
OS1			.839	
OS2			.820	.899
OS3			.875	
OS4			.828	

Notes: Extraction Method: principal component analysis; Rotation Method: Varimax with Kaiser Normalisation; rotation converged in 5 iterations.

The first and the second factor i.e. Security (SEC) and Privacy (PRV) which is common in both the scales, comprised five items and three items respectively having alpha values of 0.833 and 0.802. One item of privacy (PR1) had to be dropped because of cross loading. The third factor, Social Media Usage (SMU), and Online Shopping (ONSH) of both the scales loaded with four items each having alpha value of 0.905 and 0.899 respectively.

To gauge the gender wise difference in perception of all the factors, Independent Samples t-test was performed. The results of the t-test indicated the value of significance for all of the four variables of the study above .050 i.e. Social Media Usage (0.306), Online shopping (0.913), Security (0.764) and Privacy (0.955) which suggests that there is no significant difference with in gender (Male and Female) with respect to all of the four variables.

Confirmatory Factor Analysis (CFA)

Confirmatory factor analysis (CFA) is typically advised in order to get over the inherent constraints of exploratory factor analysis (EFA). For both models, which included the following factors: Security (SEC), Privacy (PRV), and Social Media Usage (SMU) in the first model and Security (SEC), Privacy (PRV), and Online Shopping in the second, CFA was carried out using AMOS 22. Every item showed loadings within the permissible range and significantly loaded on the associated factors (Figure 2 and Table 4).

Table 4. Standardized Regression Weights (CFA) Model 1

			Estimate
SM1	**<---**	**SMU**	**.755**
SM2	<---	SMU	.842
SM3	<---	SMU	.868
SM4	<---	SMU	.898
SE1	<---	SEC	.733
SE2	<---	SEC	.817
SE3	<---	SEC	.789
SE4	<---	SEC	.606
SE5	<---	SEC	.605
PR2	<---	PRV	.730
PR3	<---	PRV	.873
PR4	<---	PRV	.697

Table 5. Standardized Regression Weights (CFA) Model 1

			Estimate
OS1	**<---**	**ONSH**	**.789**
OS2	<---	ONSH	.833
OS3	<---	ONSH	.857
OS4	<---	ONSH	.845
SE1	<---	SEC	.741
SE2	<---	SEC	.821
SE3	<---	SEC	.774
SE4	<---	SEC	.609
SE5	<---	SEC	.607
PR2	<---	PRV	.730
PR3	<---	PRV	.872
PR4	<---	PRV	.700

Figure 2. Measurement models

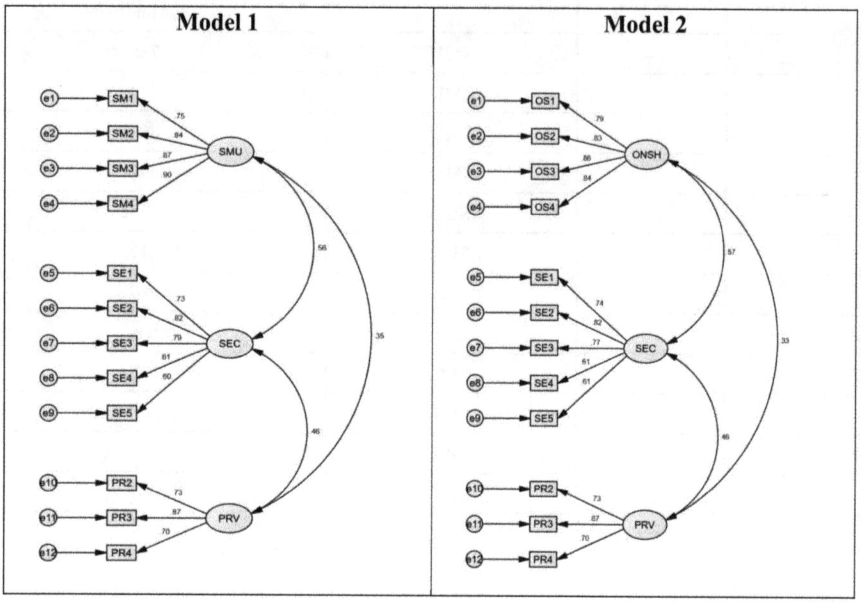

The average variance extracted (AVE) was used to confirm the discriminant and convergent validity of both scales. All of the model's constructs had AVEs greater than 0.5, which denotes good convergent validity (Khan & Adil, 2013). For each construct in Table 6, the square root of AVE (diagonal values indicated in bold) was greater than the inter-construct correlations, demonstrating sufficient discriminant validity (Fornell & Larcker 1981; Khan & Adil, 2013).

Table 6. Validity of the constructs (Model 1)

	CR	AVE	SEC	SMU	PRV
SEC	0.838	0.512	**0.716**		
SMU	0.907	0.710	0.559	**0.842**	
PRV	0.813	0.594	0.457	0.350	**0.770**

Table 7. Validity of the constructs (Model 2)

	CR	AVE	SEC	ONSH	PRV
SEC	0.838	0.512	0.716		
ONSH	0.899	0.691	0.571	0.831	
PRV	0.813	0.594	0.460	0.334	0.771

Table 6 displays the composite reliability (CR) for each factor in the two models. It was discovered that the CR for all the factor correlations was satisfactory, with values significantly above the minimum required value of 0.70 (Fornell & Larcker, 1981; Malhotra & Dash, 2011). As a result, the scale's validity and reliability are both supported by the data mentioned above. Thus, the researchers move forward with the testing of the proposed framework and hypotheses.

Structural Model

The proposed model that has been subsequently tested for its appropriateness using the data generated for the study is presented in Figure 3.

Figure 3. Structural model

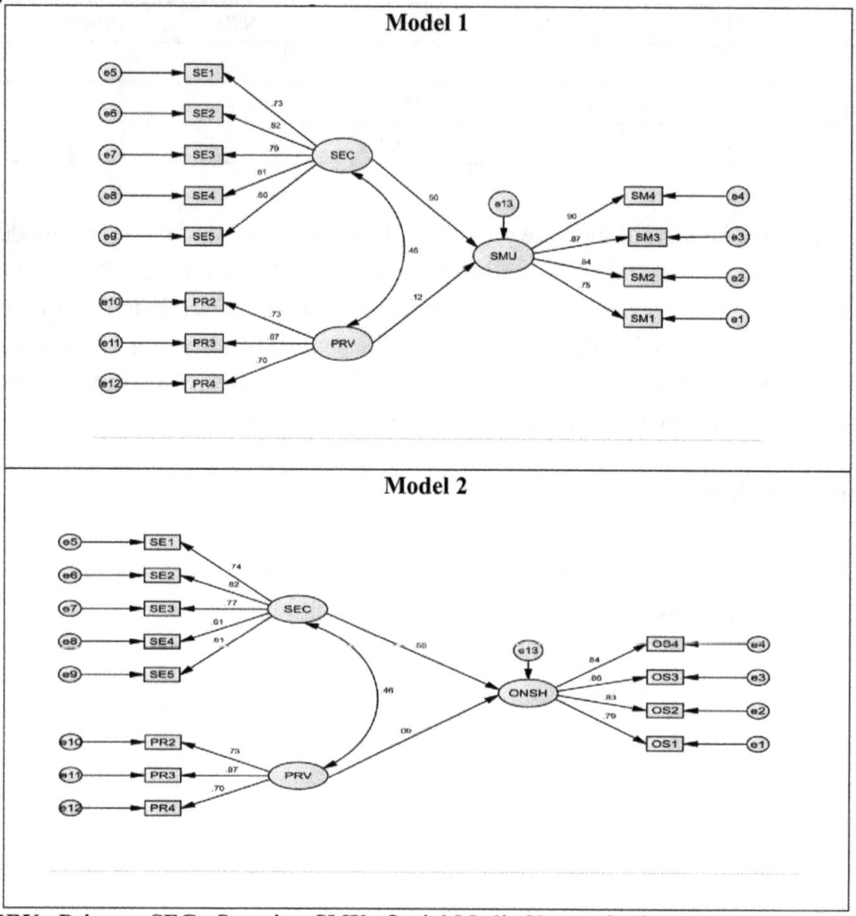

(PRV= Privacy; SEC= Security; SMU= Social Media Usage; ONSH= Online Shopping)

(PRV= Privacy; SEC= Security; SMU= Social Media Usage; ONSH= Online Shopping)

The observed values for the fit indices are presented in Table 8. The fit indices indicated a satisfactory model fit (GFI = 0.893, AGFI= .837, CFI= .938, RMSEA= .078) for model 1 and (GFI = 0.908, AGFI= .859, CFI= .958, RMSEA= .0069) for model 2. Although the value of GFI for model 1 is less than 0.90, it is within the acceptable limit (Etezadi-Amoli & Farhoomand, 1996). Thus, the overall model was found to be satisfactory.

Table 8. Fit indices of measurement model (CFA)

Fit Index	Recommended Values*	Observed Values Model 1	Observed Values Model 2
Cmin/df	< 3.0	2.259	1.803
GFI	> 0.90	.893	.908
AGFI	> 0.80	.837	.859
CFI	> 0.90	.938	.958
RMSEA	< 0.070	.080	.069

*Source: Hooper et al, 2008; Hu & Bentler, 1999; Malhotra & Dash, 2011

Of the four hypothesized relationships, two were found to be statistically significant at a significance level of 0.01 (p<0.01), supporting H_3 (Security → Social Media Usage), H_4 (Security → Online Shopping). However, the relationship of privacy Social Media Usage and Online Shopping in both the models were found to be insignificant thereby indicating not supporting H_1 (Privacy → Social Media Usage) and H_2 (Privacy → Online Shopping).

Table 9. Standardized regression weights

	Estimates	p- value
SMU ← PRV	.147	.183
SMU ← SEC	.498	.000
ONSH ← PRV	.118	.319
ONSH ← SEC	.548	.000

DISCUSSION

This study aims to investigate the relevance of security and privacy concerns brought on by the use of big data in relation to social media and online shopping. For academics and practitioners both, knowing how users view and react to these risks is essential in a time when personal data is constantly created, saved, and shared across numerous platforms. According to the study's preliminary analysis, men and women have similar views on privacy and web security issues, which is consistent with the findings of Balakrishnan (2015). This is significant because previous studies generally found that women and men differed in their levels of concern and protective behaviour when it came to privacy issues (Tifferet, 2019; Hoy & Milne, 2010; Malik et al., 2016). Particularly in the Indian setting, where internet penetration and cellphone usage have increased significantly over the past ten years, the convergence of opinions across genders in the current study may be a reflection of young people' growing digital awareness and equal exposure to online threats. According to the survey, young Indian consumers who use social media and e-commerce exhibit increased security concerns, which have a direct impact on how frequently they use social media and how they shop online. This result is consistent with research by Harris and Goode (2010), who discovered that in online settings, consumer purchase intentions are strongly influenced by both privacy and security. Their study showed that when making purchases online, customers give priority to safe systems and reliable platforms, indicating that concerns go beyond simple money security to include data security and trust in digital ecosystems. Similarly, the present research emphasizes that when it comes to e-commerce, Indian consumers- particularly the younger demographic, expect a minimum degree of security and openness.

An interesting part of this study is how security concerns have different implications on social media and online shopping. Consumers think that e-commerce platforms provide secure payment gateways and robust security procedures to protect financial transactions (Shergill & Chen, 2005). Since e-commerce directly involves financial risks, security becomes a more important factor in determining behavior and trust. Because reputable websites like Amazon and Flipkart are thought to provide better protections against fraud and financial loss, customers choose to shop from them (GVU, 1998). The findings of this study demonstrate that the level of security worries is significantly higher when purchasing online as opposed to using social media. Consumers may be cautious of social media privacy issues, but they seem to give these risks a lesser priority than the financial consequences of unsafe online transactions. This demonstrates the dichotomy of perceived risks: security is the primary worry due to the immediate financial loss associated with online shopping, even though privacy is also important.

However, there are still serious privacy risks associated with user-generated data on social media. Researchers like Beigi and Liu (2018) have noted that social media platforms' very architecture, which is built for transparency, sharing, and visibility, makes them inherently vulnerable to privacy violations. These risks are increased by big data analytics since users' casually disclosed personal information can be collected, examined, and used by outside parties for harmful purposes, targeted marketing, or even surveillance. However, the findings of current study show a somewhat contradictory trend: respondents expressed less concern about privacy, regardless of whether they were using social media or purchasing online. This finding contradicts much of the earlier literature, which consistently highlights privacy as a major deterrent to online engagement (Bansal et al., 2016).

This finding can be partly explained by privacy fatigue, wherein exposing them repeatedly to data breaches and surveillance desensitizes them to privacy risks. Second, the extensive usage of social media and e-commerce platforms in India has made data sharing so routine that privacy concerns might not be the primary consideration for customers when making decisions. Convenience, connectedness, and financial incentives (such discounts or prizes) may be more important to young consumers than abstract hazards to personal data. Third, the growing emphasis on platform reputation and brand trust may have shifted user focus away from individual privacy management to reliance on institutional responsibility, where consumers expect organizations to safeguard their information without needing constant vigilance.

The differences between the present findings and past research also show how digital behavior is changing across cultural and geographic contexts. Indian customers might exhibit a more practical approach, balancing risks against observable benefits, whereas Western research has always emphasized privacy as a top priority. In this sense, the current study contributes to the expanding literature of research that indicates cultural, technological, and economic factors moderate security and privacy concerns rather than being universal.

The overall conclusions of the study highlight the need of having a sophisticated understanding of how consumers see security and privacy in digital settings. For practitioners, this entails making investments in open and honest communication regarding security protocols, establishing credibility, and guaranteeing secure yet smooth user experiences. Young consumers' diminished emphasis on privacy issues poses significant difficulties for policymakers regarding the effectiveness of the current awareness and protection systems. As the size and reach of big data continue to grow, protecting privacy and security will be essential to preserving user confidence in social media and online shopping.

This study highlighted the need for e-commerce and social media companies to pay greater attention to security if they want to thrive in the rapidly changing big data landscape. Customers of these services must be made aware of this strict position in an open manner rather than in a concealed one. Some of the intrinsic characteristics of big data are intimately linked to certain security and privacy issues. And the majority of these problems have to do with the collection, processing, and disclosure of data to all kinds of customers and other parties. Due to the lack of formed regulatory agencies, companies need to have a well-structured big data strategy that considers the amount of risk of the data they utilize. Websites that deal with social media and e-commerce should therefore raise user awareness and be more transparent about how they use user-generated data. As was previously mentioned, it is imperative that both businesses and consumers familiarize themselves with BDA. It will serve as awareness for customers, potentially assisting them in making wiser choices when utilizing internet platforms. It is also important for the companies to have a full understanding of how it works, its scope and capabilities in order to maximize the business value and properly addressing the challenges.

IMPLICATIONS

Theoretical Implications

The results of this study contribute to the body of knowledge currently available on consumer behaviour in digital environment, privacy, and security in a number of ways. First, the result contradicts previous research that found gender differences in perceptions of security and privacy. Although earlier studies showed that women generally expressed greater concerns about online safety (Tifferet, 2019; Hoy & Milne, 2010; Malik et al., 2016), the present findings show that men and women currently see these risks similarly. This convergence points to a change in consumer behavior that could be explained by equal exposure to online platforms and growing digital literacy among genders. This suggests, theoretically, that gender is becoming less significant as a moderating factor in models of online consumer perceptions of security and trust, especially in the Indian context. Future research can further test this by integrating gender-neutral models in frameworks such as the Technology Acceptance Model (TAM) or the Unified Theory of Acceptance and Use of Technology (UTAUT).

Second, the study indicates that online shopping behavior is more influenced by security concerns than by social media use. The results here suggest that security, particularly in financial transactions, has a stronger weight in influencing customer intentions in e-commerce, even if privacy has been addressed as a core construct in privacy calculus theory. By implying that various contexts (e-commerce vs. social media) emphasize distinct aspects of customer risk perception, this adds nuance to preexisting ideas. Theoretical models of consumer digital behavior must therefore differentiate between platform-specific concerns, such as those linked to social media privacy and e-commerce security.

Third, the surprising discovery that customers are comparatively indifferent about privacy when using social media and online purchasing adds significantly to the growing conversation about privacy fatigue. According to recent research, users may become less sensitive as a result of ongoing exposure to data breaches and surveillance techniques (Bansal et al., 2016). This study provides empirical evidence in favor of this claim from an Indian viewpoint, demonstrating how young consumers may put convenience, usability, and financial incentives ahead of privacy. Theoretically, this data advances the privacy calculus theory by indicating that, particularly among younger populations, the perceived advantages of digital involvement may be outweighing the perceived risks.

Lastly, the study contributes to cross-cultural theories of digital behavior by placing consumer perceptions of big data into a regional and cultural framework. This study indicates that Indian customers place a higher priority on security, especially financial security, than privacy, despite the fact that privacy has frequently been highlighted in Western literature as the primary obstacle to online involvement. The significance of context-specific models that incorporate cultural, economic, and technological factors is highlighted by this study. In theory, it promotes a change from universal models of security and privacy to more complex frameworks that take into account regional variations in consumer psychology.

Practical Implications

From a practical standpoint, the results provide useful information for social media organizations, e-commerce platforms, and lawmakers. The significance of giving security measures top priority in e-commerce platforms is the most evident factor. Platforms must make investments in strong payment gateways, encryption technology, and multi-factor authentication to reassure users, as consumers generally identify online purchasing concerns with financial security. Businesses that successfully convey their security network and offer obvious indicators of confidence, including secure payment confirmations and branding, are probably going to attract in and keep more clients. Additionally, the preference for trustworthy e-commerce sites emphasizes the competitive edge that well-established businesses have because of their perceived reliability. Smaller or emerging platforms must therefore build credibility through partnerships, transparency, and consistent communication of their security practices.

The results point to a distinct area of attention for social media companies. Even while customers are less concerned about privacy, there are still serious concerns connected to user-generated data. Stronger user controls, more transparent data rules, and improved communication regarding the use of personal data are all requirements for businesses. Platforms must improve their privacy frameworks due to legislative demands and the possibility of reputational harm from data breaches, even though users may not now prioritize issues related to privacy. Convenience and security can be balanced by providing users with customized privacy options and informing them of the risks associated with data sharing.

From the perspective of policy and regulation, the reduced sensitivity to privacy concerns among young consumers is a matter of concern. Policymakers must recognize that the lack of consumer vigilance does not equate to the absence of risk. Instead, the heightened obligation of regulatory bodies is to maintain data protection done by effective legislative mechanisms, enforcement tools, and supervision. The Personal Data Protection Bill in India is an important milestone in enhancing consumption of safety for consumers with clear guidelines for e-commerce and social media communication with regard to data collection, storage and use. Awareness campaigns can also be launched at the educational and government levels to help young consumers understand the ongoing nature of data harm and engage in practice of being responsible in the digital space. Lastly, marketers and strategists in the digital ecosystem might also benefit from this research. Marketers should develop ads that highlight the user-friendly experience, secure payment options, and brand safety that are based receipt of consumer's choice. However, companies should avoid exploiting consumer indifference to privacy, as this could backfire in the long run. Instead, businesses can seek differentiation through company addressing security and privacy with intention and purpose and build their reputation as trustworthy stewards of consumer data. The friendly, professed work of security and privacy policies builds trust at the consumer level while the business becomes better positioned to manage future internal adjustments with continued regulatory guidelines or consumer expectation and entitlement.

Social Implications

Due to rapidly growing digital ecosystem in India, the research findings have important social implications for consumers, businesses, and society at large. First, that privacy and security concerns are no longer significantly impacted by gender suggests that democratization of technology and digital literacy programs are promoting even more equal participation in online environments. The gender-based digital difference appears to be closing as men and women display similar levels of expertise and risk perception. Given that both genders are equally confident using digital platforms, this is a positive trend for inclusion for increasing opportunities for education, employment, and entrepreneurship. This trend is also evidently present among the youth, who due to their early exposure to smartphones and affordable internet have resulted in greater confidence and proficiency in using digital platforms. As gender wise this impact is also equally present it reflects a positive development for digital literacy and inclusion.

However this growing confidence with digital platforms necessarily does not always translate into strong cyber hygiene practices, as many users contribute to reflect limited awareness of password management and importance of unique passwords, critical necessity of two factor authentication in popular platforms and updating credentials on a regular basis, the privacy settings on the social media and e commerce websites are also left at default highlighting a deeper gap between functional digital awareness and deeper understanding of the risks and need for the privacy and data protection practices

Second, the overriding concern for financial security as opposed to privacy signifies a societal change in consumer preferences. Consumers are comfortable with sharing private information for convenience and offerings, though they appear to be more cautious about exposure to financial risks. This indicates that trust is of the utmost importance with respect to monetary transactions and in order to sustain trust with consumers in India's e-commerce and digital payments. Socially, it seems to indicate the growing acceptance of cashless economies and willingness by the populace to adopt government-led digitalization initiatives, such as Digital India and the Unified Payments Interface (UPI), which are becoming more integrated in everyday consumption behaviours. But the selective caution portrays suggests that while users actively monitor alerts from banks and internet banking applications, they underestimate the long-term risks associated with reusing and utilising weak passwords, careless data sharing and application permissions.

This pattern reflects "privacy fatigue" where sustained exposure to data risks desensitizes them to security risks. Digital adoption may increase temporarily because of privacy fatigue, but people's attentiveness may decline overall, putting them at greater risk of being vulnerable to abuse. A lack of a privacy conscience can further cement imbalanced power dynamics between consumers and companies, in which companies continue to collect and make money off people's personal information with no accountability. This suggests a larger need for education and public awareness to foster the culture and practices of responsible digital citizenship.

Fourth, the study shows that contextual and cultural differences are important in shaping consumers' perceptions. Where Western context views privacy as a meaningful social right, Indian consumers seem to take a more pragmatic view of the role of privacy and have a readiness to sacrifice privacy for security and convenience. This also reflects a broader societal orientation toward collective, outcome-driven decision making, where customers may view financial risk as more tangible than informational risk. These kinds of insights respond to the need for cross-cultural dialogue and show that the context of a given society must be taken into consideration when creating global digital policies, rather than making broad universal assumptions about consumers' behaviours.

Lastly, the study's implications touch on issues of governance and societal trust. Established e-commerce companies have a disproportionate advantage since customers rely largely on reputable platforms for assurance. This could further consolidate the market and restrict prospects for new businesses. Wider societal repercussions of this tendency may include diminished diversity in the online market and heightened reliance on a small number of powerful platforms. However, in order to establish a more equitable and transparent digital environment, it also emphasizes the necessity of group trust-building processes, including independent certifications, consumer advocacy organizations, and regulatory monitoring.

DIRECTION FOR FUTURE RESEARCH

While this research has highlighted valuable information about consumer perception of security and privacy in e-commerce and social media, there are several conceptual and theoretical avenues to continue research in this area. First, there is a clear lack of research around big data analytics (BDA) and implications in the context of economies, where internet penetration and uptake of digital platforms is expanding rapidly. In developed economies, consumers are more aware of data protection rights, while consumers in developing economies, such as India, are often unaware of how their data are being used, stored, and protected. Thus, future research can examine both consumers' and businesses perceptions of privacy and security issues associated with BDA, should focus in markets that are less mature in the development of digital ecosystems and regulatory approaches (Dwivedi et al., 2021). Second, future research should critically examine why businesses may be less willing to use BDA with potential privacy and security issues. Although BDA presents business with considerable advantages regarding customer insights, customisation and operational efficiencies, adoption may still be inhibited due to concerns over data breaches and legality. Researchers might investigate this topic by relating privacy and security concerns to BDA's fundamental features, like volume, velocity, and variety, and by emphasizing solutions to these problems. This can entail looking at how corporate culture, cybersecurity infrastructure investment, and governance frameworks contribute to building confidence and lowering opposition to BDA implementation.

Third, future research can benefit from adopting a comparative perspective across regions and cultures. Since this study is limited to Indian consumers, comparative studies involving consumers in other developing economies- such as Brazil, South Africa, or Indonesia- could reveal both commonalities and differences in how privacy and security concerns are perceived. Such cross-cultural research would contribute to the development of more nuanced, context-specific theories of consumer behaviour in the digital age.

The long-term analysis of consumer attitudes is another exciting field of study. Perceptions of privacy and security are dynamic and change over time in response to exposure to cyber incidents, regulatory framework changes, and technical improvements. Longitudinal research could monitor how consumers' worries change as they become more aware of data protection regulations or following media coverage of significant breaches. Such investigations would provide valuable insights about how trust and risk perception work in digital contexts. Additionally, it might be relevant for researchers to explore the relationship between consumer decision-making and privacy fatigue. This study suggests that younger consumers are less concerned about privacy threats, which could be due to normalizing the use of data. Future research might investigate if privacy fatigue engenders risky online actions, decreases trust in digital services, or changes engagement patterns. This area of inquiry could help further theorizing the privacy calculus and provide applicable approaches for policymakers to address consumer complacency.

Lastly, future research should consider the role of new technologies, such as philosophical approaches in artificial intelligence (AI), blockchain technologies, or federated learning, in discussions of BDA, security and privacy. These technologies have the potential of exacerbating or lightening risk. For example, blockchain technologies could improve transparency and security in e-commerce transactions whereas AI analytics could create new ethical dilemmas regarding surveillance and profiling of data. The perceived trade-offs by consumers and businesses will be an important aspect in informing the next generation of research in this domain.

CONCLUSION

The purpose of this study was to explore the aspects of security and privacy that are considered when it comes to usage of big data in e-commerce and social media, specifically amongst Indian consumers. The study provided a number of compelling implications about consumer attitudes, behaviours and expectations. Notably, it appears both males and females show similar concerns about privacy and web security, contrary to previous studies that had shown differences in attitudes towards online privacy based on gender (Tifferet, 2019; Hoy & Milne, 2010; Malik et al., 2016). This similarity indicates that, in the digital age, issues of privacy and security are broadly shared societal concerns rather than gendered ones.

The study further demonstrates that young Indian consumers, especially post-graduate students, place considerable emphasis on online security when engaging with e-commerce platforms and social media. In particular, security concerns were found to have a more significant influence on online shopping behaviour compared to social media usage. This aligns with prior research highlighting the crucial role of secure payment gateways and trusted online platforms in shaping consumer confidence and purchase intentions (Shergill & Chen, 2005; Harris & Goode, 2010). Interestingly, however, consumers in this study did not display strong apprehensions about privacy, suggesting a normalization of data sharing and potential evidence of privacy fatigue, where individuals become desensitized to data misuse risks (Beigi & Liu, 2018).

The practical implications of these findings are far-reaching. For businesses, ensuring strong security measures, transparent data practices, and consumer education will be critical to building trust in digital platforms. Retailers, especially in e-commerce, must invest in secure payment gateways and advanced cybersecurity systems to reduce vulnerabilities. Social media companies, on the other hand, should focus on improving user awareness of data-sharing practices and implement stricter privacy controls to restore user confidence. From a theoretical standpoint, this research contributes to the growing body of literature on the intersection of big data, consumer behaviour, and trust. It supports and extends theories such as the privacy calculus by highlighting how security, rather than privacy, has become the dominant factor influencing consumer choices in the Indian context.

Looking forward, the chapter identifies several future research directions that can further deepen understanding in this field. In particular, there is a need for more research in developing countries, where rapid digital adoption and evolving regulatory frameworks create unique challenges. Research could also focus on organizations' reluctance to the adoption of big data analytics due to security concerns, and can provide direction for addressing such difficulties. Cross-cultural and cross-regional comparisons, tracking the evolution of consumer attitudes over time, and investigation into concepts like privacy fatigue could all add significant value to employee and consumer trust. The integration of new technologies including blockchain and artificial intelligence into discussions with respect to data security will also be a good basis for future scholars.

In conclusion, this study emphasizes that privacy may be losing its influence, while security is at the forefront for consumers considering online engagement in e-commerce, social media, or otherwise. For businesses, a failure to recognize and address these issues risks consumer nihilism at a moment when trust and engagement are paramount for business success in an increasingly digital world. For scholars, the study presents new opportunities for theoretical refinements and innovations into practical inquiries about big data, consumer behaviour, and online trust. Ultimately, finding the balance between the use of big data and the protection of consumer interests will affect the sustainability of digital platforms in future.

REFERENCES

Afzal, M., Ansari, M. S., Ahmad, N., Shahid, M., & Shoeb, M. (2024). Cyberfraud, usage intention, and cybersecurity awareness among e-banking users in India: An integrated model approach. *Journal of Financial Services Marketing*, *29*(4), 1503–1523. DOI: 10.1057/s41264-024-00279-3

Akter, S., & Wamba, S. F. (2016). Big data analytics in E-commerce: A systematic review and agenda for future research. *Electronic Markets*, *26*(2), 173–194. DOI: 10.1007/s12525-016-0219-0

Al-Debei, M. M. (2024). The era of business analytics: Identifying and ranking the differences between business intelligence and data science from practitioners' perspective using the Delphi method. *Journal of Business Analytics*, *7*(2), 94–119. DOI: 10.1080/2573234X.2023.2285483

Al-Debei, M. M., Abdeljaber, O., Ab Yajid, M. S., Khatibi, A., Al-masaeed, S., & Tham, J. (2021). The role of service quality and online trust in maintaining clients for Malaysian online enterprises. *International Journal of eBusiness and eGovernment studies, 13*(2), 149-167.

Balakrishnan, V. (2015). Cyberbullying among young adults in Malaysia: The roles of gender, age and Internet frequency. *Computers in Human Behavior*, *46*, 149–157. DOI: 10.1016/j.chb.2015.01.021

Bansal, S., Chowell, G., Simonsen, L., Vespignani, A., & Viboud, C. (2016). Big data for infectious disease surveillance and modeling. *The Journal of Infectious Diseases*, *214*(suppl_4), S375–S379. DOI: 10.1093/infdis/jiw400 PMID: 28830113

Beigi, G., & Liu, H. (2018). Privacy in social media: Identification, mitigation and applications. *arXiv preprint arXiv:1808.02191*.

Cambria, E., Grassi, M., Poria, S., & Hussain, A. (2013). Sentic computing for social media analysis, representation, and retrieval. In *Social media retrieval* (pp. 191–215). Springer. DOI: 10.1007/978-1-4471-4555-4_9

Cappa, F., Oriani, R., Peruffo, E., & McCarthy, I. (2021). Big data for creating and capturing value in the digitalized environment: Unpacking the effects of volume, variety, and veracity on firm performance. *Journal of Product Innovation Management*, *38*(1), 49–67. DOI: 10.1111/jpim.12545

Carminati, B., Ferrari, E., & Viviani, M. (2022). *Security and trust in online social networks*. Springer Nature.

Constantinides, E. (2004). Influencing the online consumer's behavior: The Web experience. *Internet Research, 14*(2), 111–126. DOI: 10.1108/10662240410530835

Dwivedi, Y. K., Hughes, L., Ismagilova, E., Aarts, G., Coombs, C., Crick, T., Duan, Y., Dwivedi, R., Edwards, J., Eirug, A., Galanos, V., Ilavarasan, P. V., Janssen, M., Jones, P., Kar, A. K., Kizgin, H., Kronemann, B., Lal, B., Lucini, B., & Williams, M. D. (2021). Artificial Intelligence (AI): Multidisciplinary perspectives on emerging challenges, opportunities, and agenda for research, practice and policy. *International Journal of Information Management, 57*, 101994. DOI: 10.1016/j.ijinfomgt.2019.08.002

Etezadi-Amoli, J., & Farhoomand, A. F. (1996). A structural model of end user computing satisfaction and user performance. *Information & Management, 30*(2), 65–73. DOI: 10.1016/0378-7206(95)00052-6

Favaretto, M., De Clercq, E., Schneble, C. O., & Elger, B. S. (2020). What is your definition of Big Data? Researchers' understanding of the phenomenon of the decade. *PLoS One, 15*(2), e0228987. DOI: 10.1371/journal.pone.0228987 PMID: 32097430

Fornell, C., & Larcker, D. F. (1981). Structural equation models with unobservable variables and measurement error: Algebra and statistics. *JMR, Journal of Marketing Research, 18*(3), 382–388. DOI: 10.1177/002224378101800313

Greenleaf, G. (2018). Global data privacy laws 2017: 120 national data privacy laws, including Indonesia and Turkey. *Privacy Laws & Business International Report, 145*, 10–13.

Gupta, A. K., & Goyal, H. (2021). Framework for implementing big data analytics in Indian manufacturing: ISM-MICMAC and Fuzzy-AHP approach. *Information Technology and Management, 22*(3), 207–229. DOI: 10.1007/s10799-021-00333-9

GVU. (1998). 10th WWW User Survey., [Web]. Graphic, Visualization, & Usability Center. Available: https://www.gvu.gatech.edu/user_surveys/survey-1998-10/ [20/05/1999].

Harris, L. C., & Goode, M. M. (2010). Online servicescapes, trust, and purchase intentions. *Journal of Services Marketing, 24*(3), 230–243. DOI: 10.1108/08876041011040631

Hassan, M. A., Shukur, Z., Hasan, M. K., & Al-Khaleefa, A. S. (2020). A review on electronic payments security. *Symmetry, 12*(8), 1344. DOI: 10.3390/sym12081344

Hoy, M. G., & Milne, G. (2010). Gender differences in privacy-related measures for young adult Facebook users. *Journal of Interactive Advertising, 10*(2), 28–45. DOI: 10.1080/15252019.2010.10722168

Indiani, N. L. P., & Fahik, G. A. (2020). Conversion of online purchase intention into actual purchase: The moderating role of transaction security and convenience. *Business: Theory and Practice*, *21*(1), 18–29. DOI: 10.3846/btp.2020.11346

Internet and Mobile Association of India, & Kantar. (2022). ICUBE 2022: India internet ecosystem. Internet and Mobile Association of India.

Khan, M. N., & Adil, M. (2013). Data analysis techniques in service quality literature: Essentials and advances. *Serbian Journal of Management*, *8*(1), 95–112.

Khan, S. (2022). Barriers of big data analytics for smart cities development: A context of emerging economies. *International Journal of Management Science and Engineering Management*, *17*(2), 123–131. DOI: 10.1080/17509653.2021.1997662

Kitchin, R. (2014). Big data, new epistemologies and paradigm shifts. *Big Data & Society*, *1*(1), 1–12. DOI: 10.1177/2053951714528481

Kshetri, N. (2014). Big data s impact on privacy, security and consumer welfare. *Telecommunications Policy*, *38*(11), 1134–1145. DOI: 10.1016/j.telpol.2014.10.002

Laudon, K., & Traver, C. G. (2009). *E-Commerce 2009: Business. Technology, and Society*. Prentice Hall.

Le, T. M., & Liaw, S. Y. (2017). Effects of pros and cons of applying big data analytics to consumers' responses in an e-commerce context. *Sustainability (Basel)*, *9*(5), 798. DOI: 10.3390/su9050798

Malhotra, N. K., & Dash, S. (2011). *Marketing Research: An Applied Orientation* (6th ed.). Pearson.

Malik, A., Hiekkanen, K., & Nieminen, M. (2016). *Privacy and trust in Facebook photo sharing: age and gender differences*. Program.

Martin, C. (2010). Social networking usage and grades among college students. A study conducted by the Whittmore School of Business and Economics University of New Hampshire.

Mikalef, P., Krogstie, J., Pappas, I. O., & Pavlou, P. (2020). Exploring the relationship between big data analytics capability and competitive performance: The mediating roles of dynamic and operational capabilities. *Information & Management*, *57*(2), 103169. DOI: 10.1016/j.im.2019.05.004

Mishra, A. A. (2010). Consumer decision-making styles and young-adult consumers: An Indian exploration. *Management & Marketing-Craiova*, (2), 229–246.

National Statistical Office. (2019). *Household social consumption on education in India (NSS 75th Round).* Ministry of Statistics and Programme Implementation, Government of India.

Ogbuke, N. J., Yusuf, Y. Y., Dharma, K., & Mercangoz, B. A. (2022). Big data supply chain analytics: Ethical, privacy and security challenges posed to business, industries and society. *Production Planning and Control, 33*(2-3), 123–137. DOI: 10.1080/09537287.2020.1810764

Patil, H. K., & Seshadri, R. (2014, June). Big data security and privacy issues in healthcare. In 2014 IEEE international congress on big data (pp. 762-765). IEEE.

Rizwan, A., Zoha, A., Zhang, R., Ahmad, W., Arshad, K., Ali, N. A., & Abbasi, Q. H. (2018). A review on the role of nano-communication in future healthcare systems: A big data analytics perspective. *IEEE Access : Practical Innovations, Open Solutions, 6*, 41903–41920. DOI: 10.1109/ACCESS.2018.2859340

Safa, N. S., & Von Solms, R. (2016). An information security knowledge sharing model in organizations. *Computers in Human Behavior, 57*, 442–451. DOI: 10.1016/j.chb.2015.12.037

Saggi, M. K., & Jain, S. (2018). A survey towards an integration of big data analytics to big insights for value-creation. *Information Processing & Management, 54*(5), 758–790. DOI: 10.1016/j.ipm.2018.01.010

Sarkar, M., & Banerjee, S. (2016). Exploring social network privacy measurement using fuzzy vector commitment. *Intelligent Decision Technologies, 10*(3), 285–297. DOI: 10.3233/IDT-160256

Seng, S., Al-Ameen, M. N., & Wright, M. (2021). A look into user privacy andthird-party applications in Facebook. *Information and Computer Security, 29*(2), 283–313.

Shergill, G. S., & Chen, Z. (2005). Web-based shopping: Consumers' Attitudes towards online shopping in New Zealand. *Journal of Electronic Commerce Research, 6*(2), 78.

Strzelecki, A., & Rizun, M. (2022). Consumers' change in trust and security after a personal data breach in online shopping. *Sustainability (Basel), 14*(10), 5866. DOI: 10.3390/su14105866

Telecom Regulatory Authority of India. (2023). *The Indian telecom services performance indicators*. Government of India.

Tifferet, S. (2019). Gender differences in privacy tendencies on social network sites: A meta-analysis. *Computers in Human Behavior, 93*, 1–12. DOI: 10.1016/j.chb.2018.11.046

Wamba, S. F., Gunasekaran, A., Akter, S., Ren, S., Dubey, R., & Childe, S. J. (2020). Big data analytics and firm performance: Effects of dynamic capabilities. *Journal of Business Research, 131*, 336–348.

Zuboff, S. (2019). *The age of surveillance capitalism: The fight for a human future at the new frontier of power*. PublicAffairs.

Chapter 6
Transparency-by-Design in Smart City Crowd Monitoring:
A Privacy-Preserving Wi-Fi Analytics Framework for Tourism and Urban Management

Ariya Namvong
http://orcid.org/0000-0001-5059-3252
Khon Kaen University, Thailand

Thalerngsak Wiangwiset
http://orcid.org/0000-0003-2384-345X
National Telecom Public Company Limited, Thailand

ABSTRACT

Smart city initiatives increasingly rely on data-driven infrastructures to support urban governance, tourism management, and public service delivery. However, data collection in public spaces continues to raise concerns regarding privacy, accountability, and public trust. Although principles such as consent, transparency, and legal compliance are widely endorsed, they are often implemented in fragmented ways, resulting in systems that may be legally defensible yet socially contested. This chapter proposes an integrated governance approach for smart city crowd monitoring through the CCTC framework, which embeds consent, control, transparency, and compliance by design across the data lifecycle. Governance is conceptualized as a structural architecture aligning legitimacy, enforceable boundaries, accountability, and ethical compliance. The framework is illustrated through

DOI: 10.4018/979-8-2600-1433-2.ch006

a municipal Wi-Fi analytics case study in Sri Chiang Mai, Thailand, demonstrating how transparency-by-design and privacy-preserving analytics can support tourism and urban management while sustaining public trust.

INTRODUCTION

Smart city initiatives increasingly rely on data-driven infrastructure to support urban governance, tourism management, and public service delivery. Systems for crowd monitoring, mobility analysis, and urban analytics are now routinely deployed in public and semi-public spaces as part of large-scale urban infrastructure. While these systems promise efficiency, safety, and improved service delivery, their expansion has intensified concerns regarding privacy, transparency, accountability, and public trust, particularly where data collection occurs continuously and without direct interaction or meaningful public understanding (Jin & Wang, 2025; Organisation for Economic Co-operation and Development, 2023).

Although principles such as consent, transparency, accountability, and legal compliance are widely endorsed in smart city policy and academic discourse, their implementation remains uneven. Empirical and governance-oriented studies show that many smart city systems satisfy formal legal or technical requirements while failing to address deeper issues of legitimacy, citizen acceptance, and democratic accountability (Organisation for Economic Co-operation and Development, 2023; van Twist et al., 2023). Transparency is frequently treated as a post hoc disclosure exercise rather than as an operational governance function, and experimental evidence demonstrates that disclosure alone does not guarantee understanding or trust. Instead, how information is designed and presented significantly shapes perceptions of intrusiveness and legitimacy (Magrizos et al., 2026; Waclawek et al., 2024).

Ethical scholarship further cautions that data-driven smart city interventions may function, intentionally or not, as forms of experimentation on urban populations. When systems operate in public space without explicit consent mechanisms, opportunities for contestation, or ongoing ethical oversight, citizens risk being treated as passive subjects rather than autonomous participants (Zimmermann, 2023). Legal compliance alone is insufficient to address these concerns, as regulatory frameworks often struggle to reconcile continuous urban data collection with consent-based data protection regimes (Jin & Wang, 2025). Taken together, this body of research indicates that the core governance challenge lies not in the absence of principles, but in weak integration and enforceability. Consent without control becomes symbolic; transparency without intelligibility fails to build trust; and compliance framed as a checklist cannot address evolving ethical and institutional risks (Zimmermann, 2023).

Against this backdrop, this chapter pursues three interrelated objectives. First, it explains how transparency and trust can be embedded in the data lifecycle of smart city systems through integrated governance arrangements rather than treated as external add-ons. Second, it presents a privacy-preserving Wi-Fi analytics approach for crowd monitoring in the context of tourism and urban management, demonstrating how actionable insights can be generated without relying on passive or intrusive data collection practices. Third, it proposes the CCTC (Consent–Control–Transparency–Compliance) framework as a governance-by-design architecture capable of strengthening institutional accountability and sustaining public trust in public-space data systems. The framework is examined through an experience-based municipal case study of a smart city Wi-Fi analytics deployment in Sri Chiang Mai, Thailand. The remainder of the chapter reviews relevant governance foundations, presents the CCTC framework, analyzes its enactment in practice, and concludes with reflections on governance trade-offs and future research directions.

LITERATURE REVIEW AND GOVERNANCE FOUNDATIONS

Consent Challenges in Smart City Data Collection

Consent has long been recognized as a foundational principle of ethical and lawful data governance, serving to protect individual autonomy and legitimize data processing practices. In smart city contexts, however, the conditions under which consent is traditionally understood are fundamentally altered. Urban data collection is increasingly embedded in large-scale, continuous infrastructure operating across public and semi-public spaces, making meaningful consent structurally difficult rather than merely procedurally complex.

A central challenge arises from the pervasive and often invisible nature of smart city data infrastructure. Sensors, connectivity networks, and analytical systems are frequently integrated into the built environment in ways that are effectively hidden from everyday perception. As a result, individuals may be subject to data processing without clear awareness, realistic opportunities for choice, or practical mechanisms for refusal. Ethical scholarship notes that when data-driven systems are embedded in everyday urban environments, conventional assumptions about informed and voluntary participation begin to break down, creating persistent tension between urban functionality and the protection of individual autonomy in public space (Novaes, 2021; Zimmermann, 2023).

This tension is reinforced by the mismatch between traditional notice-and-consent models and the operational characteristics of smart city systems. Consent mechanisms were originally designed for discrete, transactional interactions, whereas smart city infrastructure operates continuously and ubiquitously. In public space, meaningful opt-out options are often unavailable or socially costly, causing consent to function as a nominal formality rather than a substantive safeguard (Novaes, 2021). The voluntariness that consent is presumed to guarantee is therefore structurally undermined.

Scholars have consequently criticized reliance on implied or passive consent in urban data systems. Practices that infer consent from physical presence or device emissions blur the boundary between active participation and mere co-existence in public environments (van Zoonen, 2020). Because public spaces are not optional environments, requiring individuals to trade privacy for mobility, access to services, or civic participation raises significant ethical concerns. Over time, such practices risk normalizing data extraction that is difficult to contest and eroding public trust.

Notice-based consent mechanisms face additional limitations in complex smart city data ecosystems. Formal notices, privacy policies, and legal documentation are often insufficient to ensure meaningful understanding, particularly when data are aggregated, repurposed, or shared across multiple actors and lifecycle stages. Individuals rarely possess the time, expertise, or contextual knowledge needed to assess downstream data uses, weakening the validity of consent when it is treated primarily as a compliance requirement rather than as a design concern (Felzmann et al., 2020).

These challenges are compounded by institutional fragmentation. Smart city data ecosystems typically involve municipalities, infrastructure operators, technology providers, and research institutions operating under distinct mandates and accountability structures. Responsibility for consent is therefore diffused, making it difficult to attribute accountability when consent boundaries are exceeded or data are reused beyond their declared purposes. In practice, many consent frameworks implicitly rely on continuous individual vigilance, assuming that citizens can monitor complex data flows and intervene when preferences are violated. In data-intensive urban environments characterized by layered value chains and ongoing repurposing, this assumption is unrealistic and shifts governance burdens onto individuals, weakening both democratic accountability and the practical effectiveness of consent (König, 2021).

Taken together, these insights indicate that consent in smart city contexts cannot function as a one-time procedural safeguard. Instead, it must be understood as a governance condition that depends on system design, institutional responsibility, and enforceable constraints across the data lifecycle. Without such structural support, consent risks becoming symbolic, fragile, and detached from the realities of data-driven urban governance.

Control and Security in Smart City Data Governance

Control represents a central yet persistently underdeveloped dimension of smart city data governance. While many smart city initiatives articulate commitments to ethical principles, privacy protection, or legal compliance, these commitments frequently remain at the level of policy statements rather than being translated into enforceable governance mechanisms. As a result, public authorities often lack effective means to constrain how data are collected, processed, reused, and retained within complex urban data ecosystems.

A key challenge concerns governance across the data lifecycle. Smart city data typically pass through multiple stages—collection, storage, processing, aggregation, sharing, and retention—creating opportunities for downstream use that may diverge from original purposes. Research indicates that democratic control is frequently weakened when data are treated primarily as assets for administrative efficiency or innovation rather than as objects of public governance. Over time, economic and operational imperatives may overshadow initial governance commitments, leading to gradual erosion of public control over urban data practices (Franke & Gailhofer, 2021). Effective control therefore must extend beyond initial collection to encompass downstream processing, reuse, and deletion if governance commitments are to remain meaningful.

Institutional fragmentation further complicates control in smart city data ecosystems. Such systems rarely involve a single governing actor; instead, municipalities, infrastructure providers, technology vendors, and research institutions operate under distinct mandates and incentives. When decision rights over data access, modification, and reuse are unclear, control becomes diffused and accountability weakened. Ambiguity regarding who is authorized to make governance decisions increases the risk of informal practices and undermines the ability to verify whether data use aligns with declared purposes (König, 2021). In this sense, control failures reflect institutional design weaknesses as much as technical shortcomings.

Security mechanisms constitute a critical component of governance control, yet they are often treated as isolated technical safeguards. Measures such as access restrictions, encryption, and system hardening are frequently implemented to mitigate external cyber threats, while remaining weakly integrated with broader governance objectives such as purpose limitation, accountability, and lifecycle oversight. Research on smart city security governance shows that this separation limits the ability of security measures to prevent internal misuse, unauthorized repurposing, or governance drift over time (Ismagilova et al., 2022). When security is approached primarily as a technical problem rather than as a governance function, control failures may emerge through routine operational practices rather than through exceptional incidents.

These challenges are compounded by growing cybersecurity risks associated with interconnected smart city infrastructure. Centralized data platforms and expanded attack surfaces heighten exposure to both external attacks and internal misuse. Empirical studies indicate that vulnerabilities are closely linked to weaknesses in institutional coordination, lifecycle-based control, and governance oversight rather than to technical deficiencies alone (Demertzi et al., 2023). This underscores the importance of security-by-design approaches that are embedded within governance structures rather than layered onto systems post hoc.

Importantly, effective control also has a communicative dimension. Research on crowd-counting technologies suggests that public acceptance depends not only on the existence of safeguards but on citizens' understanding of how data practices are bounded and governed. Explanations that foreground purpose limitation and governance constraints foster higher levels of trust and legitimacy than purely technical descriptions (Waclawek et al., 2024). Control mechanisms therefore operate both as internal enforcement tools and as external signals of responsible governance.

Taken together, these insights indicate that control in smart city governance cannot be reduced to technical security measures or internal administrative procedures. Instead, control must be understood as a multi-layered governance function integrating institutional authority, lifecycle-based data management, and security-by-design mechanisms. Without such integration, governance commitments remain fragile and difficult to enforce within complex, multi-actor urban data ecosystems.

Transparency and Public Accountability

Transparency is widely promoted as a foundational principle of smart city governance, yet its practical implementation frequently falls short of supporting meaningful public accountability. In many initiatives, transparency is interpreted narrowly as the disclosure of policy documents, privacy notices, or technical descriptions. While such practices may satisfy formal or regulatory expectations, they often fail to render complex data practices intelligible to affected publics or to enable informed scrutiny of how data-driven systems shape public decision-making. As a result, transparency risks functioning as a symbolic requirement rather than as an effective governance mechanism.

A core limitation of prevailing transparency practices lies in their document-centric orientation. Smart city systems operate through continuous data flows, automated processing, and evolving analytical uses, yet transparency is often delivered through static disclosures detached from system operation. Governance and ethics scholarship emphasizes that transparency cannot be reduced to information availability alone but must be understood as a relational and interpretive condition shaped by how information is presented, contextualized, and understood by its audience (Cottrill et al., 2020; Felzmann et al., 2020). When transparency mechanisms fail to align with operational realities, they provide visibility without intelligibility and limit their contribution to accountability.

Recent empirical evidence reinforces the importance of designing transparency rather than merely declaring it. Experimental research demonstrates that the visual and structural presentation of privacy information significantly influences user trust and perceptions of intrusiveness. Simplified and visualized representations of data practices have been shown to improve comprehension and foster trust more effectively than text-based policies alone (Magrizos et al., 2026). Although such studies are often situated in private-sector contexts, they underscore a broader governance insight relevant to smart cities: transparency is not neutral in form, and its design directly affects whether it supports understanding, legitimacy, and trust.

Transparency challenges are further intensified by the increasing use of algorithmic and analytical systems in urban governance. As data-driven decision-making becomes embedded in public administration, opacity may arise at multiple levels, including data selection, aggregation logic, and interpretive assumptions. Empirical studies indicate that such opacity undermines public trust, particularly when individuals cannot understand how data-driven insights influence collective outcomes or public interventions (Jacobs et al., 2020). Transparency must therefore illuminate governance purposes and decision rationales, not merely technical components or datasets.

Crucially, transparency should not be equated with unrestricted openness. Governance scholarship cautions that indiscriminate disclosure may introduce new risks, including privacy breaches, misinterpretation, or secondary misuse. Effective transparency depends on selective visibility, contextual explanation, and alignment with governance objectives rather than raw data exposure (Jacobs et al., 2022). Taken together, these insights suggest that transparency in smart city governance is best understood as a design-oriented governance function that makes data practices observable and contestable without amplifying surveillance or compromising individual autonomy.

Legal, Ethical, and Institutional Compliance

Compliance is a core requirement in smart city data governance, yet it is often interpreted narrowly as adherence to legal provisions or regulatory checklists. While such approaches may satisfy minimum statutory obligations, they are frequently insufficient to address the governance challenges posed by large-scale and continuous data processing in public and semi-public spaces. Smart city systems operate at the intersection of law, ethics, and public administration, where legitimacy depends not only on formal legality but also on institutional capacity to govern data use in line with public values and accountability expectations (Jin & Wang, 2025; OECD, 2023).

From a legal perspective, smart city data practices are subject to personal data protection laws, cybersecurity regulations, and public-sector accountability requirements. Core principles such as purpose limitation, data minimization, security safeguards, and organizational responsibility are widely embedded in contemporary regulatory frameworks. However, regulatory scholarship consistently shows that formal legal compliance does not necessarily translate into social acceptance or ethical legitimacy, particularly in contexts where individuals have limited ability to avoid data collection or meaningfully exercise choice. As a result, smart city systems may remain publicly contested despite operating within legal boundaries (Jin & Wang, 2025).

Policy-oriented governance research emphasizes that compliance becomes effective only when legal requirements are integrated into institutional arrangements and operational governance practices. Rather than treating data protection as an external constraint, governance structures must align regulatory principles with how data are collected, processed, and used across the data lifecycle. Coordination, stewardship, and adaptive oversight are increasingly recognized as essential conditions for sustaining responsible data use and public legitimacy in smart city development (OECD, 2023).

Ethical considerations further extend the scope of compliance beyond formal legality. Ethical frameworks for big data and smart cities emphasize that data-driven urban systems may produce harms, including the normalization of surveillance, disproportionate monitoring, and the erosion of individual autonomy, even when such systems formally comply with existing legal requirements. From this perspective, ethical compliance requires public-sector data systems to be justified not only by efficiency or innovation gains, but also by proportionality, public interest, and democratic norms. Institutionalized ethical oversight mechanisms, including ethics committees and review boards, play a critical role in identifying risks and assessing societal impacts that legal compliance alone may fail to capture (Chang, 2021).

Governance scholarship further conceptualizes compliance as a form of institutional steering rather than mere conformity. Decisions about data access, use, and control are inherently normative, shaping power relations, policy priorities, and whose interests are ultimately served by data-driven systems. Effective compliance therefore depends on governance arrangements capable of managing trade-offs between innovation, market-driven optimization, and public-interest objectives such as sustainability and democratic accountability (Franke & Gailhofer, 2021).

Institutional complexity adds further challenges. Smart city ecosystems typically involve municipalities, infrastructure operators, technology vendors, and research institutions operating under distinct mandates and accountability structures. When compliance responsibilities are fragmented or ambiguously assigned, governance gaps emerge and accountability weakens. Research on citizen-centered data governance underscores the importance of clearly defined institutional roles, decision rights, and documentation practices to ensure that compliance obligations remain enforceable rather than symbolic (König, 2021).

Finally, empirical evidence demonstrates the limitations of document-centric compliance models in practice. Research on personal data protection compliance indicates persistent gaps between formal requirements, including the existence of privacy policies, and their actual implementation within organizational processes. In many cases, compliance becomes a documentation exercise, while user rights and effective control mechanisms remain weak or inconsistently enforced (Chatsuwan et al., 2023).

Taken together, these insights indicate that compliance in smart city data governance should be understood as a continuous, institutionally grounded, and design-oriented governance function. Effective compliance integrates legal obligations, ethical oversight, and institutional accountability into system architecture and operational workflows, providing a foundation for legitimate, enforceable, and publicly credible data governance.

Trust, Social Acceptance, and Governance Integration

Public trust and social acceptance are increasingly recognized as decisive factors in the success or failure of smart city initiatives. While data-driven technologies are often promoted for their potential to enhance efficiency and evidence-based decision-making, numerous deployments have encountered resistance when governance arrangements fail to align with public expectations and democratic norms. Empirical research consistently demonstrates that trust in smart city systems cannot be assumed as an automatic outcome of technological deployment; rather, it must be actively constructed through governance practices that are credible and intelligible to affected publics (Jacobs et al., 2020).

A central insight in the smart city governance literature is that technological performance alone is insufficient to generate trust. Citizens may acknowledge functional benefits while simultaneously expressing concerns about surveillance, loss of control, and potential misuse of data. Trust is therefore better understood as a relational and institutional condition shaped by perceptions of legitimacy, accountability, and governance integrity, rather than by system efficiency or analytical sophistication alone (Cole & Tran, 2022). Where governance arrangements are opaque, fragmented, or weakly enforced, skepticism is likely to persist even when systems formally comply with legal or procedural requirements.

Research on social acceptance further highlights the role of procedural legitimacy. Individuals are more likely to accept data-driven systems when decisions about data collection and use are perceived as justified, proportionate, and subject to meaningful oversight. Conversely, acceptance declines when consent mechanisms are unclear, purposes remain ambiguous, or affected publics feel excluded from governance processes. Evidence from contested smart city projects suggests that resistance often reflects perceived governance deficiencies rather than opposition to technology itself (Shimizu et al., 2022).

Institutional coherence also plays a critical role in shaping trust. Smart city initiatives typically involve multiple public, private, and academic actors operating under distinct mandates. When roles, responsibilities, and decision-making authority are unclear, accountability becomes diffused and governance claims lose credibility. Systematic reviews of smart city discontent indicate that citizen dissatisfaction more frequently arises from fragmented governance structures and weak oversight mechanisms than from specific technical features of deployed systems (van Twist et al., 2023).

Beyond formal governance structures, visibility of governance practices is essential for sustaining trust. Studies of public-space sensing and crowd-counting technologies show that public acceptance is strengthened when data collection boundaries, purposes, and accountability arrangements are clearly explained in accessible terms. Explanatory approaches that emphasize why data are collected, how their use is bounded, and who is responsible are more effective in fostering trust than purely technical descriptions of system functionality (Waclawek et al., 2024). Recent governance-oriented scholarship further conceptualizes trust not as an attitudinal precondition, but as an outcome of system-level design and enforceable governance arrangements. Trust emerges when data ecosystems embed stable rules for access, use, and oversight, supported by mechanisms for accountability and auditability. From this perspective, transparency or consent alone is insufficient unless governance capacities exist to ensure that commitments are respected in practice (Lomotey et al., 2022).

Taken together, these insights indicate that trust and social acceptance in smart city environments are emergent properties of integrated governance rather than products of communication strategies or public relations efforts. Trust is sustained when governance arrangements render data practices predictable, contestable, and institutionally accountable. This understanding provides a conceptual bridge to the CCTC framework, which structures consent, control, transparency, and compliance as mutually reinforcing governance functions embedded into system design and institutional practice.

Background Synthesis: From Fragmented Principles to Integrated Governance

Taken together, the preceding analysis reveals a consistent pattern in the smart city governance literature: core principles such as consent, control, transparency, compliance, and trust are widely endorsed, yet frequently operationalized in fragmented and symbolic ways. When treated as standalone safeguards, these principles lose much of their practical effectiveness.

Research on consent highlights the structural limits of notice-based models in public and semi-public spaces, where meaningful choice and refusal are often impractical. Without enforceable constraints on downstream data use and clear institutional accountability, consent risks becoming procedural rather than substantive.

Similarly, studies on control and security show that governance commitments remain weak when they are not embedded across the data lifecycle. Technical safeguards alone cannot prevent governance drift when institutional authority is fragmented and decision rights remain unclear.

Transparency scholarship further demonstrates that document-centric disclosure provides visibility without intelligibility. When transparency mechanisms are detached from system operation and public interpretation, they fail to support accountability or informed contestation.

Compliance-oriented research reinforces these concerns, showing that legal conformity alone does not secure ethical legitimacy or social acceptance. Compliance becomes fragile when reduced to documentation rather than integrated into system design, organizational roles, and operational workflows.

Across these dimensions, trust emerges not as a standalone objective but as an outcome of governance integration. When consent, control, transparency, and compliance are weakly aligned, trust erodes, even in technically sophisticated systems. Conversely, trust is strengthened when governance arrangements render data practices predictable, bounded, and accountable.

These findings suggest that the central challenge in smart city data governance lies not in the absence of principles, but in their weak integration. Addressing this gap requires an integrated governance framework that aligns these principles as mutually reinforcing components of system design and institutional practice.

THE CCTC FRAMEWORK

Framework Introduction: Positioning CCTC as an Integrated Governance Architecture

Responding to the governance gap identified above, this chapter introduces the CCTC framework as an integrated governance architecture for smart city data ecosystems. Rather than proposing new norms, CCTC operationalizes existing principles by structuring Consent, Control, Transparency, and Compliance as interdependent governance functions embedded in system design and institutional practice.

CCTC departs from checklist-based governance by adopting a design-oriented perspective. Governance is treated not as a post hoc constraint, but as a structural feature of technical architectures, organizational roles, and operational workflows. Functional integration is central to the framework: each pillar reinforces the others, reducing the risk that governance measures become symbolic or detached from practice.

Within the framework, Consent establishes legitimate participation boundaries; Control enforces those boundaries across the data lifecycle; Transparency renders governance practices intelligible and contestable; and Compliance ensures sustained alignment with legal, ethical, and institutional obligations. Trust is not assumed as an input but understood as an emergent outcome of this integrated governance structure.

The following sections elaborate each pillar of the CCTC framework, demonstrating how they function individually and collectively as components of an integrated governance architecture for smart city data systems.

Positioning CCTC Among Existing Governance Frameworks

The CCTC framework is built upon but also departs from several established governance approaches in smart city and data ethics scholarship. Existing models such as Privacy-by-Design (PbD) emphasize embedding privacy safeguards into technical architecture, particularly through data minimization, purpose limitation, and security controls. While PbD provides essential technical and regulatory guidance, it often centers primarily on privacy protection rather than on broader institutional integration across consent, transparency, and compliance functions.

Similarly, transparency toolkits and transparency-by-design approaches focus on improving intelligibility and communication of data practices, often through dashboards, visualization strategies, and disclosure mechanisms. These models strengthen accountability and public understanding but may not systematically address lifecycle-based control or enforceable institutional responsibilities across multiple actors.

Emerging governance concepts such as data trusts and citizen-centered data governance emphasize stewardship, accountability, and public value orientation. These frameworks highlight institutional responsibility and participatory governance but may not always specify how consent boundaries, technical control mechanisms, and compliance processes interact within system architecture.

The distinct contribution of CCTC lies in its explicit integration of Consent, Control, Transparency, and Compliance as mutually reinforcing governance functions embedded throughout the data lifecycle. Instead of prioritizing a single normative pillar, such as privacy, openness, or stewardship, the framework conceptualizes these principles as components of an interdependent governance architecture. Consent defines participation boundaries; control enforces those boundaries; transparency renders them intelligible and contestable; and compliance stabilizes them institutionally over time. In this sense, CCTC is not a replacement for existing models but a synthesis that operationalizes their core insights into a coherent and enforceable governance-by-design structure. As illustrated in Figure 1, the CCTC framework embeds governance functions directly in the data lifecycle rather than treating them as post hoc compliance mechanisms.

Figure 1. The CCTC governance architecture. The model illustrates the integration of consent, control, transparency, and compliance across the smart city data lifecycle, with trust emerging from enforceable governance alignment

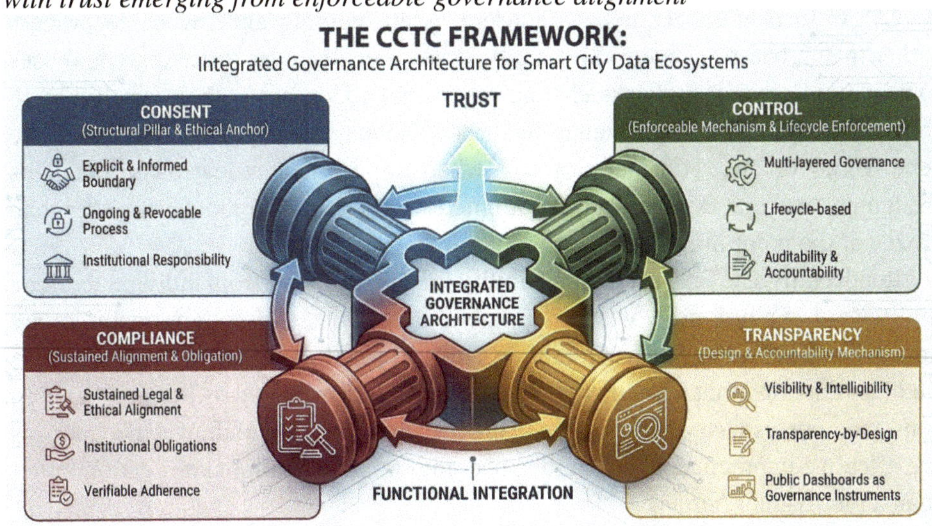

Consent as a Structural Governance Pillar

Within the CCTC framework, consent is conceptualized as a structural pillar of governance rather than a procedural or symbolic requirement. Consent is reframed as a system-level condition that determines whether data practices are legitimate, contestable, and socially acceptable. Rather than functioning as a formal checkbox or legal disclaimer, consent defines the ethical boundary of data inclusion within smart city data ecosystems.

At its core, the CCTC framework adopts a consent-first orientation. Consent is treated as a prerequisite for data inclusion, not as a post hoc justification for data processing. This approach rejects models in which mere presence in public space or passive exposure to digital infrastructure is interpreted as agreement. Instead, CCTC draws a clear distinction between physical presence and voluntary participation, particularly in public-space data systems where avoidance may be impractical or impossible.

A defining feature of consent within CCTC is its explicit and informed nature. Consent must be expressed through clear affirmative action and supported by intelligible information regarding data collection, purpose, retention, and use. Awareness alone is insufficient; information must be accessible and meaningful to non-expert audiences. Consent within CCTC therefore emphasizes understanding, agency, and legitimacy rather than formal acknowledgment.

CCTC further conceptualizes consent as an ongoing and revocable process rather than a one-time event. Smart city systems evolve over time, analytical uses expand, and governance risks change accordingly. Consent is therefore linked to the data lifecycle: material changes in purpose, scope, or analytical function require renewed governance consideration and, where appropriate, renewed consent. This design ensures that consent remains aligned with actual data practices rather than frozen at the point of initial collection.

Importantly, CCTC shifts responsibility for consent away from individuals alone and toward institutional governance. Public authorities and system operators are accountable for designing, maintaining, and enforcing consent mechanisms. This includes ensuring that non-consenting individuals are excluded by design, that consent states are respected in downstream processing, and that withdrawal mechanisms are effective in practice. Consent thus becomes an organizational obligation rather than an individual burden.

Within the CCTC framework, consent functions as the ethical and legitimacy anchor that shapes subsequent governance pillars. Control enforces consent conditions, transparency makes consent practices visible and intelligible, and compliance ensures sustained legal and ethical alignment. In this way, consent is not isolated as a standalone requirement but structurally embedded within an integrated governance architecture.

Control as an Enforceable Governance Mechanism

Within the CCTC framework, control functions as the enforceable governance mechanism that translates consent from a normative commitment into an operational reality. While consent establishes the legitimacy of participation, control ensures that agreed boundaries are respected throughout the data lifecycle. Without effective control, consent risks becoming symbolic; with control, governance commitments become technically and institutionally enforceable.

CCTC conceptualizes control as a multi-layered governance function integrating institutional authority, data management rules, and security safeguards. Control is not limited to technical access restrictions or internal administrative procedures. Instead, it encompasses the structured allocation of decision rights over data collection, processing, access, sharing, and reuse. Clearly defining who may authorize data use and under what conditions helps prevent the informal expansion of scope driven by convenience, vendor defaults, or opportunistic analytical practices.

A central design principle within CCTC is lifecycle-based control. Governance does not end once data are collected; it extends across storage, analysis, reuse, retention, and deletion. Purpose binding, retention limits, and reuse restrictions are embedded into system workflows, ensuring that data remain aligned with the consent conditions under which they were obtained. This lifecycle orientation is essential for preventing gradual shifts in data use that undermine legitimacy over time.

Security control constitutes a critical subset of governance control within CCTC. Technical safeguards, such as role-based access control, encryption of data at rest and in transit, and secure infrastructure management, are treated as governance instruments rather than purely technical features. By embedding constraints within system architecture, security controls help ensure that governance rules cannot be bypassed without detection, authorization, or traceability.

Auditability is another defining element of control in CCTC. Systems are designed to generate verifiable records of data access, processing actions, and governance decisions. Logging, documentation, and traceable workflows enable internal oversight, external review, and institutional learning over time. Control thus shifts governance from reliance on trust-based assumptions toward evidence-based accountability.

Importantly, CCTC frames control as an institutional responsibility. Public authorities retain accountability for ensuring that control mechanisms are implemented, monitored, and enforced, even when technical operations are delegated to infrastructure providers or vendors. This prevents the silent transfer of governance authority to technical actors and preserves democratic accountability within public-sector data systems.

Within the CCTC architecture, control stabilizes governance by enforcing consent conditions, supporting transparency, and enabling verifiable compliance. It is the pillar that ensures smart city data systems operate within clearly defined, enforceable, and publicly accountable boundaries.

Transparency as a Design and Accountability Mechanism

Within the CCTC framework, transparency functions as the enabling mechanism that makes consent, control, and compliance visible, intelligible, and contestable. While control enforces governance rules, transparency ensures that those rules can be understood, examined, and evaluated by relevant stakeholders. In this sense, transparency is not an optional communication practice but a structural condition for accountability and public legitimacy.

CCTC adopts a transparency-by-design orientation, rejecting approaches that treat transparency as post hoc disclosure or reactive reporting. Smart city systems often operate through complex, distributed, and automated processes that remain largely invisible to affected publics. Transparency must therefore be embedded in system architecture, governance workflows, and public interfaces from the outset, rather than added after deployment or in response to controversy.

Transparency within CCTC operates across multiple governance layers. At the data collection level, it requires visibility of sensing infrastructures, data sources, and declared purposes. At the processing and analytics level, it involves intelligibility of how data are transformed, aggregated, or analyzed, including the role of automated or algorithmic components. At the governance level, transparency encompasses clarity regarding institutional roles, decision rights, and oversight mechanisms. At the outcome level, it addresses how data-informed insights are used in policy decisions or operational interventions.

A defining feature of CCTC is the treatment of public dashboards as governance instruments rather than mere visualization tools. Dashboards translate complex data practices into accessible representations that support understanding without exposing individual-level data. Importantly, dashboard design within CCTC is constrained by consent conditions and control rules. Aggregation thresholds, temporal smoothing, and privacy-preserving transformations ensure that transparency does not undermine autonomy or security.

CCTC further distinguishes between transparency and indiscriminate openness. Open data is governed rather than automatic. Datasets are released in aggregated, contextualized, and purpose-aligned forms, accompanied by explanatory metadata and governance narratives. This approach avoids framing transparency and privacy as opposing values by positioning openness as a controlled and accountable practice.

Transparency also supports compliance verification. Without visibility, compliance claims remain difficult to substantiate. By making governance commitments observable through dashboards, documentation, and structured public reporting, CCTC enables scrutiny by regulators, civil society actors, and citizens.

Within the CCTC architecture, transparency connects consent, control, and compliance into a coherent governance system. It enables meaningful consent, renders control observable, and transforms compliance from assertion into demonstrable practice.

Compliance as a Continuous Governance Function

Within the CCTC framework, compliance is conceptualized as a continuous and verifiable governance function rather than a terminal verification step. Traditional smart city practices often approach compliance as an ex-post exercise, assessing whether systems meet formal legal requirements after deployment. CCTC rejects this model and instead embeds compliance by design, ensuring that legal, ethical, and public-sector obligations actively shape system architecture, operational workflows, and institutional oversight from the outset.

A core premise of CCTC is that legal compliance alone is insufficient to secure public legitimacy. While data protection and cybersecurity laws provide necessary regulatory baselines, compliance that is limited to formal legality may still leave data practices socially contested or ethically problematic. CCTC therefore treats compliance as a multi-layered alignment process that integrates legal requirements, ethical principles, and public-interest policy commitments into a coherent governance structure.

CCTC adopts a risk-based approach to compliance. Rather than applying uniform safeguards across all use cases, compliance obligations are calibrated to data sensitivity, scale of deployment, and potential impact on individuals and communities. Higher-risk applications—such as large-scale monitoring in public spaces or automated decision-support systems—trigger enhanced governance measures, including stricter documentation, review procedures, and oversight mechanisms. This proportionality ensures that compliance remains effective without unnecessarily constraining lower-risk innovation.

Documentation and traceability are central to compliance within CCTC. Governance decisions, consent conditions, control rules, and transparency measures are recorded in structured and auditable forms. This documentation provides evidence of compliance over time, transforming compliance from a declarative claim into a demonstrable and reviewable outcome. Traceability supports both external scrutiny and internal accountability, enabling institutions to explain and justify data practices when challenged.

Importantly, CCTC explicitly incorporates ethical compliance alongside legal compliance. Ethical review is treated as an integral component of governance rather than an optional or one-time assessment. Ethical oversight mechanisms—such as ethics committees, impact assessments, and escalation pathways—are embedded into institutional processes to evaluate proportionality, fairness, necessity, and potential societal harm. This ensures that data practices remain aligned with public values even when they are legally permissible.

Compliance within CCTC is adaptive rather than static. As systems evolve, data uses expand, and social expectations shift, compliance mechanisms are periodically revisited through structured review and reassessment. This continuous orientation guards against governance drift and ensures sustained alignment with both legal standards and ethical commitments over the system lifecycle.

Within the CCTC architecture, compliance stabilizes the framework. Consent establishes legitimacy, control enforces boundaries, transparency renders practices observable, and compliance ensures that alignment with law, ethics, and public responsibility is continuous, verifiable, and institutionally accountable.

Integrated Governance and Framework Conclusion

The CCTC framework conceptualizes Consent, Control, Transparency, and Compliance as an integrated governance architecture rather than as standalone safeguards. A core insight of the framework is that governance failures in smart city systems rarely arise from the absence of principles, but from weak integration among them. When these elements operate in isolation, legitimacy, accountability, and public trust are difficult to sustain.

By adopting a governance-by-design perspective, CCTC reframes governance as a system-level design challenge embedded in technical architecture, institutional roles, and operational practice. The framework is explicitly oriented toward public-sector smart city contexts, where participation is often unavoidable and democratic accountability is essential. Accordingly, constraints such as explicit consent, data minimization, and aggregation are treated as governance choices rather than technical limitations.

Rather than resolving all ethical or political tensions, CCTC provides a structured lens for translating governance principles into practice under real institutional conditions. The following case study examines how this integrated governance architecture was enacted within a municipal smart city deployment, highlighting how governance commitments shaped concrete design decisions and accepted trade-offs.

Methodological Approach

This chapter adopts a conceptual and practice-informed methodological approach that integrates normative governance analysis with an experience-based municipal case study. Rather than conducting a quantitative or experimental evaluation, the chapter aims to develop and operationalize an integrated governance framework for smart city data ecosystems and to illustrate its practical enactment within a real institutional context.

The analytical component of the chapter draws on recent literature in smart city governance, data ethics, transparency-by-design, and public trust. Through a structured synthesis of these strands, the chapter identifies a persistent governance gap: the fragmentation of consent, control, transparency, and compliance in public-space data systems. The CCTC framework is developed as a design-oriented governance architecture that integrates these principles across the data lifecycle.

To ground the framework in practice, the chapter examines the deployment of a municipal public Wi-Fi analytics system in Sri Chiang Mai, Thailand. The case study is based on documented system design decisions, institutional governance arrangements, ethical review processes, and operational experience associated with the project. The analysis focuses on how governance principles shaped concrete technical and organizational choices, including opt-in participation, lifecycle-based data control, aggregation strategies, and public transparency mechanisms.

As a single-case, experience-based study, the chapter does not aim to provide statistical generalization. Instead, it offers analytical generalization by demonstrating how governance-by-design can be enacted under specific institutional and regulatory conditions. The case is used to examine governance trade-offs, constraints, and decision rationales rather than to evaluate system performance metrics.

CASE STUDY

Context, Governance Setting, and Policy-to-Design: Sri Chiang Mai Smart City

The Sri Chiang Mai Smart City initiative is situated in a small municipal context along Thailand's northeastern border region. Unlike metropolitan smart city projects driven by large-scale infrastructure investment or technology-led innovation agendas, this deployment emerged from practical governance needs related to tourism management, public events, and fluctuating use of shared urban spaces. Periodic population surges during festivals and tourism seasons place pressure on public-space management, service coordination, and situational awareness.

Within this context, the need for crowd-related information was framed as a municipal management problem rather than a surveillance objective. Local authorities sought aggregated and timely insights to support event planning, spatial allocation, and coordination among municipal services. At the same time, the city's small scale, close social proximity, and visibility of public institutions heightened sensitivity toward privacy, trust, and public perception. These contextual conditions shaped governance priorities from the outset.

The system was developed through a multi-actor governance arrangement involving three institutional stakeholders. The Sri Chiang Mai Municipality provided policy direction and public-space oversight; National Telecom Public Company Limited managed network infrastructure and operational security; and a university research team was responsible for system design, data analysis, and governance alignment within approved ethical boundaries (Wiangwiset et al., 2023; Wiangwiset et al., 2025). This separation of roles was a deliberate governance choice intended to clarify accountability and prevent concentration of control within a public-sector setting.

A defining feature of the deployment was its reliance on existing municipal public Wi-Fi infrastructure rather than purpose-built sensing technologies. Leveraging existing access points reduced deployment costs and operational complexity, while avoiding the introduction of additional sensing modalities that could be perceived as disproportionate or intrusive in public space. This policy intent established a clear boundary: the system was not designed to maximize data volume or analytical granularity, but to support decision-relevant insight under conditions of institutional responsibility and public accountability.

Equally important were the technologies that were explicitly excluded. Camera-based surveillance systems and passive Wi-Fi sensing techniques that capture probe requests from nearby devices were rejected, despite their potential to increase data coverage. Although technically feasible, these approaches conflicted with the project's commitment to distinguish between physical presence in public space and voluntary participation in data collection. The system therefore accepted partial visibility as an intentional and normative design outcome.

As a result, analytical outputs focused on aggregated indicators—such as temporal crowd density patterns and access-point–level distributions—rather than individual tracking or predictive profiling. These outputs were sufficient to inform municipal planning and coordination without requiring fine-grained individual-level data. Rather than treating reduced coverage as a technical limitation, the project framed it as a governance safeguard aligned with proportionality and public legitimacy.

Taken together, the Sri Chiang Mai deployment represents a governance-intensive smart city environment in which policy intent, institutional responsibility, and system design were closely aligned. Data collection occurs in public space, participation is voluntary but uneven, and design choices reflect negotiated governance priorities rather than technological optimization. This integrated context provides the foundation for examining how the CCTC framework was enacted in practice, beginning with the operationalization of consent as the entry condition for participation in the data ecosystem.

The operationalization of the CCTC framework in the Sri Chiang Mai deployment involved translating governance principles into concrete institutional and technical design decisions. Rather than applying the framework abstractly, each pillar was embedded in specific mechanisms that shaped data collection boundaries, lifecycle control, transparency practices, and compliance processes. Table 1 summarizes how the four CCTC pillars were enacted in practice, the trade-offs accepted, and the governance risks mitigated.

Table 1. Governance-to-design mapping in the Sri Chiang Mai deployment

CCTC Pillar	Governance Principle	Design Mechanism Implemented	Accepted Trade-off	Risk Mitigated
Consent	Explicit and voluntary participation boundaries	Opt-in participation through user-initiated service access; avoidance of passive device sensing as a default design choice	Partial coverage and potential representativeness limitations	Implied surveillance; involuntary or assumed participation
Control	Lifecycle-based enforceable constraints	Data minimization and aggregation practices applied prior to analytics; restricted access to identifiable logs; role-based access controls across institutions	Reduced granularity and limited support for individual-level analytics	Function creep; unauthorized secondary use; boundary erosion
Transparency	Structured and intelligible visibility of data practices	Public dashboards using aggregated indicators with contextual explanations; on-site notices; disclosure of governance roles and system boundaries	Reduced analytical detail in public-facing outputs	Informational asymmetry; opaque decision-making
Compliance	Legal, ethical, and institutional alignment	Ethics oversight and review processes; de-identification or pseudonymization practices; documented roles, procedures, and accountability structures	Additional documentation requirements and slower change cycles	Governance drift; misalignment with legal or ethical obligations; accountability gaps

Consent in Public Space: What Was Chosen — and Why

Operationalizing consent in public space represents one of the most challenging aspects of smart city data governance. In environments where individuals move freely and participation is embedded in everyday urban infrastructure, conventional consent models—designed for discrete and voluntary interactions—become difficult to apply in practice. The Sri Chiang Mai Smart City Wi-Fi analytics system confronted this challenge directly by treating consent not as an abstract principle, but as a concrete design decision with real operational consequences.

From the outset, the project rejected approaches that infer participation from mere physical presence. Passive sensing techniques—such as capturing Wi-Fi probe requests from nearby devices—were deliberately excluded, despite their potential to significantly increase data coverage. Although technically feasible, such approaches blur the distinction between being present in public space and actively participating in data collection. In a municipal context characterized by close social proximity and heightened sensitivity to privacy, this ambiguity was considered unacceptable.

Instead, consent was operationalized through an explicit opt-in mechanism embedded in the public Wi-Fi access process. Data were generated only when individuals voluntarily connected to the municipal Wi-Fi network. Devices that did not connect—whether because users relied on mobile data, disabled Wi-Fi, or chose not to participate—were excluded from the dataset by design. This architectural choice established a clear boundary between physical presence and data participation, ensuring that inclusion in the data ecosystem required affirmative user action rather than passive exposure.

This consent-first design introduced immediate and visible trade-offs. Coverage was inherently partial, and the resulting data could not be assumed to represent the entire population present in public spaces. The system therefore sacrificed completeness and representativeness in exchange for legitimacy and clarity of participation. Rather than treating this limitation as a technical weakness to be mitigated, the project treated it as a normative constraint aligned with public-sector responsibility and proportionality.

Consent was also purpose-bound. Participation in the Wi-Fi network enabled the use of connection-related data solely for aggregated crowd analysis and tourism-related management objectives. The system was not designed to support individualized tracking, profiling, or law enforcement activities. By clearly defining and limiting the purposes of data use, the project sought to ensure that consent retained substantive meaning beyond initial network access.

Institutional responsibility for consent did not rest solely with individual users. Ethical oversight played a critical role in shaping and validating consent mechanisms. The system and its data practices were reviewed through formal research ethics procedures, which evaluated consent conditions, data minimization strategies, and potential risks associated with public-space analytics. This process shifted consent from an individual burden to an organizational obligation, reinforcing accountability at the institutional level.

The Sri Chiang Mai case illustrates that meaningful consent in public space is not achieved through procedural formality or legal disclaimers alone. Instead, it emerges from design choices that make participation explicit, bounded, and enforceable. By accepting reduced coverage as the cost of respecting autonomy and legitimacy, the system demonstrates how consent can function as a structural governance condition rather than as a symbolic or implied assumption.

This operationalization of consent establishes the foundation for subsequent governance mechanisms. Once participation boundaries are defined, the question becomes how those boundaries are enforced and stabilized over time—a role fulfilled by control mechanisms across the data lifecycle. The following section examines how control was implemented in practice to translate consent commitments into enforceable constraints.

Control in Practice: Who Controls What — and How

While consent defines the boundary of legitimate participation, control determines whether those boundaries are respected and sustained over time. In the Sri Chiang Mai Smart City Wi-Fi analytics system, control was operationalized not as a single technical safeguard, but as a distributed governance arrangement spanning institutional roles, data lifecycle management, and security design. The central challenge was to ensure that consent commitments were not eroded through downstream data handling or informal expansion of system use.

A foundational control mechanism in this deployment was the explicit allocation of institutional responsibilities. Governance authority was deliberately distributed among three actors with distinct mandates. The Sri Chiang Mai Municipality retained responsibility for policy direction, public-space deployment, and alignment with municipal objectives. National Telecom Public Company Limited was responsible for network infrastructure, server management, and operational security. The university research team was tasked with analytical design and interpretation within approved research and ethical boundaries. This separation of roles functioned as a governance control by preventing any single actor from unilaterally expanding data use or redefining system purposes.

Control was further exercised through lifecycle-based data management. Data entered the system only after explicit user connection to the public Wi-Fi network. Raw connection logs were not made directly available for analytical use. Instead, data were transformed early in the processing pipeline into aggregated representations suitable for crowd-level analysis. By constraining access to raw data and enforcing transformation at predefined stages, the system limited opportunities for secondary use or individual-level analysis that would exceed the scope of consent.

Security mechanisms played a critical role in enforcing these governance constraints. Device identifiers were subjected to privacy-preserving transformations—such as cryptographic hashing and tokenization—before analytical processing. These measures were designed to prevent reconstruction of individual identities while still allowing aggregate pattern analysis. Importantly, security controls were treated not merely as protections against external threats, but as governance instruments that made consent boundaries technically difficult to bypass.

Access restrictions reinforced institutional control. Infrastructure-level access to network logs and servers was confined to authorized National Telecom Public Company Limited personnel under operational security obligations. Analytical access was restricted to the research team operating within defined project scope and ethical approval. Municipal decision-makers interacted only with aggregated outputs through dashboards and reports, without access to device-level or trajectory data. This role-based access structure ensured that no stakeholder possessed comprehensive control over the entire data lifecycle.

Auditability provided an additional layer of governance control. Data handling procedures, analytical processes, and governance decisions were documented as part of project operations and ethical review. Any modification to system scope—such as changes in analytical objectives or data handling practices—would require renewed institutional consideration rather than informal adjustment. This documentation functioned as a safeguard against function creep, enabling oversight and accountability beyond initial deployment.

The Sri Chiang Mai case demonstrates that effective control in smart city systems emerges from the interaction of institutional design, lifecycle constraints, and security-by-design measures. Control is not exercised through trust in actors alone, but through structures that make governance commitments enforceable in practice. By stabilizing consent conditions and constraining data use across organizational and technical boundaries, control serves as the mechanism that transforms governance intent into durable operational reality.

The following section examines how these control mechanisms were made visible and intelligible to stakeholders through transparency practices, ensuring that governance arrangements could be understood, scrutinized, and held accountable in public contexts.

Transparency Through Aggregation and Public Dashboards

In the Sri Chiang Mai Smart City Wi-Fi analytics system, transparency was not treated as a secondary communication activity or a post-hoc disclosure requirement. Instead, it was implemented as a governance mechanism designed to make data practices intelligible and accountable while remaining consistent with consent and control constraints. The central challenge was to render system behavior visible without transforming transparency into an additional source of surveillance or privacy risk.

A core transparency decision concerned the level of data visibility. Rather than exposing raw connection logs or device-level records, the system communicated its outputs exclusively through aggregated indicators. Crowd density patterns, temporal distributions, and access-point–level summaries were presented in ways that conveyed situational awareness without enabling reconstruction of individual movement or behavior. Aggregation thus functioned as both a privacy safeguard and a transparency strategy, ensuring that visibility did not undermine the governance boundaries established through consent and control.

Public dashboards played a central role in operationalizing transparency. These dashboards were designed as public-facing interfaces, accessible not only to municipal officials but also to external observers. By making the same aggregated visualizations available to decision-makers and the general public, the system reduced informational asymmetry and prevented the emergence of privileged analytical views restricted to authorities. Transparency therefore operated as a structural condition for accountability rather than as an internal reporting function.

Importantly, the dashboards were not designed to maximize informational detail. They emphasized interpretability over completeness, focusing on indicators relevant to municipal planning and tourism management rather than exhaustive data representation. This design choice reflected a deliberate rejection of "illusory transparency," where excessive detail can obscure governance intent or create misleading impressions of comprehensiveness. By clearly communicating what the system could and could not represent, the dashboards supported informed interpretation rather than speculative inference.

Transparency in this case also extended beyond visualization. Documentation of system purpose, data boundaries, and institutional roles complemented dashboard outputs, providing contextual explanations necessary for meaningful understanding. On-site informational signage at Wi-Fi access locations further supported situational transparency by informing individuals about the presence and purpose of the system within the spaces where data were generated. Together, these measures ensured that transparency was encountered both digitally and physically.

Crucially, transparency was treated as bounded openness, not unrestricted access. While selected aggregated datasets and system components were made available for inspection or reuse, openness was governed to prevent re-identification, misuse, or misinterpretation. Transparency therefore did not mean exposing everything, but exposing what was necessary to support scrutiny, trust, and accountability within a public-sector context.

The Sri Chiang Mai deployment illustrates that transparency becomes meaningful when it is aligned with governance objectives rather than pursued as an end in itself. By designing transparency through aggregation, public dashboards, and contextual explanation, the system made governance practices observable without expanding the scope of data collection or eroding consent commitments. Transparency thus functioned as the outward-facing expression of internal governance discipline, linking operational control with public understanding.

The next section examines how these transparency practices were stabilized over time through legal, ethical, and institutional compliance mechanisms, ensuring that governance commitments remained credible and enforceable beyond initial deployment.

Compliance as a Continuous Governance Process

In the Sri Chiang Mai Smart City Wi-Fi analytics system, compliance was not treated as a one-time verification exercise conducted at the point of deployment. Instead, it functioned as a continuous governance process that shaped system design, constrained analytical scope, and guided institutional responsibility throughout the project lifecycle. This approach reflects the recognition that public-space data systems operate in evolving social, legal, and organizational environments where static compliance is insufficient to sustain legitimacy.

A central compliance mechanism in this case was formal ethical oversight. The system and its associated data practices underwent institutional ethical review, during which consent mechanisms, data minimization strategies, anonymization techniques, and potential risks to individuals were evaluated. The resulting ethics exemption did not signal the absence of governance concerns; rather, it confirmed that the system constituted minimal-risk data use under defined conditions. Importantly, this review process established external constraints on system evolution, ensuring that future modifications would require renewed governance consideration rather than informal expansion.

Legal compliance was embedded primarily through privacy-by-design choices rather than post hoc legal argumentation. The system was deliberately designed to avoid the collection of direct personal identifiers, individualized location trajectories, or user profiles. Device identifiers were transformed through irreversible privacy-preserving mechanisms before analytical use, and data handling was confined to controlled infrastructure environments. These architectural decisions reduced reliance on contested interpretive distinctions between personal and non-personal data by minimizing the risk of identification from the outset.

Compliance also operated through institutional role clarity. Responsibilities for infrastructure management, security operations, analytical processing, and policy alignment were distributed across distinct organizations with defined mandates. This separation of roles supported accountability by preventing the concentration of governance authority and by clarifying which actor was responsible for which aspects of compliance. In a multi-actor smart city environment, such role clarity is essential for translating abstract legal and ethical obligations into enforceable practice.

Crucially, compliance in this case was adaptive rather than static. As the system was deployed and used in real municipal contexts, adjustments were made in response to operational experience, contextual constraints, and governance considerations. Decisions regarding access point placement, data aggregation thresholds, and visualization practices were revisited to ensure continued alignment with consent commitments and proportionality. Compliance thus functioned as an ongoing process of alignment rather than as a fixed condition satisfied at system launch.

Documentation and public disclosure further reinforced compliance as a verifiable practice. By describing system design, governance choices, and limitations through peer-reviewed publications and public-facing materials, the project enabled external scrutiny beyond internal institutional review. Compliance claims were therefore supported by observable evidence rather than by internal assurances alone.

The Sri Chiang Mai case demonstrates that compliance in public-sector smart city systems cannot be reduced to legal conformity or procedural approval. Instead, it emerges from the integration of ethical oversight, privacy-preserving design, institutional accountability, and adaptive governance. By embedding compliance in system architecture and operational workflows, the project sought to ensure that governance commitments remained credible, enforceable, and responsive over time.

With compliance stabilizing the governance architecture, the case study now turns to reflective analysis, examining lessons learned, trade-offs encountered, and limitations acknowledged through the practical implementation of the CCTC framework.

Discussion: Governance Advantages, Challenges, and Ethical Considerations

The implementation of the Sri Chiang Mai Smart City Wi-Fi analytics system offers several insights into the practical enactment of governance-by-design in public-sector data systems. Rather than presenting a model solution, the case illustrates how governance priorities shape system design through negotiation, constraint, and trade-offs within real institutional contexts.

A central lesson concerns the cost of meaningful consent. Requiring explicit opt-in participation through public Wi-Fi connection significantly reduced data coverage and limited the representativeness of crowd estimates. From a technical standpoint, this constraint could be viewed as a weakness. From a governance perspective, however, it functioned as a stabilizing boundary that preserved legitimacy and public defensibility. The case demonstrates that in public-space systems, analytical completeness and proportionality are often in tension, and that prioritizing autonomy and clarity of participation may require accepting reduced analytical reach.

A second lesson highlights the role of institutional separation as a governance control. Clear allocation of responsibilities among the municipality, the telecommunications provider, and the research team reduced ambiguity over authority and limited opportunities for informal expansion of data use. This separation introduced coordination costs and slower decision-making, yet these frictions served a governance function by making data-related decisions more deliberate and accountable rather than efficient but opaque.

The case further underscores that privacy-preserving design is not a neutral technical choice but a normative commitment with operational consequences. Aggregation, identifier transformation, and access restrictions constrained the types of questions that could be asked of the data. Certain analytical ambitions—such as individual movement trajectories or fine-grained behavioral inference—were deliberately excluded. These constraints shaped not only system capability but also how outputs were interpreted and used, indicating that governance-aware design must align analytical expectations with ethical and institutional limits from the outset.

Transparency practices revealed additional trade-offs. Public dashboards enhanced accountability and reduced informational asymmetry, but required careful calibration to avoid misinterpretation or overconfidence in partial data. Making aggregated insights publicly visible increased the responsibility to communicate limitations clearly and to resist pressures to expand scope in pursuit of perceived completeness. In this sense, transparency intensified the need for disciplined governance rather than diminishing it.

Another lesson concerns the temporal dimension of governance. Commitments established at system launch did not remain static. As the system was used in practice, new questions emerged regarding data interpretation, dashboard design, and operational relevance. Ethical oversight, documentation, and institutional review provided mechanisms for reassessment, yet the experience highlighted that governance-by-design requires sustained attention rather than one-time configuration.

Finally, the case illustrates the limits of framework-based governance. While the CCTC framework offered a coherent structure for aligning consent, control, transparency, and compliance, it did not resolve all tensions inherent in public-space data use. Decisions about acceptable data loss, aggregation thresholds, and public communication required contextual judgment that could not be fully codified. Frameworks, therefore, support governance by structuring reflection and accountability, not by replacing human judgment or political responsibility.

Taken together, these reflections suggest that responsible smart city data governance is less about identifying optimal technical solutions than about sustaining principled decision-making under constraint. The Sri Chiang Mai experience illustrates how governance-by-design can guide system development while remaining sensitive to local context, institutional capacity, and public expectations. These lessons inform the broader discussion that follows, situating the CCTC framework within ongoing debates on legitimacy, accountability, and trust in data-driven urban governance.

Scalability and Transferability Across Urban Scales

While the Sri Chiang Mai deployment demonstrates the feasibility of governance-by-design in a small municipal context, questions of scalability naturally arise when considering larger metropolitan environments. Urban scale significantly shapes governance complexity, institutional coordination requirements, and data ecosystem dynamics.

In small municipalities, institutional roles are often clearly delineated and communication channels relatively direct, enabling tighter alignment between policy intent, technical design, and ethical oversight. In contrast, metropolitan smart city systems typically involve multiple municipal departments, regional authorities, private vendors, platform providers, and data intermediaries operating within layered governance structures. As scale increases, decision rights may become more fragmented, procurement processes more complex, and oversight mechanisms more distributed. These conditions may challenge the enforceability of consent boundaries, lifecycle-based control, and coherent transparency practices.

Scalability also affects consent feasibility. In dense urban settings with heterogeneous populations and overlapping infrastructures, reliance on explicit opt-in mechanisms may produce lower participation rates or uneven representation. Larger deployments may therefore require hybrid consent models, enhanced public communication strategies, or complementary governance safeguards to maintain proportionality and legitimacy.

Despite these challenges, the CCTC framework is conceptually scalable because it operates at the level of governance functions rather than specific technologies. Its principles—explicit participation boundaries, enforceable lifecycle control, transparency-by-design, and adaptive compliance—can be institutionalized across different urban scales, provided that corresponding governance capacities and accountability structures are established. The framework thus offers a structured lens for evaluating scalability trade-offs rather than prescribing a one-size-fits-all implementation model.

Technical Trade-offs and System Constraints

The Sri Chiang Mai Wi-Fi analytics system reflects deliberate governance choices that necessarily introduced technical trade-offs. These constraints were not unintended weaknesses but structured outcomes of prioritizing consent, proportionality, and privacy preservation over maximal data extraction.

A primary limitation arises from the explicit opt-in participation model. Because data are generated only when users voluntarily connect to the municipal Wi-Fi network, coverage is inherently partial. Individuals relying on mobile data networks, disabling Wi-Fi connectivity, or declining participation are excluded from the dataset. As a result, aggregated crowd indicators cannot be assumed to represent the entire population present in public spaces.

Additional constraints stem from privacy-preserving design measures. Device identifiers are transformed prior to analysis, and raw logs are not retained for individualized tracking. While these safeguards mitigate re-identification risks and prevent trajectory reconstruction, they also limit the granularity of behavioral insights. Fine-grained mobility analysis or predictive profiling was deliberately excluded from system capability.

Signal-based estimation methods further introduce technical variability. Factors such as device heterogeneity, signal fluctuation, and environmental interference may affect connection patterns. Moreover, recent operating system updates that randomize device identifiers reduce the stability of longitudinal linkage. These dynamics reinforce the importance of interpreting outputs as aggregated situational indicators rather than precise counts or individual-level measurements.

Acknowledging these constraints strengthens rather than weakens the governance argument. The system demonstrates that privacy-preserving and consent-aligned analytics require acceptance of reduced coverage and analytical scope. In this sense, technical limitations are inseparable from governance commitments, reflecting the trade-offs inherent in responsible public-space data use.

Regulatory Regime Variations and Implementation Considerations

The implementation of governance-by-design frameworks such as CCTC is inevitably shaped by differences in regulatory environments and institutional capacity. While the Sri Chiang Mai deployment operates within Thailand's Personal Data

Protection Act (PDPA) and related public-sector regulations, smart city initiatives in other jurisdictions may be subject to substantially different legal architectures.

In jurisdictions governed by comprehensive data protection regimes such as the European Union's General Data Protection Regulation (GDPR), explicit consent requirements, data minimization principles, and accountability mechanisms are legally codified and enforceable through supervisory authorities. In such contexts, the CCTC framework aligns closely with existing legal expectations, particularly in its emphasis on lifecycle control, purpose limitation, and documented compliance. However, implementation may require more formalized documentation processes, data protection impact assessments, and structured reporting obligations.

Conversely, in regulatory environments characterized by fragmented or sector-specific data governance frameworks, institutional interpretation of consent, transparency, and accountability may vary across agencies and jurisdictions. In such cases, the CCTC framework can function as a normative governance scaffold that strengthens internal coordination and clarifies decision rights even in the absence of uniform regulatory enforcement.

Implementation challenges may also arise from procurement practices, vendor ecosystems, and legacy infrastructures. Smart city systems often rely on private-sector platforms and technical intermediaries whose default configurations may prioritize efficiency or data maximization. Embedding CCTC principles therefore requires deliberate contractual design, institutional oversight, and governance capacity to ensure that public-interest objectives are not subordinated to operational convenience.

Recognizing regulatory and institutional variation underscores that governance-by-design is not a purely technical exercise but a context-sensitive institutional practice. The CCTC framework provides structured governance functions that can be adapted to different regulatory regimes, provided that corresponding accountability and oversight mechanisms are institutionally sustained.

FUTURE RESEARCH DIRECTIONS

While this chapter demonstrates the feasibility and value of the CCTC framework through conceptual analysis and a municipal case study, several directions remain for future research and practical development. Future work should extend the application of CCTC beyond Wi-Fi analytics and smart tourism to other smart city domains, such as mobility management, environmental monitoring, public safety, and digital public services, each of which presents distinct governance risks, data sensitivities, and institutional configurations. In parallel, as municipalities increasingly deploy AI-driven analytics and automated decision-support systems, further research is needed to examine how the framework can be adapted to govern algorithmic inference, model reuse, and automated outcomes. This includes rethinking consent in inferential contexts, strengthening control over model lifecycles, and developing transparency mechanisms that communicate impacts and limitations of algorithmic systems in accessible ways.

In addition, future studies may explore how deliberative and participatory governance mechanisms can complement the system-level orientation of CCTC. Citizen panels, public consultations, and co-design processes may help shape acceptable data uses, transparency practices, and governance boundaries in line with evolving public values. Further research is also needed to develop evaluation metrics and maturity models for assessing the quality of CCTC implementation across projects, as well as to examine how the framework can be institutionalized through municipal policy, procurement processes, and public-sector standards. Finally, longitudinal research will be essential to understand how governance-by-design performs over time as smart city systems scale, evolve, and integrate with new infrastructures, and to identify strategies for preventing governance drift while sustaining legitimacy and accountability.

CONCLUSION

This chapter introduced the CCTC framework as an integrated, design-oriented approach to smart city data governance that embeds Consent, Control, Transparency, and Compliance into public-sector data ecosystems by design. Addressing persistent gaps between widely endorsed governance principles and their practical implementation, the chapter reframed governance not as a peripheral regulatory obligation, but as a core architectural and institutional feature of smart city systems operating in public and semi-public spaces.

Through conceptual analysis and a municipal Wi-Fi analytics case study, the chapter demonstrated that governance failures in smart city initiatives more often arise from fragmentation than from the absence of safeguards. Consent without enforceable control becomes symbolic; control without transparency lacks accountability; transparency without credible compliance loses legitimacy; and compliance without meaningful consent risks legal formalism detached from public trust. The CCTC framework responds to these interdependencies by structuring governance as a coherent and mutually reinforcing system.

The Sri Chiang Mai municipal Wi-Fi analytics case provided practical grounding for this argument. It showed that explicit opt-in consent, lifecycle-based data control, privacy-preserving security measures, aggregated public dashboards, and ethical oversight can coexist within an operational smart city deployment. Importantly, the case highlighted that governance-by-design involves deliberate trade-offs. Constraints on data coverage and analytical granularity were treated not as technical deficiencies, but as normative design choices that enhance proportionality, accountability, and long-term legitimacy.

Overall, the contribution of this chapter lies not in proposing new governance principles, but in demonstrating how existing ones can be integrated, operationalized, and sustained within real-world public-sector systems. For policymakers and practitioners, the CCTC framework offers a decision-oriented governance architecture that supports institutional accountability and public trust without prescribing specific technologies. For researchers, it provides a structured lens for examining how governance principles are enacted in practice. By treating governance as an enabling condition rather than a constraint, CCTC shifts the focus of smart city development from technological capability toward democratic legitimacy and responsible public data use.

ACKNOWLEDGMENT

The authors gratefully acknowledge Khon Kaen University for providing academic support and an enabling research environment for this work. Sincere appreciation is also extended to the Sri Chiang Mai Municipality for the cooperation and institutional support provided in the development and deployment of the municipal smart city Wi-Fi analytics system examined in this chapter. The authors further express appreciation to National Telecom Public Company Limited for providing and managing the network infrastructure and for ensuring operational security throughout the project. The authors also thank the members of the public in Sri Chiang Mai for their cooperation and engagement, which contributed to the broader context of this work. Finally, appreciation is extended to research collaborators, colleagues, and reviewers whose insights and constructive feedback strengthened the governance perspective and conceptual framing presented in this chapter.

REFERENCES

Chang, V. (2021). An ethical framework for big data and smart cities. *Technological Forecasting and Social Change*, *165*, 120559. DOI: 10.1016/j.techfore.2020.120559

Chatsuwan, P., Phromma, T., Surasvadi, N., & Thajchayapong, S. (2023). Personal data protection compliance assessment: A privacy policy scoring approach and empirical evidence from Thailand's SMEs. *Heliyon*, *9*(10), e20648. DOI: 10.1016/j.heliyon.2023.e20648 PMID: 37886776

Cole, A., & Tran, É. (2022). Trust and the smart city. *China Perspectives*, *130*(3), 3–7. DOI: 10.4000/chinaperspectives.14024

Cottrill, C. D., Jacobs, N., Markovic, M., & Edwards, P. (2020). Sensing the city: Designing for privacy and trust in the internet of things. *Sustainable Cities and Society*, *63*, 102453. DOI: 10.1016/j.scs.2020.102453

Demertzi, V., Demertzis, S., & Demertzis, K. (2023). An overview of cyber threats, attacks and countermeasures on the primary domains of smart cities. *Applied Sciences (Basel, Switzerland)*, *13*(2), 790. DOI: 10.3390/app13020790

Felzmann, H., Fosch-Villaronga, E., Lutz, C., & Tamò-Larrieux, A. (2020). Towards transparency by design for artificial intelligence. *Science and Engineering Ethics*, *26*(6), 3333–3361. DOI: 10.1007/s11948-020-00276-4 PMID: 33196975

Franke, J., & Gailhofer, P. (2021). Data governance and regulation for sustainable smart cities. *Frontiers in Sustainable Cities*, *3*, 763788. DOI: 10.3389/frsc.2021.763788

Ismagilova, E., Hughes, L., Rana, N. P., & Dwivedi, Y. K. (2022). Security, privacy and risks within smart cities: Literature review and development of a smart city interaction framework. *Information Systems Frontiers*, *24*(2), 393–414. DOI: 10.1007/s10796-020-10044-1 PMID: 32837262

Jacobs, N., Edwards, P., Markovic, M., Cottrill, C. D., & Salt, K. (2020). Who trusts in the smart city? Transparency, governance, and the internet of things. *Data & Policy*, *2*, e11. DOI: 10.1017/dap.2020.11

Jacobs, N., Loveday, F., Markovic, M., Cottrill, C. D., Zullo, R., & Edwards, P. (2022). Prototyping an IoT transparency toolkit to support communication, governance and policy in the smart city. *The Design Journal*, *25*(3), 459–480. DOI: 10.1080/14606925.2022.2061775

Jin, Y., & Wang, Y. (2025). Reassessing smart city development and personal data protection: A regulatory framework. *International Review of Economics & Finance*, *99*, 104022. DOI: 10.1016/j.iref.2025.104022

König, P. D. (2021). Citizen-centered data governance in the smart city: From ethics to accountability. *Sustainable Cities and Society*, *75*, 103308. DOI: 10.1016/j.scs.2021.103308

Lomotey, R. K., Kumi, S., & Deters, R. (2022). Data trusts as a service: Providing a platform for multi-party data sharing. *International Journal of Information Management Data Insights*, *2*(1), 100075. DOI: 10.1016/j.jjimei.2022.100075

Magrizos, S., Campora, M., Lamprinakos, G., Giovanis, A., & Christofi, M. (2026). Transparency by design: The effect of privacy policies visualisation on brand trust and perceived intrusion. *Behaviour & Information Technology*, *45*(3), 450–462. DOI: 10.1080/0144929X.2025.2520594

Novaes, J. (2021). Private information in public spaces: Facial recognition in the times of smart urban governance. *Smart Cities and Regional Development Journal*, *5*(1), 31–43. https://scrd.eu/index.php/scrd/article/view/94

Organisation for Economic Co-operation and Development. (2023). *Smart city data governance: Challenges and the way forward*. OECD Urban Studies. OECD Publishing. DOI: 10.1787/e57ce301-en

Shimizu, Y., Osaki, S., Hashimoto, T., & Karasawa, K. (2022). Social acceptance of smart city projects: Focus on the Sidewalk Toronto case. *Frontiers in Environmental Science*, *10*, 898922. DOI: 10.3389/fenvs.2022.898922 van Twist, A., Ruijer, E., & Meijer, A. (2023). Smart cities & citizen discontent: A systematic review of the literature. *Government Information Quarterly*, *40*(2), 101799. DOI: 10.1016/j.giq.2022.101799

van Zoonen, L. (2020). Data governance and citizen participation in the digital welfare state. *Data & Policy*, *2*, e10. DOI: 10.1017/dap.2020.10

Waclawek, T., Fiedler, A., Schütz, M., & Schütz, A. (2024). Crowd-counting technology within the smart city context: Understanding, trust, and acceptance. *Frontiers in Psychology*, *15*, 1423837. DOI: 10.3389/fpsyg.2024.1423837 PMID: 39624374

Wiangwiset, T., Surawanitkun, C., Wongsinlatam, W., Remsungnen, T., Siritaratiwat, A., Srichan, C., Thepparat, P., Bunsuk, W., Kaewchan, A., & Namvong, A. (2023). Design and implementation of a real-time crowd monitoring system based on public Wi-Fi infrastructure: A case study on the Sri Chiang Mai Smart City. *Smart Cities*, *6*(2), 987–1008. DOI: 10.3390/smartcities6020048

Wiangwiset, T., Surawanitkun, C., Wongsinlatam, W., Remsungnen, T., Sorn-in, K., Siritaratiwat, A., Srichan, C., Thepparat, P., Bunsuk, W., Kaewchan, A., Supasai, W., & Namvong, A. (2025). Development of a tourist behavior analysis system using public Wi-Fi data to enhance smart tourism management: A case study of Sri Chiang Mai Smart City. *Engineering and Applied Science Research, 52*(1), 42–56. DOI: 10.14456/easr.2025.4

Zimmermann, V. (2023). Smart cities as a testbed for experimenting with humans? Applying psychological ethical guidelines to smart city interventions. *Ethics and Information Technology*, *25*(4), 54. DOI: 10.1007/s10676-023-09729-3

ADDITIONAL READING

Bozkurt, Y., Rossmann, A., Pervez, Z., & Ramzan, N. (2025). Development and evaluation of an urban data governance reference model based on design science research. *Government Information Quarterly*, *42*(2), 102025. DOI: 10.1016/j.giq.2025.102025

Haraguchi, M., Funahashi, T., & Biljecki, F. (2024). Assessing governance implications of city digital twin technology: A maturity model approach. *Technological Forecasting and Social Change*, *204*, 123409. DOI: 10.1016/j.techfore.2024.123409

Hartley, K., & Aldag, A. (2024). Public trust and support for government technology: Survey insights about Singapore's smart city policies. *Cities (London, England)*, *154*, 105368. DOI: 10.1016/j.cities.2024.105368

Merchán-Cruz, E. A., Gabelaia, I., Savrasovs, M., Hansen, M. F., Soe, S., Rodriguez-Cañizo, R. G., & Aragón-Camarasa, G. (2025). Trust by design: An ethical framework for collaborative intelligence systems in Industry 5.0. *Electronics (Basel), 14*(10), 1952. DOI: 10.3390/electronics14101952

Olsen, H. P., Hildebrandt, T. T., Wiesener, C., Larsen, M. S., & Flügge, A. W. A. (2024). The right to transparency in public governance: Freedom of information and the use of artificial intelligence by public agencies. *Digital Government: Research and Practice*, *5*(1), 8. DOI: 10.1145/3632753

KEY TERMS AND DEFINITIONS

CCTC Framework: An integrated governance framework that aligns consent, control, transparency, and compliance as mutually reinforcing mechanisms embedded into system design, institutional arrangements, and operational practice. The framework conceptualizes trust and social acceptance as emergent outcomes of effective governance integration rather than as prerequisites for system deployment.

Compliance: Compliance is defined as an institutionalized and adaptive governance function that integrates legal, ethical, and organizational requirements into system architecture and operational workflows. Beyond formal legal conformity, compliance within the CCTC framework emphasizes enforceability, proportionality, and alignment with public values over time.

Consent: In the context of smart city data governance, consent refers to a structural governance condition that defines legitimate participation boundaries in data-driven systems. Rather than a one-time procedural permission, consent is understood as a continuing condition that must be stabilized through system design, enforceable constraints, and institutional accountability across the data lifecycle.

Control: Control denotes the set of enforceable governance mechanisms that constrain how data are accessed, processed, reused, and retained across the entire data lifecycle. Within the CCTC framework, control integrates institutional authority, lifecycle-based rules, and security-by-design measures to ensure that governance commitments remain enforceable in practice.

Institutional Accountability: The clear allocation of responsibilities, decision-making authority, and oversight obligations among organizations involved in data governance. Institutional accountability supports auditability, traceability, and explainability of system operations beyond the actions of individual actors.

Public Dashboard: A public-facing interface designed to present aggregated and contextualized data insights in order to support understanding, accountability, and informed decision-making, while avoiding the exposure of individual-level or sensitive information.

Public-Space Data Collection: Data collection practices embedded in public or semi-public environments where participation is difficult to avoid and traditional consent mechanisms are structurally constrained by infrastructural and spatial conditions.

Smart City Data Governance: The institutional, legal, and organizational arrangements that shape how urban data are collected, processed, used, and governed within public and semi-public contexts.

Transparency: Transparency refers to the capacity of governance arrangements to render data practices, decision rationales, and accountability structures intelligible and contestable to appropriate audiences. In this chapter, transparency is understood as transparency-by-design, emphasizing structured visibility and explanation rather than unrestricted openness or retrospective disclosure.

Chapter 7
Transparent and Trustworthy Data Practices for Talking Head Generation: A Systematic Survey of Datasets and Ethical Implications

Vineet Kumar Rakesh
http://orcid.org/0009-0000-7102-6564
Homi Bhabha National Institute, India & Variable Energy Cyclotron Centre, India

Soumya Mazumdar
http://orcid.org/0009-0006-3521-9557
Gargi Memorial Institute of Technology, India

Research Pratim Maity
http://orcid.org/0009-0007-5326-4180
Gargi Memorial Institute of Technology, India

Tapas Samanta
http://orcid.org/0000-0003-0521-0747
Variable Energy Cyclotron Centre, India

Sarbajit Pal
http://orcid.org/0009-0004-8386-672X
Mahatma Gandhi University, India

Amitabha Das
http://orcid.org/0009-0003-1460-8308
Jadavpur University, India

ABSTRACT

Talking Head Generation (THG) needs transparent, trustworthy data: ethically sourced, recorded, annotated, licensed, and managed human data with unambiguous authorization, provenance, and subject rights. This chapter analyzes THG modalities and organizes datasets by domain, capture context, view coverage, annotation scope,

DOI: 10.4018/979-8-2600-1433-2.ch007

and access. It distills corpus strengths and gaps: language-heavy skew, frontal-view bias, coarse or artificial emotion labels, and licensing/privacy frictions. Transparency must equal technical rigor: dataset cards/datasheets, standard metadata, verifiable permission records, tiered licensing, subject-rights processes, fairness audits, and unified benchmarks with consistent preprocessing and splits. Next steps: multilingual/multicultural corpora, multi-view/3D capture, privacy-preserving pipelines, and calibrated synthetic–real co-training. Ethical, well-documented data allow generalizable THG and sustain public confidence.

INTRODUCTION

Talking Head Generation (THG) is a fast advancing area that synthesizes realistic human facial movements coordinated with numerous input modalities, speech, text, video, or still images-to construct lifelike talking faces that express articulation, emotion, and natural micro-dynamics. This multimodal ambition explains the field's growing relevance across sectors such as virtual avatars and embodied assistants in AI platforms, non-player characters and player proxies in games, remote presence in teleconferencing and telemedicine, synthetic hosts in education and entertainment, and privacy-preserving "face relays" for low-bitrate or low-connectivity scenarios. The fidelity of the output is inseparable from the trust people place in the medium; a talking face that is temporally smooth, identity-consistent, emotionally expressive, and correctly synchronized to content earns engagement and confidence, whereas uncanny outputs undermine usability and ethics alike (Peng et al., 2024; Dong & Zhang, 2025).

THG has become a cornerstone of current digital engagement. Audio-driven THG connects speech to face kinematics, seeking precise lip synchronization and prosodic alignment (Han et al., 2025). Video-driven THG transmits motion and identification signals from one sequence to another, aiming temporal coherence and identity retention under diverse stances (Liu et al., 2015). Text-driven techniques transform scripts into phonemes, prosody, and higher-level rhetorical rhythm, providing style management without any reference audio (Diao et al., 2025). Finally, image-driven approaches animate a single picture or a small series of portraits, frequently recreating a 3D or implicit representation that permits free-view control (Iandola et al., 2025). Together, these modalities illustrate THG's multimodal nature and its application breadth-from assistive communication to cinematic dubbing and metaverse avatars (Abootorabi et al., 2025).

Two causes have powered the current wave of realism: cross-pollination between generative modeling and 3D scene representation has introduced explicit or implicit geometry into the loop (Zhuang et al., 2024). Where early 2D pipelines struggled with structural plausibility, today's approaches increasingly employ 3D priors and neural radiance field (NeRF)-style formulations to handle big poses, self-occlusion, and view-consistent detail (Chen et al., 2025). One-shot and few-shot pipelines based on deformable NeRFs, for instance, retain identity while permitting free-view re-enactment, pointing to a unified approach for high-fidelity, 3D-aware talking heads appropriate for conferencing and film production (H. Ma et al., 2024).

Data affects what THG models can learn about the relationship between sound, meaning, and facial movements. High-quality, varied corpora expose models to phonetic diversity, dialects, coarticulation, emotional subtlety, and the nonverbal micro-gestures-blinks, tiny eyebrow lifts, jaw slack that make speech seem human rather than robotic (Tan et al., 2024). Conversely, restricted or noisy datasets constrain generalization and attract artifacts. Benchmark datasets perform a dual role: they are raw material for training and the yardsticks for assessment, creating the community's sense of "state-of-the-art."

The contemporary environment covers audio-driven, video-driven, text-driven, emotion-centric, and 3D/multi-view corpora (B. Li et al., 2024). VoxCeleb (Nagrani et al., 2019), VoxCeleb2, LRW/LRS, and related "in-the-wild" sets provide large-scale audiovisual recordings of unconstrained speech; video-driven needs are served by sets such as TalkingHead-1KH, HDTF, and CelebV-HQ, which deliver thousands of high-resolution clips with challenging head motions, lighting, and backgrounds. Emotionally annotated corpora supply labeled affect for expression modeling. For 3D-aware synthesis and free-view rendering, corpora with multi-view capture or explicit geometry offer spatial supervision for identity-consistent reenactment. Text-conditioned pipelines rely on multimodal sets that relate words, phonemes, rhythm, and facial movements.

However, the same datasets that enable advances also embody the field's limits. Many corpora tend toward frontal, near-frontal perspectives, lowering pose coverage and taxing models under profile or severe yaw/pitch circumstances. Others are English-dominant, underrepresenting phonemes and viseme coarticulations seen in other languages; this might worsen cross-lingual lip sync and expression timing.

THG systems are evolving from lab demonstrations to customer-facing solutions, and the concept of "good data" grows beyond representativeness and label quality to incorporate openness, accountability, and user agency. Ethical data practice is crucial to technical performance when the objective is generalizable realism that people accept and depend on. The data ethics literature spanning AI, HCI, healthcare, and public health shows consistent themes relevant to THG: establish principled processes for collection and consent; anticipate informational risk and privacy leakage; standardize documentation for interoperability and auditability; and cultivate fairness by design rather than patching bias in evaluation (Farhud & Zokaei, 2021).

Responsible curation encourages dataset authors to explain inclusion criteria; document capture circumstances, devices, demographics, and consent channels; clarify licensing in clear language; and make limits obvious (Andrews et al., 2023). For human-centric picture and video sets-THG's bread and butter-this also entails controlling identity risk and recording annotation techniques that might alter perceived emotion, identity, or lip shapes. Recent advice for human-centric datasets foregrounds privacy and bias mitigation throughout the lifespan, reframing data work as a socio-technical activity rather than a merely technological process (Mattioli & Cabitza, 2024).

Standardization is a practical lever for ethics. When metadata formats, annotation norms, and evaluation protocols converge, it becomes simpler to share data responsibly, compare approaches fairly, and repeat findings. Ethical standards borrowed from adjacent fields-sports science, healthcare imaging, and social science big data-emphasize adaptable frameworks that can respond to new capture modalities and societal expectations, along with "ethics by design" approaches that integrate value considerations at the earliest stages (Duquenoy et al., 2008).

Transparency is the connecting thread between technical rigor and ethical responsibility. Transparency encompasses (1) dataset provenance (where did the data come from, under what terms, from whom), (2) data composition (who is represented, under what conditions), (3) curation and annotation, (4) processing and preprocessing, and (5) access and governance. THG researchers already appreciate how differences in frame rate, alignment, or cropping can swing lip-sync metrics; the same level of traceability should apply to consent, usage constraints, and demographic balance so that the field can reason about risks and responsibilities as precisely as it reasons about loss curves (Olteanu et al., 2019).

The chapter examines the taxonomy and comparative analysis of THG datasets across five axes: domain and modality, capture circumstances, view coverage, annotation scope, and licensing and access restrictions. It emphasizes well-known resources such as VoxCeleb/VoxCeleb2, LRS2/LRS3-TED, TalkingHead-1KH, HDTF, CelebV-HQ, MEAD, CREMA-D, RAVDESS, BIWI 3D, Multiface, VOCA/VOCASET, MeshTalk, and CelebV-Text, while noting lesser-cited sets that fit specific requirements.

The chapter also covers the constraints and limits of existing datasets, including demographic and language imbalance, restricted emotional labeling, pose bias toward frontal views, the realism-control trade-off between wild and lab environments, and the friction of privacy/licensing. It ties these gaps to failure modes found in practice and proposes data-centric solutions to minimize them. The chapter also highlights ethical and trustworthy data practices, based on cross-domain research. It operationalizes values such as honesty, carefulness, openness, efficiency, respect for subjects, and social responsibility into THG-specific recommendations for collection, documentation, annotation, storage, and access. Practical techniques such as dataset cards, standardized consent artifacts, tiered licenses with explicit redistribution criteria, and subject rights routines are discussed. The chapter also covers governance lessons from healthcare, public health, and business AI deployments that potentially translate to THG. Future directions for THG include multilingual and multicultural corpora reflecting the world's phonetics and viseme systems, emotionally rich annotations that capture subtle, culturally situated expressions, privacy-preserving pipelines (federated collection, differential privacy, on-device preprocessing), synthetic-real co-training strategies that scale while anchoring realism, and unified benchmarking standards that align metrics, protocols, and reporting across tasks and datasets. The chapter's integrative approach is simple: reality and accountability are mutually reinforcing. Models trained on transparent, well-documented, demographically balanced, and ethically obtained data are more likely to generalize across identities, languages, and situations, and to sustain public credibility. Conversely, opacity in data provenance or consent, or restricted coverage that accentuates bias, undercuts both performance and confidence. The chapter matches technical advice with governance equivalents, including multi-view, geometry-informed datasets, high-resolution sensors and uniform calibration, and transparent reporting of device pipelines and preprocessing. For lip synchronization, it stresses phonetic variety and alignment precision, combined with annotation standards that decrease rater bias and error propagation. For natural motion, it emphasizes multi-view or motion-capture supervision, with access regimes that respect the heightened sensitivity of 3D face geometry and motion trajectories. The chapter calls for dataset cards and "datasheets" that make ethical and technical qualities first-class citizens, identifying capture settings, demographics, permission, licensing, and rights management alongside hours, speakers, FPS, resolution, and view coverage. This integration of documentation with evaluation will help the discipline transition from ad-hoc comparisons toward repeatable, fair evaluations across tasks and populations.

THG's success hinges on increasing both data quality and ethics. The same discipline used to architectural design, loss functions, and metrics should apply to the data lifecycle, from source and permission to annotation and assessment, to access, redress, and long-term stewardship.

Chapter organized as (1) THG modalities and performance criteria overview; (2) taxonomy and comparative analysis of datasets (3) obstacles and constraints (4) ethical and reliable data practices and (5) future directions.

TALKING HEAD GENERATION (THG): AN OVERVIEW

THG refers to the method of synthesizing realistic human facial motions coordinated with multiple input modalities-such as speech, text, video, or still images-to construct lifelike talking faces (Rakesh et al., 2026). It seeks to recreate human voice articulation, emotion, and natural motion in a virtual context. This technology has become a cornerstone of contemporary digital interaction, finding applications in virtual avatars, video conferencing, entertainment, healthcare, and education (Mazumdar & Chowdhury, 2025; Shin et al., 2024; Mazumdar, 2025; McCulloch & Pitts, 1943). For example, THG enables realistic digital avatars for the metaverse, increases low-bitrate video conferencing with synthetic talking faces, and supports speech therapy and remote education by providing expressive and approachable human-like interactions (Hagos et al., 2024). A typical THG pipeline incorporates many modalities-audio-driven, video-driven, text-driven, and image-driven systems-each addressing distinct input and control methods for face animation (Rakesh et al., 2026). Emerging trends include diffusion-driven talking head synthesis, federated and differential privacy-aware training strategies, and multilingual THG models designed to generalize across diverse phonemes–viseme mappings.

Audio-driven THG creates mouth and face motions based only on voice input, assuring lip synchronization and emotion alignment with the audio stream. Advanced systems such as MuseTalk (Y. Zhang et al., 2024) and RealTalk (Ji et al., 2024) enable real-time, high-fidelity lip-sync performance among unseen speakers.

Video-driven THG focuses on transferring motion and identity information from reference video sequences to new frames, retaining temporal coherence and identity consistency. Models like HiDe-NeRF (Li et al., 2023) and Neural Talking-Head (T. Wang et al., 2021) maintain precise emotions and realistic position transitions for usage in video conferencing and film dubbing.

Text-driven THG synthesizes expressive talking heads from textual scripts, translating phonemes and prosody to graphic gestures. Techniques such as TalkCLIP (Ma et al., 2025) and Text2Video (S. Zhang et al., 2022) analyze semantic and rhythmic signals from text to manage emotion and rhythm in produced speech.

Image-driven THG utilizes static portraits as input to animate faces, reconstructing and animating 3D avatars that talk and emote depending on supplied signals. Approaches like Real3DPortrait (Ye et al., 2024) and AniPortrait (Wei et al., 2024) allow the translation of still photographs into expressive 3D films, valuable in entertainment and customized media development.

Data plays a key role in defining the accuracy, realism, and generalizability of THG models. High-quality and varied datasets enable models to acquire sophisticated facial behaviors, emotional nuances, and cross-identity stability. Popular datasets such as VoxCeleb (Nagrani et al., 2019), CREMA-D, TalkingHead-1KH, and CelebV-HQ are crucial to training audio- and video-driven systems, offering multimodal input for lip-sync and emotion modeling. Datasets like RAVDESS and MEAD give emotion-rich annotations, while VOCASET and BIWI supply extensive 3D information crucial for spatial realism. The study reveals that bigger and more ethnically varied datasets boost generalization across speakers and situations, enhancing the perceived quality of produced heads. Conversely, constraints such as inadequate resolution, restricted diversity, or lack of emotional variation might contribute to prejudice, diminished realism, and poor transferability to unknown contexts. As the subject evolves, the construction of multilingual, multi-view, and emotionally varied datasets is regarded as vital to ensure fairness and robustness in future THG systems.

TAXONOMY AND COMPARATIVE ANALYSIS OF DATASETS FOR THG

THG depends on high-quality datasets to train lip synchronization, emotion synthesis, and posture control algorithms. A number of significant datasets are utilized in this area. These include audio-driven datasets like VoxCeleb (Nagrani et al., 2019), CREMA-D, LRW (Lip Reading in the Wild), MEAD, video-driven datasets like TalkingHead-1KH, HDTF, and CelebV-HQ, text-driven datasets like CelebrV-Text, emotion-specific datasets like RAVDESS and VoxCeleb (Nagrani et al., 2019)1, as well as 3D and multi-view datasets like Multiface, Vocaset, and GRD. Datasets that are driven by audio are generally focused on synchronizing face gestures with spoken inputs. VoxCeleb (Nagrani et al., 2019)1 has more than 1,251 and 6,112 speakers available on YouTube, in addition to more than 153,000 audio-video clips. Cross-identity reenactment, speaker verification, and emotion-aware synthesis are all applications that make use of these datasets. On the other hand, they have several disadvantages, such as the absence of non-frontal postures, the poor resolution, the lack of lab control, the limited ethnic variety included, the small sample size, and the laboratory setting. The process of motion transfer and identity preservation across videos is accomplished with the assistance of video-driven databases. While TalkingHead-1KH comprises more than one thousand hours of talking head movies from YouTube, HDTF features three hundred and sixty-two speakers and ten thousand footage with severe scenarios. CelebV-HQ consists of 15,653 high-resolution clips of celebrities, while BIWI-3D includes 3D scans of 14 speakers along with annotations of their head positions. The RAVDESS dataset, which features 24 artists presenting eight various emotions via voice and music, is an example of an emotion-specific dataset that focuses on complex emotional expressions. VoxCeleb (Nagrani et al., 2019)1 features 652 real Emotional conversations from 12 speakers, while 3D and Multi-View datasets allow 3D-aware synthesis and free-view viewing. Vocaset contains 3D face gestures from 12 speakers, whereas GRD delivers 33,000 videos of 34 persons saying grammatically enforced phrases. Cross-modal datasets integrate diverse modalities (text, audio, video) utilizing LRS3-TED and GRD. These datasets have limitations, notably English and restricted Emotion labels, but may enhance lip-reading models' accuracy. THG depends substantially on different, high-quality datasets for tasks like lip synchronization, Emotion synthesis, and position control. These datasets have clear drawbacks, such as a bias towards frontal viewpoints and English speakers, limited ethnic diversity, and difficulties in the utilization of several modalities. Researchers may design more efficient and economical algorithms for creating realistic and compelling talking head material by examining these datasets and discovering their limits. While dataset characteristics are examined in detail, this analysis is intended to contextualize broader technical, ethical, and deployment-related challenges rather than serve as an exhaustive catalog. Table 1 summarizes key dataset properties to support comparative understanding, allowing the subsequent discussion to focus on implications rather than raw statistics.

Table 1. Overview of various datasets

Dataset	Highlights	Year	Hours	Speakers	Sentences	Env.	View	Category	FPS	Resolution
CelebV-Text (Yu et al., 2023)	Speech-driven facial animation	2023	279	70,000	1.4M	Wild	Frontal	Video	30	512×512
MMFace4D (Wu et al., 2023)	4D motion capture for face animation	2023	36	431	11K	Lab	Frontal	Video, Audio	30	1024×1024
CelebV-HQ (Zhu et al., 2022)	High-quality celebrity videos	2022	65	15,653	150K	Wild	Frontal	Video	30	512×512
Multiface (3D) (Wuu et al., 2022)	3D facial scan dataset	2022	120	13	5K	Lab	Multi-view	Image, Audio	30	2048×1334
Responsive Listening Head (Zhou et al., 2020)	3D avatars responding to audio	2022	1.5	67	483	Wild	Frontal	Video, Audio, Image	30	384×384
BIWI (3D) (Fanelli et al., 2012)	Annotated 3D face scans	2021	1.44	14	1109	Lab	Multi-view	Video	25	1920×1080
HDTF (Zhang et al., 2021)	Head pose estimation dataset	2021	15.8	362	10K	Wild	Multi-view	Video	30	1920×1080
TalkingHead-1 KH (T. Wang et al., 2021)	Emotion-rich talking videos	2021	1000	1000+	500K	Wild	Frontal	Video	30	1280×720

continued on following page

Table 1. Continued

Dataset	Highlights	Year	Hours	Speakers	Sentences	Env.	View	Category	FPS	Resolution
MeshTalk (Richard et al., 2021)	3D talking heads driven by speech	2021	13	250	12.5K	Lab	Multi-view	Video	30	800×800
MEAD (K. Wang et al., 2020)	Emotion-labeled high-res videos	2020	39	60	20	Lab	Multi-view	Video, Audio	30	1920×1080
Face Forensics ++ (Rossler et al., 2019)	Deepfake detection corpus	2019	5.7	1000	1000+	Wild	Frontal	Video, Image	30	512×512
FFHQ (Karras et al., 2020)	GAN-ready diverse face photos	2019	120	70,000+	1M	Wild	Multi-view	Image	1	1024×1024
VOCA (Cudeiro et al., 2019)	Vocal tract visualization via video	2019	0.5	12	40	Lab	Frontal	Video, Audio	60	2000×2000
Lombard (Alghamdi et al., 2018)	Speech under noise conditions	2018	3.6	54	5400	Lab	Multi-view	Video, Audio	30	864×480
LRS2 (Chung et al., 2017)	Lip-reading dataset from BBC TV	2018	224.5	500+	1.4M	Wild	Multi-view	Video, Audio, Text	25	224×224
LRS3-TED (Shillingford et al., 2019)	TED-based AV speech dataset	2018	438	5000	152K	Wild	Multi-view	Video, Audio, Text	25	224×224
MELD (Poria et al., 2019)	Emotion-rich dialogue videos	2018	13.7	407	13K	Wild	Frontal	Video, Audio, Text	30	720×576
RAVDESS (Livingstone & Russo, 2018)	Emotion expression by actors	2018	7	24	2	Lab	Frontal	Video, Audio	30	1920×1080
MODALITY (S. Zhou et al., 2024)	Multimodal affective dataset	2017	31	35	5800	Lab	Multi-view	Audio, Video	30	1920×1080
ObamaSet (Kumar et al., 2018)	Lip-sync and deepfake dataset	2017	14	1	300	Wild	Frontal	Video	30	1280×720
VoxCeleb (Nagrani et al., 2019)	Celeb voice video collection	2017	352	1200	153.5K	Wild	Frontal	Video	25	224×224
VoxCeleb 1 (Nagrani et al., 2020)	Emotion in AV commun-ication	2016	18	12	652	Lab	Frontal	Audio, Video, Image	30	1440×1080
VoxCeleb2 (Chung et al., 2018)	Uncon-strained celeb speech data	2017	352	1251	153K	Wild	Frontal	Video	30	224×224
LRW (Yang et al., 2019)	Word-level lip-reading videos	2016	173	1000	539K	Wild	Frontal	Video, Text	30	256×256

continued on following page

Table 1. Continued

Dataset	Highlights	Year	Hours	Speakers	Sentences	Env.	View	Category	FPS	Resolution
SAVEE (W. Wang, 2010)	Emotional speech videos	2015	4	480	4800	Lab	Frontal	Video, Audio	60	720×576
TCD-TIMIT (Harte & Gillen, 2015)	AV corpus for speech recognition	2015	11.1	62	6900	Lab	Multi-view	Video, Audio	30	1920×1080
CREMA-D (Cao et al., 2014)	Emotionally expressive AV clips	2014	11.1	91	12	Lab	Frontal	Video, Audio	30	960×720
GRID (Alghamdi et al., 2018)	Speech + lip reading video corpus	2006	27.5	34	33K	Lab	Frontal	Video, Audio	25	720×576
DPCD (Xuanyuan et al., 2023)	3D Emotion + dynamic pose scans	2004	29.75	5	48.6K	Wild	Multi-view	Video, Audio, Text	25	1024×1024
CAVSR1.0 (Boulis et al., 2001)	Early lip sync + facial animation set	1998	8	123	600	Lab	Frontal	Video, Audio	30	640×480

A spectrum of training and evaluation datasets informs research on THG. The varied character of this activity is indicated by the disparities in the datasets' size, recording settings, view kinds, included modalities, motion capture data availability, and resolution. Emphasizing their key qualities required to build avatar and video synthesis algorithms, Table 1 clearly illustrates this domain's most extensively used datasets. Creating successful avatar and video synthesis algorithms relies on the number and duration of these datasets. A renowned resource for applications requiring substantial amounts of diverse audio-visual data is VoxCeleb2, which provides an impressive 2,400 hours of video featuring 6,100 voices and 1.1 million words. With 438 hours of TED Talks from 5,000 speakers and 152,000 phrases, LRS3-TED similarly provides diverse speaking styles and linguistic material for lip-reading and speech-to-text research. Conversely, CelebV-Text highlights lip sync properties, which are useful for training algorithms focused on accurate mouth movements; datasets like VOCA supply high-quality 3D face motion capture data. Recording conditions greatly alter the properties of the dataset. Many datasets are labeled as "WILD," meaning they were acquired in uncontrolled, real-world circumstances. Examples of these datasets include VoxCeleb (Nagrani et al., 2019), VoxCeleb 1 (Nagrani et al., 2019), VoxCeleb2, LRS2 (BBC), LRS3-TED, FFHQ, HDTF, TalkingHead-1KH, CelebV-HQ, and CelebrV-Text. Although it poses challenges, this change in background noise, light, and speaker placement makes models trained on such data more resilient. In contrast, datasets such as MMFace4D, BIWI (3D), VOCA, Lombard, RAVDESS, MEAD, VoxCeleb (Nagrani et al., 2019)1, SAVEE, TCD-TIMIT, CREMA-D, GRAD, and CAVSR1.0 are recorded in controlled "LAB" environments, providing cleaner data with consistent background and lighting, which can be useful for isolating particular factors like lip movements or Emotional expressions. Another key topic in the investigation of THG is view type. "FRONTAL-VIEW" recordings make up several datasets, especially those that focus on talking head construction and lip-reading, which improves the learning process for lip motions. Nonetheless, datasets such as Multiface (3D), BIWI (3D), Lombard, LRS2 (BBC), LRS3-TED, MEAD, and TCD-TIMIT supply "MULTI-VIEW" data, which is crucial to train models that can handle multiple head locations and construct talking heads that are aware of three dimensions. "N/A" is supplied for view type in datasets such as CelebV-HQ, HDTF, TalkingHead-1KH, FFHQ, VoxCeleb2, VoxCeleb (Nagrani et al., 2019), VoxCeleb (Nagrani et al., 2019)1, ObamaSet, and CREMA-D, and this shows variability or that this information is not the key focus. These datasets are frequently large-scale collections for generic face analysis or recognition. Modalities use "VIDEO" and "AUDIO" data to comprehend the link between speech and facial movements. This crucial mix is offered by a few datasets, including MMFace4D, Responsive Listening Head creation, BIWI (3D), FaceForensics++, MeshTalk, FFHQ, MODALITY, and GAN-based face generation. Motion capture data is required to train models to produce believable 3D face animations. The quality and smoothness of the produced animations are limited by frame rate (FPS). High-resolution 3D models or photos are offered via high-resolution datasets such as Multiface (3D), MEAD, RAVDESS, TCD-TIMIT, and DPCD. Additionally, another dataset that is not heavily mentioned but has an effect in the domain of THG includes Hallo3, VFHQ, and a few others.

CHALLENGES AND LIMITATIONS OF CURRENT DATASETS

THG has made great progress, but it still faces various issues that restrict its justice, realism, and generalizability. These include demographic bias, restricted emotion labeling, pose diversity concerns, synthetic and. natural data, and dataset scalability and licensing. The overrepresentation of individuals speaking the same language and hailing from the same location in current THG datasets introduces cultural and racial bias, since models developed from these datasets generally do not generalize across different ethnicities, accents, and linguistic nuances. This mismatch harms inclusion and risks reproducing prejudice in downstream applications like digital avatars and telepresence technology. Building multilingual and demographically balanced datasets is vital for furthering fair and internationally representative THG research. Limited emotion annotations in existing datasets restrict the expressiveness of THG models, resulting in avatars that frequently look lifeless or repetitive in sophisticated social interactions. A richer, effective taxonomy is vital for boosting emotional authenticity and guaranteeing that talking heads communicate with human-like complexity and empathy. Pose diversity concerns, such as dependency on frontal-view data, are another structural restriction. Many commonly accepted collections predominantly feature frontal or near-frontal head orientations, resulting in unnatural motion, distorted geometry, or loss of face identity when synthesizing off-angle viewpoints. Expanding pose variety is crucial for establishing view-consistent and spatially aware THG systems, especially for applications in immersive media and 3D telepresence. Synthetic data, such as FaceForensics++ and FFHQ, provides benefits in data management, annotation accuracy, and scalability, but typically lacks the diversity, spontaneity, and noise inherent in genuine recordings. Natural datasets recorded "in the wild" give authenticity but add issues, including irregular illumination, background noise, and uncontrolled positions. Balancing realism with experimental control is vital for strengthening the ethical trustworthiness of THG systems. Lastly, dataset scalability, privacy, and licensing continue to hamper open scientific development. Large-scale datasets, such as CelebV-HQ, TalkingHead-1KH, and HDTF, encounter use limitations that hinder redistribution or modification, frequently owing to copyright and permission considerations. Future THG data collection must emphasize ethical licensing frameworks, informed consent methods, and open-access availability to support fair innovation and assure accountability in dataset-driven research. Beyond dataset construction, practical deployment challenges—such as real-time inference constraints, consent enforcement in downstream applications, and robustness under low-resource settings—remain underexplored in current THG literature.

ETHICAL AND TRUSTWORTHY DATA PRACTICES

The evolution of ethical standards in data science has gained significant attention as the field expands and integrates into diverse sectors. Wang et al. (2018) underscore the necessity of ethical approaches within data science to mitigate negative impacts during the phases of data collection, analysis, and storage. They assert that an ethical framework is essential to ensure responsible practices in handling data. Furthermore, Harriss et al. (2022) highlight the ongoing expansion of data science, focusing on the standardization of datasets. They provide a contemporary viewpoint on ethical standards in sports and exercise science research, where adaptable ethical frameworks are essential to confront emerging challenges and advancements in technology. Padmapriya and Parthasarathy (2023) concentrate on the ethical dilemmas present in healthcare research, specifically within the realm of medical image analysis (MIA). They put forward a comprehensive approach to ethical data collection, which is pertinent given the rapid progression of data science and artificial intelligence in healthcare. Their proposed framework serves to assist data scientists in navigating potential ethical issues prior to initiating data analytics on medical datasets. In the context of THG (the specific organization or domain implied), ethical and privacy issues are not merely supplementary concerns. Rather, they are fundamental technical constraints that critically impact the usability of datasets, their readiness for deployment, and the level of public trust that can be established. This perspective positions ethical considerations as central to the practice of data science, demanding ongoing attention as the discipline evolves.

The ethical landscape in data science is influenced by technological advancements, societal and cultural contexts, and the perspectives of students and practitioners, who significantly shape ethical practices within the field. Harriss et al. (2022) emphasize the importance of dataset standardization in the ethical management of data, as it ensures interoperability and accessibility, facilitating ethical data sharing and collaboration. The evolution of ethical standards in data science is significantly shaped by growing public awareness about data privacy and security. As data becomes increasingly valuable, the ethical concerns surrounding data collection and analysis become more critical. There is a need for robust ethical guidelines, which are vital for both professional accountability and societal well-being. Additionally, due to the global nature of data science, harmonizing ethical standards across different cultures is necessary. Comparative reviews of these standards facilitate a better understanding of diverse ethical practices, promoting the creation of inclusive and universally applicable frameworks influenced by technology, societal expectations, and stakeholder perspectives. The increasing awareness of the ethical implications of data collection, analysis, and usage has led to the need for robust ethical frameworks (Kuc-Czarnecka & Olczyk, 2020).

The significance of ethical considerations in data practices is paramount, particularly as data becomes increasingly prevalent in society. Research by Zhang-Kennedy & Chiasson (2021) highlights that while consumers recognize their privacy rights, they often struggle to exercise them, indicating the need for ethical standards that are not only established but also made accessible and comprehensible to the public.

Andrews et al. (2023) highlight the ethical considerations of collecting human-centric image datasets, focusing on privacy and bias, to promote responsible data curation. Fisher et al. (2020) explore ethical challenges in eHealth HIV intervention research with an emphasis on informational risk related to recruitment and consent. Hosseini et al. (2022) explore the ethical challenges in social science research using big data, highlighting issues such as the interpretative nature of the data, complexities in managing publication risks, and a lack of regulatory oversight. Padmapriya and Parthasarathy (2023) introduce an ethical data collection framework for medical image analysis in healthcare, addressing the high-stakes ethical concerns inherent in handling sensitive data and advocating for a systematic approach for ethical data management in this field. Core ethical principles are essential for maintaining the integrity of data science practices, as underscored by Jameel and Majid (2018), who argue that ethics should be a fundamental aspect of the research process rather than a supplementary concern.

The evolution of ethical standards in data science is driven by various factors, including technological advancements, societal expectations, and the need for ethical considerations in data collection and analysis. The ethical complexities of big data present significant concerns for democracy, individual rights, and societal norms. The use of AI and big data in digital media can undermine individual agency, necessitating ethical frameworks to mitigate negative impacts and promote positive contributions to democracy. Key issues in social sciences include the interpretative nature of big data, risk management in its use, and regulatory oversights. David Resnik's research ethics framework emphasizes honesty, transparency, and social responsibility, addressing biases and individual harms in big data research. As big data evolves, addressing these ethical challenges is critical for researchers and practitioners, who must continually integrate ethical considerations into the data lifecycle and adapt to the changing regulatory landscape. Ochang et al. (2023) explore the ethical positions that underpin global brain data governance, emphasizing the need for a comprehensive global governance framework. Georgieva et al. (2022) contribute to the discourse on AI ethics by mapping AI ethical principles onto the lifecycle of AI-based digital services and products, emphasizing the gap between theoretical ethical frameworks and practical data science applications.

Austin (2023) discusses the data governance gap revealed by the COVID-19 pandemic, particularly in the context of public health emergencies, arguing for a broader framework of data governance, addressing foundational questions about decision-making, accountability, and oversight in data flows.

The research gap in data ethics is significant as data science evolves across various domains, necessitating robust regulatory and ethical frameworks to tackle complex dilemmas associated with technological advancements and large data volumes. Researchers must understand the evolving regulatory landscape and the expectations of data subjects. Key studies illustrate the intersection of big data ethics and social science research, with David Resnik proposing a research ethics framework emphasizing principles such as honesty and social responsibility. Additionally, models for data ethics instruction, like those discussed by Phan et al. (2022), address curricular disparities, while Hirsch et al. (2019) highlight corporate transformations in data ethics. Reed-Berendt et al. (2021) advocate for integrating ethical principles in the design of big data health research, specifically through a "Big Data Ethics by Design" approach. This review aims to close the data ethics research gap by offering insights into developing ethical frameworks and instructional models, ultimately promoting responsible data practices aligned with societal values and the public good.

FUTURE DIRECTIONS

THG datasets are approaching a transformational phase, as they offer the empirical underpinning for machine learning models that integrate audio and visual modalities to generate realistic, synchronized, and emotionally cohesive face animation. However, as THG technologies develop in expressive power and social consequence, the demands imposed on their underlying datasets increase proportionally. The next stage of THG corpus design and collecting must advance intentionally toward broader coverage, better contextual knowledge, and deeper care-three axes that together constitute a sustainable, trustworthy, and human-centered data ecosystem. Coverage refers to the linguistic, demographic, environmental, and behavioral breadth that guarantee a dataset accurately represents the heterogeneity of worldwide human communication. Context involves the multimodal, situational, and emotional richness that situates speech and face movement within relevant real-world settings. Care signifies the ethical, privacy-preserving, and governance frameworks that safeguard participants' rights, honor their agency, and assure data stewardship commensurate with dignity and trust. Each of these pillars interlocks: coverage without care risks exploitation; context without coverage leads to prejudice; and care without appropriate breadth may impede scientific generalizability. The next generation of THG datasets must attempt purposeful design that harmonizes all three.

Existing THG datasets are confined by their language and cultural reach. A majority of widely used corpora are English-dominant, usually relying on Western media sources such as broadcast interviews, movie snippets, or curated YouTube material. These resources, although handy, present biases that are both linguistic and performative. To surmount these restrictions, future datasets must map the world's phonetic and viseme systems. Building corpora that depict cross-linguistic phonetic variation is not just about adding additional languages; it includes capturing the audio-visual alignment specific to each.

Beyond language, demographic coverage is as vital. Age, gender, ethnicity, and face morphology all impact expressive motion fields and coarticulation geometry. Moreover, cultural traditions impact the speed, amplitude, and even permissibility of emotional manifestation. Intentional demographic balance is required, accomplished by planned sampling rather than opportunistic scraping. The predominance of English-centric datasets limits cross-lingual generalization, underscoring the need for multilingual and multicultural corpora that capture language-specific viseme dynamics and culturally grounded expressions.

Existing emotional video-speech datasets-such as MEAD, RAVDESS, CREMA-D, and MELD-have offered vital benchmarks for emotion-conditioned synthesis. Yet, these labels typically represent crude, categorized emotions, generated from actor-staged performances rather than spontaneous communication. Future datasets must represent this complexity via deeper annotation schemes that go beyond category tags. One option ahead is to embrace dimensional emotion models-such as the valence-arousal-dominance framework-augmented with discrete assessments (e.g., surprise, disdain) and cultural modifiers. Multimodal traces-audio energy contours, head nods, gaze shifts-enable models to infer emotion in context rather than from static snapshots. The future of THG datasets rests in multi-modal alignment, where emotional labels come from the dynamic interaction of speech acoustics, face movements, and social environment. The paper explores the difficulty of capturing interactional context in video-based human-centric (THG) datasets, which generally consist of solitary speakers delivering scripts or monologues. To overcome this, the future of THG data collecting rests in privacy-preserving designs, where preprocessing is conducted locally on participants' devices, and only non-identifiable representations or aggregated statistics are transferred. This assures that even disclosed datasets cannot be reverse-engineered to recreate people. Transparency is another cornerstone of care, with every THG dataset providing a detailed dataset card documenting collecting circumstances, participant demographics, recording equipment, annotation processes, and permission channels. Dataset cards should specifically describe the extent of usage approved by participants and the options for withdrawal or redress. Embedding auditable permission artifacts-cryptographically verifiable consent tokens-would enable downstream users to check compliance programmatically. Care also necessitates attention against prejudice and exclusion, since face animation models directly encode human identification traits, emerging as evident disparities in created output. Mitigating these impacts needs both dataset-level fairness analysis and model-level bias audits. Datasets should be supplemented with demographic information, fairness measurements, and benchmark splits stratified by factors such as skin tone, age, and gender expression. Reporting such information publicly creates accountability and helps the community to monitor progress toward equal performance. Data sovereignty and cultural sensitivity extend beyond individual privacy to community and cultural rights. Collecting and replicating such data without contextual consideration concerns cultural appropriation or violation of local norms. Future THG dataset efforts must interact with concepts of data sovereignty-consulting communities, obeying local data protection regulations, and offering opt-out methods for organizations as well as people. Synthetic data, created by simulation, rendering, or model-based augmentation, presents a possible answer to the scalability and privacy difficulties of human video gathering. However, synthetic corpora must be produced in cooperation with actual data, not in isolation from it, to prevent learning artifacts disconnected from human reality. Synthetic augmentation may boost variation, cover unusual viseme combinations, extreme stances, or low-resource phonemes that are difficult to record empirically. However, synthetic data comes with dangers of distributional drift-the modest divergence between created and real-world statistics. To avoid this, synthetic corpora must be calibrated against empirical distributions collected from authentic recordings. Statistical alignment guarantees that synthetic augmentations support rather than distort reality.

Future research in THG should concentrate on hybrid learning frameworks, where synthetic and real data co-train models in complimentary roles. Real data roots models in authenticity and noise realism, whereas synthetic data extends variety and inhibits overfitting. Domain adaptation approaches, such as adversarial alignment, feature disentanglement, and style transfer, may bridge the remaining gap across domains. Transparency regarding synthetic components must be necessary, and dataset cards should disclose the percentage and creation techniques of synthetic samples to preserve repeatability. Building agreed criteria for progress and replicability is critical as THG datasets expand. Evaluation techniques vary in data pretreatment, metric selection, and test-train divides, resulting to fragmented and even non-reproducible assertions. A unified benchmark should describe a limited set of core measurements that cover both objective and subjective quality characteristics. Objective measurements should evaluate alignment, smoothness, and temporal coherence, while subjective ones should assess naturalness and emotional plausibility via controlled human review processes. Each indicator should be supported by unambiguous definitions, units, and suggested statistical reporting.

Standard input preprocessing and splitting are also crucial for repeatability. Variations in face cropping, landmark detection, or audio normalization may substantially alter model outputs. Standard pipelines should be created for turning raw THG datasets into training-ready form, and fixed train/test splits must be provided to minimize unintended data leaks. Fairness and cross-domain generalization are necessary for THG technology advancement ethically and openly. Models should be assessed for demographic parity, comparing accuracy and naturalness across groups characterized by gender, race, and language. Cross-domain generalization tests give further insight on representational equality. Ablation templates and repeatable reporting will turn THG research from an artisanal endeavor into a reproducible science. Governance from data collecting to data institutions is required for sustained success in THG. Datasets should be curated, managed, and versioned by data institutions, which oversee access, changes, and ethical supervision. This institutional layer enables continuity, traceability, and community engagement, giving procedures for takedown requests, mistake rectification, and data retirement when permission expires or legal frameworks change. The future of THG datasets is not only about quantity or complexity but also about validity. Public acceptability rests on whether these systems represent the variety of the world's population, protect the rights of contributors, and function openly under responsible governance. Ethical literacy must be built into every aspect of dataset generation, setting goals jointly, documenting choices, assessing results, and interacting with impacted groups. The next generation of THG datasets will not only drive more competent and expressive models but also represent the societal ideals that make such technology respectable. Building varied, transparent, and morally demanding datasets is vital for converting the brilliance of THG algorithms into meaningful human benefit.

CONCLUSION

The chapter discusses the importance of data quality, transparency, and ethical integrity in talking head generation (THG) technologies. Advances in neural rendering, multimodal modeling, and deep generative architectures have enabled the creation of hyper-realistic, controllable, and expressive talking heads capable of mimicking human speech and emotion with striking fidelity. However, the technical progress of THG relies heavily on the datasets used to train and evaluate these models. The authors argue that the field's technical progress is inseparable from its data practices-specifically, how data are sourced, documented, annotated, and shared. Without rigorous attention to data ethics and governance, even the most elegant algorithms risk perpetuating bias, reducing inclusivity, and eroding public trust. Dataset quality and realism are crucial for the realism of a talking head model. High frame rate, consistent camera geometry, and stable alignment enable smoother temporal modeling, while diverse lighting conditions and head poses enrich the model's capacity to generalize. However, current datasets often fall short of these ideals, with many benchmark corpora remaining dominated by English-speaking subjects, captured primarily from frontal views under studio-like lighting. This narrow scope limits the realism of generated avatars when applied to multilingual, multiethnic, or spontaneous real-world scenarios. Another limitation identified is the prevalence of coarse, staged, or culturally biased emotion annotations. Many datasets categorize affect into simplified labels such as "happy," "sad," or "angry," often recorded by actors in scripted contexts rather than spontaneous interactions. These staged emotions lack ecological validity, making them poor approximations of the subtle and context-dependent ways real people express feelings. Furthermore, emotional expressions can vary dramatically across cultures, making THG models risk reproducing expressions that feel artificial or inappropriate to global audiences. The frontal-view bias prevalent in many datasets hampers the ability of THG systems to model three-dimensional head dynamics and gaze behavior. Most datasets rely on single-camera setups, resulting in flattened 2D perspectives that simplify face geometry at the expense of realism. Without multi-view or 3D capture, models struggle to reproduce natural head rotations or maintain consistent identity features under varied viewing angles. The chapter also highlights the importance of ethical analogs of technical factors in THG research. Data provenance, participant consent, demographic balance, and annotation integrity are equally critical for responsible innovation. Ethical diligence is not an external imposition but a mirror discipline to technical precision. Models trained on well-documented, demographically balanced, and ethically obtained data not only perform better across diverse conditions but also gain credibility when deployed in public-facing applications. Transparency in data lineage and curation methods builds trust among users, regulators, and peer researchers. The chapter proposes concrete practices for ethical and inclusive datasets in the field of talking head (THG) research. These practices include dataset cards and datasheets, structured documentation frameworks, and methods for labeling speech, emotion, or pose. By publishing these details, dataset creators can empower others to assess the fitness, fairness, and compliance of their data for specific research or commercial purposes. The chapter also emphasizes the importance of synthetic data, AI-generated or simulated visual and audio samples, in THG research. While synthetic data can scale coverage efficiently, it inherits biases from the generative models that produce it. Therefore, synthetic augmentation must be grounded in verified, ethically sourced real data to preserve authenticity and accountability. The chapter concludes with a collective call to action, urging all actors in the THG ecosystem to converge on shared ethical and technical standards. This includes developing unified evaluation protocols that travel across modalities and tasks, enabling apples-to-apples comparisons of model performance. Transparency should extend not only to model code but also to data preprocessing steps, train-test splits, and evaluation recipes, which are often omitted from publications despite their impact on outcomes. The authors advocate for performance reporting stratified by demographics and poses, revealing how models perform across gender, age, ethnicity, and viewing conditions. Such granular transparency helps identify systemic weaknesses and ensures that model excellence does not mask inequity. By promoting open sharing of datasets, annotations, and benchmarks under responsible licenses, the community can accelerate reproducibility and collective learning without compromising individual privacy or consent. The chapter envisions a paradigm shift in how success in talking head production is measured. Trustworthiness, transparency, and inclusivity will become as central to evaluation as perceptual quality or synchronization accuracy. Transparent data practices cultivate public confidence, enable reproducible science, and pave the way for applications that enhance human communication. The chapter closes with an appeal for collaborative stewardship, a shared commitment to make the talking head field not only a showcase of technical brilliance but also a model of ethical maturity. Only through such a balance-between performance and principle, between innovation and accountability-can the field fulfill its promise of connecting people across languages, cultures, and realities in ways that are both technologically remarkable and socially trustworthy.

REFERENCES

Abootorabi, M. M., Ghahroodi, O., Zahraei, P. S., Behzadasl, H., Mirrokni, A., Salimipanah, M., Rasouli, A., Behzadipour, B., Azarnoush, S., Maleki, B., Sadraiye, E., Feriz, K. K., Nahad, M. T., Moghadasi, A., Abianeh, A. E., Nazar, N., Rabiee, H. R., Baghshah, M. S., Ahmadi, M., & Asgari, E. (2025, April 27). *Generative AI for Character animation: A comprehensive survey of techniques, applications, and future directions*. arXiv.org. https://arxiv.org/abs/2504.19056v1

Alghamdi, N., Maddock, S., Marxer, R., Barker, J., & Brown, G. J. (2018). A corpus of audio-visual Lombard speech with frontal and profile views. *The Journal of the Acoustical Society of America, 143*(6), EL523–EL529. DOI: 10.1121/1.5042758 PMID: 29960497

Andrews, J. T. A., Sony, A. I., Zhao, D., Sony, A. I., Thong, W., Sony, A. I., Modas, A., Sony, A. I., Papakyriakopoulos, O., Sony, A. I., Xiang, A., & Sony, A. I. (2023). Ethical Considerations for Responsible Data Curation. *37th Conference on Neural Information Processing Systems (NeurIPS 2023) Track on Datasets and Benchmarks.* https://proceedings.neurips.cc/paper_files/paper/2023/file/ad3ebc951f43d1e9ed20187a7b5bc4ee-Paper-Datasets_and_Benchmarks.pdf

Austin, L. M. (2023). COVID-19 and the data governance gap. *Annual Review of Law and Social Science, 19*(1), 235–253. DOI: 10.1146/annurev-lawsocsci-050520-101947

Boulis, C., Diakoloukas, V., & Digalakis, V. (2001). Maximum likelihood stochastic transformation adaptation for medium and small data sets. *Computer Speech & Language, 15*(3), 257–285. DOI: 10.1006/csla.2001.0168

Cao, H., Cooper, D. G., Keutmann, M. K., Gur, R. C., Nenkova, A., & Verma, R. (2014). CREMA-D: Crowd-Sourced Emotional Multimodal Actors Dataset. *IEEE Transactions on Affective Computing*, *5*(4), 377–390. DOI: 10.1109/TAFFC.2014.2336244 PMID: 25653738

Chen, Z., Qi, T., Lu, C., & Zheng, W. (2025). DisenEmo: Learning disentangled emotional representation from facial motion for 3D talking head generation. *2022 IEEE International Conference on Image Processing (ICIP)*, 289-294. DOI: 10.1109/ICIP55913.2025.11084454

Chung, J. S., Nagrani, A., & Zisserman, A. (2018). VoxCeleb2: Deep Speaker Recognition. *Interspeech*, *2022*, 1086–1090. Advance online publication. DOI: 10.21437/Interspeech.2018-1929

Chung, J. S., Senior, A., Vinyals, O., & Zisserman, A. (2017). *Lip reading sentences in the wild*. IEEE., DOI: 10.1109/CVPR.2017.367

Cudeiro, D., Bolkart, T., Laidlaw, C., Ranjan, A., & Black, M. J. (2019). Capture, learning, and synthesis of 3D speaking styles. *2022 IEEE/CVF Conference on Computer Vision and Pattern Recognition (CVPR)*, 10093-10103. DOI: 10.1109/CVPR.2019.01034

Diao, X., Cheng, M., Barrios, W., & Jin, S. (2025). FT2TF: First-Person Statement Text-to-Talking Face Generation. *2022 IEEE/CVF Winter Conference on Applications of Computer Vision (WACV)*, 4821-4830. DOI: 10.1109/WACV61041.2025.00472

Dong, B., & Zhang, L. (2025). Enhanced temporal representation and spatial alignment for High-Fidelity Talking Video Generation. *The Visual Computer*, *41*(12), 9781–9792. Advance online publication. DOI: 10.1007/s00371-025-03999-2

Duquenoy, P., George, C., & Kimppa, K. (2008). Ethical, legal and social issues in medical informatics. In *IGI Global eBooks*. DOI: 10.4018/978-1-59904-780-5

Fanelli, G., Dantone, M., Gall, J., Fossati, A., & Van Gool, L. (2012). Random forests for real time 3D face analysis. *International Journal of Computer Vision*, *101*(3), 437–458. DOI: 10.1007/s11263-012-0549-0

Farhud, D. D., & Zokaei, S. (2021). Ethical issues of artificial intelligence in medicine and healthcare. *Iranian Journal of Public Health*. Advance online publication. DOI: 10.18502/ijph.v50i11.7600 PMID: 35223619

Fisher, C. B., Bragard, E., & Bloom, R. (2020). Ethical Considerations in HIV eHealth Intervention Research: Implications for informational risk in recruitment, data maintenance, and consent procedures. *Current HIV/AIDS Reports*, *17*(3), 180–189. DOI: 10.1007/s11904-020-00489-z PMID: 32358768

Georgieva, I., Lazo, C., Timan, T., & Van Veenstra, A. F. (2022). From AI ethics principles to data science practice: A reflection and a gap analysis based on recent frameworks and practical experience. *AI and Ethics*, *2*(4), 697–711. DOI: 10.1007/s43681-021-00127-3

Hagos, D. H., Battle, R., & Rawat, D. B. (2024). Recent advances in generative AI and large language models: Current status, challenges, and perspectives. *IEEE Transactions on Artificial Intelligence*, *5*(12), 5873–5893. DOI: 10.1109/TAI.2024.3444742

Han, Z., Teye, M., Yadgaroff, D., & Bütepage, J. (2025). Tiny is not small enough: High quality, low-resource facial animation models through hybrid knowledge distillation. *ACM Transactions on Graphics*, *44*(4), 1–18. DOI: 10.1145/3730929

Harriss, D. J., Jones, C., & MacSween, A. (2022). Ethical Standards in Sport and Exercise Science Research: 2022 update. *International Journal of Sports Medicine*, *43*(13), 1065–1070. DOI: 10.1055/a-1957-2356 PMID: 36495253

Harte, N., & Gillen, E. (2015). TCD-TIMIT: An Audio-Visual Corpus of Continuous Speech. *IEEE Transactions on Multimedia*, *17*(5), 603–615. DOI: 10.1109/TMM.2015.2407694

Hirsch, D. D., Bartley, T., Chandrasekaran, A., Parthasarathy, S., Turner, P. N., Norris, D., Lamont, K., & Drummond, C. (2019). Corporate Data Ethics: Data Governance Transformations for the age of advanced Analytics and AI. SSRN *Electronic Journal*. DOI: 10.2139/ssrn.3478826

Hosseini, M., Wieczorek, M., & Gordijn, B. (2022). Ethical issues in social science research employing big data. *Science and Engineering Ethics*, *28*(3), 29. Advance online publication. DOI: 10.1007/s11948-022-00380-7 PMID: 35705883

Iandola, F., Pidhorskyi, S., Santesteban, I., Gupta, D., Pahuja, A., Bartolovic, N., Yu, F., Garbin, E., Simon, T., & Saito, S. (2025). SqueezeMe: Mobile-Ready distillation of Gaussian Full-Body Avatars. *SIGGRAPH Conference Papers '25: Proceedings of the Special Interest Group on Computer Graphics and Interactive Techniques Conference Conference Papers*, 1-11. DOI: 10.1145/3721238.3730599

Jameel, B., & Majid, U. (2018). Research fundamentals: Data collection, data analysis, and ethics. *Undergraduate Research in Natural and Clinical Science and Technology (URNCST). Journal*, *2*(4), 1–8. DOI: 10.26685/urncst.39

Ji, X., Lin, C., Ding, Z., Tai, Y., Yang, J., Zhu, J., Hu, X., Zhang, J., Luo, D., & Wang, C. (2024). RealTalk: Real-time and Realistic Audio-driven Face Generation with 3D Facial Prior-guided Identity Alignment Network. *arXiv (Cornell University)*. / arxiv.2406.18284DOI: 10.48550

Karras, T., Laine, S., & Aila, T. (2020). A Style-Based generator architecture for generative adversarial networks. *IEEE Transactions on Pattern Analysis and Machine Intelligence*, *43*(12), 4217–4228. DOI: 10.1109/TPAMI.2020.2970919 PMID: 32012000

Kuc-Czarnecka, M., & Olczyk, M. (2020). How ethics combine with big data: A bibliometric analysis. *Humanities & Social Sciences Communications*, *7*(1), 137. Advance online publication. DOI: 10.1057/s41599-020-00638-0

Kumar, R., Sotelo, J., Kumar, K., De Brébisson, A., & Bengio, Y. (2018). ObamaNet: Photo-realistic lip-sync from text. *arXiv (Cornell University)*. /arxiv.1801.01442DOI: 10.48550

Li, B., Wei, X., Liu, B., He, Z., Cao, J., & Lai, Y. (2024). Pose-Aware 3D Talking Face Synthesis using Geometry-guided Audio-Vertices Attention. *IEEE Transactions on Visualization and Computer Graphics*, *31*(3), 1758–1771. DOI: 10.1109/TVCG.2024.3371064 PMID: 38416616

Li, W., Zhang, L., Wang, D., Zhao, B., Wang, Z., Chen, M., Zhang, B., Wang, Z., Bo, L., & Li, X. (2023). One-Shot High-Fidelity Talking-Head Synthesis with Deformable Neural Radiance Field. *arXiv (Cornell University)*. /arxiv.2304.05097DOI: 10.1109/CVPR52729.2023.01723

Liu, Y., Xu, F., Chai, J., Tong, X., Wang, L., & Huo, Q. (2015). Video-audio driven real-time facial animation. *ACM Transactions on Graphics*, *34*(6), 1–10. DOI: 10.1145/2816795.2818122

Livingstone, S. R., & Russo, F. A. (2018). The Ryerson Audio-Visual Database of Emotional Speech and Song (RAVDESS): A dynamic, multimodal set of facial and vocal expressions in North American English. *PLoS One*, *13*(5), e0196391. DOI: 10.1371/journal.pone.0196391 PMID: 29768426

Ma, H., Zhang, T., Sun, S., Yan, X., Han, K., & Xie, X. (2024). CVTHead: One-shot Controllable Head Avatar with Vertex-feature Transformer. *2022 IEEE/CVF Winter Conference on Applications of Computer Vision (WACV)*, 6119-6129. DOI: 10.1109/WACV57701.2024.00602

Ma, Y., Wang, S., Ding, Y., Ma, B., Lv, T., Fan, C., Hu, Z., Deng, Z., & Yu, X. (2025). TalkCLIP: Talking Head Generation with Text-Guided Expressive Speaking Styles. *IEEE Transactions on Multimedia*, *27*, 1–12. DOI: 10.1109/TMM.2025.3581808

Mattioli, M., & Cabitza, F. (2024). Not in my face: Challenges and ethical considerations in automatic face emotion recognition technology. *Machine Learning and Knowledge Extraction*, *6*(4), 2201–2231. DOI: 10.3390/make6040109

Mazumdar, S. (2025). Educational implications of 6G technology for society 5.0. In *Elsevier eBooks* (pp. 255-265). DOI: 10.1016/B978-0-443-27434-3.00017-9

Mazumdar, S., & Chowdhury, I. (2025). Integration of machine learning, deep learning, and Internet of Things technologies for stress management and identification: a systematic analysis. In *Elsevier eBooks* (pp. 407-418). DOI: 10.1016/B978-0-443-33498-6.00023-6

McCulloch, W. S., & Pitts, W. (1943). A logical calculus of the ideas immanent in nervous activity. *The Bulletin of Mathematical Biophysics*, *5*(4), 115–133. DOI: 10.1007/BF02478259

Nagrani, A., Chung, J. S., Xie, W., & Zisserman, A. (2019). Voxceleb: Large-scale speaker verification in the wild. *Computer Speech & Language*, *60*, 101027. DOI: 10.1016/j.csl.2019.101027

Nagrani, A., Chung, J. S., Xie, W., & Zisserman, A. (2020). Voxceleb: Large-scale speaker verification in the wild. *Computer Speech & Language*, *60*, 101027. DOI: 10.1016/j.csl.2019.101027

Ochang, P., Eke, D., & Stahl, B. C. (2023). Towards an understanding of global brain data governance: Ethical positions that underpin global brain data governance discourse. *Frontiers in Big Data*, *6*, 1240660. Advance online publication. DOI: 10.3389/fdata.2023.1240660 PMID: 38025947

Olteanu, A., Castillo, C., Diaz, F., & Kıcıman, E. (2019). Social data: Biases, methodological pitfalls, and ethical boundaries. *Frontiers in Big Data*, *2*, 13. Advance online publication. DOI: 10.3389/fdata.2019.00013 PMID: 33693336

Padmapriya, S. T., & Parthasarathy, S. (2023). Ethical Data Collection for Medical Image Analysis: A Structured Approach. *Asian Bioethics Review*, *16*(1), 95–108. DOI: 10.1007/s41649-023-00250-9 PMID: 37361687

Peng, W., Zhang, K., & Zhang, S. Q. (2024). T3M: Text Guided 3D Human Motion Synthesis from Speech. *Findings of the Association for Computational Linguistics: NAACL, 2022*, 1168–1177. DOI: 10.18653/v1/2024.findings-naacl.74

Phan, L., Ali, I., Labou, S., & Foster, E. (2022). A model for data ethics instruction for non-experts. *IASSIST Quarterly*, *46*(4). Advance online publication. DOI: 10.29173/iq1028

Poria, S., Hazarika, D., Majumder, N., Naik, G., Cambria, E., & Mihalcea, R. (2019). MELD: a multimodal Multi-Party dataset for emotion recognition in conversations. In *Proceedings of the 57th Annual Meeting of the Association for Computational Linguistics*. Association for Computational Linguistics. DOI: 10.18653/v1/P19-1050

Rakesh, V. K., Mazumdar, S., Maity, R. P., Pal, S., Das, A., & Samanta, T. (2026). Advancements in talking head generation: A comprehensive review of techniques, metrics, and challenges. *The Visual Computer*, *42*(1), 9. Advance online publication. DOI: 10.1007/s00371-025-04232-w

Reed-Berendt, R., Dove, E. S., & Pareek, M. (2021). The ethical implications of big data research in public health: "Big Data Ethics by Design" in the UK-REACH study. *Ethics & Human Research*, *44*(1), 2–17. DOI: 10.1002/eahr.500111 PMID: 34936235

Richard, A., Zollhofer, M., Wen, Y., De La Torre, F., & Sheikh, Y. (2021). MeshTalk: 3D Face Animation from Speech using Cross-Modality Disentanglement. *2021 IEEE/CVF International Conference on Computer Vision (ICCV)*, 1153-1162. DOI: 10.1109/ICCV48922.2021.00121

Rossler, A., Cozzolino, D., Verdoliva, L., Riess, C., Thies, J., & Niessner, M. (2019). FaceForensics++: Learning to Detect Manipulated Facial Images. *2021 IEEE/CVF International Conference on Computer Vision (ICCV)*, 1-11. DOI: 10.1109/ICCV.2019.00009

Shillingford, B., Assael, Y., Hoffman, M. W., Paine, T., Hughes, C., Prabhu, U., Liao, H., Sak, H., Rao, K., Bennett, L., Mulville, M., Denil, M., Coppin, B., Laurie, B., Senior, A., & De Freitas, N. (2019). Large-Scale visual speech recognition. *Interspeech, 2022*, 4135–4139. Advance online publication. DOI: 10.21437/Interspeech.2019-1669

Shin, A., Lee, J., Hwang, J., Kim, Y., & Park, G. (2024). Wav2NeRF: Audio-driven realistic talking head generation via wavelet-based NeRF. *Image and Vision Computing, 148*, 105104. DOI: 10.1016/j.imavis.2024.105104

Tan, S., Ji, B., Bi, M., & Pan, Y. (2024). EDTaLK: Efficient Disentanglement for Emotional Talking head synthesis. In *Lecture notes in computer science* (pp. 398-416). DOI: 10.1007/978-3-031-72658-3_23

Wang, K., Wu, Q., Song, L., Yang, Z., Wu, W., Qian, C., He, R., Qiao, Y., & Loy, C. C. (2020). MEAD: a Large-Scale Audio-Visual dataset for Emotional Talking-Face Generation. In *Lecture notes in computer science* (pp. 700-717). DOI: 10.1007/978-3-030-58589-1_42

Wang, T., Mallya, A., & Liu, M. (2021). One-Shot Free-View neural Talking-Head synthesis for video conferencing. *2022 IEEE/CVF Conference on Computer Vision and Pattern Recognition (CVPR)*. DOI: 10.1109/CVPR46437.2021.00991

Wang, W. (2010). *Machine Audition: Principles, algorithms and systems*. IGI Global., DOI: 10.4018/978-1-61520-919-4

Wang, Y., Shaw, E., Kruse, B., & Ghods, M. (2018). On identifying factors affecting ethical practices in data science domains. *SMU Data Science Review, 1*(2). https://scholar.smu.edu/datasciencereview/vol1/iss2/2/

Wei, H., Yang, Z., & Wang, Z. (2024). AniPortrait: Audio-Driven Synthesis of Photorealistic Portrait Animation. *arXiv (Cornell University)*. /arxiv.2403.17694DOI: 10.48550

Wu, H., Jia, J., Xing, J., Xu, H., Wang, X., & Wang, J. (2023, March 17). *MMFace4D: a Large-Scale Multi-Modal 4D face dataset for Audio-Driven 3D face animation.* arXiv.org. https://arxiv.org/abs/2303.09797

Wuu, C., Zheng, N., Ardisson, S., Bali, R., Belko, D., Brockmeyer, E., Evans, L., Godisart, T., Ha, H., Hypes, A., Koska, T., Krenn, S., Lombardi, S., Luo, X., McPhail, K., Millerschoen, L., Perdoch, M., Pitts, M., Richard, A., . . . Sheikh, Y. (2022). Multiface: a dataset for neural face rendering. *arXiv (Cornell University).* /arxiv.2207.11243DOI: 10.48550

Xuanyuan, M., Wang, Y., Guo, H., Ma, X., Guo, Y., Yu, T., & Dai, Q. (2023). Hi Sheldon! Creating Deep Personalized Characters from TV Shows. *arXiv (Cornell University).* /arxiv.2304.11093DOI: 10.48550

Yang, S., Zhang, Y., Feng, D., Yang, M., Wang, C., Xiao, J., Long, K., Shan, S., & Chen, X. (2019). *LRW-1000: A Naturally-Distributed Large-Scale Benchmark for Lip Reading in the Wild.* IEEE., DOI: 10.1109/FG.2019.8756582

Ye, Z., Zhong, T., Ren, Y., Yang, J., Li, W., Huang, J., Jiang, Z., He, J., Huang, R., Liu, J., Zhang, C., Yin, X., Ma, Z., & Zhao, Z. (2024). Real3D-Portrait: One-shot realistic 3D talking portrait synthesis. *arXiv (Cornell University).* /arxiv.2401.08503DOI: 10.48550

Yu, J., Zhu, H., Jiang, L., Loy, C. C., Cai, W., & Wu, W. (2023). CelebV-Text: A Large-Scale facial Text-Video dataset. *2022 IEEE/CVF Conference on Computer Vision and Pattern Recognition (CVPR).* DOI: 10.1109/CVPR52729.2023.01422

Zhang, S., Yuan, J., Liao, M., & Zhang, L. (2022). Text2video: Text-Driven Talking-Head Video Synthesis with Personalized Phoneme - Pose Dictionary. *ICASSP 2022 - 2022 IEEE International Conference on Acoustics, Speech and Signal Processing (ICASSP)*, 2659-2663. DOI: 10.1109/ICASSP43922.2022.9747380

Zhang, Y., Liu, M., Chen, Z., Wu, B., Zeng, Y., Zhan, C., He, Y., Huang, J., & Zhou, W. (2024). MuseTalk: Real-Time High Quality Lip Synchronization with Latent Space Inpainting. *arXiv (Cornell University).* /arxiv.2410.10122DOI: 10.48550

Zhang, Z., Li, L., Ding, Y., & Fan, C. (2021). Flow-guided One-shot Talking Face Generation with a High-resolution Audio-visual Dataset. *2022 IEEE/CVF Conference on Computer Vision and Pattern Recognition (CVPR)*, 3660-3669. DOI: 10.1109/CVPR46437.2021.00366

Zhang-Kennedy, L., & Chiasson, S. (Eds.). (2021). "Whether it's moral is a whole other story": consumer perspectives on privacy regulations and corporate data practices. In the Seventeenth *Symposium on Usable Privacy and Security*. USENIX Association. https://www.usenix.org/conference/soups2021/presentation/zhang-kennedy

Zhou, S., Yang, B., Yuan, M., Jiang, R., Yan, R., Pan, G., & Tang, H. (2024). Enhancing SNN-based spatio-temporal learning: A benchmark dataset and Cross-Modality Attention model. *Neural Networks*, *180*, 106677. DOI: 10.1016/j.neunet.2024.106677 PMID: 39260008

Zhou, Y., Han, X., Shechtman, E., Echevarria, J., Kalogerakis, E., & Li, D. (2020). MakeItTalk. *ACM Transactions on Graphics*, *39*(6), 1–15. DOI: 10.1145/3414685.3417774

Zhu, H., Wu, W., Zhu, W., Jiang, L., Tang, S., Zhang, L., Liu, Z., & Loy, C. C. (2022). CelebV-HQ: a Large-Scale Video Facial Attributes Dataset. In *Lecture notes in computer science* (pp. 650-667). DOI: 10.1007/978-3-031-20071-7_38

Zhuang, Y., Cheng, B., Cheng, Y., Jin, Y., Liu, R., Li, C., Cheng, X., Liao, J., & Lin, J. (2024). Learn2Talk: 3D Talking Face Learns from 2D Talking Face. *IEEE Transactions on Visualization and Computer Graphics*, **•••**, 1–13. DOI: 10.1109/TVCG.2024.3476275 PMID: 39374282

ADDITIONAL READING

Chen, L., Cui, G., Kou, Z., Zheng, H., & Xu, C. (2020). What comprises a good talking-head video generation?: A Survey and Benchmark. *arXiv (Cornell University)*. /arxiv.2005.03201DOI: 10.48550

Gowda, S. N., Pandey, D., & Gowda, S. N. (2023). From Pixels to Portraits: A comprehensive survey of talking head generation techniques and applications. *arXiv (Cornell University)*. /arxiv.2308.16041DOI: 10.48550

Michelsanti, D., Tan, Z., Zhang, S., Xu, Y., Yu, M., Yu, D., & Jensen, J. (2021). An Overview of Deep-Learning-Based Audio-Visual Speech Enhancement and Separation. *IEEE/ACM Transactions on Audio, Speech, and Language Processing*, *29*, 1368–1396. DOI: 10.1109/TASLP.2021.3066303

Nguyen-Le, H., Tran, V., Nguyen, D., & Le-Khac, N. (2024). Passive Deepfake Detection across Multi-modalities: A Comprehensive survey. *arXiv (Cornell University)*. /arxiv.2411.17911DOI: 10.36227/techrxiv.173273016.63626046/v1

Toshpulatov, M., Lee, W., & Lee, S. (2023). Talking human face generation: A survey. *Expert Systems with Applications, 219*, 119678. DOI: 10.1016/j.eswa.2023.119678

Wang, R., Cao, Y., Han, K., & Wong, K. K. (2024). A survey on 3D human avatar modeling — From Reconstruction to generation. *arXiv (Cornell University)*. /arxiv.2406.04253DOI: 10.48550

Zhen, R., Song, W., He, Q., Cao, J., Shi, L., & Luo, J. (2023). Human-Computer Interaction System: A survey of Talking-Head Generation. *Electronics (Basel), 12*(1), 218. DOI: 10.3390/electronics12010218

KEY TERMS AND DEFINITIONS

Audio-/Video-/Text-/Image-Driven THG: The four input modes: drive faces from voice, transmit motion from video, produce from text (via phonemes/prosody), or animate a still portrait-often mixed in one pipeline.

Data Institutions & Governance: Stewardship entities that version, gate, and audit datasets throughout time-managing access, changes, and ethical supervision as laws and consent develop.

Dataset Cards / Datasheets: Standardized, public "nutrition labels" for datasets that specify out capture circumstances, demographics, permission, licensing, rights, and technical specifications (hours, FPS, resolution, splits).

Emotion Annotation Limits: Many settings utilize harsh, acted descriptors ("happy/sad/angry"). The chapter advocates for deeper, context-aware schemes (e.g., valence-arousal) to capture actual emotional complexity.

Frontal-View Bias: A typical dataset tilt toward front-facing pictures that hampers performance on profile angles and rich head motion. Fixing it required multi-view/3D capture and larger stances.

Multilingual & Multicultural Coverage: Designing datasets that represent global phonetics, visemes, accents, and expressive conventions so models generalize across languages and cultures.

Privacy-Preserving Pipelines: Collect and process data using strategies like on-device preprocessing or differential privacy/federation to decrease identity risk while still facilitating research.

Synthetic-genuine Co-Training: Use synthetic data to increase coverage (unusual visemes, extreme positions) but calibrate it against genuine recordings to prevent wandering from human authenticity.

Talking Head Generation (THG): Tech that synthesizes realistic talking faces from inputs including voice, text, video, or a single picture, striving for natural lip-sync, emotion, and identity consistency.

Tiered Licensing & Subject Rights: Licenses that explicitly identify permissible uses/redistribution, including realistic mechanisms for data access, takedowns, withdrawal, and recourse for participants.

Transparency (in Datasets): Clear documentation of where data originated from, who's represented, how it was collected/annotated/processed, and under what access and governance rules-so others can audit and trust findings.

Trustworthy Data Practices: Ethical sourcing, express consent, meticulous annotation, unambiguous licensing, and governance that safeguard subject rights and make research replicable and accountable.

Unified Benchmarks & Standard Splits: Shared preprocessing, metrics, and fixed train/test splits so results are comparable and repeatable across tasks, datasets, and demographics.

Verifiable Consent Artifacts: Storing auditable evidence of participant consent (e.g., cryptographically checkable tokens) so downstream users may programmatically validate approved usage.

Chapter 8
The Ecosystem of State Support for Science in Slovakia and Scientific Data

Danica Zendulková
http://orcid.org/0000-0003-2487-0177
Slovak Centre of Scientific and Technical Information, Slovakia

Gabriela Gavurníková
http://orcid.org/0000-0001-7096-6378
Slovak Centre of Scientific and Technical Information, Slovakia

Ján Turňa
http://orcid.org/0000-0001-5813-566X
Slovak Centre of Scientific and Technical Information, Slovakia

ABSTRACT

The chapter examines the science and research ecosystem in Slovakia, including its constituent elements, actors, processes, and instruments, with particular emphasis on the organization of research information and research data management. Credibility and transparency constitute fundamental pillars of the contemporary scientific ecosystem. In a context where science increasingly depends on open data, interdisciplinary collaboration, and public funding, these principles acquire critical significance for the effective functioning of research and innovation. The first section explores national science policy and its key principles such as open science, research ethics, and gender equality in science and research. The second section focuses on the prerequisites for data-driven policymaking in the field of science and research.

DOI: 10.4018/979-8-2600-1433-2.ch008

It addresses standards and models for data recording within information systems supporting scientific activity, the processing of research data, and the integration of such systems as essential conditions for producing high-quality and trustworthy data.

INTRODUCTION

The science and research ecosystem is understood as the set of institutions, actors, processes, and instruments that collectively ensure the functioning of scientific research activities. Credibility and transparency constitute fundamental pillars of the modern scientific ecosystem. In an environment where science increasingly relies on open data, interdisciplinary collaboration, and public funding, these principles acquire critical importance for the effective operation of research and innovation.

The ecosystem of scientific information and its governance is currently regarded as essential for ensuring that science functions effectively and serves its intended purpose (Altman & Cohen, 2022). According to these authors, fundamental principles and values also include fairness and equity, as well as adherence **to** information ethics and sustainability.

In Slovakia, the ecosystem of state support for science and scientific data comprises several interconnected levels: from policy-makers, through funding and evaluation bodies, to institutions, researchers, and research infrastructures. This ecosystem is gradually being shaped by reforms aimed at increasing openness, fairness, and accountability in the allocation of financial resources and in making research outputs accessible to the public.

Transparency in science encompasses not only the accessibility of data, methodologies, and research results, but also clearly defined and verifiable procedures for decision-making on research funding. The credibility of the system, in turn, depends on its integrity, the professional quality of evaluation processes, and independence from political or institutional influences. Together, these elements form the foundation of an environment in which researchers, institutions, and the broader public can trust that public resources are used efficiently and in accordance with the public interest.

In the Slovak context, issues of credibility and transparency relate particularly to the functioning of grant agencies, the management of scientific data, open access, and the implementation of open science principles. However, a robust ecosystem is needed not only where research outputs are openly shared, but also where transparency permeates the research process from the outset, enabling more rigorous and collaborative research (Thibault et al., 2023).

The aim of this section is to characterize the fundamental components of state support for science and of the processes of collecting, processing, preserving, and disseminating scientific information and data in Slovakia, and to analyse the extent to which trust and transparency are embedded within the existing ecosystem.

STATE SCIENCE POLICY

State science policy in Slovakia may be defined as the set of objectives, principles, and instruments through which the state directs and supports research, development, and innovation. It encompasses the creation of legislative and financial instruments, the coordination of activities among various public bodies, and the funding of research and development.

The state science policy of the Slovak Republic focuses primarily on:

- the development of research, development, and innovation (RDI) as key determinants of competitiveness;
- the support of excellent science and applied research;
- the interconnection of the academic sector, the business community, and public administration;
- the development of human resources in science;
- the internationalization of Slovak research (cooperation with the EU and OECD);
- the transfer of knowledge into practice (technology transfer, start-ups, patents).

In addition to the reorganisation of the system, a central priority is increasing public investment in research, development, and innovation in line with the national strategy, as well as simplifying procedures—specifically public procurement, auditing, and financial control in the area of research, development, and innovation.

The governance system for science and research in Slovakia has a multi-level structure, which will be examined in greater detail in the following paragraphs.

Model of State Support for Research and Development

The model of state science policy in Slovakia represents the system through which the state governs, supports, and advances science, research, and innovation. This system is coordinated by the state through a range of institutions, strategic documents, and financial instruments. It combines direct and indirect support from the state budget, complemented by European funding sources and private investment. The model is grounded in the principles of strategic management (setting priorities and objectives), programme-based financing (support through grants, projects, and programmes), competitiveness and quality evaluation, and cooperation between the academic and business sectors.

Its purpose is to ensure the interconnection of strategic decision-making, coordination, implementation, and evaluation of scientific activities.

Figure 1 provides a graphical representation of the model of state support.

Figure 1. Main stakeholders of the R&D ecosystem in Slovakia

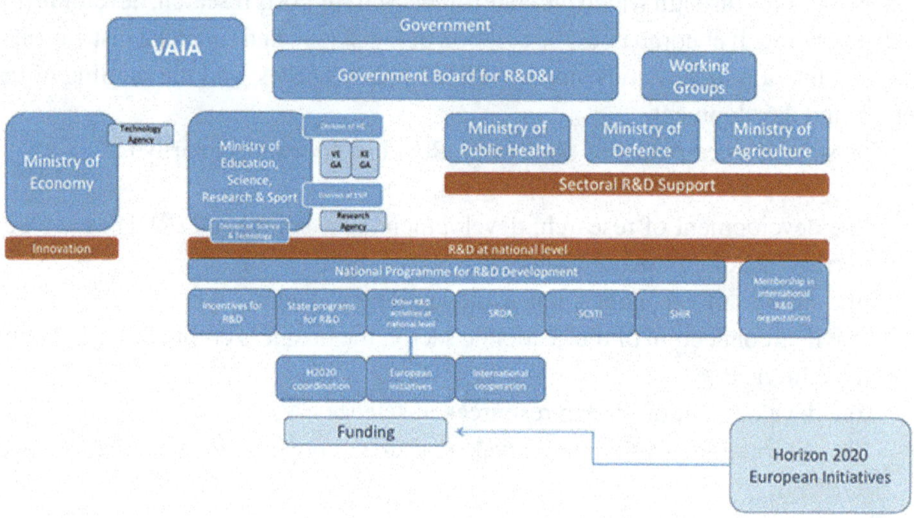

At the strategic level, which determines the overall direction, priorities, and objectives of state science and innovation policy, the central authorities of public administration operate. These include, above all, the Government of the Slovak Republic, the Government Council for Research, Development and Innovation, and the Ministry of Education, Research, Development and Youth of the Slovak Republic (MŠVVaM SR), which has historically been responsible for state science policy (Ministry of Education, Research, Development and Youth of the Slovak Republic, 2024a). A gradual shift is currently taking place, with responsibility for strategy formation and coordination moving from the ministerial level to the supra-ministerial level, specifically to the Office of the Government of the Slovak Republic.

In 2021, the Research and Innovation Authority (VAIA) was established within the Office of the Government as a coordination body tasked with reforming state support for science, research, and the innovation ecosystem. VAIA was created in response to the need to strategically guide and coordinate research and innovation policies in areas that do not clearly fall within the competences of existing ministries. It functions as the executive body and secretariat of the Government Council for Science, Technology, and Innovation.

Since 2025, VAIA has been incorporated into the Office of the Deputy Prime Minister of the Slovak Republic for the Recovery Plan and the Knowledge Economy. Its primary role is the implementation of the *National Strategy for Research, Development and Innovation 2030*, as well as the coordination and management of the Government Council for Science, Technology, and Innovation, whose competences were transferred from the Ministry of Education. In addition to introducing international expert evaluation of research and innovation, VAIA is responsible for developing talent policies and designing a new model of governance and funding for research and development under the Government Council for Science, Technology, and Innovation. However, the process of transferring competences has not yet been completed or fully embedded in legislation. Planned steps include drafting a new Act on Research, Development and Innovation and reorganising and consolidating ministries, agencies, and institutions responsible for policymaking and support in R&D&I.

The executive or implementation level consists of grant agencies that provide funding for science and research through grants, programmes, and projects.

The operational level is where research and development are carried out; it comprises the institutions and organisations engaged in scientific research across various sectors.

Another level consists of monitoring, evaluation, control, and support activities, in which research information and the tools for processing it, namely information systems supporting science, play a crucial role.

Strategic Documents

National strategic documents in the field of science policy build upon EU-wide guidelines and methodological frameworks intended for the Member States.

The central document of the science and research ecosystem in Slovakia is the *National Strategy for Research, Development and Innovation* (VAIA, 2023), which outlines the objectives, priorities, and intentions of the Slovak Republic, as well as principles of good governance and effectiveness in the field of research, development and innovation. The strategy is accompanied by an **Action Plan**, which is updated on an ongoing basis. The implementation of the strategy is overseen by the Government Council for Science, Technology and Innovation.

The *Roadmap of Research Infrastructures – SK VI Roadmap 2020–2030* (Ministry of Education, Science, Research and Sport, 2021a) constitutes a key national document for research infrastructures. It maps not only the historical development but also the current status of major public and private research infrastructures in Slovakia.

Since June 2021, Slovakia has implemented the *National Strategy for Open Science 2021–2028* (Ministry of Education, Science, Research and Sport, 2021b), approved by the Government of the Slovak Republic. This strategy defines the steps necessary to implement the principles of open science. Its objective is to create a sustainable model enabling all actors in the Slovak research ecosystem to participate in adopting global open science principles: promoting the dissemination, exchange, reuse, and accessibility of research outputs. In doing so, it aims to strengthen domestic and international scientific collaboration, foster cooperation between the public and private sectors, enhance research infrastructure, support the education of new generations of researchers and university educators, and create conditions for effective strategic governance of research and education. The strategy is implemented through biennial Action Plans.

On 28 August 2024, the Government of the Slovak Republic approved the *Code of Research Integrity and Ethics in Slovakia* (Ministry of Education, Research, Development and Youth, 2024b). This Code is a binding document that establishes ethical requirements and principles for all individuals working in science and research, as well as for organisations involved in research activities. Its aim is to strengthen the quality, credibility, and professionalism of scientific research in Slovakia.

Strategic documents also include Gender Equality Plans (GEPs), which set objectives and measures to promote gender equality within research institutions. Their development is aligned with the activities of the European Commission, which issued the *Gender Equality Strategy 2020–2025* (European Commission, 2020). Since 2022, the existence of a Gender Equality Plan has been a mandatory requirement for participation in the Horizon Europe funding programme.

Legislation

The research, development, and innovation ecosystem in Slovakia is governed by several laws:

- Act No. 172/2005 Coll. on the Organisation of State Support for Research and Development
- Act No. 185/2009 Coll. on Incentives for Research and Development
- Act No. 131/2002 on Universities
- Act No. 133/2002 Coll. on the Slovak Academy of Sciences
- Act No. 243/2017 on Public Research Institutions

The fundamental law is the Act on State Support for Research and Development, which defines the legal framework for supporting science. The Act on Incentives regulates the operation of one of the grant schemes for funding research. The Act on

Universities and the Act on the Slovak Academy of Sciences govern the functioning of key research organisations in Slovakia. The latter law complements the Act on the Slovak Academy of Sciences and defines the transformation of SAS institutes, which prior to its enactment operated as budgetary and contributory organisations, into public research institutions. The significance of this law lies primarily in the regulation of research infrastructure management and financing, enabling these institutions to become competitive within the European Research Area.

Sectoral Structure of Research and Development Actors

The sectoral structure of science and research refers to the way in which entities conducting research and development (R&D) activities are classified according to their founding authority, legal status, and primary mission. This concept enables the analysis and comparison of different components of the research system—for example, the university sector, the government sector, the business sector, and non-profit organisations. The purpose of sectoral classification is to provide an overview of which actors participate in R&D, what resources they use, and what outputs they generate. Such classification is also essential for the development of science and technology policy, research funding, and international statistical comparison following OECD and Eurostat methodologies.

The sectoral structure of Slovak science and research is defined by the Act No. 172/2005 Coll. on State Support for Research and Development as follows:

- **Government sector**, comprising legal entities established by central government authorities;
- **Public research institutions sector**, consisting of institutes of the Slovak Academy of Sciences;
- **Higher education sector**, including public, state, and private universities, as well as legal entities founded by them that carry out research and development;
- **Non-profit sector**, comprising non-profit organisations, civic associations, and associations of legal entities engaged in research and development;
- **Business enterprise sector**, consisting of business organisations conducting research and development as part of their activities.

The most significant actors are the Slovak Academy of Sciences, with its 47 institutes functioning as public research institutions, and universities. In Slovakia, there are 20 public universities, 3 state universities, 10 private universities, and 2 foreign universities.

Other organisations (state, private, or non-profit) declare their involvement in science and research in several ways. First, research and development must be explicitly stated in their founding charter (in the case of state organisations) or in their business activity description (for private or commercial entities).

In addition, all such entities must apply for a certificate of eligibility to conduct research and development if they wish to apply for state support. The certificate is issued based on meeting several requirements, including laboratory infrastructure, personnel capacity, previous research activities, and research plans.

This process results in the creation of a database of research organisations within the SK CRIS system, which serves as a reference register for Slovak grant agencies. Before awarding a grant, agencies verify through the database whether the applicant organisation holds a valid certificate of eligibility to conduct R&D. The number of certificate holders has remained relatively stable over time at around 700, the majority of which are business enterprises.

Open Science

Open Science "represents an approach to the research process based on collaboration, sharing, and the open dissemination of knowledge through the optimal use of digital technologies and the application of openness principles in every aspect of the research cycle" (Foster Open Science, 2020). The term *Open Science* is often used as an umbrella concept encompassing various other "movements aimed at removing barriers to the sharing of any outputs, resources, methods, or tools at any stage of the research process" (Foster Open Science, 2020). It also includes numerous related concepts, as illustrated in Figure 2.

Figure 2. Open Science

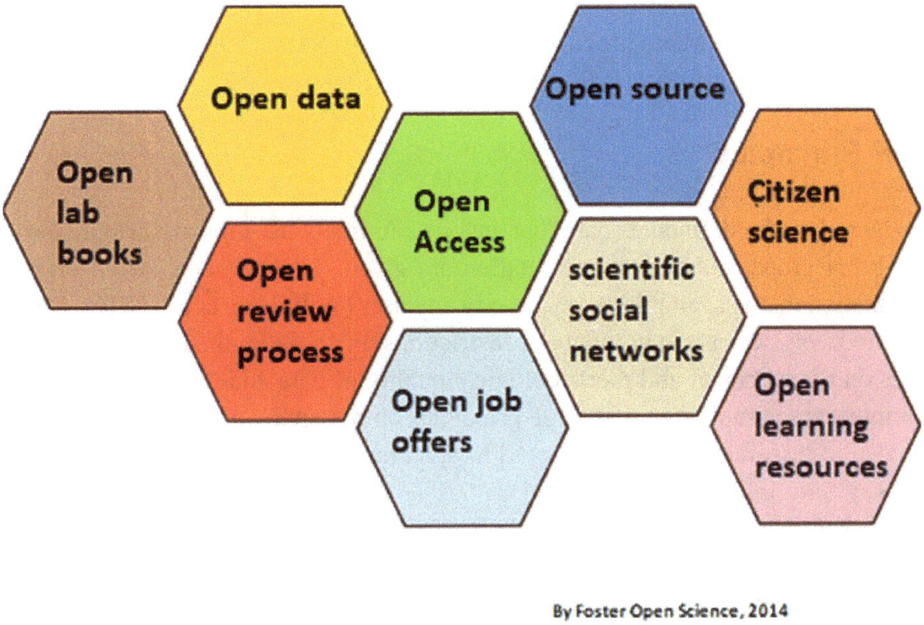

UNESCO, in its *Recommendation on Open Science* (2021), defines Open Science as an inclusive concept that brings together different movements and practices aimed at making multilingual scientific knowledge openly accessible and reusable for everyone. To enhancing scientific collaboration and information sharing for the benefit of science and society, and opening the processes of knowledge creation, evaluation, and communication to societal actors beyond the traditional scientific community. Open Science spans all scientific disciplines and aspects of scientific practice, including basic and applied sciences, natural and social sciences, and the humanities, and rests on the following key pillars: open scientific knowledge, open scientific infrastructures, scientific communication, open engagement of societal actors, and open dialogue with other knowledge systems.

Open Science promotes transparency, collaboration, and free access to research outputs (Mons, 2019). It increases the efficiency, reliability, and societal responsiveness of scientific research (Bordons et al., 2023).

Individual countries develop Open Science policies, a set of guidelines, rules, regulations, laws, principles, or instructions—intended to implement the values and principles of Open Science in practice. In Slovakia, research institutions have access to the document *Methodological Recommendations for the Development and Implementation of Institutional Open Science Policies for Research Institutions* when formulating their own Open Science policies.

Open Science also provides an organisational and policy framework for implementing the FAIR principles (Burgelman et al., 2019).

FAIR Principles

Open data are defined as data that anyone can freely use and redistribute, provided that proper attribution and citation are given. They are considered digital information that is available at any time to any user (Wilkinson et al., 2016). Open data are freely accessible without any restrictions. In addition, the FAIR principles focus on the technical and methodological quality of data and their reusability. It is important to emphasize that these principles do not apply only to research data, but also to research information stored in open research infrastructures, including CRIS systems (Hauschke et al., 2021).

The key characteristics of open data are accessibility, reusability, and universal participation without discrimination. In the context of open data, the concept of FAIR data is frequently mentioned. FAIR data are an essential component of Open Science and describe some of the central principles of good data management and open access to research data.

FAIR is an acronym representing four principles that ensure that data are:

Findable

The first step in using data is their findability. Data should be described with metadata that includes information about the context, quality, conditions, and characteristics of the data. This enhances data discovery, reuse, and citation. Metadata should be assigned a persistent identifier, which helps eliminate ambiguity in published data. Metadata should also be registered or indexed in a discoverable source, as identifiers and metadata alone do not guarantee easy findability on the internet.

Accessible

Once a user has found the required data, they need to know how to access it. Metadata should be retrievable using a standard communication protocol that is open and universally implementable. Metadata should remain accessible even if the data itself is no longer available.

Interoperable

Metadata should use a formal, accessible, shared, and broadly applicable language for knowledge representation. To ensure automated findability and interoperability of data files, ontologies, thesauri, and data models should be applied. Metadata should also include references to other metadata. Creating links between metadata sources improves understanding of the data context.

Reusable

The main goal of FAIR principles is to optimize the reuse of data. Therefore, both data and metadata should be well described. Metadata should be richly annotated with precise and relevant attributes to enable reuse in a specific context. Key attributes include clear and accessible data usage licenses and precise provenance information. Data should be organised in standardized formats, supported by established and sustainable formats and controlled vocabularies.

In Slovakia, the importance of applying FAIR principles to research information and the corresponding systems for their management and processing is well recognized. The Current Research Information System (CRIS) is a key part of the research infrastructure, specifically designed to support and operationalize the implementation of FAIR principles (Azeroual et al., 2022).

Ethics in Science

Ethics in science in Slovakia is an essential part of both national science policy and everyday scientific practice. It constitutes a system of rules, principles, and institutions that ensure research is conducted honestly, transparently, and with respect for human rights, the environment, and societal values. Ethical principles also apply to the processing of scientific information and research data (Schöpfel & Azeroual, 2023), including their relationship to the application of Open Science principles (Schöpfel et al., 2022). The importance of these principles is increasing in light of the emerging trend of artificial intelligence utilization (Azeroual et al., 2024).

Scientific ethics concerns researchers' behaviour, the protection of research integrity, respect for the rights of research participants, accountability to society and the environment, and the prevention of research misconduct, including data falsification and plagiarism.

The institutional framework for ethics in science is provided by the Ethics Committee for Research and Development of the Slovak Republic, a national body established under the Ministry of Education, Science, Research, and Sport of the Slovak Republic. The Committee oversees adherence to ethical principles in science and research, issues opinions on disputed cases, and provides recommendations and methodological guidance. The fundamental document is the Code of Research Integrity and Ethics in Slovakia. Every major research organisation maintains its own ethics committee.

Ethics in science is based on internationally recognized principles such as honesty, responsibility, objectivity, transparency, and respect. Applying these principles safeguards the credibility of science and its contribution to society.

Data Protection

Data protection in science involves compliance with the European General Data Protection Regulation (GDPR) and national legislation, particularly the right to personal data protection, as well as the Act on the Protection of Personal Rights. Scientific research may process personal data only under conditions such as obtaining consent from the data subject or fulfilling tasks in the public interest, while respecting the right to object to data processing.

In Slovakia, the relevant legislation on personal data protection includes:

- Regulation (EU) 2016/679 of the European Parliament and Council of 27 April 2016 on the protection of natural persons with regard to the processing of personal data and on the free movement of such data, repealing Directive 95/46/EC.
- Act No. 18/2018 Coll. on the Protection of Personal Data, as amended.

Regarding the collection of data on research, development, and innovation within the ecosystem, the legal basis for such data collection is the fulfillment of statutory obligations of the ministry (Act 172/2005 on State Support for Research and Development) and the execution of the Slovak Centre of Scientific and Technical Information (CVTI SR) tasks carried out in the public interest. The public interest is understood as the lawful processing of information on research and development activities funded by state budget resources (Zendulkova & Azeroual, 2022).

Gender Equality

Gender equality in science and research is a key priority of the new European Research Area (ERA). Promoting equality between women and men is a fundamental responsibility of the European Union in all its activities as required by the treaties. Gender equality is a core value of the EU, a fundamental right, and a key principle of the European Pillar of Social Rights. It is also a crucial condition for an innovative, competitive, and prosperous European economy.

Institutional change strategies implemented through gender equality plans have had a very positive impact in EU countries over the last decade. According to the latest report on progress in the European Research Area, these strategies have acted as a catalyst for improvements in the quality of research and innovation.

In Slovakia, the key document is the *National Strategy for Gender Equality and Equal Opportunities in the Slovak Republic for 2021–2027* (Ministry of Labour, Social Affairs, and Family SR, 2021), which includes a dedicated chapter on gender equality in science, research, and education. This document is followed by institutional gender equality plans, which are mandatory for organisations applying for funding under certain EU programs.

The objectives of gender equality measures in science and research are to:

- Improve the representation of women in research and decision-making bodies.
- Eliminate gender bias in the evaluation of scientific work.
- Support work–life balance for researchers (ERAPortál, 2025).

Monitoring the state of gender equality is carried out both through statistical surveys and based on data from information systems (Zendulková et al., 2022).

Science and research policy defines the strategic direction of a country's scientific development. Its significance lies in effectively focusing research on areas with the greatest societal and economic impact.

A trustworthy and responsible science policy seeks to create transparent and stable funding sources for scientific and innovation activities, and it promotes Slovakia's integration into European and global research spaces. It aims to link science with practice and the economy so that research outcomes contribute to economic growth, new products, and value-added services. It also fosters social responsibility in science, transparency, and ethical research practices.

Data-driven decision-making ensures that policy is based on measurable, verifiable evidence. The availability and quality of data allow for better analyses, predictive modelling, impact monitoring, and decision transparency. A trustworthy, transparent, and responsible science policy must therefore be based on high-quality and accessible data. As Numajiri & Hayashi (2024) emphasize, the availability of open data and their use in analyses is a critical prerequisite not only for any data-driven research but also for credible science policy.

DATA ON SCIENCE AND RESEARCH AND THEIR PROCESSING

Data on science and research constitute a fundamental element of the modern governance of the research and innovation ecosystem. They enable the systematic monitoring of scientific capacities, activities, outputs and impacts, thereby forming the basis for effective policy-making, long-term strategic planning and international benchmarking.

A key actor in the field of science and research data processing in Slovakia is the CVTI SR. As an organisation directly managed by the Ministry of Education, Research, Development and Youth of the Slovak Republic (MŠVVaM SR), CVTI SR serves as the national information centre for science, technology, innovation and education, as well as the country's specialised scientific library. It coordinates and operates interdisciplinary research and development centres and national infrastructures for research, development, innovation and education. Its mission is to support the development of science, technology and education. Its tasks include the operation of research information systems, the management of library and information resources, the provision of information services for the expert community, methodological and analytical work to support governance and evaluation in research, development and higher education, the delivery of projects supporting research and education, and the popularisation of science and technology.

CVTI SR has long been responsible for building, developing and operating several nationwide information systems, tools and registers serving research institutions within the remit of the Ministry. These responsibilities are carried out on the basis of authorisations and delegated mandates. CVTI SR operates these systems within its own ICT infrastructure, the Data Centre for Research and Development.

Competencies of CVTI SR are derived from several tasks:

- Official international cooperation in the development of the European Open Science Cloud (EOSC).
- Delegated responsibility from the Ministry for operating and developing national information systems supporting research and development.
- Delegated responsibility for processing and providing access to data from national information systems and from global scientific databases.
- Cooperation with OpenAIRE in supporting open science and the dissemination of scientific information and data.

The operation of key national information systems for science and research in Slovakia addresses complex and globally relevant challenges: research data processing, support for open science, interoperability of information systems, the 'once-only' principle, open research data publishing, FAIR data management, support for research evaluation, master data management, central identity management and the provision of ICT infrastructure services.

Among the key information systems and registers operated by CVTI SR are:

CREPČ – Central Register of Publication Activity, a comprehensive bibliographic database of publications produced by Slovak higher education institutions, used for the evaluation of publication activity, statistical reporting for university funding, accreditation processes, periodic evaluation of research, development, artistic and other creative outputs, and for the implementation of performance-based funding.

CREUČ – Central Register of Artistic Activity, a bibliographic database of artistic outputs of Slovak higher education institutions.

SK CRIS – National Research Information System, containing structured data on research projects undertaken by Slovak organisations, their outputs, a map of research infrastructure, a register of research organisations and a database of researchers. It supports capability assessments and statistical surveys of research and development potential and has previously been used to administer selected national grant schemes.

CIP VVI – Central Information Portal for Research, Development and Innovation, a core information, management and oversight tool of national science and technology policy.

CRZP and ANTIPLAG – Central Register of Theses and Dissertations and Antiplagiarism System, which securely stores digital theses and performs automated originality checks.

SCIDAP – National Open Digital Repository for Publications, preserving and providing access to full-text publications produced by Slovak research institutions.

SVD – National Open Digital Repository for Research Data, enabling the secure storage and open dissemination of research datasets.

OAPP – Open Access Publishing Platform, supporting the publication of open access journals and monographs.

Analytical and Statistical Module for Research Evaluation, which provides tools for complex analyses, benchmarking, predictive modelling and evaluation of the quantitative and qualitative performance of Slovak research. It integrates both internal and external data sources including Web of Science, citation databases, SCIDAP, SVD, CRZP, SK CRIS and electronic information resources.

ISS CVTI SR – Integrated Service System, providing ICT infrastructure services, access to integrated applications and tools supporting research and technology transfer, including PRIMO, HAN, ERMS, Mediainfo, the Open Data Platform and the NARCOS national system for respiratory diseases.

Beyond CVTI SR, several other institutions operate relevant information systems within the Slovak research ecosystem, particularly research funding agencies:

The **Slovak Research and Development Agency (APVV)**, established in 2005, is the sole national grant agency providing state funding for research projects, agency programmes and international cooperation initiatives. Its mission is to support high-quality basic and applied research, to contribute to the objectives of national science and technology policy and to stimulate participation in European and international research programmes.

The **Scientific Grant Agency (VEGA)** of the Ministry and the Slovak Academy of Sciences coordinates the evaluation of basic research projects undertaken at universities and research institutes.

The **Cultural and Educational Grant Agency (KEGA)** supports applied research in education, pedagogy and the arts.

In addition, the **ITMS governmental information system** provides a unified platform for recording, processing and monitoring EU structural funds programmes.

Many research organisations also operate their own institutional systems, such as the Slovak Academy of Sciences' databases of publications, projects and personnel, and university systems (e.g., the STU Academic Information System and the University of Žilina Institutional CRIS).

Data processing within these systems is shaped by different legislative frameworks and serves diverse purposes, resulting in heterogeneous processes and varying degrees of obligation for research actors.

Despite this heterogeneity, these data sources form a coherent ecosystem due to the use of international standards, data models and classifications for describing the entities and attributes represented in the databases. These shared principles provide the foundation for the development of a robust and high-quality research information infrastructure.

Metadata on Research and Development

The term *metadata,* that is, data about data, is generally used to describe the data structures in which information about individual objects is stored. In the context of metadata, a variety of data models and standards are employed to enable the integration of heterogeneous databases that contain similar types of content.

Metadata, together with their creation, standardisation and use, are themselves the subject of research. For example, Mayernik (2019) discusses metadata in a broad sense within the sociology of science, examining how researchers document, describe, annotate, organise and manage data in their everyday scientific practice. It is beyond doubt that the use of metadata standards enhances research reproducibility, and not only in computer science (Leipzig et al., 2021). In library and information science, a typical example of metadata is the "catalogue card", or, in contemporary settings, a database record of a library information system describing a library document (Ukropová, 2002).

Metadata are often reduced to descriptive or administrative elements. In the case of a research project, this includes information such as the project title, project code, start and end dates, funding source, as well as a substantive description of the research in the form of an abstract, keywords and similar descriptors.

A clear overlap with library science emerges particularly in databases of research outputs (publications, patents, products). These outputs are linked to research actors (organisations, researchers) and to research activities (projects).

At this point, it is necessary to highlight standardisation as a mechanism that ensures uniform recording of such information by diverse stakeholders at the international level. The multidisciplinary application of metadata standards is addressed, for instance, by the Committee on Data for Science and Technology (CODATA), which also identifies numerous challenges in this area (Rumble et al., 2019). Traditional metadata standards for research data, used by Datacite, Dataverse Network, Dryad or FigShare, are examined by Farnel and Shiri (2014). However, these classical approaches, which historically focused on the organisation, classification and reuse of resources, are now undergoing rapid transformation with the increasing integration of artificial intelligence technologies (Yang et al., 2025).

Among the metadata standards used for research and development information in Slovakia, the most important is the specialised CERIF format, alongside Dublin Core, designed for the description of electronic resources and commonly used by memory institutions. The MARC21 format for bibliographic metadata is also widely applied, primarily within library information systems, although it is supported by some research output databases as well.

CERIF (Common European Research Information Format) is an XML data format intended for the organisation of data on science and research. It is recommended by the European Commission as the standard for the automation of research information management (Interoperable Europe, Common European Research Information Format, 2017). At its core, CERIF provides a data model that enables metadata-based representation of research entities, their activities, relationships and outputs.

The elements of CERIF (Figure 3) have a defined structure, semantics and set of relationships, and are organised into hierarchically ordered categories:

1. **Core Entities** (Person, Project, Organisation)
2. **Result Entities** (Publications, Patents, Products)
3. **Second-Level Entities**
4. **Link Entities**

Figure 3. CERIF 1.6 (Dvořák, 2025)

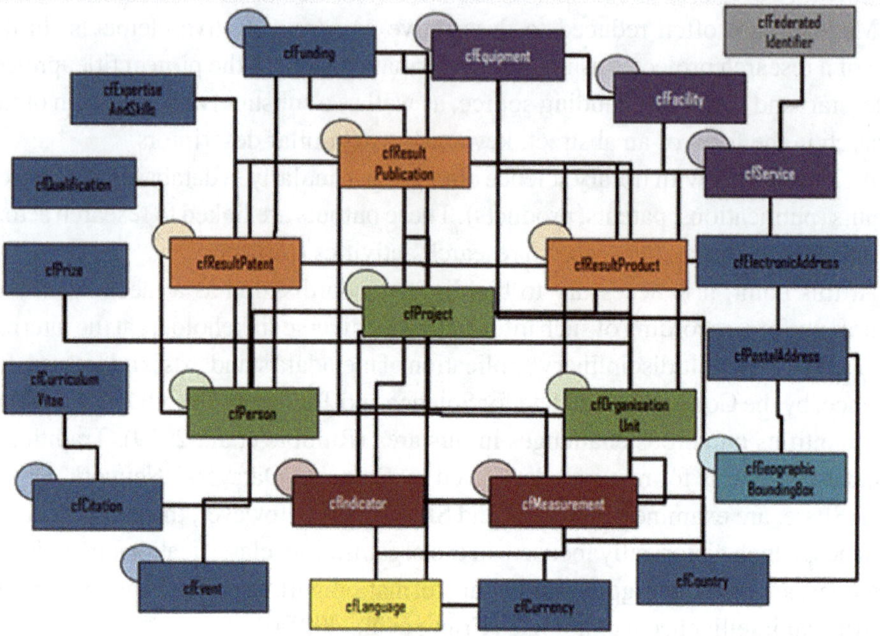

The complete CERIF data model comprises several subsystems, a semantic layer, XML schemas, SQL scripts and implementation examples. An exchange format for metadata CERIF_XML has been developed. The use of the model, which is continuously being updated and expanded, is subject to a Creative Commons licence.

CRIS systems are capable of collecting a wide range of metadata for multiple entities related to research activities. However, as the open-science environment becomes increasingly complex, new opportunities arise for these systems to store even greater volumes of information in a highly interconnected manner, characteristic of the CERIF data model (de Castro, 2024).

Based on more than ten years of experience with the use of the relational CERIF data format, we can conclude that it has proven highly effective. The implementation of metadata within research information systems in Slovakia enables:

- improved discovery and sharing of research information and data;
- thorough documentation of the provenance and context of research;
- assessment of the quality and reproducibility of research outputs;
- compliance with the requirements of open science and those of funding agencies;
- international comparability of research activities;

- participation in international research infrastructures and projects.

Scientific Data, Their Processing and Secure Storage

In Slovakia, scientific data are systematically collected across most scientific disciplines. In the natural sciences, these include genetic and molecular data, monitoring of populations and invasive species, climate and environmental data, as well as geological mapping and various laboratory measurements. Scientific data also encompass data models in artificial intelligence, data from transport and energy systems, economic indicators and meteorological data. A distinct category comprises scientific data in the fields of medical sciences, biomedicine, genetics and bioinformatics.

The processing and secure storage of scientific data in Slovakia are carried out in accordance with the latest European trends and requirements, with a strong emphasis on the FAIR principles. Data governance follows international Open Science principles and legislation on personal data protection. The processing of personal data is regulated by the General Data Protection Regulation (GDPR), with compliance monitored by the Office for Personal Data Protection of the Slovak Republic.

The Ministry of Education, Research, Development and Youth of the Slovak Republic has issued methodological guidelines and is developing specialised infrastructure for data management and archiving. A key instrument for managing data throughout the entire research lifecycle is the Data Management Plan (DMP).

Data are stored in scientific repositories within the SANET network, within the computational capacities of the Slovak Academy of Sciences, in departmental data centres, and in various repositories such as the international ZENODO repository, the Central Data Archive, the Slovakiana archive, the national repositories SCIDAP and SVD, as well as university repositories.

Secure data storage includes the use of appropriate technological solutions and adherence to ethical principles. For secure and long-term storage, digital repositories are used (including technological solutions such as DSpace, EPrints, Invenio, etc.) along with university archives. The Slovak Centre of Scientific and Technical Information (CVTI SR) and the Slovak Academy of Sciences contribute to the development of infrastructure for research data. For example, the SAS operates the Slovak Archive of Social Data (SASD), which serves for non-commercial use and archiving of data from international sociological surveys. Emphasis is placed on protecting identities and maintaining data confidentiality, particularly when working with sensitive personal data.

Biomedical data have their own particular characteristics. In the Slovak sectors of biomedicine, genomics and bioinformatics, data processing and storage focus on handling vast amounts of data (so-called BIG DATA) and on the sensitivity of the information. Strict ethical and legal standards, as well as specialised infrastructure, play a crucial role. The massive accumulation of extensive molecular and clinical datasets in recent decades has radically transformed personalised medicine and raised high expectations regarding its impact on biomedical research and healthcare. Extremely large collections of biomedical "omics" data (genomics, proteomics, transcriptomics, metabolomics, glycomics, etc.) and clinical data pose major challenges for analysis and interpretation and require the development of new robust algorithms capable of correctly analysing such high-volume datasets while accounting for individual genetic variability—an essential prerequisite for advancing personalised medicine (Hassan et al., 2022).

The processing of biomedical and genomic data demands substantial computational power and adherence to international standards to ensure accuracy and reproducibility. Bioinformatic analyses rely on advanced tools and software for processing sequencing data (e.g., DNA, RNA), genome mapping, variant identification and functional annotation. These processes are carried out on high-performance computing (HPC) infrastructures, where standardisation and data quality are crucial. Strict quality control (QC) and standardised data-processing protocols are implemented in accordance with the requirements of clinical research or diagnostics. From an ethical and legal perspective, working with genetic data requires particular attention to informed consent, as well as anonymisation and/or pseudonymisation to protect individual privacy. Legislation is stringent and follows EU directives.

The definition of "big data" encompasses several dimensions: volume, velocity, variety, value, variability, visualisation, virality and veracity (Figure 4) which describe the enormous scale of structured, semi-structured and unstructured datasets (Bibault, 2020; Normandeau, 2013; Gandomi & Haider, 2015; Diebold et al., 2012).

Given the sensitivity and scale of genomic data, secure storage and underlying infrastructure are critical. Data are stored in specialised, secure digital repositories and biobanks that meet strict security and long-term archiving requirements. In Slovakia, biobanks exist that store not only biological material (e.g., tissue and blood samples) but also associated clinical and genomic data. A crucial aspect is the computational infrastructure for genomic data, which requires a combination of high-performance hardware, specialised software and efficient storage and data-management solutions.

Figure 4. Representation of distinct dimensions of big data

(Hassan, M. et al, 2022)

Among the key components and requirements for processing these data are:

- High-Performance Computing (HPC): Genome analysis is extremely computationally demanding. It requires servers with a high number of CPU cores and often GPU acceleration to speed up tasks such as sequence mapping and variant calling.
- Sufficient Memory (RAM): Some bioinformatics tools—particularly those working with reference genomes—require large amounts of operational memory (often tens to hundreds of gigabytes of RAM).
- Scalable Storage: Genomic data (for example from next-generation sequencing – NGS) generate enormous volumes of data (terabytes to petabytes). The infrastructure must include high-speed, scalable storage systems (such as parallel file systems or cloud storage) with adequate backup and archiving capabilities.
- Network Connectivity: Fast data transfer between storage and compute nodes is critical for minimising processing times.
- Specialised Software and Tools: A range of bioinformatics platforms and analysis tools is used. Examples include platforms such as Galaxy (a web-based analysis platform requiring no command-line interaction) or specific libraries and packages in programming languages such as R or Python, as well as tools like GATK or Samtools.

- Cloud Computing: Many organisations use commercial cloud providers (such as AWS, Microsoft Azure or Google Cloud Platform) for their flexibility, scalability and accessibility of HPC-as-a-Service.
- Data Security and Management: The sensitivity of genomic data requires strict security measures, compliance with ethical and legal requirements, and adherence to established standards (for example within initiatives such as the European Genomic Data Infrastructure – GDI).

Data security is essential due to the sensitive nature of genomic data, which pose a significant risk of re-identification. Key functions and safeguards include:

- Pseudonymisation and Anonymisation: These are standard practices for protecting identity. Pseudonymised data (codes replacing direct identifiers) are still classified as personal data under the GDPR and require additional safeguards. Anonymised data, where re-identification is not possible, may be shared more freely.
- Access Control: Access is restricted to authorised and qualified users. Multifactor authentication (MFA) and structured access levels are implemented (e.g., tiered access, in which data are processed in a secure environment without direct access to raw data).
- Encryption: Data are encrypted both at rest and in transit. Advanced cryptographic techniques are applied to ensure confidentiality.
- Secure Processing Environments: Analyses are often carried out in specially protected, trusted environments ("secure processing environments") that ensure that data do not leave the controlled infrastructure.
- Auditing and Monitoring: Access logs and data-processing records are regularly reviewed to prevent misuse and to monitor compliance.
- Controlled Access: The scientific community does not receive open access to raw sensitive data. Instead, access is granted in a controlled manner based on approved research projects and after signing agreements on confidentiality and responsible data use.
- International Protocols: Slovak researchers follow international data-sharing protocols and tools, including those developed by the Global Alliance for Genomics and Health (GA4GH).

Academic and research institutions in Slovakia, such as the Slovak Academy of Sciences and selected universities possess the necessary IT infrastructure for processing and storing big data. We can mention Pavol Jozef Šafárik University in Košice, Comenius University in Bratislava, the Comenius University Science Park,

Matej Bel University in Banská Bystrica, the Slovak University of Technology in Bratislava, and the Technical University of Košice.

They are able to ensure access for the scientific and research community through controlled mechanisms and international cooperation, in line with the FAIR principles.

The processing of biomedical and genetic data in Slovakia is subject to strict regulation and is fully harmonised with European Union law. Slovak legislation reflects all major EU directives and regulations in the areas of genetic technologies, biomedicine, personal data protection and the handling of human tissues and cells. The Office for Personal Data Protection of the Slovak Republic plays a central role in supervising compliance of processing activities with the GDPR and national legislation. Slovakia also transposes EU directives into its domestic legal framework and directly applies EU regulations with immediate effect.

1. General Data Protection Regulation (GDPR)

Regulation (EU) 2016/679 is the fundamental pillar of the protection of personal data, including sensitive health and genetic data. Slovak legislation, in particular Act No. 18/2018 Coll. on the Protection of Personal Data, fully implements the requirements of the GDPR. In biomedical research, this means obtaining unambiguous and specific consent from persons whose genetic data are processed with a clear determination of the purpose of use (informed consent), pseudonymisation, anonymization, technical and organizational measures to protect against unauthorized access or misuse.

2. Regulation on the European Health Data Space (EHDS)

Regulation (EU) 2025/327 (adopted in May 2024) creates a specific data environment for the health sector across the EU. It is intended to improve individuals' access to their data (primary use) and at the same time enable the secure cross-border use of anonymised data for research and innovation purposes (secondary use). The National Centre for Health Information (NCHI, 2025) is actively working on the implementation of the EHDS. The regulation will require a significant amendment of the Slovak healthcare system and the establishment of specialised access authorities for health data, thereby standardising and simplifying the sharing of biomedical data at the European level.

3. Legislation on Genetic Technologies and GMOs

Directive 2001/18/EC on the deliberate release into the environment of genetically modified organisms (GMOs) and other related EU regulations (e.g. Regulation

1829/2003 on genetically modified food and feed) regulate the work with GMOs in research and their placing on the market. These directives are transposed into Act No. 151/2002 Coll. on the use of genetic technologies and genetically modified organisms and related decrees (e.g. Decree of the Ministry of the Environment of the Slovak Republic No. 274/2019 Coll.). The Slovak Environmental Inspection (SIŽP) and the Ministry of the Environment of the Slovak Republic supervise compliance with these rules, which are crucial for laboratories working with genetic modifications.

4. Directives on Human Tissues and Cells (HTC)

Directive 2004/23/EC and subsequent technical guidelines set quality and safety standards for the donation, testing, processing, preservation, storage and distribution of human tissues and cells (HoC) intended for clinical use. These will be replaced by the new Regulation (EU) 2024/1938 from August 2027. Within the framework of Slovak legislation, Act No. 578/2004 Coll. on healthcare providers regulates the functioning of tissue facilities and biobanks in accordance with these requirements, thus ensuring safety and ethics when working with human biological material and associated data. Excellent research infrastructure within Slovakia, the biobank complex together with the built Martin Center for Biomedicine and Martin University Hospital represent the potential for state-of-the-art research and clinical testing. Long-term and systematic collection of samples, storage and provision of biological material for scientific research with respect for all the rights of donors contributes to improving the quality of life of the next generation and to the development of personalized medicine. The aim is that the benefit of all activities is primarily for the patient in terms of effective, modern and targeted therapy. (JLF UK, 2023)

Overall, the Slovak legal framework reflects the effort to comply with European standards, balancing the need for innovation and data sharing in research with strict privacy and ethical principles. The security of large-scale genomic data repositories in Slovakia and their availability to the scientific research community are regulated by a strict framework. It combines national legislation with binding European regulations and initiatives such as the GDPR, the EHDS and the 1+MG initiative. The EU flagship initiative "1+ Million Genomes" (1+MG) aims to enable secure access to genomics and corresponding clinical data across Europe in order to support breakthrough research and health policy-making and stimulate personalized healthcare with the potential to improve disease prevention and balance privacy protection with the need for data sharing for the advancement of research and clinical practice. (European Commission, 2025)

Overall, the system is designed to enable scientific progress through data sharing, but only within a strictly controlled and secure environment that protects the rights and privacy of Slovak and EU citizens.

Slovakia is involved in ESFRI infrastructures as part of international cooperation. The European Strategy Forum on Research Infrastructures (ESFRI) aims to build European research and development and support a common approach to science policy-making in research infrastructures in Europe. The ESFRI Forum has prepared a European indicative plan for research infrastructures of pan-European interest, which create a strategic tool for the development of scientific integration in Europe and strengthen their international reach. The last update in 2012 identified 48 research infrastructures (European Strategy Forum on Research Infrastructures, 2015).

The Slovak Republic is involved in the position of a member or a guest member in various ESFRI research infrastructures.

For biomedical research in Slovakia, it is important that the Slovak Republic has become a full member of the pan-European research infrastructure ELIXIR. This step followed Slovakia's previous activities as an observer or prospective member in this and other ESFRI infrastructures (e.g. BBMRI ERIC, EATRIS ERIC). ELIXIR (European Life Science Infrastructure for Biological Information) is a distributed international research infrastructure that brings together resources on life sciences. From all over Europe. These resources include databases, software tools, training materials, cloud storage and supercomputers and expertise. By joining the international infrastructure, Slovakia has committed to building and operating its own national node (ELIXIR SK), which is compatible with the central requirements of ELIXIR and provides services to the Slovak and international research community. An extremely valuable benefit of full membership is to enable Slovak scientists to fully use the resources and services, actively participate in building and managing the infrastructure and collaborate on international projects in the field of biomedicine, bioinformatics and genomics (SK4ERA, 2025).

ELIXIR coordinates these resources to form a unified infrastructure. This infrastructure makes it easier for scientists to find and share data, exchange expertise and agree on best practices. Ultimately, this helps them gain new knowledge about the functioning of living organisms.

CVTI SR, academic institutions and SAS play a key role in the development of the national node and the promotion of the ELIXIR infrastructure in Slovakia. Slovakia's entry into ELIXIR is an important step in strengthening the country's position in the European Research Area and supporting open science and data management in biomedical fields. In Slovakia, the computational infrastructure for biomedical data, including genomic data, is being developed mainly within academic and research institutions and is often linked to funding from EU funds.

For Slovakia, membership in the research infrastructure of EMBL (European Molecular Biology Laboratory) is a significant contribution to research in the life sciences. Slovakia became a full member of EMBL in 2018 after a period of prospective membership that began in 2014. Since then, the Slovak scientific community has been actively involved in EMBL within its missions, engaging in excellent collaborative research at individual EMBL sites, educating a new generation of Slovak scientists, using new scientific services and technologies, and striving for innovation and research valorisation. We are following a positive trend in the involvement of Slovak scientists in EMBL from the period 2021-2024.

The cooperation between the Slovak scientific community and EMBL continues to grow in the context of the current EMBL program Molecules for Ecosystems. Within this five-year program, EMBL is expanding existing opportunities for its member states to engage, from joint research projects and training modalities to new cutting-edge services. The increase in participation of Slovak scientists observed since the launch of the program proves that these opportunities are actively used by Slovak researchers and that EMBL activities within its missions are of great importance for Slovakia.

Of importance for Slovakia is the cooperation with the excellent bioinformatics institute EMBL-EBI in Hinxton. EMBL-EBI develops and maintains the world's most comprehensive collection of freely available and up-to-date molecular data resources. Created in collaboration with scientists globally, this includes over 40 open databases and hundreds of bioinformatics tools and software, all accessible at EMBL-EBI services to anyone worldwide.

Open life science databases provided by EMBL-EBI form the foundation for much of modern life science research. They save researchers thousands of hours and enable the pursuit of research questions that would be impossible without such comprehensive resources. In 2021, an independent assessment highlighted their critical role in research and development, with 70 percent of participants indicating that not being able to access EMBL-EBI data resources would have a major or severe impact on their work. To capture this value, EMBL has been collecting country-level bibliometric data on publications enabled by EMBL-EBI data resources, showcasing their significance to the scientific community.

In 2024, EMBL-EBI received over 10 million web access requests2 from Slovakia, showcasing that EMBL-EBI data resources are indispensable for Slovak life scientists, both in the academic and industrial sectors. The requests originated from 39,812 unique Slovak IP hosts, each representing a distinct device, such as a computer or a server. Additionally, in 2024, 30 publications3 by authors affiliated with Slovak institutions were enabled by EMBL-EBI data resources. The most frequently cited resources were the European Nucleotide Archive, the Protein Data Bank and UniProt.

The software tools used in Slovakia are typical for the international bioinformatics community, specific commercial platforms vary by workplace.

Open-source tools such as GATK (Genome Analysis Toolkit), samtools, BWA, and various libraries and packages in the R and Python programming languages predominate. These are used to process and analyse sequencing data obtained by NGS sequencing. (NGS - next generation sequencing).

Some workplaces use web platforms such as Galaxy for simplified analysis without the need for advanced command line skills. To a lesser extent, specialized commercial software solutions for medical data management and analysis are also used.

Slovakia has specific hardware, which is concentrated in larger research centres and universities where HPC centres have been established. Research institutions such as the Slovak Academy of Sciences and technical universities (e.g. TUKE, STU, UMB) and also CVTI SR operate high-performance computing (HPC) clusters for processing computational tasks. These include servers with a high number of CPU cores, large operating memory and high-speed storage. Local servers and storage serve smaller laboratories and healthcare facilities for data collection and temporary processing. The Slovak academic and scientific network SANET provides high-speed connectivity between institutions, which is crucial for the transfer of large volumes of biomedical data.

In the biomedical sector, it is essential to support and develop cloud solutions. Within commercial clouds, global providers such as: "Amazon Web Services" (AWS), "Microsoft Azure", and "Google Cloud Platform" are used for their scalability and flexibility. Currently, there is an effort in Slovakia to develop a state academic cloud infrastructure and provide data services in accordance with EU regulations (e.g. GDPR) for the secure storage and sharing of sensitive medical data.

The projects, which are co-funded by the EU, are aimed at creating digital bio-banks that use cloud technologies to support systemic public research infrastructure and testing of new treatment strategies.

Slovakia is involved in European initiatives such as the "1+ Million Genomes" (1+MG) Initiative and the European Health Data Space (EHDS). These initiatives aim to create a federated and secure infrastructure that will enable cross-border access to popular genomic data in the EU for research purposes, while maintaining high standards of security and privacy.

A prerequisite for international cooperation is a high-quality national infrastructure. Slovak institutions (CVTI SR, SAS) are working on building national nodes (e.g. EOSC-SK), which will connect to the European Open Science Cloud Infrastructure (EOSC) and enable data sharing in accordance with EU standards.

Integration of Data and Systems as a Foundation for High-Quality and Trustworthy Information

In contemporary science and public administration, there is an increasing emphasis on the need for interconnected, interoperable and trustworthy data ecosystems.

Data integration, the coordinated linkage of data from different sources, formats and domains, constitutes a fundamental prerequisite for ensuring the quality, consistency and reliability of information (Turning FAIR into reality, 2018).

Data integration is crucial from several perspectives. In terms of data quality, integration makes it possible to detect errors, duplications and incomplete records across systems. High-quality data must be not only accurate but also consistent and up-to-date. Transparent interconnection of sources simultaneously enhances their traceability, which is important for building trust in their origin and correctness. Data integration also increases the efficiency of research and research management: integrated data systems enable automated processing, analytics and the re-use of data, thereby reducing administrative and scientific redundancy (Wilkinson et al., 2016).

In Slovakia, we have undertaken the implementation of Open Science and the FAIR principles for research data collected not only within SK CRIS, across all systems under our management. We focus on the implementation of unique identifiers, data management, metadata quality control, and the integration of various data sources into broader units with the character of research infrastructures. The aim is to ensure that collected data are used not only at the national level, but also it be made available for international comparison.

To support these integration efforts, the Slovak Centre of Scientific and Technical Information (CVTI SR) has developed the Comprehensive Information System for the Acquisition, Processing, Preservation and Dissemination of Scientific and Bibliometric Data and Publications, and for Providing Access to Tools and Applications Supporting Research and Development (abbreviated as KOMIS).

The resulting national research infrastructure aggregates systems supporting research operated by CVTI SR and provides access to services of the Data Centre for Research and Development, such as storage capacity, data processing, and the use of various installed software applications (Software as a Service – SaaS), mainly in the fields of mathematics, statistics and bioinformatics. The solution also includes analytical tools for data processing and a module for searching available data and information resources.

The entry point to the system is a presentation platform (Figure 5) with an implemented Single Sign-On (SSO) authentication process, which allows users to share their credentials easily across various systems and applications. For identity and access management, the open-source tool Keycloak has been deployed. The solution is linked to a local Active Directory identity management system and also enables authentication via an ORCID identifier.

Multiple metadata standards are used within KOMIS. In addition to the CERIF format implemented in SK CRIS, these include mainly DataCite, Dublin Core and MARC21, all processed in JSON. These formats are also supported for data export, particularly from repositories.

KOMIS has defined open API calls using REST-API protocols. These API interfaces are used for communication with external systems as well as for internal communication between the individual components of KOMIS. KOMIS is currently in pilot operation, and its beta version does not yet support full production deployment of all functionalities.

Figure 5. KOMIS presentation platform

As part of strengthening integration objectives, several related functionalities have been implemented in the Slovak Research Information System (SK CRIS), specifically:

- Implementation of researcher ID federation. The system now supports internationally used persistent identifiers (PIDs), specifically ORCID, ResearcherID and Scopus ID, as well as the national identifier ID of a Higher Education Teacher from the register of university employees.
- Integration with the Register of Legal Entities (using a national-level PID for organisations, namely the Identification Number of an Organisation – IČO). The Register of Legal Entities is a reference register. Integration with this register enables SK CRIS to retrieve data on organisations by validating their IČO. This applies the "once only" principle, ensuring that users do not need to re-enter information already available in the national register.
- Extension of recorded research outputs to include DOIs and URLs of the full text of publications.

It should be emphasised that researcher identification is already technically implemented in several other research-support systems. However, the provision of an identifier is not yet mandatory, as not all researchers currently possess one of the commonly used persistent identifiers. Full implementation of unique personal identification in practice is contingent upon legislative anchoring.

For research organisations, unique identification has already been put into practice. Slovakia operates a legally mandated Register of Legal Entities, which ensures authoritative identification. Unique identification of Slovak organisations is provided through the national identifier IČO. In addition, Slovak organisations are generally also included in the international Research Organisation Registry (ROR).

Among the controlled vocabularies or thesauri used for the substantive categorisation of recorded objects, the most important are those derived from Slovak legislation: the Classification of Science and Technology Fields and the Classification of Study Fields.

The system integration scheme for research-support systems is presented in Figure 6.

Figure 6. Integration of systems for supporting science in Slovakia

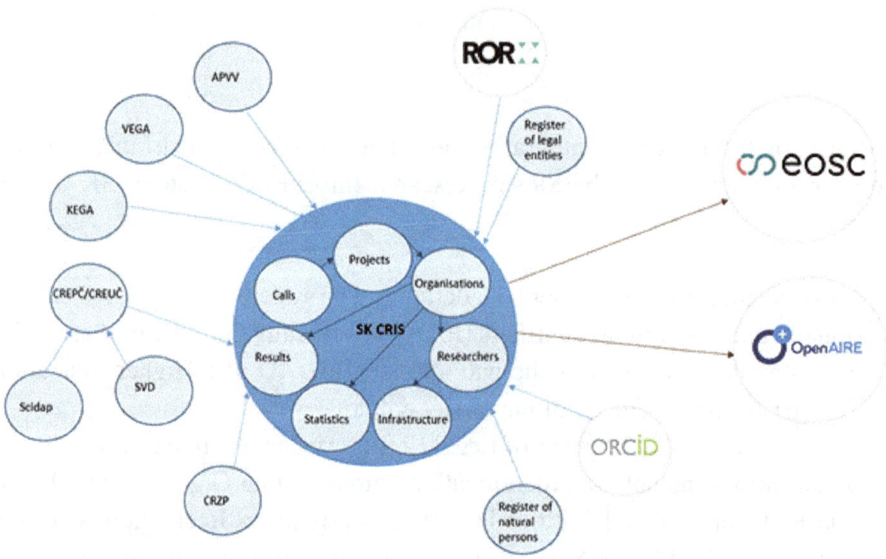

Within international initiatives aimed at the integration of science and research data, Slovakia participates not only in the activities of the international organisation for research information euroCRIS, but primarily in the OpenAIRE project and in the EOSC federation.

Data and systems integration is not merely a technical task, but a strategic pillar of open, trustworthy and reproducible science.

It ensures that data are:

- High-quality – accurate, complete and consistent,
- Trustworthy – with clearly defined provenance and governance,
- Reusable – thanks to shared standards, metadata and interoperable infrastructures.

In a well-integrated data environment, quality and trust do not become additional features, but a natural result of the design of the data ecosystem.

CONCLUSION

Statistical indicators comparing the position of EU countries in science and research place Slovakia only in the lower third.

Slovakia has long exhibited very low expenditure on science and research—both as a share of GDP and in terms of private-sector investment. Other indicators also fall below the EU average, for example the PISA tests for pupils and students, and Slovakia similarly performs worse in innovation outcomes and in linking research with industry.

On the other hand, a new national strategy (VAIA, 2023) has been adopted, defining three fundamental transformations of the research and development ecosystem.

The first concerns investment in a high-quality system. Alongside the necessary increase in funding for research, development and innovation, the mechanisms for allocating and drawing these resources will be reformed.

The second area focuses on talent. The research and innovation ecosystem can flourish only if it is staffed with high-quality, strategically important talent from Slovakia and abroad. The intention is to support the development of domestic talent, attract and retain existing and foreign talent, and purposefully enhance the quality of life and work in Slovak cities where the vast majority of research and innovation resources are concentrated.

The third area introduces a comprehensive framework for setting priorities in the support of research, development and innovation in Slovakia.

The planned reforms also address research information and data. The objective is to strengthen support for open data and open science, and to make data from public administration and research more widely accessible in order to stimulate innovation. To realise the planned measures in the field of open data, it is necessary to translate strategic intentions into concrete actions:

- Legislative support, including the introduction of motivational and/or restrictive measures for entities obliged to provide data.
- Optimisation of data and information collection processes, in line with the *"once only"* principle, with the aim of reducing excessive administrative burden.
- Support for the creation of high-quality metadata, including metadata quality control and the implementation of data curation and data management tasks.
- Implementation of persistent identifiers, international standards and integration tools within modern software solutions developed in accordance with contemporary trends in digitalisation and the use of artificial intelligence tools in science, research and public administration.

The implementation of measures in research policy and in the area of open research information and data will be accompanied by increasing trust among the actors of the research and innovation ecosystem towards the state and, conversely, the trust of the state towards researchers and innovators. A trust-based, transparent, collaborative and stimulating research ecosystem, firmly embedded in the international context, is a prerequisite for successfully addressing the economic and technological challenges of the present.

Funding

This publication was written thanks to the generous support for the project Integration of Genomic Data Resources for National Security in the Human, Food, and Environmental Sectors, Project No. 401101C603

REFERENCES

Altman, M., & Cohen, P. N. (2022). The Scholarly Knowledge Ecosystem: Challenges and Opportunities for the Field of Information. *Frontiers in Research Metrics and Analytics*, *6*, 751553. Advance online publication. DOI: 10.3389/frma.2021.751553 PMID: 35178498

Azeroual, O., & Schöpfel, J., Pölönen, & J. Nikiforova, A. (2022). Putting FAIR Principles in the Context of Research Information: FAIRness for CRIS and CRIS for FAIRness. In *Proceedings of the 14th International Joint Conference on Knowledge Discovery, Knowledge Engineering and Knowledge Management (IC3K 2022)*. SciTePress, 63-71. DOI: 10.5220/0011548700003335

Azeroual, O., Schöpfel, J., Störl, U., & Marušić, A. (2024). Ethical aspects using AI in CRIS. *Procedia Computer Science*, *249*, 150–159. DOI: 10.1016/j.procs.2024.11.058

Bibault, J.-E. (2020). Real-life clinical data mining: Generating hypotheses for evidence-based medicine. *Annals of Translational Medicine*, *8*(4), 69. Advance online publication. DOI: 10.21037/atm.2019.10.99 PMID: 32175362

Bordons, M., González-Albo, B., & Moreno-Solano, L. (2023). Improving our understanding of open access: How it relates to funding, internationality of research and scientific leadership. *Scientometrics*, *128*(8), 4651–4676. DOI: 10.1007/s11192-023-04726-1

Burgelman, J. C., Pascu, C., Szkuta, K., Von Schomberg, R., Karalopoulos, A., Repanas, K., & Schouppe, M. (2019). Open Science, Open Data, and Open Scholarship: European Policies to Make Science Fit for the Twenty-First Century. *Frontiers in Big Data*, *2*, 43. Advance online publication. DOI: 10.3389/fdata.2019.00043 PMID: 33693366

Castro, P. (2024). Improving CRIS features to support new Open Access implementation workflows at institutions. *Procedia Computer Science*, *249*, 179–185. DOI: 10.1016/j.procs.2024.11.062

Diebold, F. X., Cheng, X., Diebold, S., Foster, D., Halperin, M., Lohr, S., Mashey, J., Nickolas, T., Pai, M., & Pospiech, M. A. (2012). *Personal Perspective on the Origin (s) and Development of "Big Data": The Phenomenon, the Term, and the Discipline*. CiteSeer.

Dvořák, J. (2025). *CERIF Tutorial.* euroCRIS Membership Meeting Leuven, Belgium. http://hdl.handle.net/11366/2727

ERAPortál. (2025). *Rodová rovnosť vo výskume. Politický rámec a základné definície.* [Gender equality in research. Policy framework and basic definitions.] https://eraportal.sk/eraportal/rodova-rovnost-vo-vyskume/politicky-ramec-a-zakladne-definicie/

euroCRIS. (2025) *Directory of Research Information Systems – DRIS.* https://dspacecris.eurocris.org/browse?type=driscountry&order=ASC&rpp=20&authority=824

European Commission. (2020). *Únia rovnosti: stratégia pre rodovú rovnosť na roky 2020 – 2025.* [A Union of Equality: Gender Equality Strategy 2020-2025.] https://commission.europa.eu/strategy-and-policy/policies/justice-and-fundamental-rights/gender-equality/gender-equality-strategy_sk

European Commission. (2025). *European '1+ Million Genomes' initiative.* https://digital-strategy.ec.europa.eu/en/policies/1-million-genomes

European Strategy Forum on Research Infrastructures. (2015). *Európske strategické fórum o výskumných infraštruktúrach (ESFRI roadmap) v interakcii s pripravovanou cestovnou mapou infraštruktúr výskumu a vývoja (SVK roadmap).* [The European Strategy Forum on Research Infrastructures (ESFRI roadmap) in interaction with the upcoming roadmap for research and development infrastructures (SVK roadmap).] https://www.minedu.sk/data/att/8d3/8662.3ee4cb.pdf

Farnel, S., & Shiri, A. (2014). Metadata for Research Data: Current Practices and Trends. *International Conference on Dublin Core and Metadata Applications,* 2014. DOI: 10.23106/dcmi.952136534

Gandomi, A., & Haider, M. (2015). Beyond the hype: Big data concepts, methods, and analytics. *International Journal of Information Management*, *35*(2), 137–144. DOI: 10.1016/j.ijinfomgt.2014.10.007

Hassan, M., Awan, F. M., Naz, A., deAndrés-Galiana, E. J., Alvarez, O., Cernea, A., Fernández-Brillet, L., Fernández-Martínez, J. L., & Kloczkowski, A. (2022). Innovations in Genomics and Big Data Analytics for Personalized Medicine and Health Care: A Review. *International Journal of Molecular Sciences*, *23*(9), 4645. Advance online publication. DOI: 10.3390/ijms23094645 PMID: 35563034

Hauschke, C., Nazarovets, S., Altemeier, F., & Kaliuzhna, N. (2021). Roadmap to FAIR Research Information in Open Infrastructures. *Journal of Library Metadata*, *21*(1–2), 45–61. DOI: 10.1080/19386389.2021.1999156

JLF UK. (2023). *Systémová verejná výskumná infraštruktúra – biobanka pre nádorové a zriedkavé ochorenia.* [Systemic public research infrastructure – biobank for cancer and rare diseases.] https://www.jfmed.uniba.sk/uploads/media/Systemova_verejna_vyskumna_infrastruktura_biobanka_pre_nadorove_a_zriedkave_ochorenia_II_faza.pdf

Leipzig, J., Nüst, D., Hoyt, C. T., Ram, K., & Greenberg, J. (2021). The role of metadata in reproducible computational research. *Patterns (New York, N.Y.), 2*(9), 100322. Advance online publication. DOI: 10.1016/j.patter.2021.100322 PMID: 34553169

Mayernik, M. S. (2019). Metadata accounts: Achieving data and evidence in scientific research. *Social Studies of Science, 49*(5), 732–757. DOI: 10.1177/0306312719863494 PMID: 31354073

Ministry of Education. Science, Research and Sports of SR (2021a). *Cestovná mapa výskumných infraštruktúr - SK VI Roadmap 2020 – 2030.* [Roadmap of research infrastructures - SK RI Roadmap 2020 - 2030.] https://www.minedu.sk/data/att/c28/25884.f33c49.pdf

Ministry of Education. Science, Research and Sports of SR (2021b). *Národná stratégia pre otvorenú vedu na roky 2021-2028.* [National Strategy for Open Science for 2021-2028.] https://www.minedu.sk/data/files/10833_narodna-strategia-pre-otvorenu-vedu-na-roky-2021--2028.pdf

Ministry of Education. Science, Research and Sports of SR (2022). *Metodické odporúčanie na tvorbu a implementáciu inštitucionálnej politiky otvorenej vedy pre inštitúcie vykonávajúce vedu a výskum.* [Methodological recommendation for the creation and implementation of an institutional open science policy for institutions conducting science and research.] https://www.minedu.sk/data/att/62e/33212.73cb3f.pdf

Ministry of Education. Research, Development and Youth of SR (2024a). *Správa o stave výskumu a vývoja v Slovenskej republike a jeho porovnanie so zahraničím za rok 2023.* [Report on the state of research and development in the Slovak Republic and its comparison with abroad for 2023.] https://www.minedu.sk/data/att/108/33300.81834d.pdf

Ministry of Education. Research, Development and Youth of SR (2024 b). *Kódex výskumnej integrity a etiky na Slovensku.* [Code of Research Integrity and Ethics in Slovakia.] https://www.minedu.sk/data/att/155/32501.fe9bf4.pdf

Ministry of Labor. Social Affairs and Family of SR. (2021). *Celoštátna stratégia rovnosti žien a mužov a rovnosti príležitostí v Slovenskej republike na roky 2021 – 2027*. [National Strategy for Equality between Women and Men and Equal Opportunities in the Slovak Republic for 2021-2027.] https://www.employment.gov.sk/files/sk/ministerstvo/spolocny-sekretariat-vyborov/vybor-rodovu-rovnost/dokumenty-udalosti/strategia-rovnosti-z-m-2021-27.pdf

Mons, B. (2019). FAIR Science for Social Machines: Let's Share Metadata Knowlets in the Internet of FAIR Data and Services. *Data Intelligence*, *1*(1), 21–42. DOI: 10.1162/dint_a_00002

NCZI. (2025). *Slovensko napreduje v implementácii EHDS*. [Slovakia is making progress in implementing the EHDS] https://www.nczisk.sk/Aktuality/Pages/Slovensko-napreduje-v-implementacii-EHDS.aspx

Normandeau, K. (2013). *Beyond Volume, Variety and Velocity is the Issue of Big Data Veracity. Inside Big Data.* https://insidebigdata.com/2013/09/12/beyond-volume-variety-velocity-issue-big-data-veracity

Numajiri, H., & Hayashi, T. (2024). Analysis on open data as a foundation for data-driven research. *Scientometrics*, *129*(10), 6315–6332. DOI: 10.1007/s11192-024-04956-x

Rumble, J.Jr, Broome, J., & Hodson, S. (2019). Building an International Consensus on Multi-Disciplinary Metadata Standards: A CODATA Case History in Nanotechnology. *Data Science Journal*, *18*(1), 12. Advance online publication. DOI: 10.5334/dsj-2019-012

SK4ERA (2025). *Elixir.* https://eraportal.sk/eraportal/oblasti-nasej-podpory/pristup-k-vyskumnym-infrastrukturam/elixir/

Schöpfel, J., & Azeroual, O. (2023). Ethical Issues of the Organization and Management of Research Information. *Communication, technologies et développement*, *14*. DOI: 10.4000/ctd.9857

Schöpfel, J., Azeroual, O., & Castro, P. (2022). Research Information Systems and Ethics relating to Open Science. *Procedia Computer Science*, *211*, 36–46. DOI: 10.1016/j.procs.2022.10.174

Thibault, R. T., Amaral, O. B., Argolo, F., Bandrowski, A. E., Davidson, A. R., & Drude, N. I. (2023). Open Science 2.0: Towards a truly collaborative research ecosystem. *PLoS Biology*, *21*(10), e3002362. Advance online publication. DOI: 10.1371/journal.pbio.3002362 PMID: 37856538

Ukropová, D. (2002) Metadáta v slovenských knižniciach. [Metadata in Slovak Libraries] *IT Lib. Informačné technológie a knižnice, 6* (4). https://itlib.cvtisr.sk/clanky/clanek2107/

UNESCO (2021). *UNESCO Recommendation on Open Science.* DOI: 10.54677/MNMH8546

VAIA. (2023). *Národná stratégia výskumu, vývoja a inovácií.* [National Strategy for Research, Development and Innovation.] https://vaia.gov.sk/wp-content/uploads/2023/05/01_Narodna-strategia-vyskumu-vyvoja-a-inovacii_vlastny-material_V2.pdf

Wilkinson, M. D., Dumontier, M., Aalbersberg, I. J., Appleton, G., Axton, M., Baak, A., Blomberg, N., Boiten, J. W., Bonino da Silva Santos, L., Bourne, P. E., Bouwman, J., Brookes, A. J., Clark, T., Crosas, M., Dillo, I., Dumon, O., Edmunds, S., Evelo, C. T., Finkers, R., & Mons, B. (2016). The FAIR Guiding Principles for scientific data management and stewardship. *Scientific Data, 3*(1), 160018. Advance online publication. DOI: 10.1038/sdata.2016.18 PMID: 26978244

Yang, W., Fu, R., Amin, M. B., & Kang, B. (2025). The Impact of Modern AI in Metadata Management. *Human-Centric Intelligent Systems, 5*(3), 323–350. DOI: 10.1007/s44230-025-00106-5

Zendulková, D., & Azeroual, O. (2022). Legal aspects and data protection in relation to the CRIS system. *Procedia Computer Science, 211*, 17–27. DOI: 10.1016/j.procs.2022.10.172

Zendulková, D., Gavurníková, G., Krivjanska, A., Staňáková, Z., Putalová, A., & Janková, M. (2022). Representation of Women in Slovak Science and Research: An Analysis Based on the CRIS System Data. *Information (Basel), 13*(10), 482. DOI: 10.3390/info13100482

Compilation of References

Abayomi-Alli, O., Misra, S., & Abayomi-Alli, A. (2022). A deep learning method for automatic SMS spam classification: Performance of learning algorithms on indigenous dataset. *Concurrency and Computation: Practice and Experience, 34*(17), e6989. h<ps://dl.acm.org/doi/10.1145/2034691.2034742

Abdelhafeez, A., & Aziz, A. S. (2025). *Enhanced Email Spam Detection Using Fine-Tuned Transformer Models and Classical Machine Learning Techniques.* Multicriteria Algorithms with Applications. DOI: 10.61356/j.mawa.2025.8597

Abidallah, N., Ailane, A., Bourekkache, S., Kahloul, L., Khalgui, M., & Azzaoui, N. (2025, January). Blockchain and Genetic Algorithms Interactions: A Brief Review. *In 2025 International Symposium on iNnovative Informatics of Biskra* (ISNIB) (pp. 1-6). IEEE.

Abootorabi, M. M., Ghahroodi, O., Zahraei, P. S., Behzadasl, H., Mirrokni, A., Salimipanah, M., Rasouli, A., Behzadipour, B., Azarnoush, S., Maleki, B., Sadraiye, E., Feriz, K. K., Nahad, M. T., Moghadasi, A., Abianeh, A. E., Nazar, N., Rabiee, H. R., Baghshah, M. S., Ahmadi, M., & Asgari, E. (2025, April 27). *Generative AI for Character animation: A comprehensive survey of techniques, applications, and future directions*. arXiv.org. https://arxiv.org/abs/2504.19056v1

Afzal, M., Ansari, M. S., Ahmad, N., Shahid, M., & Shoeb, M. (2024). Cyberfraud, usage intention, and cybersecurity awareness among e-banking users in India: An integrated model approach. *Journal of Financial Services Marketing*, *29*(4), 1503–1523. DOI: 10.1057/s41264-024-00279-3

Ahmed, S. F., Sharmin, S., Kuldeep, S. A., Lameesa, A., Alam, M. S. B., Liu, G., & Gandomi, A. H. (2024). Transformative impacts of the internet of medical things on modern healthcare. *Results in Engineering*, *25*, 103787. DOI: 10.1016/j.rineng.2024.103787

Akter, S., & Wamba, S. F. (2016). Big data analytics in E-commerce: A systematic review and agenda for future research. *Electronic Markets, 26*(2), 173–194. DOI: 10.1007/s12525-016-0219-0

Al-Debei, M. M., Abdeljaber, O., Ab Yajid, M. S., Khatibi, A., Al-masaeed, S., & Tham, J. (2021). The role of service quality and online trust in maintaining clients for Malaysian online enterprises. *International Journal of eBusiness and eGovernment studies, 13*(2), 149-167.

Al-Debei, M. M. (2024). The era of business analytics: Identifying and ranking the differences between business intelligence and data science from practitioners' perspective using the Delphi method. *Journal of Business Analytics, 7*(2), 94–119. DOI: 10.1080/2573234X.2023.2285483

Aldoseri, A., Al-Khalifa, K. N., & Hamouda, A. M. (2024). AI-powered innovation in digital transformation: Key pillars and industry impact. *Sustainability (Basel), 16*(5), 1790. DOI: 10.3390/su16051790

Alghamdi, N., Maddock, S., Marxer, R., Barker, J., & Brown, G. J. (2018). A corpus of audio-visual Lombard speech with frontal and profile views. *The Journal of the Acoustical Society of America, 143*(6), EL523–EL529. DOI: 10.1121/1.5042758 PMID: 29960497

Ali, H., Jawad, T., & Zuhair, H. (2021). Data Security Using Random Dynamic Salting And AES Based on Master-Slave Keys for Iraqi Dam Management System. *Indonesian Journal of Electrical Engineering and Computer Science, 23*(2), 1018–1029. DOI: 10.11591/ijeecs.v23.i2.pp1018-1029

Almeida, T. A., Hidalgo, J. M. G., & Yamakami, A. (2011, September). Contributions to the study of SMS spam filtering: new collection and results. In *Proceedings of the 11th ACM symposium on Document engineering* (pp. 259-262). DOI: 10.1145/2034691.2034742

Al-Tameemi, et al. (2025). A Systematic Review of Metaverse Cybersecurity: Frameworks, Challenges, and Strategic Approaches in A Quantum-Driven Era. *Mesopotamian Journal of CyberSecurity, 5*(2), 770–803.

Altherwi, A., Ahmad, M. T., Alam, M. M., Mirza, H., Sultana, N., Pasha, A. A., Sultana, N., Khan, A. I., Alam, M. M., & Azim, R. (2024). A hybrid optimization approach for securing cloud-based e-health systems. *Multimedia Tools and Applications, 84*(16), 16525–16560. DOI: 10.1007/s11042-024-19688-6

Altman, M., & Cohen, P. N. (2022). The Scholarly Knowledge Ecosystem: Challenges and Opportunities for the Field of Information. *Frontiers in Research Metrics and Analytics*, *6*, 751553. Advance online publication. DOI: 10.3389/frma.2021.751553 PMID: 35178498

Al-Zubaidie, M. (2025). A Critical Reliable Model for Promoting Patient Medical Wireless Sensors Information Security. *Procedia Computer Science*, *263*, 17–24. DOI: 10.1016/j.procs.2025.07.003

Al-Zubaidie, M., & Jebbar, W. A. (2024). Providing Security for Flash Loan System Using Cryptocurrency Wallets Supported by XSalsa20 in a Blockchain Environment. *Applied Sciences (Basel, Switzerland)*, *14*(14), 6361. DOI: 10.3390/app14146361

Al-Zubaidie, M., & Jebbar, W. A. (2025). Blockchain-powered dynamic segmentation in personal health record. *Mesopotamian Journal of Cybersecurity*, *5*(3), 953–976. DOI: 10.58496/MJCS/2025/054

Andrews, J. T. A., Sony, A. I., Zhao, D., Sony, A. I., Thong, W., Sony, A. I., Modas, A., Sony, A. I., Papakyriakopoulos, O., Sony, A. I., Xiang, A., & Sony, A. I. (2023). Ethical Considerations for Responsible Data Curation. *37th Conference on Neural Information Processing Systems (NeurIPS 2023) Track on Datasets and Benchmarks*. https://proceedings.neurips.cc/paper_files/paper/2023/file/ad3ebc951f43d1e9ed20187a7b5bc4ee-Paper-Datasets_and_Benchmarks.pdf

Anshori, M., Karya, D., & Gita, M. (2022). A Study on The Reuse Intention of E-Commerce Platform Applications: Security, Privacy, Perceived Value, and Trust. *J. Manaj. Teor. Dan Ter. J. Theory Appl. Manag.*, *15*(1), 13–24. DOI: 10.20473/jmtt.v15i1.34923

Atiyah, R. G.(2024). Intermediary Decentralized Computing and Private Blockchain Mechanisms for Privacy Preservation in The Internet of Medical *Things. Mesopotamian Journal of CyberSecurity*, *4*(3), 152–165. DOI: 10.58496/MJCS/2024/020

Austin, L. M. (2023). COVID-19 and the data governance gap. *Annual Review of Law and Social Science*, *19*(1), 235–253. DOI: 10.1146/annurev-lawsocsci-050520-101947

Awad, W. A., & Elseuofi, S. M. (2011). Machine Learning methods for E-mail Classification. *International Journal of Computer Applications*, *16*(1), 39–45. DOI: 10.5120/1974-2646

Awosika, T., Shukla, R. M., & Pranggono, B. (2024). Transparency and privacy: The role of explainable AI and federated learning in financial fraud detection. *IEEE Access : Practical Innovations, Open Solutions, 12*, 64551–64560. DOI: 10.1109/ACCESS.2024.3394528

Azeroual, O., & Schöpfel, J., Pölönen, & J. Nikiforova, A. (2022). Putting FAIR Principles in the Context of Research Information: FAIRness for CRIS and CRIS for FAIRness. In *Proceedings of the 14th International Joint Conference on Knowledge Discovery, Knowledge Engineering and Knowledge Management (IC3K 2022)*. SciTePress, 63-71. DOI: 10.5220/0011548700003335

Azeroual, O. (2025). *Von der Literaturflut zur Erkenntnis: Research Guru AI als Katalysator für die Zukunft wissenschaftlicher Analyse*. Information – Wissenschaft & Praxis., DOI: 10.1515/iwp-2025-2050

Azeroual, O., Schöpfel, J., Störl, U., & Marušić, A. (2024). Ethical aspects using AI in CRIS. *Procedia Computer Science, 249*, 150–159. DOI: 10.1016/j.procs.2024.11.058

Balakrishnan, V. (2015). Cyberbullying among young adults in Malaysia: The roles of gender, age and Internet frequency. *Computers in Human Behavior, 46*, 149–157. DOI: 10.1016/j.chb.2015.01.021

Banabilah, S., Aloqaily, M., Alsayed, E., Malik, N., & Jararweh, Y. (2022). Federated learning review: Fundamentals, enabling technologies, and future applications. *Information Processing & Management, 59*(6), 103061. DOI: 10.1016/j.ipm.2022.103061

Banday, M. T., & Jan, T. R. (2009). Effectiveness and limitations of statistical spam filters. *arXiv preprint arXiv:0910.2540.*

Bansal, S., Chowell, G., Simonsen, L., Vespignani, A., & Viboud, C. (2016). Big data for infectious disease surveillance and modeling. *The Journal of Infectious Diseases, 214*(suppl_4), S375–S379. DOI: 10.1093/infdis/jiw400 PMID: 28830113

Beigi, G., & Liu, H. (2018). Privacy in social media: Identification, mitigation and applications. *arXiv preprint arXiv:1808.02191.*

Bennett, C. H., & Brassard, G. (2014). Quantum cryptography: Public key distribution and coin tossing. *Theoretical Computer Science, 560*, 7–11. DOI: 10.1016/j.tcs.2014.05.025

Bhatia, A. S., & Neira, D. E. B. (2024). Federated hierarchical tensor networks: A collaborative learning quantum AI-driven framework for healthcare. arXiv preprint arXiv:2405.07735.

Bhatia, A. S., Kais, S., & Alam, M. A. (2023). Federated quanvolutional neural network: A new paradigm for collaborative quantum learning. *Quantum Science and Technology*, *8*(4), 045032. DOI: 10.1088/2058-9565/acfc61

Bhatia, A. S., Saggi, M. K., & Kais, S. (2025). Application of quantum-inspired tensor networks to optimize federated learning systems. *Quantum Machine Intelligence*, *7*(1), 12. DOI: 10.1007/s42484-025-00243-x

Biamonte, J., Wittek, P., Pancotti, N., Rebentrost, P., Wiebe, N., & Lloyd, S. (2017). Quantum machine learning. *Nature*, *549*(7671), 195–202. DOI: 10.1038/nature23474 PMID: 28905917

Bibault, J.-E. (2020). Real-life clinical data mining: Generating hypotheses for evidence-based medicine. *Annals of Translational Medicine*, *8*(4), 69. Advance online publication. DOI: 10.21037/atm.2019.10.99 PMID: 32175362

Bonawitz, K., Ivanov, V., Kreuter, B., Marcedone, A., McMahan, H. B., Patel, S., Ramage, D., Segal, A., & Seth, K. (2019). Practical secure aggregation for privacy-preserving machine learning. In *Proceedings of the ACM SIGSAC Conference on Computer and Communications Security* (pp. xxx–xxx). London, United Kingdom.

Bordons, M., González-Albo, B., & Moreno-Solano, L. (2023). Improving our understanding of open access: How it relates to funding, internationality of research and scientific leadership. *Scientometrics*, *128*(8), 4651–4676. DOI: 10.1007/s11192-023-04726-1

Boulis, C., Diakoloukas, V., & Digalakis, V. (2001). Maximum likelihood stochastic transformation adaptation for medium and small data sets. *Computer Speech & Language*, *15*(3), 257–285. DOI: 10.1006/csla.2001.0168

Bowles, J., Ahmed, S., & Schuld, M. (2024). Better than classical? The subtle art of benchmarking quantum machine learning models. arXiv preprint arXiv:2403.07059.

Burgelman, J. C., Pascu, C., Szkuta, K., Von Schomberg, R., Karalopoulos, A., Repanas, K., & Schouppe, M. (2019). Open Science, Open Data, and Open Scholarship: European Policies to Make Science Fit for the Twenty-First Century. *Frontiers in Big Data*, *2*, 43. Advance online publication. DOI: 10.3389/fdata.2019.00043 PMID: 33693366

Cai, L., Hu, Q., Jiang, T., & Niyato, D. (2024). Blockchain-enabled secure federated learning for digital twin networks. *IEEE Wireless Communications*.

Cambria, E., Grassi, M., Poria, S., & Hussain, A. (2013). Sentic computing for social media analysis, representation, and retrieval. In *Social media retrieval* (pp. 191–215). Springer. DOI: 10.1007/978-1-4471-4555-4_9

Cao, H., Cooper, D. G., Keutmann, M. K., Gur, R. C., Nenkova, A., & Verma, R. (2014). CREMA-D: Crowd-Sourced Emotional Multimodal Actors Dataset. *IEEE Transactions on Affective Computing*, *5*(4), 377–390. DOI: 10.1109/TAFFC.2014.2336244 PMID: 25653738

Cappa, F., Oriani, R., Peruffo, E., & McCarthy, I. (2021). Big data for creating and capturing value in the digitalized environment: Unpacking the effects of volume, variety, and veracity on firm performance. *Journal of Product Innovation Management*, *38*(1), 49–67. DOI: 10.1111/jpim.12545

Carminati, B., Ferrari, E., & Viviani, M. (2022). *Security and trust in online social networks*. Springer Nature.

Castro, P. (2024). Improving CRIS features to support new Open Access implementation workflows at institutions. *Procedia Computer Science*, *249*, 179–185. DOI: 10.1016/j.procs.2024.11.062

Chang, V. (2021). An ethical framework for big data and smart cities. *Technological Forecasting and Social Change*, *165*, 120559. DOI: 10.1016/j.techfore.2020.120559

Chani, A., & Bhagwan, J. (2025). *Email Spam Detection: Comparative Review of Deep, Transformer, and LLM Techniques*. IJRASET.

Chapman, A. L., Morgan, L. C., & Gartlehner, G. (2010). Semi-automating the manual literature search for systematic reviews increases efficiency. *Health Information and Libraries Journal*, *27*(1), 22–27. DOI: 10.1111/j.1471-1842.2009.00865.x PMID: 20402801

Chatsuwan, P., Phromma, T., Surasvadi, N., & Thajchayapong, S. (2023). Personal data protection compliance assessment: A privacy policy scoring approach and empirical evidence from Thailand's SMEs. *Heliyon*, *9*(10), e20648. DOI: 10.1016/j.heliyon.2023.e20648 PMID: 37886776

Chen, Z., Qi, T., Lu, C., & Zheng, W. (2025). DisenEmo: Learning disentangled emotional representation from facial motion for 3D talking head generation. *2022 IEEE International Conference on Image Processing (ICIP)*, 289-294. DOI: 10.1109/ICIP55913.2025.11084454

Cho, K., Van Merriënboer, B., Gulcehre, C., Bahdanau, D., Bougares, F., Schwenk, H., & Bengio, Y. (2014). Learning phrase representations using RNN encoder-decoder for statistical machine translation. *arXiv preprint arXiv:1406.1078*. DOI: 10.3115/v1/D14-1179

Chung, J., Gulcehre, C., Cho, K., & Bengio, Y. (2014). Empirical evaluation of gated recurrent neural networks on sequence modeling. *arXiv preprint arXiv:1412.3555*.

Chung, J. S., Nagrani, A., & Zisserman, A. (2018). VoxCeleb2: Deep Speaker Recognition. *Interspeech, 2022*, 1086–1090. Advance online publication. DOI: 10.21437/Interspeech.2018-1929

Chung, J. S., Senior, A., Vinyals, O., & Zisserman, A. (2017). *Lip reading sentences in the wild.* IEEE., DOI: 10.1109/CVPR.2017.367

Cole, A., & Tran, É. (2022). Trust and the smart city. *China Perspectives, 130*(3), 3–7. DOI: 10.4000/chinaperspectives.14024

Constantinides, E. (2004). Influencing the online consumer's behavior: The Web experience. *Internet Research, 14*(2), 111–126. DOI: 10.1108/10662240410530835

Cottrill, C. D., Jacobs, N., Markovic, M., & Edwards, P. (2020). Sensing the city: Designing for privacy and trust in the internet of things. *Sustainable Cities and Society, 63*, 102453. DOI: 10.1016/j.scs.2020.102453

Cudeiro, D., Bolkart, T., Laidlaw, C., Ranjan, A., & Black, M. J. (2019). Capture, learning, and synthesis of 3D speaking styles. *2022 IEEE/CVF Conference on Computer Vision and Pattern Recognition (CVPR)*, 10093-10103. DOI: 10.1109/CVPR.2019.01034

Dada, E. G., Bassi, J. S., Chiroma, H., Abdulhamid, S. I. M., Adetunmbi, A. O., & Ajibuwa, O. E. (2019). Machine learning for email spam filtering: Review, approaches and open research problems. *Heliyon, 5*(6), e01802. DOI: 10.1016/j.heliyon.2019.e01802 PMID: 31211254

de la Torre-López, J., Ramírez, A., & Romero, J. R. (2023). Artificial intelligence to automate the systematic review of scientific literature. *Computing, 105*(10), 2171–2194. DOI: 10.1007/s00607-023-01181-x

Delgado-Chaves, F. M., Jennings, M. J., Atalaia, A., Wolff, J., Horvath, R., Mamdouh, Z. M., Baumbach, J., & Baumbach, L. (2025). Transforming literature screening: The emerging role of large language models in systematic reviews. *Proceedings of the National Academy of Sciences of the United States of America, 122*(2), e2411962122. DOI: 10.1073/pnas.2411962122 PMID: 39761403

Demertzi, V., Demertzis, S., & Demertzis, K. (2023). An overview of cyber threats, attacks and countermeasures on the primary domains of smart cities. *Applied Sciences (Basel, Switzerland), 13*(2), 790. DOI: 10.3390/app13020790

Devlin, J., Chang, M. W., Lee, K., & Toutanova, K. (2019, June). Bert: Pre-training of deep bidirectional transformers for language understanding. In *Proceedings of the 2019 conference of the North American chapter of the association for computational linguistics: human language technologies, volume 1 (long and short papers)* (pp. 4171-4186).

Diao, X., Cheng, M., Barrios, W., & Jin, S. (2025). FT2TF: First-Person Statement Text-to-Talking Face Generation. *2022 IEEE/CVF Winter Conference on Applications of Computer Vision (WACV)*, 4821-4830. DOI: 10.1109/WACV61041.2025.00472

Diebold, F. X., Cheng, X., Diebold, S., Foster, D., Halperin, M., Lohr, S., Mashey, J., Nickolas, T., Pai, M., & Pospiech, M. A. (2012). *Personal Perspective on the Origin (s) and Development of "Big Data": The Phenomenon, the Term, and the Discipline*. CiteSeer.

Dong, B., & Zhang, L. (2025). Enhanced temporal representation and spatial alignment for High-Fidelity Talking Video Generation. *The Visual Computer*, *41*(12), 9781–9792. Advance online publication. DOI: 10.1007/s00371-025-03999-2

Dritsas, E., & Trigka, M. (2025). Machine Learning in e-Commerce: Trends, Applications, and Future Challenges. *IEEE Access : Practical Innovations, Open Solutions*, *13*, 99048–99067. DOI: 10.1109/ACCESS.2025.3572865

Duaa, T., et al. (2024). Enhancing Electronic Agriculture Data Security with A Blockchain-Based Search Method And E-Signatures. *Mesopotamian journal of Cybersecurity*, 4(3), 1-21.

Duquenoy, P., George, C., & Kimppa, K. (2008). Ethical, legal and social issues in medical informatics. In *IGI Global eBooks*. DOI: 10.4018/978-1-59904-780-5

Dvořák, J. (2025). *CERIF Tutorial*. euroCRIS Membership Meeting Leuven, Belgium. http://hdl.handle.net/11366/2727

Dwivedi, Y. K., Hughes, L., Ismagilova, E., Aarts, G., Coombs, C., Crick, T., Duan, Y., Dwivedi, R., Edwards, J., Eirug, A., Galanos, V., Ilavarasan, P. V., Janssen, M., Jones, P., Kar, A. K., Kizgin, H., Kronemann, B., Lal, B., Lucini, B., & Williams, M. D. (2021). Artificial Intelligence (AI): Multidisciplinary perspectives on emerging challenges, opportunities, and agenda for research, practice and policy. *International Journal of Information Management*, *57*, 101994. DOI: 10.1016/j.ijinfomgt.2019.08.002

ERAPortál. (2025). *Rodová rovnosť vo výskume. Politický rámec a základné definície.* [Gender equality in research. Policy framework and basic definitions.] https://eraportal.sk/eraportal/rodova-rovnost-vo-vyskume/politicky-ramec-a-zakladne-definicie/

Etezadi-Amoli, J., & Farhoomand, A. F. (1996). A structural model of end user computing satisfaction and user performance. *Information & Management, 30*(2), 65–73. DOI: 10.1016/0378-7206(95)00052-6

euroCRIS. (2025) *Directory of Research Information Systems – DRIS.* https://dspacecris.eurocris.org/browse?type=driscountry&order=ASC&rpp=20&authority=824

European Commission. (2020). *Únia rovnosti: stratégia pre rodovú rovnosť na roky 2020 – 2025.* [A Union of Equality: Gender Equality Strategy 2020-2025.] https://commission.europa.eu/strategy-and-policy/policies/justice-and-fundamental-rights/gender-equality/gender-equality-strategy_sk

European Commission. (2025). *European '1+ Million Genomes' initiative.* https://digital-strategy.ec.europa.eu/en/policies/1-million-genomes

European Strategy Forum on Research Infrastructures. (2015). *Európske strategické fórum o výskumných infraštruktúrach (ESFRI roadmap) v interakcii s pripravovanou cestovnou mapou infraštruktúr výskumu a vývoja (SVK roadmap).* [The European Strategy Forum on Research Infrastructures (ESFRI roadmap) in interaction with the upcoming roadmap for research and development infrastructures (SVK roadmap).] https://www.minedu.sk/data/att/8d3/8662.3ee4cb.pdf

Fanelli, G., Dantone, M., Gall, J., Fossati, A., & Van Gool, L. (2012). Random forests for real time 3D face analysis. *International Journal of Computer Vision, 101*(3), 437–458. DOI: 10.1007/s11263-012-0549-0

Farhud, D. D., & Zokaei, S. (2021). Ethical issues of artificial intelligence in medicine and healthcare. *Iranian Journal of Public Health.* Advance online publication. DOI: 10.18502/ijph.v50i11.7600 PMID: 35223619

Farnel, S., & Shiri, A. (2014). Metadata for Research Data: Current Practices and Trends. *International Conference on Dublin Core and Metadata Applications,* 2014. DOI: 10.23106/dcmi.952136534

Favaretto, M., De Clercq, E., Schneble, C. O., & Elger, B. S. (2020). What is your definition of Big Data? Researchers' understanding of the phenomenon of the decade. *PLoS One, 15*(2), e0228987. DOI: 10.1371/journal.pone.0228987 PMID: 32097430

Felzmann, H., Fosch-Villaronga, E., Lutz, C., & Tamò-Larrieux, A. (2020). Towards transparency by design for artificial intelligence. *Science and Engineering Ethics, 26*(6), 3333–3361. DOI: 10.1007/s11948-020-00276-4 PMID: 33196975

Fisher, C. B., Bragard, E., & Bloom, R. (2020). Ethical Considerations in HIV eHealth Intervention Research: Implications for informational risk in recruitment, data maintenance, and consent procedures. *Current HIV/AIDS Reports*, *17*(3), 180–189. DOI: 10.1007/s11904-020-00489-z PMID: 32358768

Fornell, C., & Larcker, D. F. (1981). Structural equation models with unobservable variables and measurement error: Algebra and statistics. *JMR, Journal of Marketing Research*, *18*(3), 382–388. DOI: 10.1177/002224378101800313

Franke, J., & Gailhofer, P. (2021). Data governance and regulation for sustainable smart cities. *Frontiers in Sustainable Cities*, *3*, 763788. DOI: 10.3389/frsc.2021.763788

Gandomi, A., & Haider, M. (2015). Beyond the hype: Big data concepts, methods, and analytics. *International Journal of Information Management*, *35*(2), 137–144. DOI: 10.1016/j.ijinfomgt.2014.10.007

Gangwani, P., Perez-Pons, A., Bhardwaj, T., Upadhyay, H., Joshi, S., & Lagos, L. (2021). Securing environmental IoT data using masked authentication messaging protocol in a DAG-based blockchain: IOTA tangle. *Future Internet*, *13*(12), 312. DOI: 10.3390/fi13120312

Gangwani, P., Perez-Pons, A., Braccia, P., Upadhyay, H., & Lagos, L. (2023). Integration of data science and IoT with blockchain for Industry 4.0. In *Blockchain and its applications in Industry 4.0* (pp. 139–177). Springer. DOI: 10.1007/978-981-19-8730-4_6

Georgieva, I., Lazo, C., Timan, T., & Van Veenstra, A. F. (2022). From AI ethics principles to data science practice: A reflection and a gap analysis based on recent frameworks and practical experience. *AI and Ethics*, *2*(4), 697–711. DOI: 10.1007/s43681-021-00127-3

Greenleaf, G. (2018). Global data privacy laws 2017: 120 national data privacy laws, including Indonesia and Turkey. *Privacy Laws & Business International Report*, *145*, 10–13.

Gupta, A. K., & Goyal, H. (2021). Framework for implementing big data analytics in Indian manufacturing: ISM-MICMAC and Fuzzy-AHP approach. *Information Technology and Management*, *22*(3), 207–229. DOI: 10.1007/s10799-021-00333-9

Guzella, T. S., & Caminhas, W. M. (2009). A review of machine learning approaches to spam filtering. *Expert Systems with Applications*, *36*(7), 10206–10222. DOI: 10.1016/j.eswa.2009.02.037

GVU. (1998). 10th WWW User Survey., [Web]. Graphic, Visualization, & Usability Center. Available: https://www.gvu.gatech.edu/user_surveys/survey-1998-10/ [20/05/1999].

Haddaway, N. R., Bethel, A., Dicks, L. V., Koricheva, J., Macura, B., Petrokofsky, G., Pullin, A. S., Savilaakso, S., & Stewart, G. B. (2020). Eight problems with literature reviews and how to fix them. *Nature Ecology & Evolution*, *4*(12), 1582–1589. DOI: 10.1038/s41559-020-01295-x PMID: 33046871

Haddaway, N. R., Woodcock, P., Macura, B., & Collins, A. (2015). Making literature reviews more reliable through application of lessons from systematic reviews. *Conservation Biology*, *29*(6), 1596–1605. DOI: 10.1111/cobi.12541 PMID: 26032263

Hagos, D. H., Battle, R., & Rawat, D. B. (2024). Recent advances in generative AI and large language models: Current status, challenges, and perspectives. *IEEE Transactions on Artificial Intelligence*, *5*(12), 5873–5893. DOI: 10.1109/TAI.2024.3444742

Han, Z., Teye, M., Yadgaroff, D., & Bütepage, J. (2025). Tiny is not small enough: High quality, low-resource facial animation models through hybrid knowledge distillation. *ACM Transactions on Graphics*, *44*(4), 1–18. DOI: 10.1145/3730929

Hardwicke, T. E., Mathur, M. B., MacDonald, K., Nilsonne, G., Banks, G. C., Kidwell, M. C., Hofelich Mohr, A., Clayton, E., Yoon, E. J., Henry Tessler, M., Lenne, R. L., Altman, S., Long, B., & Frank, M. C. (2018). Data availability, reusability, and analytic reproducibility: Evaluating the impact of a mandatory open data policy at the journal Cognition. *Royal Society Open Science*, *5*(8), 180448. DOI: 10.1098/rsos.180448 PMID: 30225032

Harris, L. C., & Goode, M. M. (2010). Online servicescapes, trust, and purchase intentions. *Journal of Services Marketing*, *24*(3), 230–243. DOI: 10.1108/08876041011040631

Harriss, D. J., Jones, C., & MacSween, A. (2022). Ethical Standards in Sport and Exercise Science Research: 2022 update. *International Journal of Sports Medicine*, *43*(13), 1065–1070. DOI: 10.1055/a-1957-2356 PMID: 36495253

Harte, N., & Gillen, E. (2015). TCD-TIMIT: An Audio-Visual Corpus of Continuous Speech. *IEEE Transactions on Multimedia*, *17*(5), 603–615. DOI: 10.1109/TMM.2015.2407694

Hassan, M. A., Shukur, Z., Hasan, M. K., & Al-Khaleefa, A. S. (2020). A review on electronic payments security. *Symmetry*, *12*(8), 1344. DOI: 10.3390/sym12081344

Hassan, M., Awan, F. M., Naz, A., deAndrés-Galiana, E. J., Alvarez, O., Cernea, A., Fernández-Brillet, L., Fernández-Martínez, J. L., & Kloczkowski, A. (2022). Innovations in Genomics and Big Data Analytics for Personalized Medicine and Health Care: A Review. *International Journal of Molecular Sciences*, *23*(9), 4645. Advance online publication. DOI: 10.3390/ijms23094645 PMID: 35563034

Hauschke, C., Nazarovets, S., Altemeier, F., & Kaliuzhna, N. (2021). Roadmap to FAIR Research Information in Open Infrastructures. *Journal of Library Metadata*, *21*(1–2), 45–61. DOI: 10.1080/19386389.2021.1999156

Himdi, T. (2024). A blockchain and AI-driven security framework for cognitive cities. *Advances in Artificial Intelligence and Machine Learning*, *4*, 2908–2925. DOI: 10.54364/AAIML.2024.44169

Hirsch, D. D., Bartley, T., Chandrasekaran, A., Parthasarathy, S., Turner, P. N., Norris, D., Lamont, K., & Drummond, C. (2019). Corporate Data Ethics: Data Governance Transformations for the age of advanced Analytics and AI. SSRN *Electronic Journal*. DOI: 10.2139/ssrn.3478826

Hossain, S. M. M., Kamal, K. M. A., Sen, A., & Sarker, I. H. (2023). Tf-idf feature-based spam filtering of mobile sms using a machine learning approach. In *Applied Intelligence for Industry 4.0* (pp. 162–175). Chapman and Hall/CRC. DOI: 10.1201/9781003256083-13

Hosseini, M., Wieczorek, M., & Gordijn, B. (2022). Ethical issues in social science research employing big data. *Science and Engineering Ethics*, *28*(3), 29. Advance online publication. DOI: 10.1007/s11948-022-00380-7 PMID: 35705883

Hoy, M. G., & Milne, G. (2010). Gender differences in privacy-related measures for young adult Facebook users. *Journal of Interactive Advertising*, *10*(2), 28–45. DOI: 10.1080/15252019.2010.10722168

Hu, J., Hoang, X., & Khalil, I. (2011). An Embedded DSP Hardware Encryption Module for Secure E-Commerce Transactions. *Security and Communication Networks*, *4*(8), 902–909. DOI: 10.1002/sec.221

Iandola, F., Pidhorskyi, S., Santesteban, I., Gupta, D., Pahuja, A., Bartolovic, N., Yu, F., Garbin, E., Simon, T., & Saito, S. (2025). SqueezeMe: Mobile-Ready distillation of Gaussian Full-Body Avatars. *SIGGRAPH Conference Papers '25: Proceedings of the Special Interest Group on Computer Graphics and Interactive Techniques Conference Conference Papers*, 1-11. DOI: 10.1145/3721238.3730599

Imperva. (2023). The State of Security within Ecommerce in 2022. Available online: https://www.imperva.com/resources/reports/The-State-of-Security-Within-eCommerce-in-2022_report.pdf (accessed on 19 March 2023).

Imran, O., Yousif, S., Hameed, I., Abed, W., & Hammid, A. (2020). Implementation of El-Gamal Algorithm for Speech Signals Encryption and Decryption. *Procedia Computer Science*, *2020*(167), 1028–1037. DOI: 10.1016/j.procs.2020.03.402

Indiani, N. L. P., & Fahik, G. A. (2020). Conversion of online purchase intention into actual purchase: The moderating role of transaction security and convenience. *Business: Theory and Practice*, *21*(1), 18–29. DOI: 10.3846/btp.2020.11346

Internet and Mobile Association of India, & Kantar. (2022). ICUBE 2022: India internet ecosystem. Internet and Mobile Association of India.

Ioannidis, J. P., Salholz-Hillel, M., Boyack, K. W., & Baas, J. (2021). The rapid, massive growth of COVID-19 authors in the scientific literature. *Royal Society Open Science*, *8*(9), 210389. DOI: 10.1098/rsos.210389 PMID: 34527271

IoT Analytics. (2021). The state of IoT: 2021 edition. Retrieved July 1, 2025, from https://iot-analytics.com/product/state-of-iot-summer-2021/

Ismagilova, E., Hughes, L., Rana, N. P., & Dwivedi, Y. K. (2022). Security, privacy and risks within smart cities: Literature review and development of a smart city interaction framework. *Information Systems Frontiers*, *24*(2), 393–414. DOI: 10.1007/s10796-020-10044-1 PMID: 32837262

Jacobs, N., Edwards, P., Markovic, M., Cottrill, C. D., & Salt, K. (2020). Who trusts in the smart city? Transparency, governance, and the internet of things. *Data & Policy*, *2*, e11. DOI: 10.1017/dap.2020.11

Jacobs, N., Loveday, F., Markovic, M., Cottrill, C. D., Zullo, R., & Edwards, P. (2022). Prototyping an IoT transparency toolkit to support communication, governance and policy in the smart city. *The Design Journal*, *25*(3), 459–480. DOI: 10.1080/14606925.2022.2061775

Jameel, B., & Majid, U. (2018). Research fundamentals: Data collection, data analysis, and ethics. *Undergraduate Research in Natural and Clinical Science and Technology (URNCST). Journal*, *2*(4), 1–8. DOI: 10.26685/urncst.39

Jebbar, W. A., & Al-Zubaidie, M. (2024). Transaction-Based Blockchain Systems Security Improvement Employing Micro-Segmentation Controlled By Smart Contracts and Detection of Saddle Goatfish. *SN Computer Science*, *5*(7), 898. DOI: 10.1007/s42979-024-03239-9

Ji, X., Lin, C., Ding, Z., Tai, Y., Yang, J., Zhu, J., Hu, X., Zhang, J., Luo, D., & Wang, C. (2024). RealTalk: Real-time and Realistic Audio-driven Face Generation with 3D Facial Prior-guided Identity Alignment Network. *arXiv (Cornell University)*. / arxiv.2406.18284DOI: 10.48550

Jiang, L., Zheng, H., Tian, H., Xie, S., & Zhang, Y. (2021). Cooperative federated learning and model update verification in blockchain-empowered digital twin edge networks. *IEEE Internet of Things Journal*, *9*(13), 11154–11167. DOI: 10.1109/JIOT.2021.3126207

Jin, Y., & Wang, Y. (2025). Reassessing smart city development and personal data protection: A regulatory framework. *International Review of Economics & Finance*, *99*, 104022. DOI: 10.1016/j.iref.2025.104022

JLF UK. (2023). *Systémová verejná výskumná infraštruktúra – biobanka pre nádorové a zriedkavé ochorenia.* [Systemic public research infrastructure – biobank for cancer and rare diseases.] https://www.jfmed.uniba.sk/uploads/media/Systemova_verejna_vyskumna_infrastruktura_biobanka_pre_nadorove_a_zriedkave_ochorenia_II_faza.pdf

Karras, T., Laine, S., & Aila, T. (2020). A Style-Based generator architecture for generative adversarial networks. *IEEE Transactions on Pattern Analysis and Machine Intelligence*, *43*(12), 4217–4228. DOI: 10.1109/TPAMI.2020.2970919 PMID: 32012000

Kaspersky Lab. Phishing and Spam Annual Report 2024. 2025. Available online: https://www.kaspersky.co.za/about/pressreleases/kaspersky-reports-nearly-900-million-phishing-attempts-in-2024-as-cyber-threats-increase?utm_source=chatgpt.com (accessed on 1 August 2025).

Khan, M. N., & Adil, M. (2013). Data analysis techniques in service quality literature: Essentials and advances. *Serbian Journal of Management*, *8*(1), 95–112.

Khan, S. (2022). Barriers of big data analytics for smart cities development: A context of emerging economies. *International Journal of Management Science and Engineering Management*, *17*(2), 123–131. DOI: 10.1080/17509653.2021.1997662

Kim, Y. (2014). Convolutional neural networks for sentence classification. *arXiv preprint arXiv:1408.5882*. DOI: 10.3115/v1/D14-1181

Kitchin, R. (2014). Big data, new epistemologies and paradigm shifts. *Big Data & Society*, *1*(1), 1–12. DOI: 10.1177/2053951714528481

König, P. D. (2021). Citizen-centered data governance in the smart city: From ethics to accountability. *Sustainable Cities and Society*, *75*, 103308. DOI: 10.1016/j.scs.2021.103308

Kshetri, N. (2014). Big data s impact on privacy, security and consumer welfare. *Telecommunications Policy*, *38*(11), 1134–1145. DOI: 10.1016/j.telpol.2014.10.002

Kuc-Czarnecka, M., & Olczyk, M. (2020). How ethics combine with big data: A bibliometric analysis. *Humanities & Social Sciences Communications*, *7*(1), 137. Advance online publication. DOI: 10.1057/s41599-020-00638-0

Kumar, N., & Sonowal, S. (2020, July). Email spam detection using machine learning algorithms. In *2020 Second International Conference on Inventive Research in Computing Applications (ICIRCA)* (pp. 108-113). IEEE. DOI: 10.1109/ICIRCA48905.2020.9183098

Kumar, P., Kumar, R., Kumar, A., Franklin, A. A., Garg, S., & Singh, S. (2022). Blockchain and deep learning for secure communication in digital twin empowered industrial IoT network. *IEEE Transactions on Network Science and Engineering*, *10*(5), 2802–2813. DOI: 10.1109/TNSE.2022.3191601

Kumar, V., & Sinha, D. (2021). A Robust Intelligent Zero-Day Cyber-Attack Detection Technique. *Complex & Intelligent Systems*, *7*(5), 2211–2234. DOI: 10.1007/s40747-021-00396-9

Kusa, W., Hanbury, A., & Knoth, P. (2022). Automation of citation screening for systematic literature reviews using neural networks: A replicability study. In *European Conference on Information Retrieval* (pp. 584-598). Cham: Springer International Publishing. DOI: 10.1007/978-3-030-99736-6_39

Lame, G. (2019). Systematic literature reviews: An introduction. In *Proceedings of the design society: international conference on engineering design* (Vol. 1, No. 1, pp. 1633-1642). Cambridge University Press.

Laorden, C., Santos, I., Sanz, B., Alvarez, G., & Bringas, P. G. (2012). Word sense disambiguation for spam filtering. *Electronic Commerce Research and Applications*, *11*(3), 290–298. DOI: 10.1016/j.elerap.2011.11.004

Laudon, K., & Traver, C. G. (2009). *E-Commerce 2009: Business. Technology, and Society*. Prentice Hall.

Leipzig, J., Nüst, D., Hoyt, C. T., Ram, K., & Greenberg, J. (2021). The role of metadata in reproducible computational research. *Patterns (New York, N.Y.)*, *2*(9), 100322. Advance online publication. DOI: 10.1016/j.patter.2021.100322 PMID: 34553169

Le, T. M., & Liaw, S. Y. (2017). Effects of pros and cons of applying big data analytics to consumers' responses in an e-commerce context. *Sustainability (Basel), 9*(5), 798. DOI: 10.3390/su9050798

Li, L. (2024, October). Using The Ripple Consensus Algorithm to Achieve Transparent Cross-Border Payments in E-Commerce. *In 6th International Conference on Artificial Intelligence and Advanced Manufacturing* (AIAM 2024) (Vol. 2024, pp. 295-299). IET.

Li, W., Zhang, L., Wang, D., Zhao, B., Wang, Z., Chen, M., Zhang, B., Wang, Z., Bo, L., & Li, X. (2023). One-Shot High-Fidelity Talking-Head Synthesis with Deformable Neural Radiance Field. *arXiv (Cornell University)*. /arxiv.2304.05097DOI: 10.1109/CVPR52729.2023.01723

Li, W., Zhong, N., Yao, Y. Y., Liu, J., & Liu, C. (2006, December). Spam filtering and email-mediated applications. In International workshop on web intelligence meets brain informatics (pp. 382-405). Berlin, Heidelberg: Springer Berlin Heidelberg. DOI: 10.1007/978-3-540-77028-2_23

Li, B., Wei, X., Liu, B., He, Z., Cao, J., & Lai, Y. (2024). Pose-Aware 3D Talking Face Synthesis using Geometry-guided Audio-Vertices Attention. *IEEE Transactions on Visualization and Computer Graphics, 31*(3), 1758–1771. DOI: 10.1109/TVCG.2024.3371064 PMID: 38416616

Liu, Y., Xu, F., Chai, J., Tong, X., Wang, L., & Huo, Q. (2015). Video-audio driven real-time facial animation. *ACM Transactions on Graphics, 34*(6), 1–10. DOI: 10.1145/2816795.2818122

Livingstone, S. R., & Russo, F. A. (2018). The Ryerson Audio-Visual Database of Emotional Speech and Song (RAVDESS): A dynamic, multimodal set of facial and vocal expressions in North American English. *PLoS One, 13*(5), e0196391. DOI: 10.1371/journal.pone.0196391 PMID: 29768426

Lomotey, R. K., Kumi, S., & Deters, R. (2022). Data trusts as a service: Providing a platform for multi-party data sharing. *International Journal of Information Management Data Insights, 2*(1), 100075. DOI: 10.1016/j.jjimei.2022.100075

Lueg, C. P. (2005). From spam filtering to information retrieval and back: Seeking conceptual foundations for spam filtering. *Proceedings of the American Society for Information Science and Technology, 42*(1), meet.14504201146. Advance online publication. DOI: 10.1002/meet.14504201146

Magrizos, S., Campora, M., Lamprinakos, G., Giovanis, A., & Christofi, M. (2026). Transparency by design: The effect of privacy policies visualisation on brand trust and perceived intrusion. *Behaviour & Information Technology*, *45*(3), 450–462. DOI: 10.1080/0144929X.2025.2520594

Ma, H., Zhang, T., Sun, S., Yan, X., Han, K., & Xie, X. (2024). CVTHead: One-shot Controllable Head Avatar with Vertex-feature Transformer. *2022 IEEE/CVF Winter Conference on Applications of Computer Vision (WACV)*, 6119-6129. DOI: 10.1109/WACV57701.2024.00602

Malhotra, N. K., & Dash, S. (2011). *Marketing Research: An Applied Orientation* (6th ed.). Pearson.

Malik, A., Hiekkanen, K., & Nieminen, M. (2016). *Privacy and trust in Facebook photo sharing: age and gender differences*. Program.

Mallampati, D. (2018). An efficient spam filtering using supervised machine learning techniques. *International Journal of Scientific Research in Computer Science and Engineering*, *6*(2), 33–37. DOI: 10.26438/ijsrcse/v6i2.3337

Manjare, S. O. (2025). E-Security Evolution: Navigating The E-Commerce Cybersecurity Landscape. In *Artificial Intelligence for Cyber Security and Industry 4.0* (pp. 292–318). CRC Press.

Martin, C. (2010). Social networking usage and grades among college students. A study conducted by the Whittmore School of Business and Economics University of New Hampshire.

Mattioli, M., & Cabitza, F. (2024). Not in my face: Challenges and ethical considerations in automatic face emotion recognition technology. *Machine Learning and Knowledge Extraction*, *6*(4), 2201–2231. DOI: 10.3390/make6040109

Maurya, S., Joseph, S., Asokan, A., Algethami, A. A., Hamdi, M., & Rauf, H. T. (2021). Federated transfer learning for authentication and privacy preservation using novel supportive twin delayed DDPG (S-TD3) algorithm for IIoT. *Sensors (Basel)*, *21*(23), 7793. DOI: 10.3390/s21237793 PMID: 34883794

Ma, Y., Wang, S., Ding, Y., Ma, B., Lv, T., Fan, C., Hu, Z., Deng, Z., & Yu, X. (2025). TalkCLIP: Talking Head Generation with Text-Guided Expressive Speaking Styles. *IEEE Transactions on Multimedia*, *27*, 1–12. DOI: 10.1109/TMM.2025.3581808

Mayernik, M. S. (2019). Metadata accounts: Achieving data and evidence in scientific research. *Social Studies of Science*, *49*(5), 732–757. DOI: 10.1177/0306312719863494 PMID: 31354073

Mazumdar, S. (2025). Educational implications of 6G technology for society 5.0. In *Elsevier eBooks* (pp. 255-265). DOI: 10.1016/B978-0-443-27434-3.00017-9

Mazumdar, S., & Chowdhury, I. (2025). Integration of machine learning, deep learning, and Internet of Things technologies for stress management and identification: a systematic analysis. In *Elsevier eBooks* (pp. 407-418). DOI: 10.1016/B978-0-443-33498-6.00023-6

McCulloch, W. S., & Pitts, W. (1943). A logical calculus of the ideas immanent in nervous activity. *The Bulletin of Mathematical Biophysics*, *5*(4), 115–133. DOI: 10.1007/BF02478259

McMahan, B., Moore, E., Ramage, D., Hampson, S., & Arcas, B. A. y. (2017). Communication-efficient learning of deep networks from decentralized data. In *Proceedings of the Artificial Intelligence and Statistics Conference* (pp. xxx–xxx). Fort Lauderdale, FL, United States.

Mehta, S., Khurana, M., Dogra, A., & Hariharan, S. (2024). Advancing IoT security through federated learning: A comprehensive approach. In *Proceedings of the International Conference on Applied Artificial Intelligence and Computing (ICAAIC)* (pp. 561–566). IEEE. DOI: 10.1109/ICAAIC60222.2024.10575903

Méndez, J. R., Fdez-Riverola, F., Díaz, F., Iglesias, E. L., & Corchado, J. M. (2006, July). A comparative performance study of feature selection methods for the anti-spam filtering domain. In *Industrial conference on data mining* (pp. 106–120). Springer Berlin Heidelberg. Springer. DOI: 10.1007/11790853_9

Meyer, T. A., & Whateley, B. (2004, July). SpamBayes: Effective open-source, Bayesian based, email classification system. In *CEAS*.

Mikalef, P., Krogstie, J., Pappas, I. O., & Pavlou, P. (2020). Exploring the relationship between big data analytics capability and competitive performance: The mediating roles of dynamic and operational capabilities. *Information & Management*, *57*(2), 103169. DOI: 10.1016/j.im.2019.05.004

Ministry of Education. Research, Development and Youth of SR (2024 b). *Kódex výskumnej integrity a etiky na Slovensku.* [Code of Research Integrity and Ethics in Slovakia.] https://www.minedu.sk/data/att/155/32501.fe9bf4.pdf

Ministry of Education. Research, Development and Youth of SR (2024a). *Správa o stave výskumu a vývoja v Slovenskej republike a jeho porovnanie so zahraničím za rok 2023.* [Report on the state of research and development in the Slovak Republic and its comparison with abroad for 2023.] https://www.minedu.sk/data/att/108/33300.81834d.pdf

Ministry of Education. Science, Research and Sports of SR (2021a). *Cestovná mapa výskumných infraštruktúr - SK VI Roadmap 2020 – 2030.* [Roadmap of research infrastructures - SK RI Roadmap 2020 - 2030.] https://www.minedu.sk/data/att/c28/25884.f33c49.pdf

Ministry of Education. Science, Research and Sports of SR (2021b). *Národná stratégia pre otvorenú vedu na roky 2021-2028.* [National Strategy for Open Science for 2021-2028.] https://www.minedu.sk/data/files/10833_narodna-strategia-pre-otvorenu-vedu-na-roky-2021--2028.pdf

Ministry of Education. Science, Research and Sports of SR (2022). *Metodické odporúčanie na tvorbu a implementáciu inštitucionálnej politiky otvorenej vedy pre inštitúcie vykonávajúce vedu a výskum.* [Methodological recommendation for the creation and implementation of an institutional open science policy for institutions conducting science and research.] https://www.minedu.sk/data/att/62e/33212.73cb3f.pdf

Ministry of Labor. Social Affairs and Family of SR. (2021). *Celoštátna stratégia rovnosti žien a mužov a rovnosti príležitostí v Slovenskej republike na roky 2021 – 2027.* [National Strategy for Equality between Women and Men and Equal Opportunities in the Slovak Republic for 2021-2027.] https://www.employment.gov.sk/files/sk/ministerstvo/spolocny-sekretariat-vyborov/vybor-rodovu-rovnost/dokumenty-udalosti/strategia-rovnosti-z-m-2021-27.pdf

Mishra, A. A. (2010). Consumer decision-making styles and young-adult consumers: An Indian exploration. *Management & Marketing-Craiova*, (2), 229–246.

Mitra, D., Kulkarni, P., Pathak, P., & Natrai, N. (2022). Importance of Coping with Cyber Security Challenges in E Commerce Business. *In Proceedings of the 2022 International Interdisciplinary Humanitarian Conference for Sustainability* (IIHC), Bengaluru, India, 18–19 November 2022; pp. 1596–1601.

Mohajan, H. K. (2018). Qualitative research methodology in social sciences and related subjects. *Journal of economic development, environment and people, 7*(1), 23-48.

Mohammed, S., Mohammed, O., Fiaidhi, J., Fong, S., & Kim, T. H. (2013). Classifying unsolicited bulk email (UBE) using python machine learning techniques. *International Journal of Hybrid Information Technology*, *6*(1), 43–56.

Mohd, N., & Ashawesh, A. (2021). Enhanced AES Algorithm Based on 14 Rounds in Securing Data and Minimizing Processing Time. *Journal of Physics: Conference Series, 2021*(1793), 012066. DOI: 10.1088/1742-6596/1793/1/012066

Mons, B. (2019). FAIR Science for Social Machines: Let's Share Metadata Knowlets in the Internet of FAIR Data and Services. *Data Intelligence*, *1*(1), 21–42. DOI: 10.1162/dint_a_00002

Morriss, J., Brindle, T., Rösman, J. B., Reibsamen, D., & Enz, A. (2024). The Literature Review Network: An Explainable Artificial Intelligence for Systematic Literature Reviews, Meta-analyses, and Method Development. *arXiv preprint arXiv:2408.05239*.

Muhajjar, R. A.. (2024). Integrating Trustworthy Mechanisms to Support Data and Information Security in Health Sensors. *Procedia Computer Science*, *237*, 43–52. DOI: 10.1016/j.procs.2024.05.078

Mutemi, A., & Bacao, F. (2024). E-Commerce Fraud Detection Based on Machine Learning Techniques: Systematic Literature Review. *Big Data Mining and Analytics*, *7*(2), 419–444. DOI: 10.26599/BDMA.2023.9020023

Nagrani, A., Chung, J. S., Xie, W., & Zisserman, A. (2019). Voxceleb: Large-scale speaker verification in the wild. *Computer Speech & Language*, *60*, 101027. DOI: 10.1016/j.csl.2019.101027

National Statistical Office. (2019). *Household social consumption on education in India (NSS 75th Round)*. Ministry of Statistics and Programme Implementation, Government of India.

Naveenkumar, C., & Venkataramana, K. (2025). SMS SPAM Filtering With Machine Learning Model Distilbert. International Journal of Scientific Research in Computer Science. *Engineering and Information Technology*, *11*(3), 170–175.

NCZI. (2025). *Slovensko napreduje v implementácii EHDS*. [Slovakia is making progress in implementing the EHDS] https://www.nczisk.sk/Aktuality/Pages/Slovensko-napreduje-v-implementacii-EHDS.aspx

Nguyen-Trung, K., Saeri, A. K., & Kaufman, S. (2024). Applying ChatGPT and AI-Powered Tools to Accelerate Evidence Reviews. *Human Behavior and Emerging Technologies*, *2024*(1), 8815424. DOI: 10.1155/2024/8815424

Normandeau, K. (2013). *Beyond Volume, Variety and Velocity is the Issue of Big Data Veracity. Inside Big Data*. https://insidebigdata.com/2013/09/12/beyond-volume-variety-velocity-issue-big-data-veracity

Novaes, J. (2021). Private information in public spaces: Facial recognition in the times of smart urban governance. *Smart Cities and Regional Development Journal*, *5*(1), 31–43. https://scrd.eu/index.php/scrd/article/view/94

Numajiri, H., & Hayashi, T. (2024). Analysis on open data as a foundation for data-driven research. *Scientometrics, 129*(10), 6315–6332. DOI: 10.1007/s11192-024-04956-x

Ochang, P., Eke, D., & Stahl, B. C. (2023). Towards an understanding of global brain data governance: Ethical positions that underpin global brain data governance discourse. *Frontiers in Big Data, 6*, 1240660. Advance online publication. DOI: 10.3389/fdata.2023.1240660 PMID: 38025947

Ogbuke, N. J., Yusuf, Y. Y., Dharma, K., & Mercangoz, B. A. (2022). Big data supply chain analytics: Ethical, privacy and security challenges posed to business, industries and society. *Production Planning and Control, 33*(2-3), 123–137. DOI: 10.1080/09537287.2020.1810764

Olteanu, A., Castillo, C., Diaz, F., & Kıcıman, E. (2019). Social data: Biases, methodological pitfalls, and ethical boundaries. *Frontiers in Big Data, 2*, 13. Advance online publication. DOI: 10.3389/fdata.2019.00013 PMID: 33693336

Organisation for Economic Co-operation and Development. (2023). *Smart city data governance: Challenges and the way forward.* OECD Urban Studies. OECD Publishing. DOI: 10.1787/e57ce301-en

Padmapriya, S. T., & Parthasarathy, S. (2023). Ethical Data Collection for Medical Image Analysis: A Structured Approach. *Asian Bioethics Review, 16*(1), 95–108. DOI: 10.1007/s41649-023-00250-9 PMID: 37361687

Patil, H. K., & Seshadri, R. (2014, June). Big data security and privacy issues in healthcare. In 2014 IEEE international congress on big data (pp. 762-765). IEEE.

Peng, W., Zhang, K., & Zhang, S. Q. (2024). T3M: Text Guided 3D Human Motion Synthesis from Speech. *Findings of the Association for Computational Linguistics: NAACL, 2022*, 1168–1177. DOI: 10.18653/v1/2024.findings-naacl.74

Phan, L., Ali, I., Labou, S., & Foster, E. (2022). A model for data ethics instruction for non-experts. *IASSIST Quarterly, 46*(4). Advance online publication. DOI: 10.29173/iq1028

Phillips-Wren, G., & Hoskisson, A. (2015). An analytical journey towards big data. *Journal of Decision Systems, 24*(1), 87–102. DOI: 10.1080/12460125.2015.994333

Poria, S., Hazarika, D., Majumder, N., Naik, G., Cambria, E., & Mihalcea, R. (2019). MELD: a multimodal Multi-Party dataset for emotion recognition in conversations. In *Proceedings of the 57th Annual Meeting of the Association for Computational Linguistics*. Association for Computational Linguistics. DOI: 10.18653/v1/P19-1050

Prathiba, S. B., Govindarajan, Y., Ganesan, V. P. A., Ramachandran, A., Selvaraj, A. K., Bashir, A. K., & Gadekallu, T. R. (2024). Fortifying federated learning in IIoT: Leveraging blockchain and digital twin innovations for enhanced security and resilience. *IEEE Access : Practical Innovations, Open Solutions*, *12*, 68968–68980. DOI: 10.1109/ACCESS.2024.3401039

Rakesh, V. K., Mazumdar, S., Maity, R. P., Pal, S., Das, A., & Samanta, T. (2026). Advancements in talking head generation: A comprehensive review of techniques, metrics, and challenges. *The Visual Computer*, *42*(1), 9. Advance online publication. DOI: 10.1007/s00371-025-04232-w

Rakotomalala, R. (2005, February). TANAGRA: a free software for research and academic purposes. In *Proceedings of EGC* (Vol. 2, pp. 697-702).

Rasha, H. R.. (2025). Sturdy Blockchain Combined with E-apps Repositories Based on Reliable Camouflaging and Integrating Mechanisms. *IJ Computer Network and Information Security*, *17*(3), 35–53. DOI: 10.5815/ijcnis.2025.03.03

Razzaq, R. H., & Al-Zubaidie, M. (2024). Maintaining Security of Patient Data By Employing Private Blockchain and Fog Computing Technologies Based on Internet of Medical Things. *Informatica (Vilnius)*, *48*(12).

Reed-Berendt, R., Dove, E. S., & Pareek, M. (2021). The ethical implications of big data research in public health: “Big Data Ethics by Design” in the UK-REACH study. *Ethics & Human Research*, *44*(1), 2–17. DOI: 10.1002/eahr.500111 PMID: 34936235

Richard, A., Zollhofer, M., Wen, Y., De La Torre, F., & Sheikh, Y. (2021). MeshTalk: 3D Face Animation from Speech using Cross-Modality Disentanglement. *2021 IEEE/CVF International Conference on Computer Vision (ICCV)*, 1153-1162. DOI: 10.1109/ICCV48922.2021.00121

Rizwan, A., Zoha, A., Zhang, R., Ahmad, W., Arshad, K., Ali, N. A., & Abbasi, Q. H. (2018). A review on the role of nano-communication in future healthcare systems: A big data analytics perspective. *IEEE Access : Practical Innovations, Open Solutions*, *6*, 41903–41920. DOI: 10.1109/ACCESS.2018.2859340

Rossler, A., Cozzolino, D., Verdoliva, L., Riess, C., Thies, J., & Niessner, M. (2019). FaceForensics++: Learning to Detect Manipulated Facial Images. *2021 IEEE/CVF International Conference on Computer Vision (ICCV)*, 1-11. DOI: 10.1109/ICCV.2019.00009

Rumble, J.Jr, Broome, J., & Hodson, S. (2019). Building an International Consensus on Multi-Disciplinary Metadata Standards: A CODATA Case History in Nanotechnology. *Data Science Journal, 18*(1), 12. Advance online publication. DOI: 10.5334/dsj-2019-012

Sadri, H., Yitmen, I., Tagliabue, L. C., & Westphal, F. (2023). A conceptual framework for blockchain and AI-driven digital twins for predictive operation and maintenance. In Proceedings of the European Conference on Computing in Construction and the International CIB W78 Conference (Vol. 4).

Safa, N. S., & Von Solms, R. (2016). An information security knowledge sharing model in organizations. *Computers in Human Behavior, 57*, 442–451. DOI: 10.1016/j.chb.2015.12.037

Saggi, M. K., & Jain, S. (2018). A survey towards an integration of big data analytics to big insights for value-creation. *Information Processing & Management, 54*(5), 758–790. DOI: 10.1016/j.ipm.2018.01.010

Sahami, M., Dumais, S., Heckerman, D., & Horvitz, E. (1998, July). A Bayesian approach to filtering junk e-mail. In *Learning for Text Categorization: Papers from the 1998 workshop* (Vol. 62, pp. 98-105).

Saha, R., Geetha, G., Kumar, G., & Kim, T. (2018). RK-AES: An Improved Version of Aes Using A New Key Generation Process with Random Keys. *Security and Communication Networks, 2018*(2018), 9802475. DOI: 10.1155/2018/9802475

Saleem, S., Islam, Z. U., Hasan, S. S. U., Akbar, H., Khan, M. F., & Ibrar, S. A. (2025). Spam email detection using long short-term memory and gated recurrent unit. *Applied Sciences (Basel, Switzerland), 15*(13), 7407. DOI: 10.3390/app15137407

Salman, M., Ikram, M., Basta, N., & Kaafar, M. A. (2025). Spallm-guard: Pairing sms spam detection using open-source and commercial llms. *arXiv preprint arXiv:2501.04985*.[REMOVED HYPERLINK FIELD]

Sarkar, M., & Banerjee, S. (2016). Exploring social network privacy measurement using fuzzy vector commitment. *Intelligent Decision Technologies, 10*(3), 285–297. DOI: 10.3233/IDT-160256

Sasikumar, A., Vairavasundaram, S., Kotecha, K., Indragandhi, V., Ravi, L., Selvachandran, G., & Abraham, A. (2023). Blockchain-based trust mechanism for digital twin empowered industrial internet of things. *Future Generation Computer Systems, 141*, 16–27. DOI: 10.1016/j.future.2022.11.002

Saxe, J., & Berlin, K. (2017). eXpose: A character-level convolutional neural network with embeddings for detecting malicious URLs, file paths and registry keys. *arXiv preprint arXiv:1702.08568*.

Schneider, K. M. (2003, April). A comparison of event models for Naive Bayes anti-spam e-mail filtering. In *10th conference of the European chapter of the association for computational linguistics*. DOI: 10.3115/1067807.1067848

Schöpfel, J., & Azeroual, O. (2023). Ethical Issues of the Organization and Management of Research Information. *Communication, technologies et développement, 14*. DOI: 10.4000/ctd.9857

Schöpfel, J., Azeroual, O., & Castro, P. (2022). Research Information Systems and Ethics relating to Open Science. *Procedia Computer Science, 211*, 36–46. DOI: 10.1016/j.procs.2022.10.174

Seng, S., Al-Ameen, M. N., & Wright, M. (2021). A look into user privacy andthird-party applications in Facebook. *Information and Computer Security, 29*(2), 283–313.

Shafique, M., Marchisio, A., Putra, R. V. W., & Hanif, M. A. (2021). Towards energy-efficient and secure edge AI: A cross-layer framework. In *Proceedings of the IEEE/ACM International Conference on Computer-Aided Design (ICCAD)* (pp. 1–9).

Shergill, G. S., & Chen, Z. (2005). Web-based shopping: Consumers' Attitudes towards online shopping in New Zealand. *Journal of Electronic Commerce Research, 6*(2), 78.

Shillingford, B., Assael, Y., Hoffman, M. W., Paine, T., Hughes, C., Prabhu, U., Liao, H., Sak, H., Rao, K., Bennett, L., Mulville, M., Denil, M., Coppin, B., Laurie, B., Senior, A., & De Freitas, N. (2019). Large-Scale visual speech recognition. *Interspeech, 2022*, 4135–4139. Advance online publication. DOI: 10.21437/Interspeech.2019-1669

Shimizu, Y., Osaki, S., Hashimoto, T., & Karasawa, K. (2022). Social acceptance of smart city projects: Focus on the Sidewalk Toronto case. *Frontiers in Environmental Science, 10*, 898922. DOI: 10.3389/fenvs.2022.898922

Shin, A., Lee, J., Hwang, J., Kim, Y., & Park, G. (2024). Wav2NeRF: Audio-driven realistic talking head generation via wavelet-based NeRF. *Image and Vision Computing, 148*, 105104. DOI: 10.1016/j.imavis.2024.105104

SHirvani. G., & Ghasemshirazi, S. (2025). Advancing Email Spam Detection: Leveraging Zero-Shot Learning and Large Language Models. *arXiv preprint arXiv:2505.02362*.

Shyaa, G. S., & Al-Zubaidie, M. (2023). Utilizing Trusted Lightweight Ciphers to Support Electronic-Commerce Transaction Cryptography. *Applied Sciences (Basel, Switzerland), 13*(12), 7085. DOI: 10.3390/app13127085

Sidi, Y., & Harel, O. (2018). The treatment of incomplete data: Reporting, analysis, reproducibility, and replicability. *Social Science & Medicine, 209*, 169–173. DOI: 10.1016/j.socscimed.2018.05.037 PMID: 29807627

Sinha, A., Sharma, N., Kumar, S., Lande, A., & Iqbal, M. I. (2024). AI-enhanced living: The future of smart homes. In *Proceedings of the International Conference on Smart Devices (ICSD)*. Dehradun, India. DOI: 10.1109/ICSD60021.2024.10751168

SK4ERA (2025). *Elixir.* https://eraportal.sk/eraportal/oblasti-nasej-podpory/pristup-k-vyskumnym-infrastrukturam/elixir/

Spezi, V., Wakeling, S., Pinfield, S., Creaser, C., Fry, J., & Willett, P. (2017). Open-access mega-journals: The future of scholarly communication or academic dumping ground? A review. *The Journal of Documentation, 73*(2), 263–283. DOI: 10.1108/JD-06-2016-0082

Strzelecki, A., & Rizun, M. (2022). Consumers' change in trust and security after a personal data breach in online shopping. *Sustainability (Basel), 14*(10), 5866. DOI: 10.3390/su14105866

Tahayur, D. H.. (2025). Security Cooperation in the Protection Concerns of Agriculture Data Using Efficient Signatures and Artificial Bee Colony Manner. In *Sustainable Information Security in the Age of AI and Green Computing* (pp. 439–460). IGI Global Scientific Publishing.

Tajudeen, K. O., Ameen, A. O., & Adeniyi, A. E. (2025). A Systematic Review on Advanced Encryption Standard Cryptography to Enhance Message Security. *Multimedia Tools and Applications, 84*(40), 1–26. DOI: 10.1007/s11042-025-21041-4

Taloba, A. I., & Ismail, S. S. (2019, December). An intelligent hybrid technique of decision tree and genetic algorithm for e-mail spam detection. In *2019 Ninth International Conference on Intelligent Computing and Information Systems (ICICIS)* (pp. 99-104). IEEE. DOI: 10.1109/ICICIS46948.2019.9014756

Tan, S., Ji, B., Bi, M., & Pan, Y. (2024). EDTaLK: Efficient Disentanglement for Emotional Talking head synthesis. In *Lecture notes in computer science* (pp. 398-416). DOI: 10.1007/978-3-031-72658-3_23

Telecom Regulatory Authority of India. (2023). *The Indian telecom services performance indicators*. Government of India.

Temitayo, F., Stephen, O., & Abimbola, A. (2012). Hybrid GA-SVM for efficient feature selection in e-mail classification. *Computer Engineering and Intelligent Systems*, *3*(3), 17–28.

Thibault, R. T., Amaral, O. B., Argolo, F., Bandrowski, A. E., Davidson, A. R., & Drude, N. I. (2023). Open Science 2.0: Towards a truly collaborative research ecosystem. *PLoS Biology*, *21*(10), e3002362. Advance online publication. DOI: 10.1371/journal.pbio.3002362 PMID: 37856538

Tifferet, S. (2019). Gender differences in privacy tendencies on social network sites: A meta-analysis. *Computers in Human Behavior*, *93*, 1–12. DOI: 10.1016/j.chb.2018.11.046

Torres, J., Mulligan, C., Jorge, J., & Moreira, C. (2025). PROMPTHEUS: A Human-Centered Pipeline to Streamline Systematic Literature Reviews with Large Language Models. *Information (Basel)*, *16*(5), 420. DOI: 10.3390/info16050420

Tregi, T. G., & Al-Zubaidie, M. (2025). Enhancing Traffic Data Security in Smart Cities Using Optimized Quantum-Based Digital Signatures and Privacy-Preserving Techniques. *Mesopotamian Journal of CyberSecurity*, *5*(1), 256–272. DOI: 10.58496/MJCS/2025/017

Ukropová, D. (2002) Metadáta v slovenských knižniciach. [Metadata in Slovak Libraries] *IT Lib. Informačné technológie a knižnice, 6* (4). https://itlib.cvtisr.sk/clanky/clanek2107/

UNESCO (2021). *UNESCO Recommendation on Open Science*. DOI: 10.54677/MNMH8546

VAIA. (2023). *Národná stratégia výskumu, vývoja a inovácií.* [National Strategy for Research, Development and Innovation.] https://vaia.gov.sk/wp-content/uploads/2023/05/01_Narodna-strategia-vyskumu-vyvoja-a-inovacii_vlastny-material_V2.pdf

Van Tilborg, H. C. (2025). *Chinese Remainder Theorem. In Encyclopedia of Cryptography, Security and Privacy*. Springer Nature Switzerland.

van Twist, A., Ruijer, E., & Meijer, A. (2023). Smart cities & citizen discontent: A systematic review of the literature. *Government Information Quarterly*, *40*(2), 101799. DOI: 10.1016/j.giq.2022.101799

van Zoonen, L. (2020). Data governance and citizen participation in the digital welfare state. *Data & Policy*, *2*, e10. DOI: 10.1017/dap.2020.10

Waclawek, T., Fiedler, A., Schütz, M., & Schütz, A. (2024). Crowd-counting technology within the smart city context: Understanding, trust, and acceptance. *Frontiers in Psychology, 15*, 1423837. DOI: 10.3389/fpsyg.2024.1423837 PMID: 39624374

Wamba, S. F., Gunasekaran, A., Akter, S., Ren, S., Dubey, R., & Childe, S. J. (2020). Big data analytics and firm performance: Effects of dynamic capabilities. *Journal of Business Research, 131*, 336–348.

Wang, K., Wu, Q., Song, L., Yang, Z., Wu, W., Qian, C., He, R., Qiao, Y., & Loy, C. C. (2020). MEAD: a Large-Scale Audio-Visual dataset for Emotional Talking-Face Generation. In *Lecture notes in computer science* (pp. 700-717). DOI: 10.1007/978-3-030-58589-1_42

Wang, X. L. (2005, August). Learning to classify email: a survey. In 2005 International conference on machine learning and cybernetics (Vol. 9, pp. 5716-5719). IEEE. doi:DOI: 10.1109/ICMLC.2005.1527956

Wang, Y., Shaw, E., Kruse, B., & Ghods, M. (2018). On identifying factors affecting ethical practices in data science domains. *SMU Data Science Review, 1*(2). https://scholar.smu.edu/datasciencereview/vol1/iss2/2/

Wang, T., Mallya, A., & Liu, M. (2021). One-Shot Free-View neural Talking-Head synthesis for video conferencing. *2022 IEEE/CVF Conference on Computer Vision and Pattern Recognition (CVPR)*. DOI: 10.1109/CVPR46437.2021.00991

Wang, W. (2010). *Machine Audition: Principles, algorithms and systems*. IGI Global., DOI: 10.4018/978-1-61520-919-4

WEBSCALE. The Global Ecommerce Security Report 2022. 2022. Available online: https://www.webscale.com/global-ecommercesecurity-report-2022/ (accessed on 18 March 2023).

Wellmon, C. (2015). *Organizing enlightenment: Information overload and the invention of the modern research university*. JHU Press.

Wiangwiset, T., Surawanitkun, C., Wongsinlatam, W., Remsungnen, T., Siritaratiwat, A., Srichan, C., Thepparat, P., Bunsuk, W., Kaewchan, A., & Namvong, A. (2023). Design and implementation of a real-time crowd monitoring system based on public Wi-Fi infrastructure: A case study on the Sri Chiang Mai Smart City. *Smart Cities, 6*(2), 987–1008. DOI: 10.3390/smartcities6020048

Wiangwiset, T., Surawanitkun, C., Wongsinlatam, W., Remsungnen, T., Sorn-in, K., Siritaratiwat, A., Srichan, C., Thepparat, P., Bunsuk, W., Kaewchan, A., Supasai, W., & Namvong, A. (2025). Development of a tourist behavior analysis system using public Wi-Fi data to enhance smart tourism management: A case study of Sri Chiang Mai Smart City. *Engineering and Applied Science Research, 52*(1), 42–56. DOI: 10.14456/easr.2025.4

Wilkinson, M. D., Dumontier, M., Aalbersberg, I. J., Appleton, G., Axton, M., Baak, A., Blomberg, N., Boiten, J. W., Bonino da Silva Santos, L., Bourne, P. E., Bouwman, J., Brookes, A. J., Clark, T., Crosas, M., Dillo, I., Dumon, O., Edmunds, S., Evelo, C. T., Finkers, R., & Mons, B. (2016). The FAIR Guiding Principles for scientific data management and stewardship. *Scientific Data*, *3*(1), 160018. Advance online publication. DOI: 10.1038/sdata.2016.18 PMID: 26978244

Wu, H., Jia, J., Xing, J., Xu, H., Wang, X., & Wang, J. (2023, March 17). *MMFace4D: a Large-Scale Multi-Modal 4D face dataset for Audio-Driven 3D face animation.* arXiv.org. https://arxiv.org/abs/2303.09797

Yang, S., Zhang, Y., Feng, D., Yang, M., Wang, C., Xiao, J., Long, K., Shan, S., & Chen, X. (2019). *LRW-1000: A Naturally-Distributed Large-Scale Benchmark for Lip Reading in the Wild.* IEEE., DOI: 10.1109/FG.2019.8756582

Yang, W., Fu, R., Amin, M. B., & Kang, B. (2025). The Impact of Modern AI in Metadata Management. *Human-Centric Intelligent Systems*, *5*(3), 323–350. DOI: 10.1007/s44230-025-00106-5

Yousif, S., Abboud, A., & Radhi, H. (2020). Robust Image Encryption with Scanning Technology, The El-Gamal Algorithm and Chaos Theory. *IEEE Access : Practical Innovations, Open Solutions*, *8*, 155184–155209. DOI: 10.1109/ACCESS.2020.3019216

Yu, J., Zhu, H., Jiang, L., Loy, C. C., Cai, W., & Wu, W. (2023). CelebV-Text: A Large-Scale facial Text-Video dataset. *2022 IEEE/CVF Conference on Computer Vision and Pattern Recognition (CVPR)*. DOI: 10.1109/CVPR52729.2023.01422

Zendulková, D., & Azeroual, O. (2022). Legal aspects and data protection in relation to the CRIS system. *Procedia Computer Science*, *211*, 17–27. DOI: 10.1016/j.procs.2022.10.172

Zendulková, D., Gavurníková, G., Krivjanska, A., Staňáková, Z., Putalová, A., & Janková, M. (2022). Representation of Women in Slovak Science and Research: An Analysis Based on the CRIS System Data. *Information (Basel)*, *13*(10), 482. DOI: 10.3390/info13100482

Zhang, S., Yuan, J., Liao, M., & Zhang, L. (2022). Text2video: Text-Driven Talking-Head Video Synthesis with Personalized Phoneme - Pose Dictionary. *ICASSP 2022 - 2022 IEEE International Conference on Acoustics, Speech and Signal Processing (ICASSP)*, 2659-2663. DOI: 10.1109/ICASSP43922.2022.9747380

Zhang-Kennedy, L., & Chiasson, S. (Eds.). (2021). "Whether it's moral is a whole other story": consumer perspectives on privacy regulations and corporate data practices. In the Seventeenth *Symposium on Usable Privacy and Security*. USENIX Association. https://www.usenix.org/conference/soups2021/presentation/zhang-kennedy

Zhang, X., Zhao, J., & LeCun, Y. (2015). Character-level convolutional networks for text classification. *Advances in Neural Information Processing Systems*, •••, 28.

Zhang, Z.(2019). Efficient and Secure ECDSA Algorithm and Its Applications: A Survey. [IJCNIS]. *International Journal of Communication Networks and Information Security*, *9*(1).

Zhang, Z., Li, L., Ding, Y., & Fan, C. (2021). Flow-guided One-shot Talking Face Generation with a High-resolution Audio-visual Dataset. *2022 IEEE/CVF Conference on Computer Vision and Pattern Recognition (CVPR)*, 3660-3669. DOI: 10.1109/CVPR46437.2021.00366

Zhao, W., Aldyaflah, I. M., Gangwani, P., Joshi, S., Upadhyay, H., & Lagos, L. (2023). A blockchain-facilitated secure sensing data processing and logging system. *IEEE Access : Practical Innovations, Open Solutions*, *11*, 21712–21728. DOI: 10.1109/ACCESS.2023.3252030

Zhou, S., Yang, B., Yuan, M., Jiang, R., Yan, R., Pan, G., & Tang, H. (2024). Enhancing SNN-based spatio-temporal learning: A benchmark dataset and Cross-Modality Attention model. *Neural Networks*, *180*, 106677. DOI: 10.1016/j.neunet.2024.106677 PMID: 39260008

Zhou, Y., Han, X., Shechtman, E., Echevarria, J., Kalogerakis, E., & Li, D. (2020). MakeItTalk. *ACM Transactions on Graphics*, *39*(6), 1–15. DOI: 10.1145/3414685.3417774

Zhu, H., Wu, W., Zhu, W., Jiang, L., Tang, S., Zhang, L., Liu, Z., & Loy, C. C. (2022). CelebV-HQ: a Large-Scale Video Facial Attributes Dataset. In *Lecture notes in computer science* (pp. 650-667). DOI: 10.1007/978-3-031-20071-7_38

Zhuang, Y., Cheng, B., Cheng, Y., Jin, Y., Liu, R., Li, C., Cheng, X., Liao, J., & Lin, J. (2024). Learn2Talk: 3D Talking Face Learns from 2D Talking Face. *IEEE Transactions on Visualization and Computer Graphics*, •••, 1–13. DOI: 10.1109/TVCG.2024.3476275 PMID: 39374282

Zimmermann, V. (2023). Smart cities as a testbed for experimenting with humans? Applying psychological ethical guidelines to smart city interventions. *Ethics and Information Technology*, *25*(4), 54. DOI: 10.1007/s10676-023-09729-3

Zuboff, S. (2019). *The age of surveillance capitalism: The fight for a human future at the new frontier of power*. PublicAffairs.

About the Contributors

Otmane Azeroual is a world-renowned senior researcher, lecturer, and thought leader in digital transformation, artificial intelligence, and advanced data-driven research infrastructures. His groundbreaking interdisciplinary work at the nexus of computer science, higher education research, innovation management, and industry has set new standards in how data and AI reshape science and society. His research on the design, deployment, and critical evaluation of Current Research Information Systems (CRIS) — combined with cutting-edge AI-powered analytics — is internationally acclaimed and among the most cited in the field. Dr. Azeroual's pioneering contributions drive the evolution of intelligent data ecosystems that empower Open Science, elevate transparency, and revolutionize strategic decision-making in science policy worldwide. Holding a Ph.D. in Engineering Informatics and a robust foundation in business information systems and software engineering, he has authored numerous high-impact publications in top-tier journals and has been a sought-after keynote and plenary speaker at prestigious global conferences. His expertise is recognized by editorial boards and scientific committees internationally, where he shapes the future agenda of research data science. Bridging academia and private industry, Dr. Azeroual uniquely fuses rigorous theoretical insight with practical innovation. His leadership in both sectors fuels transformative digital strategies and sustainable technological solutions. As an inspiring educator, he equips emerging researchers and professionals with cutting-edge knowledge in AI, data science, research analytics, and project management — preparing them to excel in complex, dynamic environments. Passionate about harnessing AI for evidence-based governance, Dr. Azeroual actively collaborates across disciplines to build resilient, transparent, and data-driven research infrastructures that set global benchmarks. His visionary work not only advances scientific understanding but also catalyzes paradigm shifts that benefit institutions, governments, and society at large.

***

Mishall Al-Zubaidie received the bachelor's degree in computer science from Basrah University, Iraq, in 2004 the master's degree in the security of the wireless network from Basrah University, Iraq, in 2010 and the PhD degree with the School of Agricultural, Computational and Environmental Sciences, Faculty of Health, Engineering, and Sciences, University of Southern Queensland, Toowoomba, QLD, Australia in 2020. His current research interests are - Network communications - Authorising and authenticating users in Electronic Medical Record (EMR) - Authorising and authenticating users in Electronic Health Record (EHR) - Incorporating security and privacy into Health Wireless Sensor Network (HWSN) - Public-Key cryptography - Lightweight hash functions - Anonymity and pseudonymity techniques - XML/XACML policies and authorisation - Keys exchange and session keys - WSN performance - Protection of MAC address - Routing protocols (LEACH/SPIN) - Keys exchange/agreement algorithm in the health system, security, and privacy challenges in smart cities, security and forensics, blockchain and integrity techniques, quantum cryptography keys and signatures, multi factors authentication for modern applications. He has published many research papers in the field of security and privacy in addition to reviewing more than 1292 research papers for different journals and publishers. Also, he worked as an editor role for over 63 assignments.

Ravikumar Ch is an accomplished professional in the field of Computer Science & Engineering, recognized for his contributions to both academia and research. He earned his B.Tech. Degree from Jawaharlal Nehru Technological University in 2004, followed by an M.Tech in Computer Science & Engineering in 2011. Recently, he successfully defended his Ph.D. in Computer Science & Engineering from Lovely Professional University in 2024, focusing on innovative approaches in Cloud Cryptography and blockchain security. With over 14 years of teaching experience and 5 years dedicated to research, Dr. Ravikumar's academic journey includes notable achievements such as receiving the Best Teacher Award from Anurag Engineering College in 2011 for his exceptional delivery of the Operating System subject. His research prowess is evidenced by his authorship of 20 Scopus indexed papers and 5 Web of Science indexed papers, alongside securing 2 patents in areas spanning cloud computing and blockchain technology. Dr. Ravikumar's expertise extends to the forefront of technological advancements, particularly in cloud computing and blockchain.

Amitabha Das is the Director and Head of the School of Nuclear Studies and Application at Jadavpur University, Kolkata. He specializes in nuclear instrumentation, embedded systems, and reactor control systems. Dr. Das has led research on FPGA-based real-time data acquisition systems for high-resolution nuclear spectroscopy and has contributed to AI-driven applications such as lipreading and sign language recognition. He has supervised advanced research in nuclear reactor control, including LPV-based switching MRAC techniques.

Zainab Fatima is an adjunct faculty in Department of Management Studies, Jamia Millia Islamia, New Delhi. She has done her PhD from Department of Management Studies, Jamia Millia Islamia, New Delhi. Her research areas are consumer behaviour, ecological buying behaviour and green marketing. With an excellent academic performance throughout her school and college, she holds two gold medals in BSc (Hons.) specializing in chemistry from Aligarh Muslim University, followed by an MBA from the same university before joining Jamia Millia for PhD. Her area of research is consumer buying behaviour in e-commerce industry, analysing effect of big data analytics on consumers' response in the form of their purchase behaviour.

Richard Khan is an experienced information management and technology professional with over two decades of experience leading technology operations, delivering large-scale IT projects, and providing solutions to optimize infrastructure, ensure compliance, and scale business processes. His expertise spans strategic planning, technology migration and integration, software development, and other core areas critical to achieving organizational goals and increasing profitability. Throughout his career, Richard has led multiple onshore and offshore teams, built strong professional relationships, and successfully executed strategic business objectives. He has extensive experience in stakeholder communication, project leadership, performance improvement, and value stream optimization. His experience covers public, private, and nonprofit sectors, with particular expertise in QA/DevOps/automation, process and value stream analysis, requirements management, project lifecycle management, product development, change and risk management, and system and solution architecture. Richard recently completed an MBA with a focus on Artificial Intelligence (AI). His dedication to AI and machine learning in a business context has also led him to create a comprehensive AI glossary, highlighting his passion for innovative technologies and responsible AI applications.

Research Maity is an undergraduate student in Computer Science and Business Systems at Gargi Memorial Institute of Technology. His research interests include machine learning, computer vision, and speech synthesis. He is actively involved in research projects and technical events.

Soumya Mazumdar is currently pursuing a dual degree a B.Tech in Computer Science and Business Systems from Gargi Memorial Institute of Technology, and a B.S. in Data Science from the Indian Institute of Technology Madras. He has made significant contributions to interdisciplinary research, with multiple publications in reputed journals and edited volumes by Elsevier, Springer, IEEE, Wiley, and CRC Press. His primary research interests include artificial intelligence, machine learning, 6G communications, healthcare technologies, and industrial automation.

Sarbajit Pal is a retired senior scientist and former Head of C&I Group at the Variable Energy Cyclotron Centre (VECC), a premier R&D unit under the Department of Atomic Energy, Government of India . With a Ph.D. in Electronics Engineering, he has significantly contributed to the development of control and instrumentation systems for particle accelerators, including the K500 Superconducting Cyclotron . His expertise encompasses embedded systems, experimental physics, and control systems, with a focus on implementing EPICS-based control architectures . Dr. Pal has authored over 30 publications and has mentored several Ph.D. students in electronics and computer science.

Vineet Rakesh is a Technical Officer (Scientific Category) at the Variable Energy Cyclotron Centre (VECC), Department of Atomic Energy, India, with over 22 years of experience in software engineering, database systems, and artificial intelligence. His research interest on cutting-edge research in talking head generation, lipreading, and ultra-low-bitrate video compression for real-time teleconferencing. Currently pursuing a Ph.D. at Homi Bhabha National Institute, Mumbai, his work integrates deep learning, computer vision, and GPU-accelerated computing. Mr. Rakesh has also contributed to office automation, OCR systems, and digital transformation projects at VECC. He is an Associate Member of the Institution of Engineers (India) and has received the DAE Group Achievement Award.

Tapas Samanta is a senior scientist and Head of the Computer and Informatics Group at the Variable Energy Cyclotron Centre (VECC), Department of Atomic Energy, India. With a strong background in Electronics, Computer Science, and over two decades of experience, he leads initiatives in artificial intelligence, industrial automation, and control systems for particle accelerators. His work spans embedded systems, high-performance computing, and public technology outreach. Dr. Samanta also heads Technology Transfer Division and Public Awareness Cell of VECC, promoting scientific innovation for societal benefit.

Mohd Abdul Moid Siddiqui is currently an Assistant Professor at IILM Graduate School of Management, Greater Noida. Prior to this, he worked as an Assistant Professor & Head Academics, Faculty of Management, Asian Business School, Noida and Subject Expert and Faculty at Institute of Development Studies, University of Lucknow. He has a PhD in Business Administration from Faculty of Management Studies and Research, AMU. He is a Commerce graduate from the

University of Lucknow, post that, he has done MBA and PG Diploma in Personnel Management from Aligarh Muslim University. He has presented and published research in journals of repute and premier institutions in India and abroad, such as SC Johnson School of Business, Cornell University, New York, Prague Technical University—Czech Republic, IIM Lucknow to name a few.

Danica Zendulková holds the position of Director of the Department of Administration and Operation of R&D Portal at the Slovak Centre of Scientific and Technical Information which is the national information centre for science, technology, innovation and education and it also serves as the scientific library of the Slovak Republic. Her major job tasks include the nation-wide collection, processing and analysis of data on science and research, as well as the evaluation of publication outputs of academic institutions in the Slovak Republic and reporting on them. She has actively attended a number of domestic and international conferences and meetings with impactful presentations. Some of her lectures, she gave abroad, had been invited., She takes part in national and international research projects and some of her publications are indexed in the Web of Science/Scopus databases. She also represents the Slovak Republic in some international organisations as a member. She did as a member of the International organisation on research information EuroCRIS board. ORCID: 0000-0003-2487-0177 Scopus Author ID: 56278062400

Index

B

Big Data 67, 90, 123, 124, 125, 126, 127, 128, 129, 130, 131, 134, 141, 142, 143, 145, 148, 149, 150, 151, 152, 153, 154, 155, 164, 190, 198, 207, 208, 216, 218, 243, 244, 246, 257, 258, 260

C

CCTC Framework 157, 159, 166, 168, 169, 170, 171, 172, 173, 174, 175, 177, 183, 184, 185, 187, 188, 189, 193
CERIF Format 241, 252
Chinese Remainder Theorem 31, 42, 67
Current Research Information System 235

D

Data Governance 88, 159, 161, 163, 165, 167, 169, 178, 185, 187, 188, 190, 191, 192, 193, 194, 208, 214, 216, 218, 243
Dataset 52, 77, 81, 97, 98, 100, 101, 102, 103, 106, 113, 116, 118, 178, 186, 196, 198, 199, 201, 202, 203, 204, 205, 206, 207, 209, 210, 211, 212, 213, 214, 218, 219, 220, 221, 222
Deep Learning 18, 20, 28, 72, 91, 95, 96, 100, 101, 104, 105, 106, 107, 115, 116, 118, 127, 217
Digital Communication 91
DL 91, 95, 96, 97, 99, 100, 101, 102, 104, 105, 107, 111, 112, 113, 116, 118

E

E-Commerce 32, 33, 34, 35, 36, 37, 38, 43, 44, 45, 47, 49, 50, 52, 53, 54, 55, 56, 57, 58, 63, 64, 65, 66, 67, 68, 123, 124, 125, 126, 127, 128, 129, 130, 131, 133, 142, 143, 144, 145, 146, 147, 148, 149, 150, 151, 153
E-Commerce Attacks 33, 52
Ethical 2, 3, 8, 9, 11, 19, 24, 25, 83, 86, 96, 106, 127, 128, 129, 131, 149, 154, 157, 158, 159, 160, 161, 163, 164, 165, 167, 168, 170, 173, 174, 175, 176, 177, 178, 179, 180, 182, 183, 184, 185, 188, 190, 192, 193, 195, 196, 197, 198, 199, 202, 206, 207, 208, 209, 211, 212, 213, 214, 215, 216, 217, 218, 219, 222, 223, 230, 235, 237, 243, 244, 246, 248, 257, 260
Ethical Oversight 158, 164, 165, 174, 178, 182, 183, 184, 185, 188

F

FAIR Principles 234, 235, 243, 247, 252, 257

I

Institutional Accountability 159, 165, 167, 183, 189, 193

L

Literature Analysis 73, 76, 79, 84, 88

M

Metadata Standards 240, 241, 252, 260
ML 91, 93, 97, 98, 99, 100, 101, 103, 105

O

Open Science 69, 70, 72, 75, 77, 78, 79, 80, 81, 83, 84, 85, 87, 89, 225, 226, 230, 232, 233, 234, 235, 238, 242, 243, 249, 251, 252, 255, 257, 259, 260, 261

P

Privacy 1, 2, 3, 4, 5, 6, 8, 9, 10, 11, 13, 16, 17, 18, 19, 20, 21, 22, 23, 26, 27, 28, 33, 35, 65, 67, 83, 86, 93, 96, 104, 123, 124, 125, 126, 127, 128, 129, 130, 131, 132, 134, 135, 136, 141, 142, 143, 144, 145, 146, 147, 148,

149, 150, 151, 152, 153, 154, 155, 157, 158, 159, 160, 161, 162, 163, 165, 168, 169, 172, 173, 176, 178, 180, 181, 182, 183, 184, 186, 188, 190, 191, 196, 197, 198, 199, 200, 206, 207, 209, 210, 213, 221, 222, 244, 248, 251
Privacy Preservation 13, 19, 28, 65, 186
Public Key 27, 33, 34, 38, 39, 44, 45, 47, 49, 59, 62, 64, 68
Public-Space Data Collection 194
Public Trust 3, 157, 158, 159, 160, 163, 165, 174, 175, 188, 189, 192, 207, 212

R

Reproducible Research 81
Research Guru AI 69, 71, 72, 73, 74, 75, 76, 77, 78, 79, 80, 81, 82, 83, 84, 85, 86, 87, 88, 89

S

Science Policy 225, 227, 228, 229, 235, 237, 249, 259
Scientific Information 226, 227, 235, 238
Scientific Workflows 74
Security 1, 2, 3, 4, 5, 7, 8, 9, 10, 11, 13, 14, 15, 16, 17, 18, 19, 20, 21, 22, 24, 25, 26, 28, 29, 31, 32, 33, 34, 35, 36, 38, 39, 40, 41, 43, 49, 51, 52, 53, 54, 56, 57, 58, 63, 64, 65, 66, 67, 68, 83, 92, 94, 96, 102, 103, 123, 124, 125, 126, 127, 128, 129, 130, 131, 132, 134, 135, 136, 141, 142, 143, 144, 145, 146, 147, 148, 149, 150, 151, 152, 153, 154, 161, 162, 164, 167, 168, 171, 172, 176, 179, 180, 183, 188, 190, 191, 193, 207, 221, 244, 246, 248, 251, 256
Security Protocol 57
Smart City Governance 162, 163, 165, 167, 175
Social Acceptance 164, 165, 166, 167, 191, 193
Social Media 123, 124, 125, 126, 127, 128, 129, 130, 131, 132, 133, 134, 136, 141, 142, 143, 144, 145, 146, 148, 149, 150, 151
Spam Email 92, 96, 97, 99, 100, 102, 116, 120
Sri Chiang Mai 158, 159, 175, 176, 177, 178, 179, 180, 181, 182, 183, 185, 186, 188, 190, 192
Systematic Review 65, 67, 89, 128, 151, 192
System Integration 254

T

Talking Head Generation 195, 196, 200, 212, 214, 217, 218, 219, 221, 222
Transparent 2, 4, 5, 8, 18, 19, 23, 24, 25, 66, 71, 72, 77, 78, 80, 81, 83, 84, 85, 86, 87, 88, 126, 129, 143, 145, 148, 150, 195, 199, 212, 213, 237, 252, 256
Trustworthy 1, 2, 13, 16, 18, 19, 20, 23, 25, 67, 73, 91, 116, 126, 145, 146, 195, 198, 202, 206, 209, 223, 226, 237, 251, 255

www.ingramcontent.com/pod-product-compliance
Lightning Source LLC
LaVergne TN
LVHW081525300926
849161LV00006B/1297